D0472429

Just a few of the many excellent book reviews our products I

Top 50 book reviewers for **Amazon.com** have given this book the highest rating of **5 stars!**

⭐⭐⭐⭐⭐ **A thorough exposition of how to appraise real estate.**
Amazon Top 50 Book Reviewer: Harold McFarland from Florida

Real Estate Appraising from A to Z - delivers up exactly what it promises - a thorough, understandable course on appraising. The author discusses appraisals as a business and how to get into the appraisal business, but it is much more that just that. If you are looking at purchasing property for investing. If you are looking at purchasing a new home, wanting to know the value of vacant property, etc. this is an excellent book. It covers all the bases when valuing a property. Some of the subjects discussed include community factors, market influences, potential hidden problems and how to find them, building inspection, the cost approach to valuation, the income approach to valuation, and writing a proposal. Given the thorough coverage and easy to understand writing style, this book is a highly recommended purchase for anyone who might be interested in appraisals (either doing them or understanding someone else's), or investing in real estate.

⭐⭐⭐⭐⭐ **Appraisal Know-How.**
Reviewer: Author/Reviewer Denise Clark from California

Real Estate Appraising from A to Z
Denise's Pieces Author Site & Book Reviews
www.denisemclark.com

Real estate appraisers are in demand these days, and get paid hundreds of dollars for their services. The best thing about becoming an appraiser is that you don't need a Master's Degree or any special schooling to become one. What you do need, however, is knowledge. In his extensively researched and illustrated Real Estate Appraising from A to Z, author Cozzi sets out to give anyone interested in moving into this quickly growing field the tools he or she will need, not only to do the job, but to do it right.

Mr. Cozzi starts with the very basics. For instance, the purpose, benefits and explanation of what an appraiser is, what he does and how to become a certified appraiser. From there, he guides the reader step by step through what appraisers look for when inspecting homes, both their exteriors and interiors. He explains how to determine home values of not only single-dwelling homes, but condominiums as well.

But Mr. Cozzi doesn't stop there. In basic, easily understood terms, he explains such topics as depreciation, the different types of home mortgages and appraisal accounts such as original home loan and refinance loan appraisals and foreclosure appraisals.

Real Estate Appraising from A to Z is just what the title implies. Mr. Cozzi's ability to instruct without 'talking down' to his audience is a plus and a rare treat - even for those who know absolutely nothing about the 'home' business. Homeowners would do well to have a copy of this book on hand before obtaining an appraisal, and use Cozzi's inspection guidelines within the actual appraising section of the book to obtain the most favorable value for their homes. Mr. Cozzi's easy to read, friendly writing style offers expert and timely advice and instruction for both homeowners and aspiring appraisers. If you want to work for yourself, earn extra money, or increase the value of your home, this edition is a definite must.

(Continued on page 2)

(Continued from page 1)

★★★★☆ **Appraiser's Dream Book for beginners or experts!**
Reviewer: Author/Reviewer C. Robbinson from New York

Real Estate Appraising from A to Z - We have one of the busiest appraisal and home inspection companies in our area. We exclusively work for mortgage lenders and banks who are very picky about getting high quality reports and evaluations. We have been using this "A to Z" appraisal book and the "A to Z" inspection book for years as MANDATORY reading for all of our appraisers and home inspectors when we hire and train them. It's the simplest to understand and the most thorough covering all necessary topics that we have found on the market. This book will tell you the realities of evaluating real estate without giving you a bunch of fluff - that's why we like it so much. Our appraisers and inspectors get years of expertise and knowledge in one book without having to make the mistakes they would to learn from their own experiences. It saves us a lot of time in getting our employees up to speed doing professional reports and evaluations for our banking clients. We can't afford to send our clients poor quality reports since there's a lot of competition in our business. This book keeps us at the top of our game and keeps our clients happy.

Real Estate Press - "...the Real Estate from A to Z books and videos are the best we've ever seen."

New Home Construction Journal – "...the best selling reference books available for home builders and buyers and cover every topic from A to Z."

Seminar Progress Report - "...top-notch real estate investors, inspectors and appraisers agree the Real Estate from A to Z series is a great value."

Home-Based Business Monthly - "If you're looking to become a knowledgeable home inspector or appraiser, Real Estate from A to Z series is crucial."

Real Estate Investors Journal - "...Real Estate from A to Z series is by far the most in-depth resource for every investor, beginner to expert."

What's In This For You?

 Real Estate Appraisers earn **$300** or more for each appraisal. Many appraisers are so busy that they do two appraisals per day!

 You don't need to have any background in real estate to become a highly paid real estate appraiser. All you need is to obtain the right knowledge and business plan, *(which we'll give you)*. Male or female, and your current age doesn't matter either, since there is *no* manual labor or hard work involved.

Here's just a few of the
benefits you get from our products:

 Earn Money in one of the fastest growing businesses in the country.

 Be Your Own Boss and work part-time or full-time. <u>*You*</u> set your own hours.

 Save Money when you buy, sell, or renovate your own home.

 Eliminate Safety Hazards to make your home safe for you and your family.

 Real Estate Related knowledge to help people with the *biggest* investment they will ever make - their own home.

What's The Income Potential?

Are you wondering about the income and growth potential of the real estate appraisal business? Then look below because a picture is worth a thousand words. Many appraisers earn **high** incomes every year while working right out of their home. The appraisal industry has been growing by leaps and bounds every year. And remember, this growth has gone on during one of the worst economic recessions in history! Our textbook manual shows you the reasons why your appraisal business can grow during a recession.

Grow th Of The Appraisal Industry

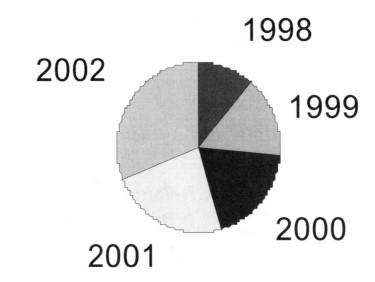

What Houses Need Appraisals?

Are you wondering about the need for appraisals? Then look below because this data has been taken from evaluating thousands of homes. The graph shows the probability of finding aspects that can negatively affect the market value of any house, *(including yours!)* Our textbook manual shows you the reasons why <u>all</u> homes need to be appraised. Do you really know the true market value of your house?

Probability of Changes to Market Value

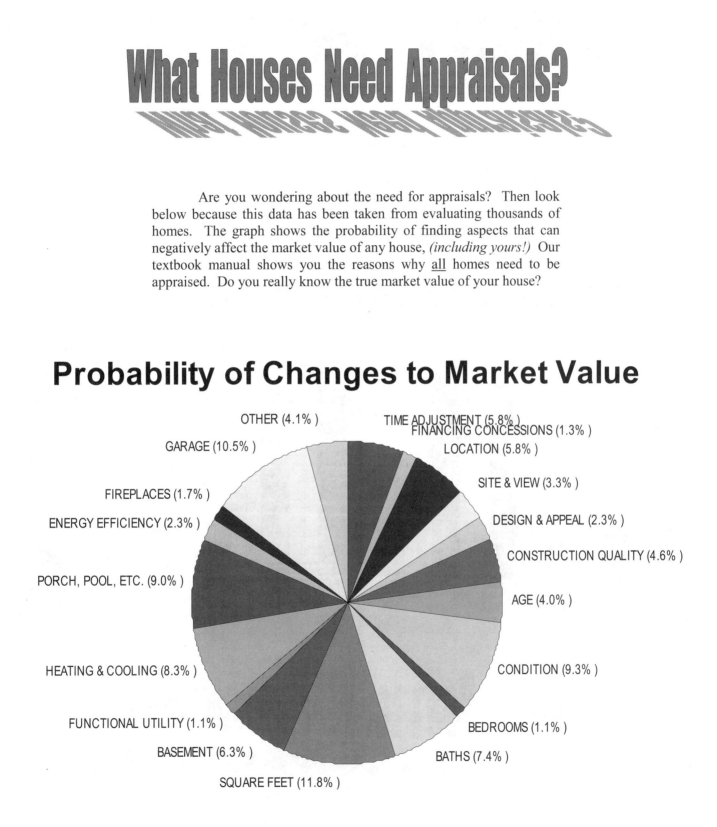

OTHER (4.1%)
TIME ADJUSTMENT (5.8%)
FINANCING CONCESSIONS (1.3%)
GARAGE (10.5%)
LOCATION (5.8%)
FIREPLACES (1.7%)
SITE & VIEW (3.3%)
ENERGY EFFICIENCY (2.3%)
DESIGN & APPEAL (2.3%)
PORCH, POOL, ETC. (9.0%)
CONSTRUCTION QUALITY (4.6%)
AGE (4.0%)
HEATING & COOLING (8.3%)
CONDITION (9.3%)
FUNCTIONAL UTILITY (1.1%)
BEDROOMS (1.1%)
BASEMENT (6.3%)
BATHS (7.4%)
SQUARE FEET (11.8%)

So you don't want a career change? That's fine, but would you be interested in saving thousands of dollars when you buy your own home? Then look below. This graph shows some potential market value adjustments found when buying your home. By identifying any negative aspects *before* you buy, you'll be able to negotiate a lower purchase price.

Potential $ Savings for Home Buyers

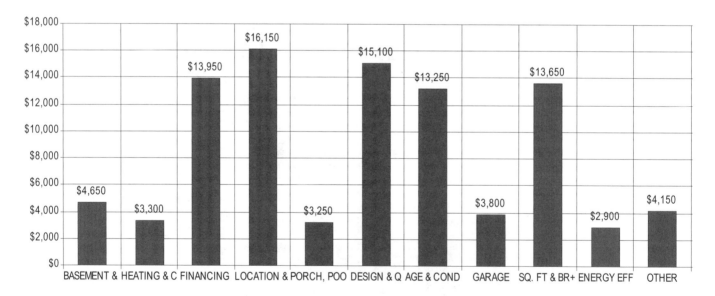

What's A Seller's Savings?

You're not buying a house at this time? Okay, but would you be interested in saving thousands of dollars when you renovate or sell your own home? Then look down. This graph shows your potential profit when selling your home. By properly evaluating these typical market value adjustments ahead of time, you can earn an additional $1.60 for each $1.00 you have invested in your home. This $1.60 figure is based on an annual appreciation rate of only 10% over five years.

Potential $ Savings for Home Sellers

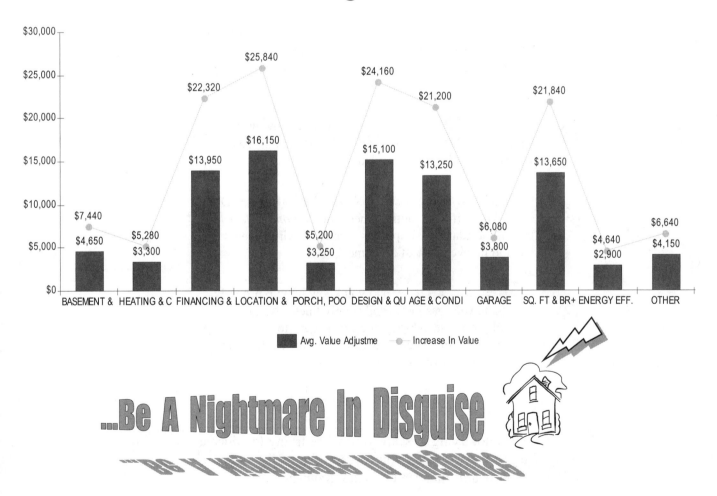

...Be A Nightmare In Disguise

What Safety Hazards?

So you think there are no safety hazards
around your home? Well, think again.

 Lead In Water & Paint - Do you know
how to check for lead in your home? Lead poisoning
is the *number one* childhood disease in America!

 Radon Gas - Is it in your house? The EPA,
(Environmental Protection Agency), has determined
that radon is the *number two* leading cause of lung
cancer behind cigarette smoking!

 Asbestos & UFFI - Do you know what
they look like? Asbestos and UFFI insulations have
caused countless cancer related deaths.

 Improper Electrical Wiring - Do
you know if your outlets meet the *National Electric
Code* standards? Improper electrical wiring can be
found in over 90% of all homes!

 Gas Leaks - Do you know how to properly
evaluate your gas meter and supply lines? Natural gas
is colorless and odorless before it gets to the utility
company. An undetected gas leak can explode and
blow up an entire building!

We're not trying to scare you, we're trying to educate
you. We just want to open your eyes to the reality of some
of the safety hazards that can be found in *any* home.

Customer Comments & Recommendations

From the Author,

Thank you very much for purchasing my book. I invite you to view our web site at **www.nemmar.com** to see the other real estate products we offer that will save you thousands of dollars when you buy, sell, or renovate a home. Please email me and let me know what you think of my book after you have time to review it. Customer feedback and recommendations are greatly appreciated and help me to improve all of our products.

Thank you,

Guy Cozzi
Nemmar Real Estate Training
*"Everything You Need To Know About Real Estate
From Asbestos to Zoning"*

Nemmar Real Estate Training is ranked as one of the most exclusive real estate appraisal and home inspection training services since 1988. Our top selling products have taught thousands of real estate professionals and homeowners nationwide. You too can learn everything you need to know about Real Estate - from Asbestos to Zoning. With this knowledge you will save thousands of dollars when you buy, sell, or renovate your home. You will also learn how to eliminate safety hazards and properly maintain a home. Statistics show an average savings of at least **$4,700.00** per home for customers who have read our books. Both of our books are the **number one** seller's in the *Real Estate Appraisal* and *Home Inspection* categories nationwide and they have been called the "Bible" of the real estate industry. Written by Guy Cozzi who has decades of experience as a licensed appraiser, home inspector, consultant, and real estate investor. This top selling author has been quoted as a real estate expert by the *New York Times* and many other publications. He has been a guest speaker on real estate investment TV shows for years. Guy Cozzi has taught thousands of people how to inspect, appraise and invest in real estate and provides advice to many banks and mortgage lenders.

The real facts other books don't tell you! ***You'll learn everything that your Realtor doesn't want you to know.*** Realtors "sugar coat" the problem conditions in a house in order to close the deal and get paid their sales commission. This is unquestionably the only book of its kind that teaches you how to prevent those pitfalls. You get information that the professionals use to make you an educated consumer enabling you to negotiate a much better price on the purchase, renovation, or sale of your home.

Don't let your dream house be a nightmare in disguise! These fourth edition "A to Z" books will assist you with the biggest investment of your life - your own home! These products were originally designed to train top-notch, professional home inspectors, appraisers, investors, and Realtors and are now available at a price affordable to everyone. **All** homes need to be inspected and appraised for safety hazards and maintenance.

Table of Contents

The *Operating Systems, Lower Level, Interior* and *Exterior Inspection* sections are condensed versions of those found in our home inspection book:
Home Inspection Business From A to Z

THE OPERATING SYSTEMS INSPECTION

THE LOWER LEVEL INSPECTION

THE INTERIOR INSPECTION

THE EXTERIOR INSPECTION

APPRAISING REAL ESTATE

(Continued on page 11)

(Continued from page 10)

THE DIRECT SALES COMPARISON APPROACH

SAMPLE APPRAISAL REPORTS

THE COST APPROACH

THE INCOME APPROACH

MISCELLANEOUS APPRAISAL INFORMATION

FINISHING THE APPRAISAL REPORT

THE APPRAISAL COURSE SPP

REALITY, MOTIVATIONAL AND STRAIGHT TALK

This fourth edition of my book is dedicated to *Gianfranco Scalise* who died at age 29 in a car accident on Sunday, August 17, 2003.
The same day I finished editing this book.

Life is short and precious. If you live an honest life and leave this world a little better off then when you got here, then you can consider yourself a success. *Gianfranco* was a success and he will be missed by his family and friends.

Introduction

This book is going to cover every aspect of the real estate appraisal business. I'm not going to paint some fairy tale, rosy picture or give you any fluff. I'm going to tell it like it is without holding anything back, so you can definitely sink your teeth into this book. This book was originally designed to train top-notch, professional real estate appraisers. However, the book is extremely helpful to anyone involved in real estate. This includes a home buyer, homeowner, home seller, Realtor, home inspector, etc. Refer to the **Benefits Of Knowledge Of Appraisals** section to see the reasons why **anyone** can benefit by knowing this material. A lot of the information in this educational material goes well beyond what's covered in other books. That's why I say it's "the *real facts* other books don't tell you!"

You may have purchased some of my other books, such as **Home Inspection Business From A to Z**. If you have, then you will find that some of the information contained in this book is similar. This is because there are many important aspects that pertain to both the real estate appraisal and the home inspection businesses, as well as, real estate investing. I hope you don't feel that some information is redundant. It will only benefit you to read it several times to make sure you know the information well enough so it doesn't cost you time and money later. If you haven't purchased some of our other products, then do it now! I'm serious about that because our products are worth much more than the price we sell them for.

There will be information in this book that you'll find very surprising and enlightening as to the inner workings of the real estate business. I certainly found it surprising when I got involved in real estate. The only problem was I had to find out the hard way. I'm going to tell you about it so you don't have to make the same mistakes that I made. They say a *Wise Man* learns by his mistakes, but a *Genius* learns by the mistakes of others. So I'll do the best I can to make you a genius!

I had a strong motivating factor for writing this book in the first place. I wrote it because I think there's a very important need for good, honest and thorough real estate appraisers. I sincerely want people to be more informed about the realities involved with the biggest investment decision they make - the purchase and sale of their own home. There is also an urgent need to improve the integrity and professionalism of the real estate business overall. By being in the real estate business, I've seen firsthand that there are many aspects about it that need to be improved upon. These improvements would be for the benefit of everyone involved, not just appraisers. I hope this book will help increase the integrity and professionalism of the real estate business. If it does, then I will feel that this information provides a much needed service and well worth my efforts.

To get the most benefit, you have to read this book from cover-to-cover. So don't get lazy and cut corners; read everything! You have to read the book enough times until you've memorized enough of the information so you know what you're doing. You can't just read it once and expect to know enough to do a proper and thorough real estate appraisal. You can't "wing it" on an appraisal job because sometimes you'll get a client who asks a lot of questions. If you're fumbling for answers then you'll lose credibility and the client's respect.

This doesn't mean that you have to know the answer to every question the client asks. However, you need to be able to answer the vast majority of their questions. There are times that I tell clients *"I don't know"* when asked about a particular item. Because I know the answers to the vast majority of their questions, I have the client's respect for being so knowledgeable. They realize that I can't be a walking encyclopedia.

Don't expect to make big money overnight in this business, it's not a get rich quick scheme. It takes time to build up a referral business that brings in a lot of money. But don't worry. If you learn this material well enough and keep feeding your mind with new literature and training courses, you can make big money. Your referrals will begin to come automatically, without even advertising. The whole key to making a lot of money on a steady basis is to have satisfied clients. This is the same concept in every profession and not just the real estate appraisal business. Satisfied clients will refer their friends and business associates to you for appraisals. You'll become one of the best and busiest appraisers in your area if your knowledgeable and honest.

You will eventually get to the point when you're doing a lot of real estate appraisals. When you get to this point, don't book more than two appraisals in one day. If you try to do too many appraisals, you'll be rushing to get to the next appointment or you'll be tired before the end of the day. This can cause you to miss something that could create problems later with an angry phone call from your client.

Please send me an email and let me know what you think of this book and any recommendations you might have for improvements or new products. I accept positive and negative comments since both help me to improve the next version of the book. I am always looking to improve my products and services and I greatly appreciate customer feedback and suggestions.

> *I had a strong motivating factor for writing this educational material in the first place. I wrote it because I think there's a very important need for good, honest and thorough appraisers. I sincerely want people to be more informed about the realities involved with the biggest investment decision they make - the purchase and sale of their home.*

About The Author

I'll briefly walk you through my background so you'll see how I ended up in the real estate appraisal business. My father died of cancer when I was 15, and as a result, I had to pay my own way through high school and college. I've worked many different types of service industry jobs to help pay my bills. I worked with a tree service company, a moving company, a house painting company, as a security guard, a day camp counselor, a golf caddie, in a restaurant as a dishwasher, a busboy, a waiter and a bartender and the list goes on and on.

I studied art history in college. When I graduated college I was working as a waiter at a local restaurant. You can see from my education and training, I had no experience in real estate and I knew virtually nothing about it. I didn't even know what a mortgage was! I knew a mortgage had something to do with real estate, but I didn't know exactly what it had to do with it. One day I saw an Infomercial TV show advertising cassette tapes dealing with real estate investing. The show peaked my curiosity because it talked about buying real estate with "no money down." I ended up buying that cassette tape series and I listened to the tapes and read the books that came with it about 10 times over. I memorized just about everything in that material.

In 1988, while I was working as a waiter, my brother and I took out small personal loans to get down payment money to buy a rundown, old single-family house. This house was located in a low-income area of New York and it needed *a lot* of work. We gradually fixed this house up in our spare time, learning the ropes as we went along by trial and error. When we were finished, the house was appraised for <u>twice</u> what we paid for it. As a result, we refinanced the house. We used the money from this loan as a down payment to buy a two-family house that was in just as bad condition as the first house. We renovated the two-family house and then it was also appraised for <u>twice</u> what we paid for it. We refinanced this house and used the extra money to buy a six-family house. The six-family also needed a lot of work in repairs. So we did the same thing again, except this time when we were finished with the renovations, the house didn't appraise for twice what we paid for it. The six-family was appraised for <u>four times</u> what we paid for it!!

We hired the best home inspector we could find to check these houses out before we purchased them. This inspector also inspected other houses we had planned on buying, however, things came up in the inspection that made us change our minds. We were beginning to learn the ropes about real estate and construction from buying, renovating and managing our own rental properties. This inspector coincidentally offered to train us to go into the home inspection business ourselves. The only catch was that we had to pay him $10,000 to do it! We saw that this inspector was earning over $135,000 per year while working right out of his home, and so we decided to take him up on his offer. I'm glad we did, because that $10,000 investment may have seemed like a lot of money back then, but it's paid for itself many times over.

I trained under this home inspector and did a lot of reading, research and memorization. This learning process took a long time before I really felt that I knew what I was doing. I took many classes dealing with the different aspects of real estate and construction. I then went on to pass the exams offered by ASHI, The *American Society of Home Inspectors*. After I passed the exams, I became a full member of ASHI. This gave me even more knowledge and expertise in the home inspection business.

After getting into the home inspection business, I ran into a friend of mine from high school, named Mike, who was a real estate appraiser in the area. Mike had become a very qualified real estate appraiser. I was curious about how Mike trained to become an appraiser and what type of income someone could make in that profession. So I asked Mike some questions and found out that many appraisers earn over $140,000 per year while working out of their homes. He told me some other interesting things about the appraisal business but I just stored it all in the back of my mind and didn't think much about it.

Shortly after that, I received a phone call from another friend of mine from college, named Phil. Phil told me he was working for a bank in their foreclosure department. Phil said that he didn't hire home inspectors as much as he did appraisers for the properties the bank would foreclose on. After a bank forecloses on a property, they have an appraisal done to determine what the present market value is. A bank needs to estimate the market value to know what to try and sell the property for. Sometimes they need to have a home inspection done as well, but not as often. Anyway, this really got me thinking about learning how to do real estate appraisals. I was making a lot of money with my rental properties and home inspection business. However, I'm always looking for new opportunities to make an additional income *(and you should too)*. My friend Phil at the bank said that if I learned how to do appraisals well enough, he could give me plenty of work. This **really** set the wheels turning in my head.

I called back my other friend Mike, who was an appraiser, and asked if he could train me to do appraisals for a reasonable fee. Mike agreed to train me for one-half of the fee that I would charge the bank for each appraisal. This ended up amounting to over $8,500! I called Phil at the bank and told him I could do appraisals for him. I said that I will be getting trained by a qualified appraiser who had been in the business for years. This appraiser would also review all of my appraisals before they were mailed to the bank. Phil then agreed to give me some appraisal work since I would have all of my appraisals reviewed by a qualified appraiser during my training.

It took about six months of working with Mike and writing up and reviewing many appraisals before I really felt that I knew what I was doing. I then went on to take the State Appraisal classes to get even more knowledge and expertise in real estate appraising. Some of the classes I took are: Course 1, Course 2, and the Course Standards of Professional Practice Part A and Part B. To continue building up my credentials and experience, I passed the State Appraisal examination to become a State Certified Real Estate Appraiser. With all of this training combined with my experience in the business, I know that I have a big edge on many of the appraisers. This is because I have such an extensive and diverse background in many different aspects of real estate.

In this book and educational series I'm going to tell you about all of the information and training I learned from a top notch home inspector, a highly qualified appraiser, and the home inspection and appraisal classes. Plus I'll tell you about all of the information I've learned from my own experiences in real estate and in the appraisal and inspection business. The only part of that training I'm going to leave out is the $20,000 in up front fees and class tuition that I had to pay when I first started!! I hope you don't mind me leaving that part out.

Purpose Of A
Real Estate Appraisal

An appraisal is needed to determine the estimated *market value* of a house or condominium. It is used to assist someone in making a decision. They may be considering purchasing, selling or lending money on a house, condo or a commercial property. Appraisals are also used for tax purposes to estimate how much money a property owner has to pay in taxes.

Banks need appraisals to assist them in figuring out how much money to lend someone for a mortgage loan application. There are many different aspects of a loan application that the banker has to consider, but the bank *always* requires an appraisal.

People get very emotional and excited about purchasing a house. When they're in this highly

> A house is usually the biggest investment most people will make, so it's prudent for them not to take any chances. They should try to eliminate as much risk as possible.

emotional and excited state, they tend to just look at the cosmetic appeal of a house instead of the important factors. They forget that they're not buying a car; they're buying a house! By becoming too emotionally attached to a deal, people often pay above market value for a home. This can cost them tens of thousands of dollars in an overpriced purchase. A house is the biggest investment most people will make, so it's prudent for them not to take any chances. They should try to eliminate as much risk as possible. It's a great feeling to have a client thank you for helping them out with the biggest investment they'll ever make.

A pre-purchase appraisal will inform people of the true market value of a house. This will enable them to make an educated and intelligent decision on whether or not to purchase the home. They will also know the approximate amount to pay for it.

All houses and condos should have a home inspection performed by a well qualified and thorough home inspector, before signing any contracts. The appraisal is generally done after the contracts are signed and the bank financing application has been filled out. There will be repairs or upgrading needed in all homes, even brand new ones. Sometimes people think that because a house is new it doesn't need to be inspected. They don't realize that builders are

businessmen trying to make a profit. Any builder who doesn't do quality construction can cut corners to save a few dollars to try to try to increase their profit. When a house is built *"up to code"* it doesn't ensure a perfect house. Local building codes are the minimum standards that a builder or contractor has to follow to obtain a building permit or a Certificate of Occupancy for the work done. There's nothing to stop a builder or a contractor from exceeding the building codes other than saving some money for themselves or their client.

Pre-sale appraisals are recommended. Before someone puts their house up for sale they should have it appraised to estimate the true market value. This will prevent any last minute holdups because of problems found during the bank's appraisal. Any last minute problems will delay the sale or kill the deal altogether.

Homeowners can hire an appraiser to dispute the amount of their property taxes. Many people don't realize that they can be over charged for their property tax assessments. Homeowners need to hire an appraiser if they believe their property taxes are too high. An appraiser can estimate the market value of their house and then the homeowner can try to have their property taxes reduced.

An **"A to Z Appraiser"** provides a much needed and highly respected service. People are trusting you to help them with the biggest decision they'll ever make!!

Benefits Of Knowledge Of Appraisals

Being an *"A to Z Appraiser"* will enable you to be involved in a recession-proof business! Real Estate is still bought and sold during a recession in the economy. In addition to the typical home sales, there are foreclosure sales, relocations, and distressed sales. The only difference about a recession is that houses are sold for a lower price. Also, during a recession the mortgage loan interest rates tend to drop. As a result, many people refinance their existing mortgages to take advantage of the lower rates. All of these houses still need to be appraised, and as a result, your business can grow during a slow economy.

Unfortunately, there are people who lose their homes due to tragic circumstances in their lives. However, you're not taking advantage of anyone or being unethical by appraising properties that are the result of a distressed sale or a foreclosure. All of these properties have to be appraised. Therefore, someone is going to be hired to do the job. Everyone will be much better off if the client hires an *"A to Z Appraiser"* who does top quality work.

Being an *"A to Z Appraiser"* can make you a much better home buyer or real estate investor. Before you buy a house or a rental property you can check it from top to bottom to figure out what it's worth. You can save up to tens of thousands of dollars by determining what price to pay. Many home buyers simply pay close to the asking price that the seller lists the house for. They tend to assume that the "listing price" must be close to the market value of the property. Often this is not so. The seller can ask any price they want for their property. However, the true market value could be much less than their asking price. If you have the knowledge of how to perform good, thorough appraisals then you can negotiate some price reduction or concessions. You can intelligently inform a seller if the asking price is too high.

Being an *"A to Z Appraiser"* can make you a much better home seller. Before you sell your house you can find out what the present market value is ahead of time. An awful lot of real estate deals are killed before the real estate appraisal or home inspection is done. The buyer and seller may come to an agreement on price and terms pending the appraisal or inspection. If the appraiser is thorough, they may find that the sales price agreed upon is too high. This ends up throwing a monkey wrench into the works by lowering the sales price or killing the deal. You can also learn if the asking price for your house is too low! You don't want to sell your house for a lot less than what it's worth, do you?

Being an *"A to Z Appraiser"* can make you a much better homeowner. You can make your house safe for you and your family. You'll be able to identify electrical hazards, radon, asbestos, carbon monoxide and gas leaks, etc. Prevent accidents *before* they happen! Also, eliminate building code violations or from being cheated by contractors.

Being an *"A to Z Appraiser"* can make you a much better Realtor. If you're presently a Real Estate Agent or Broker, you already know how a low appraisal or problems found during the home inspection can kill a deal. You can greatly increase the percentages of the deals you close. You can show the seller what the current market value is at the time you take the listing for the house or condo. As a Realtor, you can inform the home seller yourself without waiting for the bank appraiser to do it later.

I'm sure all of you that are presently Realtors are aware of houses that just sit on the market for long periods of time without selling. The *major* reason a house or condo doesn't sell within a reasonable amount of time is due to the asking price of the seller. Even if a house is in a bad area and needs work, someone will buy it if the price is right!! As a Realtor, you can help to reduce your headaches and wasted time showing

> *So you see, I've got this baby set on automatic pilot. There's something in this material for just about anyone to benefit from.*

clients' an overpriced house with a seller that won't come down in price. You can get more listings due to your knowledge and expertise, which any home buyer or seller will respect. This will enable you to increase your business and income.

Being an *"A to Z Appraiser"* can make you a much better real estate consultant. If you do any consulting work, you can gain much more respect and business due to your expertise and knowledge.

Being an *"A to Z Appraiser"* can make you a much better home inspector. I do inspections as well as appraisals and I can see things that 90% of the inspectors in the business don't even know about. My inspections are much more thorough and informative for the client. Therefore, I can charge a lot more for my work than other inspectors can.

So you see, I've got this baby set on automatic pilot. There's something in this material for just about anyone to benefit from. There's only one type of individual that I can think of that can't benefit from this material. That's someone who has no intention of going into the real estate business in any way, shape or form. They also would need to have no intention of ever owning their own house or condo. If that description fits you, then throw this book away right now because it's not for you.

Description Of A Real Estate Appraisal

A real estate appraisal is a little different depending on your regional area and the type of appraisal that is being done. However, you'll be dealing with the same general appraisal process and business. There are many different types of appraisers, some of which include: commercial real estate appraisers, residential real estate appraisers, furniture appraisers, jewelry appraisers, art appraisers, automobile appraisers, and the list goes on and on. We're going to concentrate on residential real estate appraising in this book.

A real estate appraisal is an **estimate** of market value based upon the **opinion** of the appraiser. You're not stating the *exact* price that the property is worth in your appraisal report. You only give an estimate of the market value. Two separate appraisers are considered accurate if their value estimates differ by a maximum of 10% for the same property. The reason for this is that generally no two people will pay the identical price for a property. One buyer might like the house a little bit more than another buyer and so he would pay more, and vice versa. Therefore, when you estimate market value, you're merely giving your opinion. Your opinion will be based upon all of your field work and data. The estimated value in your appraisal report is the price you feel that the majority of the *typical buyers* in the area would pay for the subject property.

An appraisal involves a visual, limited time, nondestructive inspection of the subject property that you're appraising. There's no dismantling or using tools to take things apart. However, you will need some tools to help you on the appraisal. I'll tell you what tools you need a little further on in this book.

You're a real estate appraiser, you're not a repairman. Tell the client to have something checked out by a licensed contractor if it's not operating properly, or if you have any doubts about its present condition. This means that you don't need to know how to fix everything in a house. All you need to do is to be able to identify a problem, or identify whether the operating systems are working properly. To make this point more clear, I'll use an analogy with your car. Normally, you know when your car isn't running properly or if there's a problem with it. However, you don't need to know how to fix the car. All you need to do is identify that something is wrong and that a repairman needs to check it out further. You just bring the car to an auto mechanic and let them tell you exactly what's wrong and what it will cost to repair the problem.

As a real estate appraiser, you're not required to be the **Wizard of Oz**. You're not required to have a *magic wand* that reveals every, single problem with the house and site. You're not required to have *X-ray vision* to see things behind walls, ceilings or other finished areas. You're not required to have a *crystal ball* to foresee **all** potential problems that will arise in the future with the subject property. *(However some people expect you to)*.

As an appraiser you check all visible, accessible areas and operating systems, such as, heating, air-conditioning, electrical, plumbing, the roof, etc. Everything should appear to be operating properly and in satisfactory condition at the time of the appraisal.

You'll find that real estate appraising is a very interesting career. There are many different aspects that go into an appraisal report. There are photographs, some field work, some analysis of different data sources, some math calculations, etc. It's a very satisfying feeling to know that you can do very thorough appraisals.

Often when people find out that you're an appraiser they'll ask you, *"What's my house worth?"* For some strange reason people think that appraisers have some magical power. They believe an appraiser can just look at a property and be able to tell you what it's worth. You will get asked that question, *(many times if you go into this business)*. If you do, just politely tell them that an appraisal is a lot of field work. It's similar to doing a written report for school. There are no shortcuts to doing a good appraisal.

Being A State Certified Real Estate Appraiser

To do real estate appraisals for federally related transactions, there are Federal and State licenses and/or certification requirements in all states. The regulations generally require you to work under someone else's wing until you learn the basics of the business and get some training. They also may require you to take some basic appraisal classes to teach you the ropes as well. You'll find the appraisal classes to be very interesting if you have knowledgeable instructors for the courses.

If you decide to work with someone else's appraisal company, you'll find this will help you a lot in the beginning stages. You won't be calling the shots for a while, but you also won't have the overhead or liability problems. You will benefit by working with an experienced appraiser until you learn the basics.

This book is a very in-depth look at the different aspects of real estate appraising. I think that you'll find it to be very helpful and enlightening. However, it will benefit you to get some field work training alongside an experienced appraiser. That's because there are some aspects that are easier to understand if they are shown in person. If you're shown certain aspects on an actual appraisal assignment, it will be easier to understand and apply them properly. Although, the better the appraisal training manual, then the better your head start will be at becoming a qualified appraiser. I hope you find this book to be a good head start to being an appraiser!

Starting Out And Setting Up A Business

Set up a corporation in the state that you will be doing business in. This isn't a big expense. Consult an attorney in your area to assist you. You can use your home as an office. This is the most common way to start out. There's very little overhead and you don't have to pay rent and utilities for office space. Set up a separate phone line. You don't have to hire a secretary if you can't afford one, just use an answering machine. **You** set your own hours and you can work part-time or full-time, whichever you prefer.

Have business cards, stationary and brochures made up at a local printer and drop them off and introduce yourself at: the local real estate offices, law offices, banks, home inspection offices and any businesses involved in real estate. I did this for months in my beginning stages. Banks are by far your best source of appraisal business. They need to order appraisals constantly for their mortgage loans. If you get on a bank's approved appraiser list you should have more than enough business to keep you busy and keep your own savings account growing.

Relocation companies are a great source of appraisals. I had a friend who was doing over a million dollars a year in business with relocation companies for appraisals and inspections. Get the relocation directories for the phone numbers and addresses of the people to contact. When a company relocates one of their employees they generally have two appraisals and two home inspections done. The company hires one appraiser and inspector, and the employee of the company hires the other appraiser and home inspector. The purpose of this is that they get two different opinions as to the current market value and condition of the employee's house. They then agree to a sales price and the company will reimburse their employee by buying the house from them. This enables the employee to move to the new location and buy a home. Sometimes when the first two appraisals are very different in estimating market value, they hire a *third* appraiser to settle the matter!

Some insurance companies hire appraisers before they write certain homeowner's policies. Contact some of the insurance agents in your area and see if they need appraisers. Attorneys and Accountants often hire appraisers to help settle an estate. An estate is created when someone dies and the heirs have to file the tax returns and disburse or manage the personal property and assets of the deceased person. The IRS requires an appraisal to figure out what the *estate tax* will be. The family members and/or relatives are taxed on the inheritance of the personal property and assets of the deceased person.

Rent mailing lists of real estate offices, law offices, relocation companies, etc. to send out brochures and cards with a cover letter. Local billboards and radio ads can be inexpensive for the exposure you get.

Work with another appraisal company. This is a great way to start out because you get to learn the business from someone who has been doing appraisals for years. You will be building up contacts as well during your training. There are many benefits to doing this. You get to learn the basics of the business and you don't have the liability and overhead costs.

R.E. Appraisal Education

It's very important to keep educating yourself to stay up to date and knowledgeable. Join appraisal organizations and meet other appraisers. Some appraisal organizations have Errors and Omissions insurance offered to their members. Errors and Omissions insurance is <u>not</u> to be used as a safety net. Don't think that you can do bad appraisals and not have to worry about paying any penalties from lawsuits because you have E and O insurance. The purpose of E and O insurance is only in the event that you accidentally miss something on an appraisal. It's also used in the event that you get an unreasonable client who sues you for no-good reason. It only takes one or two bad and dishonest appraisers that get a few really big lawsuits against them to cancel the E and O insurance program for everyone. So don't ruin Errors and Omissions insurance for everyone else. Do good, thorough and honest appraisals.

I'll give you a perfect example of what you don't want to do concerning E and O insurance. There was recently some **Bozo** in my area who jumped into the home inspection business without knowing anything about it. Anyway, this new home inspector must have figured that he could learn the business overnight. He was telling potential customers, while giving them price quotes over the phone, that they should hire him because he had insurance. These customers would call

me and ask me if my company carried E and O insurance. I said yes but then I asked them why. When they told me what this other inspector was telling people, I was amazed at the absurdity and ignorance of this new inspector.

Just because someone has Errors and Omissions insurance doesn't mean that their insurance company is going to send checks out to anyone who wants one! If an inspector or appraiser gets slapped with too many lawsuits, then his insurance carrier will drop him like a bad habit. If that happens, then who is going to compensate all of his other clients who had totally useless home inspections or appraisals from this clown? Also, who would want to buy a house and then find out later about some major problems that should have been identified during the home inspection or appraisal? If the problems are overwhelming, then you wouldn't want to buy the house anyway, regardless of whether an insurance company was willing to compensate you for some damages.

The best insurance policy and client referral potential is to do good, honest and thorough appraisals. Each of your appraisals should take about one to two days to complete. This includes the on-site inspection, taking your field notes and photographs, finding comparable sales, gathering the pertinent data, and then writing up the appraisal report. I've heard of some appraisers doing three to four appraisals in one day. I could not believe it when I heard that. I couldn't even get all of the information and photographs together for just <u>one</u> appraisal in that amount of time, let alone write up the entire report! So don't be a *"Walk-Thru"* appraiser by taking people's money and running. Do

> Errors and Omissions insurance is <u>not</u> to be used as a safety net. Don't think that you can do bad appraisals not have to worry about paying any losses from lawsuits because you have E and O insurance.

yourself and your clients a favor. Spend enough time to check everything out properly at the job site, in obtaining the comparable sales, in gathering the data, and in putting together the written report.

Some appraisal organizations have annual national seminars. They also have classes and real estate appraisal exams that are very good for keeping you on your toes and up to date. There are monthly newsletters that keep you up to date. You can get education credits for taking real estate appraisal classes. You need education credits to renew your

Federal and State licenses and certifications, as well as, for any appraisal designation that you have.

I highly recommend you take some of the appraisal courses needed to obtain a state appraisers license. They have a class called *The Standards Of Professional Practice* that they require state licensed appraisers to take. This class will really open your eyes to the ethical and honest conduct that's required and expected of anyone in the real estate profession.

Join ASHI, the American Society of Home Inspectors, and meet other inspectors. I believe that the best home inspection organization in the country is ASHI. ASHI has the best Standards of Practice, and inspectors, and is growing very rapidly. Their Standards have reportedly been used in court cases because they're very good. I happen to be a member of the American Society of Home Inspectors as well as a State Certified Appraiser. That's something you may want to consider. Being a member of ASHI gives you much more credibility in a potential client's eyes. You will have the edge over the competition when a client is calling around for price quotes and comparing the appraisal company services in your area. There are very, very, few people that are good home inspectors *and* appraisers. I mean ASHI member inspectors and State Certified appraisers and not some guy who says he does both but has no extensive training in either.

Read books, listen to tapes, and talk to local appraisers, builders, contractors and building department inspectors to keep informed and educate your mind. There are constantly new technologies being applied to housing construction that you need to keep on top of. You also have to keep informed about the trends in the local real estate market.

Take some knowledgeable local contractors and appraisers out to lunch occasionally. This will enable you to find out about the new trends and technologies being used in new housing construction and you can compare your appraisal war stories. You may even be able to deduct it as a business expense! You'll be *amazed* at what you can learn from a contractor who specializes in a particular field. There are times when I come across something new that I haven't seen before during an appraisal. When this happens, I'll call a contractor who installs or repairs that item. I'll also call another appraiser and ask questions about it. People love to share their expertise with someone who's interested and willing to listen.

Take continuing education classes at local colleges. You may want to take a local building inspectors licensing course or test. This isn't required but it will give you more credibility and education.

Tools That Are Helpful

◊ Road maps of your area and a car compass to find the job site.
◊ A clipboard with a notepad and pens to take your field notes.
◊ Standard appraisal forms.
◊ A measuring wheel or 50-100 foot long measuring tape that can be reeled in for easy use and storage.
◊ Reliable camera and plenty of film to take interior, exterior and other photographs of the subject property, comparable sales and the neighborhood.
◊ Tool box to carry any tools.
◊ Reliable, powerful flashlight is a necessity.
◊ Lighted magnifying glass to view any data plates that are hard to read.
◊ Large probe and an awl to check wood for rot and termite damage.
◊ Hard hat, knee pads and a jump suit to wear in narrow crawl spaces.
◊ A marble and a six inch and a four-foot level to check walls and floors for being level.
◊ Pliers to help in necessary situations, such as lifting the corner of a rug to see the floor underneath.
◊ Binoculars to view the roof, chimney, siding and other parts of the house that you can't see clear enough from the ground.
◊ Folding ladder to look at the roof from a closer view.

Booking Real Estate Appraisal Jobs

To give a price quote you have to determine the amount of time and liability that's involved with the appraisal. There are appointment and price quote cards that are available from our company for a small fee. These index cards will help you give price quotes and keep track of your appraisal appointments. Contact us if you need some of these cards.

Explain to the client what's involved in doing a thorough appraisal. If you do work for banks, then they will already know the basics of what an appraisal report looks like. Let them know you're a very good, thorough real estate appraiser. Tell them how you give your clients much more data and photographs in your reports as compared to what other appraisers provide. This will help them with their decision about the subject property.

Don't make them think that your estimate of market value will be accurate to the penny because no appraisal report can be that accurate. Just make them realize how thorough you are and the realities of what an appraisal report involves. If you do this, then everything is up front for your clients to understand. They'll realize that your appraisal isn't some kind of guarantee that will exactly tell them the market value of the subject property. Remember it's an *estimate* of market value.

Sometimes you'll book jobs to appraise vacant houses. Some houses are left vacant when being sold for a number of different reasons. The homeowner could have died and it's an estate sale; the owner may have been relocated by his company for a new job position; the owner may be away for a long vacation; it could be a bank foreclosure sale, etc. If the subject property is vacant, then there are important items to be aware of. Often, vacant houses will have the utilities turned off. You should notify the client of this when booking the job. I've arrived at houses many times to do a home inspection or appraisal and the utilities were turned off. This limits what you can evaluate. For example, without electricity you can't check the outlets and switches; without gas or oil you can't test the boiler/furnace or water heater; without the water supply turned on you can't test the plumbing pressure and drainage. There's another aspect to be aware of with vacant houses. If the property is located in cold weather areas, then the heating system must be kept on all winter or else the water pipes must be winterized. This protects the pipes from water freezing, expanding and cracking the pipes.

Beginning The Appraisal

I'll go through the appraisal process. You can modify it to meet your own needs or desires. You'll be nervous for the first ten or so appraisals. This is normal. Just remember that you need to learn this material well enough, and keep up to date with all the new real estate and construction trends. If you do then you will earn the respect of the client and all third parties to the transaction by being so knowledgeable.

When I say third party people, I'm talking about people involved in the transaction, not including your client. This could be any number of people. The list includes but isn't limited to: the seller, the Realtor, the home inspector, the mortgage lender, the attorney, the seller's dog or cat, and anyone else who has an interest in the deal. I also want to make it clear that throughout this book both males and females are being referred to whenever the pronouns *he* or *she* are used. Both males and females are also referred to when I give examples of war stories that I've encountered in the real estate business. The pronouns "he" or "she" are only used for the sake of brevity.

On your way to the subject property you should drive around the area before you get there. This will enable you to get a feel for the neighborhood. Take a good look around the neighborhood to see what condition and style the houses are in. See if there are any recreational facilities, such as, parks and playgrounds nearby. Check for the distance to any local transportation, shopping and employment centers. What are the negative and positive aspects of living in this area? Etc. Take note of the condition of the exterior of the house or condo, the terrain, if there are any ponds or streams, etc. Mark down the time the on-site appraisal work begins and ends. Mark down the weather conditions. Any snow covered areas will not be visible for inspection. Rain may have signs, or lack of signs, of water in the lower level and any roof leaks.

Greet the owner and Realtor and just tell them you have to ask some questions about the house or condo to get some background. You need this info to help you with the report and the appraisal. There are some aspects of the house that you can't always detect or verify without some additional information from the seller or Realtor. Often you'll find that you can't get all the information you need from the questions you ask the owner or Realtor. Just get whatever information you can and keep a record of it. Make sure that you put their answers in the written report to CYA, which stands for Cover Your Assets. *(You can remove some letters off the end of Assets if you like)*. This will help in the event that you find out later that someone misrepresented the house or condo. You'll be able to show proof about what was stated and represented to you and your client at the time of the appraisal. This is why you want to stress to the client to arrange the on-site work at a time when the owner of the house is home. It's important to tell your client this when you're booking the appraisal. This way they'll have time to notify the owner to arrange the appointment. You should also get a copy of any real estate listing sheets, surveys, etc. See if there's anything important in these documents to help you or your client.

You have to be very gentle when you ask the seller of the house the following questions. Sometimes they get very upset and worried about all these questions. Just tell them that it's nothing personal or that you don't trust them, you just need this information to assist you with the appraisal. There are many aspects about a house that only the owner may know about and that's what you're trying to find out. If they (the seller) were buying the house, they'd want you to find out the same information from the seller as well. **Just remember that you're a guest in someone else's house! So don't be rude or get into an argument with anyone at the inspection site**. You have to always be very diplomatic and professional in this or any other business to be successful.

Some of the questions to ask:

◊ Age of House/Condo
◊ How long they lived there
◊ Any damaged areas to the floors, walls, and/or ceilings that they know about. Are any damaged areas hidden by carpets, furniture, sheetrock, etc.
◊ Any insulation added or removed to the floors, walls, and/or ceilings. Any UFFI foam or asbestos insulation removed must have licensed EPA contractor certification.
◊ Any past or present problems with the water pressure and drainage.
◊ Any past or present problems with electrical overloads, outlets, switches, etc.

◊ Does the fireplace draft properly and how often do they use it *(if applicable)*.
◊ Any exterior siding added after the original construction. What's behind it.
◊ Roof age and any past or present leaks.
◊ Any decks or additions added. If yes, are all valid permits and Certificate of Occupancies, *(C of O)*, filed at town hall.
◊ Any structural renovations done. If yes, is there a C of O for the work done.
◊ Furnace/Boiler Age. Dates and how often serviced. Are all rooms heated. Any oil tanks, used or unused, and their location. The age of any oil tanks.
◊ Age of the air-conditioning compressor. If it's too cold to test, did it operate properly last season. Dates and how often the system was serviced.
◊ Have they ever treated for termites or wood destroying insects. Date treated. Any damage from wood destroying insects, *(WDI)*. Any guarantees or documentation for any treatments performed.
◊ Any sump pumps in the house. Any water problems.
◊ Is house/condo connected to Municipal water & sewer systems. This is very important to get from them since there is no way to determine this at the site without checking the town hall records.

◊ Septic System:
◊ Any survey or plot plan showing the system.
◊ Any renovations or additions to the house that need septic system approvals, such as bathrooms added.
◊ Construction and size of septic tank.
◊ Is the tank original or was it upgraded.
◊ Date the tank was last pumped out and the times prior to this cleaning.
◊ Name of the septic service company for more info.

◊ Well Water System:
◊ Any survey or plot plan showing the system.
◊ Depth of the well.
◊ Is the well water pressure and volume adequate for normal use.
◊ Date the well pump was last serviced or replaced.
◊ Date the well water storage tank was last serviced and the age of the tank.
◊ Name of the well service company for more info.

◊ Swimming Pool:
◊ Age of the pool, filter, heater and liner.
◊ Do they have a Certificate of Occupancy and all valid permits.

◊ Any known leaks in the pool walls.
◊ Has it been properly winterized *(if applicable)*.
◊ Name of the pool service company for more info.

◊ Are there any outstanding building, zoning or other violations or any missing permits and/or approvals.
◊ Can I test all operating systems in the house or are there any that are being repaired or aren't functioning properly. Operating Systems refers to items such as the heating, air-conditioning, plumbing, electrical, wells, septics, etc.

When you ask these preinspection questions, make sure that you ask the owner or Realtor about information from any prior owners of the house. Meaning that if the seller tells you, *"No, we have never made any changes to the foundation or septic system,"* then ask them if they know of any prior owners having made any changes, repairs, etc.

The On-Site Appraisal Inspection

Some areas of the country, like Florida, don't have basements in the houses due to a high groundwater table that would cause flooding. These houses are built on a concrete slab and therefore there is no lower level. As you move from the lower level through the interior and up to the attic, move in a clockwise direction. This will help prevent you from bouncing around from room to room which may cause you to skip a room by accident.

Another *very important* item to carry is your camera with plenty of film. I take at least one full roll of twenty-four photographs for each appraisal I do. If you do this then you'll have plenty of pictures to help you when you write up the report. Don't just take the minimum number of photographs that are required to

> *Another very important item to carry is your camera with plenty of film. I take at least one full roll of twenty-four photographs for each appraisal I do.*
> *If you do this then you'll have plenty of pictures to help you when you write up the report.*

do a form appraisal report. Make the extra effort and take photos of interior rooms, the lower level, the operating systems, the attic and the exterior of the

house. You should also take photos of the neighborhood and anything else needed to help your client in reading the appraisal report. If you include these photos with your appraisal your clients will appreciate the fact that you provide them with more than the minimum requirements in your reports.

You have to remember to bring a 50-100 foot long measuring tape or an appraisal measuring wheel to take any pertinent dimensions. Some of the items that must be measured are: the outside dimensions of the house to estimate square footage, any decks, patios or pools, any garages, etc. You have to also bring a notepad so that you can write down the dimensions and a diagram of the exterior and the interior of the house. On the interior you'll be drawing a diagram with the layout of the floor plan to include in your written report. You don't have to measure the interior rooms, except for the basement. You measure the *outside* of a building to estimate the square footage. If you take measurements on the interior of the house you should add about six inches to the figures. This is done because generally you should measure from the outside of the finished walls.

I'll always start the on-site inspection in the lower level because this is usually where the operating systems are located. For an appraisal, I usually spend at least 20 minutes in the lower level of a house looking at the operating systems and for structural, water and termite problems. Take a good look around, the lower level is an area that can really show a lack of maintenance and some problems that need to be repaired. We'll go into much more detail about how to do the on-site inspection in the following pages. But for now I'll go through some of the basics.

Some signs of structural problems are large cracks in the foundation walls that are wider than 1/4 of an inch. Large horizontal cracks are **very** serious and must be evaluated by a licensed contractor. Signs of water problems are indicated by *efflorescence* on the walls and floors. Efflorescence is the white mineral salts that are the residue left on masonry construction materials due to moisture. Another indication of water problems is rotted wood members on the floors and walls. Check the base of any stored items in the lower level and underneath the corners of any carpets or floor coverings. Signs of wood destroying insect damage are indicated by wood beams that appear hollow and decayed. Probe the wood structural beams where visible and accessible.

When you look at the operating systems, check for any signs of aging and a lack of proper maintenance. Obviously if the boiler, or any other operating system, looks like they're on their last leg then you have to take this into account when determining the overall condition of the house. Check for insulation in the ceiling and if there is any heat or air-conditioning provided to finished rooms in the lower level. Look at the main electrical panel and all subpanels to see if there is any rust on them. I'll go into much more detail in the following pages to really show you how to evaluate the condition of the house. If you learn this material well enough, you'll be *light years* ahead of the competition!!

If there are any finished rooms or structural changes noted, make sure you find out if all valid permits and approvals have been obtained for this work. If there are no permits then this could be a building code violation that has to be corrected.

Before leaving this area, don't forget to take your measurements and photographs of the basement and all operating systems. This way when you get back to your office, you can refer to them while writing up the appraisal report. Just use your eyes and common sense when you're doing your inspections and make notes on anything that affects the value of the subject property.

The Operating Systems, Lower Level, Interior and Exterior Inspection sections are very condensed versions of those found in our home inspection book:

Home Inspection Business From A to Z

The Operating Systems Inspection

Heating Systems

The average homeowner often improperly uses the term *furnace* when discussing their *boiler*. This same confusion happens with *heat pumps*. I'll explain the difference between a Furnace, Boiler and a Heat Pump:

◊ A *furnace* has a burner that heats the air and then blows it out of vents, sometimes called registers. You won't find any radiators if a furnace heats the house. Both a furnace and a heat pump use vents to discharge warm air in the house.

◊ A *boiler* heats by boiling water to create steam in a steam system. In a hot water system, a boiler heats water without reaching the boiling temperature and then circulates it in the pipes. The heated water or steam is sent through radiators to heat the house.

◊ A *heat pump* is a central air-conditioning system that works in reverse in the winter time. No matter how cold it is outside, there's always some heat in the air. The freon in the heat pump can absorb this heat. The air is then blown over the freon coils and the house is heated with warm air through vents.

Check for a service card showing the last date of maintenance service for the heating system. The ceiling over the heating system should have a covering of sheetmetal or 5/8 inch fireproof sheetrock to help

> The flue pipe is used to safely discharge the carbon monoxide and other products of combustion. These gases _must be safely discharged_ from the house. They're _lethal gases!!!_

prevent the spread of fires in this area.

Check the flue pipe on gas and oil fired heating systems. The flue pipe is usually located at the rear of the unit. The flue pipe is used to safely discharge the carbon monoxide and other products of combustion. All gas and oil fired burners discharge these products of combustion. These gases _must be safely discharged_ from the house. They're _lethal gases_!!! It's similar to

having the exhaust fumes from your car discharge inside your house. It'll kill everyone in the house! The flue pipe sections _must_ be screwed together for safety. They must have an upward pitch. They should not be within four inches of any combustible material, such as wood, to help prevent fires.

Check the oil tank if it's located in the interior of the house and is visible. I prefer interior oil tanks more than underground tanks due to the potential expense of a leak. There have been recent Environmental Protection Agency court rulings about leaking oil tanks that incur stiff fines for the owner of the leaking tanks. It's also expensive to dispose of oil tanks because they're considered a contaminated waste like asbestos and toxic chemicals. If there's an underground oil tank, recommend that a licensed environmental contractor perform tests to find out if there are any leaks. There are a number of different tests to detect a leaking oil tank. Each test has positive and negative aspects to it. A Petro Test by a reputable oil contractor be performed to find out if there are any leaks. A Petro-Test is a pressure test that an oil contractor performs. What they do is seal off the oil tank vents and feed lines and pump air into the tank. They then monitor the pressure in the tank to determine if it drops which would indicate a leak. Another test is a Water Test. If an oil tank leaks there's a good chance water will enter it. The oil contractor will check the tank to find out if there's any water in it.

Determine if any C of O's, *(Certificate of Occupancy)*, permits or surveys are needed in the local municipality with underground oil tanks. Interior and underground oil tanks generally last about 25 to 30 years and longer if they're maintained. If there are a lot of evergreen trees around the area where an oil tank is buried it'll cut down the life expectancy of the tank. This is because these trees add a lot of acid into the soil that rots the tanks quicker.

Check all heating pipe joints for rust or leaking conditions that'll require repairs. You'll usually find some rust unless it's a new unit.

Important

Air-Conditioning Systems

Don't turn on any central or window or wall air-conditioning units when the outdoor air temperature is 65 degrees Fahrenheit or lower. The interior pressure that's required to properly operate an air-conditioning system is too low when the temperature is 65 degrees or lower. If the unit is turned on, there are a number of ways that you could damage the compressor or the other components and end up buying the owner a new air-conditioning system.

Don't listen to anyone that says you can test the system anyway when the temperature is too cold. Let them turn on the system so if it blows, then they have to pay for it. I've heard a few war stories about poorly trained home inspectors that turned on A/C systems in the winter time and ended up blowing the compressors. Don't let this happen to you.

Check the exterior compressor unit while the air-conditioning system is on. See if it's making any unusual noises or if it's very old and rusty. Check the data plate to try to figure out the age and size of the unit. The life expectancy of a compressor is about 10 years depending upon the amount of usage. The life expectancy also depends on the quality of the unit and the maintenance given to the system.

> *Don't turn on any central or window or wall A/C units when the outdoor air temperature is 65 degrees Fahrenheit or lower. If the unit is turned on, there are a number of ways that you could damage the compressor or other components.*

Domestic Water Heaters

Usually the water heaters are a separate unit but can be immersion coils inside boilers. Separate water heater units can be gas, oil or electrically heated. An immersion coil system has water pipes that carry cold water inside a coil located in the side of the boiler. The coils are *immersed* in the hot boiler water, hence you get the name *immersion coils*.

The standard size water heater for a single family house is 40 gallons. Sometimes you'll find an oversized water heater in the house. It's not as energy efficient because a lot of water will be heated and then it will just sit in the tank without being used.

Check for any rust or water leaking conditions on the unit. The water heater should be kept on the warm setting for maximum efficiency and life expectancy. The life expectancy of a water heater is 10-12 years. A high temperature setting will cause the unit to constantly be heating water higher than is necessary which can cause premature failure.

During your interior inspection, check the water at some of the faucets and tubs. You want to make sure that adequate hot water is available.

Plumbing System

Look at all visible plumbing lines. There will be very little to view in a finished basement or behind walls and ceilings. Check for any corrosion, leaks or any buildup of mineral deposits. There are several types of plumbing line materials including Copper, Brass, Galvanized Iron, Lead, PVC, and Cast Iron.

Often you'll see water stains on some of the floor joists, which are the beams that support the floor above. You'll also see water stains on the subflooring, which is the base for the floor above. Minor water stains are normal, especially underneath kitchens and baths. You need to be concerned about extensive water damage. If any doubts exist, check the floor above the damaged or stained areas. Try bouncing on the floor above during your interior inspection.

Check the water main line where it enters the house. The water main for a house connected to a city water system is usually located in the lower level at the base of the foundation wall facing the street. The water main for a house connected to an on-site well water system is usually located in the lower level at the base of any of the foundation walls. Ask the owner or Realtor if you can't find the main water line. Sometimes they're behind personal items or finished walls in the lower level.

Find out what type of pipe material the main water line is made of. Usually it'll be copper for a house with city water and it may be plastic for a house with well water. *Lead* piping is very rarely found in my area. It's not used any longer because the lead content can seep into the water supply which is very hazardous. These

> *Also, recommend that all lead piping be replaced with a new pipe for safety. The reason for this is that lead poisoning is the NUMBER ONE childhood disease in the USA.*

pipes will **always** leak some amount of lead content into the house water supply. A lead main entry line will be silver in color and may have a small bubble-type bulge in the beginning of the line. This bulge is known as a "wiped" joint. If you see a lead main water line or any lead piping in the house, highly recommend that the client have a laboratory water analysis done for safety. Also, recommend that all lead piping be replaced with a new pipe for safety. The reason for this is that lead poisoning is the ***NUMBER ONE*** childhood disease in the USA. Lead is an element that doesn't break down when it gets in your system. The effects of lead poisoning in children are *irreversible!!* Lead poisoning can damage the kidneys, nervous system and blood, and can cause permanent brain damage. So don't take any chances with this stuff.

In older houses there will be lead in some of the soldered pipe joints. Gradually, over time the amount of lead in the solder will be reduced from leaching into the drinking water. Ice makers are prone to very high lead levels. The water in a freezer ice maker can sit in the pipe for days. This allows enough time for the lead to leach into the water at high levels. A lead abatement contractor told me that he's tested houses where the children had extremely high levels of lead in their bodies. He said that after the test results came back, almost all the lead in their bodies was coming from the ice cubes!

I telling you ahead of time, that if you come across any lead piping in a house, some Realtors and other third parties will try to sugarcoat the problem. They're going to tell your client that *"they only need to install a water filter and it'll be fine."* Don't let your client be snowed with that line! Tell them to remove all lead piping and eliminate the problem for good.

Check for an electrical grounding wire. This is a **very important** safety item!!! It should be located by the water meter or the entry of the water main line. The purpose of this is to ground the house electrical system for safety. Electrical systems can also be grounded to an exterior metal rod driven 8-10 feet into the ground. The grounding wire doesn't have to be insulated like most electrical wiring because there's normally no current passing through this wire. It may be enclosed in BX cable or a conduit, which is a metal covering for protection from damage.

The grounding clamps should not be rusty or loose, but often they are. The grounding wire should be clamped on both sides of the water meter, if there is a water meter installed. If there is no water meter, then the grounding wire should be clamped on both sides of the water main shutoff valve. Often it will only be clamped to one side of the water meter or main shutoff valve. Tell the client that they need to have a *jumper cable* installed with clamps to span the water meter.

> *Check for an electrical grounding wire. This is a very important safety item!!! It should be located by the water meter or the water main line entry.*

This is an inexpensive item to install and it's a safety requirement of the National Electric Code. A jumper cable is merely an additional heavy gauge wire about three feet long that's attached on both sides of the water meter. A jumper cable normally doesn't need to be an insulated wire because no electrical current should be passing through this wire unless there is a problem condition.

During the interior inspection check the water pressure and drainage by briefly running the faucets and tubs. In the bathrooms run the sink faucet, the tub or shower faucet and flush the toilet simultaneously. Watch the faucets to see if the pressure drops significantly. A minor pressure drop is normal but a large pressure drop can indicate either poor water pressure or clogged supply lines. Poor water pressure in some supply lines may be due to the street water pressure being too low. However, it's most likely caused by some supply pipes inside the house that have clogged over the years. Tell the client to have a licensed plumber check it out to determine if there are many clogged lines or just a small section that needs replacing.

Don't forget to turn off any faucets that you're testing during the inspection. You don't want to flood someone's house. Water damage can be very messy and expensive to repair.

Well Water Systems

The main components of a well water system consist of a well pump, the water lines, the pressure gauge and the water storage tank. Well pumps are usually located inside the well and aren't visible. The life expectancy of a well pump is about 7-10 years but can be longer if the pump isn't overworked or neglected. The life expectancy also depends upon the type and quality of the pump installed and the acidity of the well water. Generally you should use the 7-10 year range during an inspection.

Try to get as much information as you can about the well from the owner or Realtor. Use the preinspection questions that I mentioned earlier for a guideline but don't be afraid to ask any other questions for further information. Don't be surprised if they don't know very much about the well system. Unfortunately, this is often the case. Don't be surprised if the answers you get don't seem to be the truth from the results of the well test.

Look at the well water lines to determine their condition. Take a look at the well water storage tank, if it's visible. Check for any rust or aging signs. The

> The minimum acceptable flow for a well system is five gallons per minute, (GPM). Some local area codes may require a higher GPM rating, so check with your local building department.

water storage tank should be painted and insulated to prevent any condensation from building up on the outside. The condensation causes rust. There should always be a pressure relief valve for safety in case the pressure in the system gets too high. It's usually set at 75 psi, *(pounds per square inch)*, depending upon the type and capacity of the storage tank. Make sure the tank has an air fill valve to adjust the air-to-water ratio inside during periodic maintenance.

The minimum acceptable flow for a well system is five gallons per minute, *(GPM)*. Some local codes may require a higher GPM rating, so check with your local building department. What you need to be concerned about, is an abnormal drop in pressure. Just ask yourself and the client, if they're present: Are the pressure and volume of the water flow enough to take a shower with? If the answer is no, then tell the client to have the system checked out by a licensed well service contractor.

Check to find out if there's a water filter installed on the system. I even recommend that the client use water filters when their house is connected to the city water system. Water filters are *highly* recommended for health reasons, especially with all of the pollutants going into the water supply these days.

Septic Systems

The main components of a septic system consist of the drainage lines, the holding tank and the leaching fields or seepage pits. The life expectancy of a septic system is about 30 years depending upon the type of construction and the maintenance given it. Try to get as much information as you can about the septic from the owner or Realtor. Use the preinspection questions that I mentioned earlier for a guideline but don't be afraid to ask any other questions for further information. Don't be surprised if they don't know very much about the septic system. Unfortunately, this is often the case.

I'll tell you a war story I heard that oughta jar ya a little bit. I know an inspector who did an inspection where the client, the Realtor, the seller, and the real estate listing all stated that the house was connected to the municipal sewer system. About four months later, the inspector got a letter from the client. The letter stated that the client went to town hall to find out about installing a pool in his backyard. He was awfully surprised to find out that the house had a septic system and was **not** connected to the city sewer system.

✗ VERY IMPORTANT INFO

There's no way to tell for sure if a main drainage line leads to a septic system or a city sewer system because they're identical. The point I'm trying to make, is that there's no way to know for sure whether or not the house is connected to the municipal sewer system. So you want to mention to the client that the only way for him to determine this is to check with the local building or health departments at town hall. Now do you see what I mean about being thorough and Covering Your Assets. This is why you need to ask the owner the preinspection questions and be up front and honest with your client.

Septic systems <u>must</u> be pumped out clean and inspected internally every two to three years at least. It should be more frequent than every two years if there are many people in the house or they do a lot of entertaining. I know a septic cleaning contractor in my area who has one customer that gets their tank cleaned every 3-4 *months* because they have a very high water usage.

You will encounter some homeowners who think you don't have to pump septic tanks clean. They believe in the fairy tale myth that the bacterial action inside the septic tank decomposes all the solid waste away. There are some products sold that claim to help the decomposition in septic tanks. Some homeowners think you merely have to use these products instead of pumping the tank periodically. You must tell your client that this is totally incorrect and the client needs to have the tank pumped and internally inspected. When this occurs you'll often have a third party say, *"If it's not broken, don't fix it."* My response to that is, *"Should you wait until you're terminally ill before going to the doctor for a physical?"*

> *The point I'm trying to make, is that there's no way to know for sure whether or not the house is connected to the municipal sewer system.*
> *So you want to mention to the client that the only way for him to determine this is to check with town hall.*

Electrical Syst

The main components of the electrical system consist of: the service entrance lines, the electrical conduit lines, the electrical meter, the main electrical panel and any subpanels, fuses or circuit breakers, the interior electrical wiring and the electrical system grounding cable.

<u>**Remember that electricity can kill you!!**</u> Before touching the main panel or any subpanels check them with a voltage tester to make sure that it's not electrified. Voltage testers can be purchased very inexpensively at a local hardware or electrical supply store. There was a story in the ASHI monthly newsletter about one inspector who noticed that the insulation on the service entrance line had worn off at the top of the main panel. This caused the main panel to be electrified. Luckily he tested the panel before touching it.

Also, don't go near any exposed wiring or any electrical panels or wiring if there's water on the floor or near the wires. Water and electricity *don't* mix! You're not paid to get electrocuted; you're paid to appraise the house. The ASHI and the state appraisal standards state very clearly that home inspectors and/or appraisers are not required to do anything that can be hazardous to themselves or to others.

Check the main panel for any rust or corrosion. If there's excessive rust or corrosion, then recommend that a licensed electrician evaluate the system. After testing the electrical panel with a voltage tester check to make sure it's installed on the wall securely by *gently* trying to shake the panel. Be careful - you don't want to loosen the electrical panel nor any wiring, you just want to see if it's secured properly. See if there are any hazardous conditions around the panel. Some hazards to watch out for are: potential water, objects in the way, the panel being too high to reach safely, etc.

Check to see whether the system has fuses or circuit breakers. Newer houses have *circuit breakers* which are the plastic switches that can easily be turned on or off by the homeowner. Older houses have *fuses* which are the glass screw-in type. <u>Do not turn any circuit breakers off or on or replace any fuses!!</u> Sometimes a circuit will be off because the homeowner is making repairs or the circuit was overloaded. Just inform the client of this and tell them to check with the owner or a licensed electrician to figure out the cause. You aren't allowed to turn any circuits on or off or replace any fuses for safety reasons.

Check to see if there are any open circuit breaker or fuse slots in the main panel or any subpanels. Open slots need to be covered with *blanks* or spare circuit breakers or fuses. This will prevent anyone from sticking their fingers or any objects inside the main panel and getting electrocuted. *Subpanels* are small electrical panels that branch off from the main electrical panel. The purpose of subpanels is to prevent very long branch circuit runs in the house. Long branch wires can cause a *"drop"* in the electrical current.

> All two prong outlets should be upgraded to the modern three prong grounded outlets by a licensed electrician.

In the main panel you'll see the main disconnect for the entire electrical system in the house. This is similar to the water and gas main shutoff valves. Sometimes the main disconnect is located outside the house, next to the electrical meter. Check the main disconnect for an amperage rating number. It should be written right on the circuit breaker or fuse. Fuse systems have either a *pullout* fuse box or a *cartridge* fuse for a main disconnect. A pullout fuse box is simply a cartridge fuse inside a small box that's pulled out to shut off all the electrical power to the house. A cartridge fuse is a fuse that looks like a miniature stick of dynamite that has metal blades at the top and bottom.

Do not remove any electrical panel covers!! Do not pull out the main disconnect box or touch the cartridge fuse if you can't see their rating number!! Just tell the client that you can't determine the amperage on these disconnects due to the type of system that it is. Tell them to have a licensed electrician find out the amperage for them.

It's **extremely** important that the electrical system be grounded to a properly working grounding cable attached to the water main line or a grounding rod in the soil. Make sure the client understands the importance of maintaining a properly operating grounding system of the electrical service for safety. Review the plumbing section that details the attachment of the electrical ground cable near the water meter.

As you go through the interior and exterior of the house check for any loose wiring that needs to be

secured or any electrical hazards. Make sure you warn the client and the homeowner of any hazards. Remember, electricity can kill people so be very thorough and careful during the inspection. Check for loose electrical switches and outlets that need to be secured. Also, check for any "do-it-yourself" work in the house. All electrical repairs **must** be performed by a licensed electrician. All valid permits and building department approvals must be obtained for any work done. As a safety precaution, check to make sure that the outlets and switches in the bathroom **are not** reachable from the tub or shower. Remember that water and electricity don't mix! Remind your client of this.

Older houses will have the two pronged outlets as opposed to the modern three prong types. The third prong is used for the grounding prong in electrical cord plugs. The purpose of this grounding prong is that most appliances today have an internal ground. All two prong outlets should be upgraded to the modern three prong grounded outlets by a licensed electrician.

In newer construction or recently renovated houses you may find *Ground Fault Circuit Interrupters* in some outlets. They're also called GFCI's for short. GFCI outlets have two buttons in the middle that are marked *test* and *reset.* A Ground Fault Circuit Interrupter is an electronic device that will trip or turn off the circuit when it senses a potentially hazardous condition. It's very sensitive and operates very quickly. The National Electric Code recommends that GFCI's be installed anywhere near water for safety. Water prone areas include basements, garages, kitchens, bathrooms and all exterior outlets. You should recommend the installation of GFCI's to all of your clients for safety reasons. They're an inexpensive item

> The National Electric Code recommends that GFCI's be installed anywhere near water for safety.
> Water prone areas include basements, garages, kitchens, bathrooms and all exterior outlets.

to have installed and they significantly increase electrical safety in the home.

If the client has children, recommend that they install child proof caps for the electrical outlets. These are small plastic plugs to cover any unused outlets so a child won't stick anything into them and get electrocuted. You should also recommend that they use child guards for all cabinets to prevent children from opening cabinets that have cleansers and sharp objects inside.

The Lower Level Inspection

Lower Level

Some houses are built on a concrete slab and therefore there's no lower level to inspect. When you're inspecting the lower level of a house move in a clockwise or counter clockwise direction so you make sure you don't miss anything. Some lower level areas will be finished with rugs on the floors and sheetrock on the walls and ceilings and you can't view behind these finished coverings. Finished lower level areas add more value in price to a home but they make inspections more difficult for home inspectors and appraisers. Some lower level areas will be inaccessible due to personal items of the seller put there for storage. Just tell the client that you don't have X-ray vision and you'll try to evaluate as much as possible. Any inaccessible areas can't be evaluated so just do the best you can.

Check the lower level steps and any entrances to make sure they're in good condition and safe. All stairs need to have handrails and evenly spaced steps for safety. This will help prevent any tripping hazards.

Check the construction materials used for the foundation walls. The foundation will be made of poured concrete in new construction. Concrete block foundation walls are also common to find. Brick and stone constructed walls are usually found in older houses. Due to the cost of construction today, you probably won't find brick or stone foundation walls in newer houses.

The floor of the lower level should have a concrete covering. The vast majority of the time it will have a concrete covering. If there is a dirt floor, you should recommend that a concrete covering be installed. This will help prevent water, termite and radon entry in the house. Covering a dirt floor with concrete can be expensive, so tell the client to obtain an estimate before closing on the house.

Check for any large cracks in the walls and floors. You'll always find some minor settlement cracks in the walls and floors. These minor cracks are caused by the settling of the house and the expansion and contraction of the construction materials. As long as the settlement cracks are less the 1/4 inch wide, then it's a normal condition. Just tell the client to have the cracks caulked and sealed to prevent water entry and to monitor these cracks for future or further movement.

All construction materials will expand and contract with the weather and temperature changes during the year. This can also create these minor cracks that you'll find. However, the cracks that you're looking for are long horizontal cracks or cracks over 1/4 inch in width. These cracks are much more serious, and if you find any, tell the client to have a licensed contractor evaluate them and give estimates for any repairs needed. Cracks over 1/4 inch wide indicate excessive differential settlement of the house and aren't normal. You'll find large cracks from time to time, so just remember to be careful and not to rush the inspection where you'll overlook them.

Long horizontal cracks are another indication of potentially serious problems with the foundation. You won't find these cracks as often, but if you do you better recommend that a licensed contractor evaluate the foundation for the client. Long horizontal cracks can indicate that the foundation wall is being pushed inward by the soil. The wall **will** collapse if this movement continues. Obviously, you can't see any cracks behind finished areas or personal items in the lower level. That's why you have to notify the client of the limits of the inspection due to inaccessible areas.

See if there are any areas of the foundation that have been altered from the time of the original construction of the house. If you notice any alterations, then recommend that the client check with town hall to make sure all valid permits and approvals have been obtained for the work performed. The last thing you need is to have someone buy a house and find out that the do-it-yourself work done to the original foundation doesn't pass the local codes and is unsafe.

Check the main girder beams, all support posts, the floor joists, and the subflooring where visible and accessible. Probe all wood members for rot or wood destroying insect damage. Sometimes in some newer construction you'll find a steel *"I"* beam as the main girder of the house. This is superior construction because the steel *"I"* beams have tremendous structural support. Check any steel beams for rust that will require painting or repairs.

Probe some wood floor joists for rot or wood destroying insect damage. Often you'll find damage from rot due to water leaks over the years in a bathroom or kitchen above. Check for any sagging sections of the floor joists that will suggest unusual settlement and sloping floors in the rooms above.

Crawl Spaces

Some houses will have crawl spaces which are small areas underneath the house that aren't high enough to stand up in. You should ask the owner if there are any crawl spaces before starting your inspection. Ask this because the entrances to crawl space areas can be hidden by personal items or wall finishings.

You should use a jumpsuit, kneepads, a hardhat, gloves, and a flashlight to enter any crawl space areas that aren't too narrow for you to safely enter. A crawl space is an area that **demands** attention. Crawl spaces need attention because there's a higher risk of rot and

> *A crawl space is an area that demands attention. There's a higher risk of rot and termite infestation due to these areas being dark and damp.*

termite infestation due to these areas being dark and damp most of the time. So don't get lazy and just assume everything is OK in the crawl space. You may end up regretting it if the client might call you up six months later to complain about the termite damage they found in the crawl space. You'll have a hard time defending yourself if you didn't check this area if it was accessible at the time of your inspection.

Check for the condition of the foundation walls, support posts, main girder, floor joists and subflooring in the crawl space. Look for the same problems that were discussed in the lower level section.

Gas Service

If the house is connected to the local gas utility lines in the street, check the condition of the gas meter and gas lines. If the house isn't connected to any gas service lines, recommend to the client that they check with the local utility company. They'll need to find out what the costs are to hook up or if it's even possible to

> *If you smell or detect any gas leaks IMMEDIATELY tell the client, all third parties and the homeowner to contact the local utility company to make repairs.*
> *Leaking gas will explode!!!*

get gas service in the house. Some areas don't have natural gas service and the client might not know this. Don't just assume your client is aware of the lack of gas service lines in the street. You don't want him to be confronted with any surprises after he moves into the house.

The gas meter is usually located in the lower level or just outside the house next to the foundation. All gas service lines should be approved black iron gas piping. There should not be any copper or other types of metals being used for gas supply lines. If there are, then you should recommend that they have a licensed plumber make any necessary repairs to bring the gas lines up to the building codes.

If the gas lines are rusty, recommend that they be painted. Make sure that there's a main shutoff valve near the gas meter for safety. You might want to purchase a hand held combustible gas detector to check the visible gas lines and the meter for any gas leaks. If you smell or detect any gas leaks **IMMEDIATELY** tell the client, all third parties and the homeowner to contact the local utility company to make repairs. Any leaking gas will explode!!! Don't take any chances.

Natural gas is colorless and odorless when it comes from the earth. The gas utility companies put the odor into the gas before it reaches your house. The reason they put the odor in the gas is so that it's easier to detect a gas leak. If you couldn't see nor smell a gas leak, then you wouldn't be aware of a problem until *after* an explosion occurred.

Some houses have *Propane Gas* or *Liquid Petroleum Gas* service, also called LPG for short. This is similar to getting oil deliveries because the tanks are filled by a local LPG gas supplier. Check the condition of the LPG gas tanks for any rust or corrosion. Also, make sure that the tank is properly leveled on a sturdy foundation. Recommend that the client check with town hall to make sure all valid permits are on file for the LPG tanks on the site.

Also, remind the client not to bring any gas tanks into the house, such as barbecue tanks or automobile gas cans. Barbecue gas tanks are under extreme pressure, like scuba diving tanks. *If they ever exploded, they'd blow up the entire house and everyone in it!!*

Auxiliary Systems

Check for the existence of any alarm systems, fire detection systems, intercoms, burglar alarms, central vacuum systems, lawn sprinklers, etc. Often the control panels for these devices are located in the lower level.

You're not required to evaluate these systems during an appraisal. Just tell the client to get any manuals from the owner and find out how to operate these systems. Tell the client to find out if any fire or alarm systems are hooked up to any monitoring services and/or the local police or fire departments. Also, have them check to see what the fees are for this service.

Water Penetration

While you're in the lower level you want to check for any signs of water problems in the house. This is something you *don't* want to forget. It certainly isn't life threatening to the occupant of the house to overlook water problems during an inspection. However, you will get phone calls from angry clients who have discovered that they get water in the lower level of their new home. Fortunately, I never got any angry phone calls but I know some inspectors who have. People get very upset if they get water in their basement.

If you're inspecting the house during the rainy season, then the groundwater table will be higher than normal. You should always tell your client to visit the house after it rains, before the closing. This way they will be able to see for themselves if there is a potential problem with water penetration. Signs of water penetration can be white mineral salts on the concrete walls and floors. This is called *efflorescence* and it's caused by water seeping through the concrete and then drying on the exterior portion. After the water dries, it leaves the white, mineral salt from the concrete as a residue. Most lower level areas will get some minor efflorescence on the lower portion of the walls and floors. This is from the normal humidity in the lower level because these rooms are located underground. Recommend that the client use a dehumidifier to help prevent moisture.

In the corners you may see indications of water stains. Often the cause of these stains is due to the lack of gutters and downspouts on the house. Another cause is that the downspouts are draining right next to the foundation walls on the exterior. All downspouts should be piped away from the house about five feet so

You're looking for excessive or abnormal signs of water problems, not just normal humidity and condensation stains.

the rainwater won't drain next to the foundation and enter the lower level. Sometimes the downspouts drain into underground drain lines. These lines can become clogged due to leaves or small animals becoming stuck in them. Underground drain lines need to be checked periodically for proper operation.

The grading of the soil next to the exterior of the house can also cause minor water stains on the lower level walls and floors. All soil next to the foundation should slope away from the side of the house to help prevent rainwater from entering the lower level. We'll talk more about gutters, downspouts, and soil grading in the exterior section of the book.

Another way to check for water problems is to probe the wood members that are in contact with the floor, such as, workbench posts, storage items, wood shelves, etc. Check under the corner of any carpeting or floor coverings in the lower level. If there's a water problem, then these areas will have signs of it. You're looking for excessive or abnormal signs of water problems, not just normal humidity and condensation stains. Be wary of recently painted lower level walls and floors. Sometimes the homeowner will paint just before selling a house. This can hide any indications of water problems.

Check for the existence of any sump pumps. *Sump pumps* are pumps that help carry water away from the house. Sump pumps are located in small pits dug into the lower level floor and have a drainage pipe to carry water to a more desirable location. When sump pumps are installed, it usually indicates that the lower level has a water penetration problem. Sometimes, you'll find a sump pump in a lower level that doesn't have any water problems. One reason for this is that some builders and homeowners install these pumps as a precautionary measure, even if they haven't had water penetration.

Check with the local building department to find out if the subject property is located in a designated flood hazard zone. A *flood hazard zone* is a designated area by the government. These areas have a certain potential of becoming flooded from time to time. Flood maps are located in every town hall and are available to the public to view for free. If a house is located in a flood hazard zone, the homeowner should obtain flood hazard insurance on top of the regular homeowner and title insurance for safety.

The Interior Inspection

Kitchen

After finishing in the lower level you're ready to begin inspecting the livable areas of the house. I usually start with the kitchen and move from room to room but feel free to adapt the inspection procedure to any method you like. Check the kitchen walls and floors for any structural problems or settlement cracks. Check the condition of the kitchen floor covering. The majority of houses have vinyl linoleum or ceramic tile floor coverings. In some houses you'll find hardwood on the kitchen floors. Hardwood isn't used as a kitchen floor often because of the possibility of it getting wet and damaged in this area. Be careful when inspecting older houses that have 9 inch x 9 inch floor tiles made of a very hard material. These tiles are usually a Vinyl and Asbestos material so you want to notify your client about the possible asbestos problems with them.

Check the kitchen cabinets by opening and closing a few of them. Make sure the cabinets are securely fastened to the wall and floor. I know an inspector who was inspecting one home and the entire kitchen cabinet came right off the wall when he was checking it.

See if there are enough electrical outlets for modern usage and that they have Ground Fault Circuit Interrupter protection. Run the kitchen faucet hot and cold lines to make sure there's adequate hot water and there are no leaks underneath the sink. If there's a spray attachment in the sink area, check that as well. Sometimes they won't be operating properly.

Ask the client, the seller or Realtor if the appliances are being sold with the house. Most of the time they are. If they're sold with the house, then spot check the appliances by turning them on and off briefly. For refrigerators, just open the doors to make sure they're cold inside. Tell the client you're very limited in what you can evaluate as to the life expectancy of appliances. This way the client won't think you're guaranteeing that the appliances will work for many years to come.

Note the condition and age of the appliances and recommend that any older units be upgraded for energy efficiency and convenience.

Bathrooms

Check the bathroom walls and floors for any structural problems or settlement cracks. Check the condition of the bathroom wall and floor coverings. Most houses have ceramic tile floor coverings and part of the walls may have tile coverings. In some houses you'll find carpeting on the bathroom floors. Carpeting isn't used very often because of the possibility of it getting wet. Lift up a corner of the carpet to see what's underneath. Sometimes there are cracked and damaged tiles or water stains.

Press on some tiles, especially in the bathtub and shower area to see if any are loose. Check to see if the tiles need to be caulked between the joints to help prevent water leaks behind the walls. Some shower and tub areas are made of a premolded plastic and fiberglass material. Check these for any cracks and proper caulking around the edges.

Check the condition of the bathroom sink area for any cracks or loose sections. Make sure the drain stop mechanism in the sink is working. Often they won't be. Test any bathroom ventilation fans for proper operation. See if there's at least one electrical outlet and that it has Ground Fault Circuit Interrupter protection. Sometimes in older houses there won't be any grounded outlets in the bathroom which is an inconvenience.

Check the water pressure and drainage. There are usually local guidelines about what the minimum allowable water pressure should be, but generally, most houses will always meet the minimum criteria.

After running the water for a few minutes check to see if the sink and tub drain properly. Sometimes they'll drain very slowly and need to be unclogged.

Floors and Stairs

As you go through the house check the floors for any sagging or uneven areas that'll indicate structural settlement. Jump on the floor in each room to make sure they're sound. Don't jump so hard that you knock things off the walls, just do it lightly. Also, remember to look above you before you jump to test the floors. One time I forget to do this and I hit my head on a light fixture above me. Also, remember to look above you before you jump to test the floors. One time I forget to do this and I hit my head on a light fixture above me.

If there are hardwood floors, see if you notice any damaged areas or bowed sections. If there are carpets, check for signs of aging and worn areas that'll show the need for replacement. Check under the corner of some carpeting, if you can, to find out what's underneath. It's usually hardwood or plywood underneath but check to make sure and notify the client of what you see. The reason for this is that some people think that there's always hardwood floors underneath the carpeting. After they move into the house they may want to remove the carpets and leave the hardwood floors visible. You don't want them to be surprised about finding plywood as opposed to nice hardwood floors under the carpets.

You also have to be careful about carpets that hide damaged areas underneath. I did an inspection once, where the client bought the house from a dishonest seller. After the client moved in, they found damage under the carpeting. The seller intentionally hid the

> *Check underneath the corner of some carpeting, if you can, to find out what's underneath. It's usually hardwood or plywood underneath but check to make sure and notify the client of what you see.*

damage during the home inspection. The seller had placed a couch over one section and put a large pile of toys and boxes over another section. I told the client to do a "walk-thru" inspection before the closing. This would enable them to check for any damaged areas after all furniture and personal items were removed from the house. The client did a walk-thru but they still

didn't see this damage until after they removed the carpeting.

You also have to be careful to see if there are any moisture problems underneath hardwood floors. Moisture from basements, crawl spaces, water leaks, etc. will cause a hardwood floor to buckle. The reason the floor buckles, is that the wood absorbs the moisture and when it dries out, the wood will expand. If there are no gaps between the wood boards to allow for this expansion, then the boards will buckle upwards.

Check all staircases for sturdiness and secure handrails. Always recommend that they install handrails on both sides of the staircases for safety. There should be a light fixture and a light switch at the top and bottom of all stairways for safety. If there's a window at the base of a staircase its sill should be at least 36 inches above the floor. This will help prevent someone from falling through the window in the event they fell down the stairs. If the sill is less than 36 inches high, a window guard should be installed as a precautionary measure.

Walls and Ceilings

Check all of the walls and ceilings for any structural problems or settlement cracks. You'll usually find some minor settlement cracks but you're looking for any major problems that could be hazardous. In older houses the walls will be made of *lath and plaster* which is also called *stucco*. Lath and plaster consists of an underlying layer of metal wiring, or lath, which has a layer of concrete over it. Lath and plaster walls are very rigid and have good sound insulating and fireproofing qualities. However, since these walls are so rigid they can develop cracks from any minor settlement in the house or with the temperature changes. Also, the metal lath can rust out over time and sections of the plaster can fall off which can be hazardous.

In newer houses the walls will be made of *sheetrock* which is also called *drywall*. Sheetrock consists of a gypsum material on the interior, usually about 1/2 inch thick, with exterior layers of a lightweight cardboard paper. The gypsum is a clay and plaster mixture. Sheetrock panels are sold in four feet by eight feet sections and are installed on the walls and ceilings with nails or screws. Screws are preferred to nails because they hold longer. Nails can pop loose over time which you'll see sometimes during an inspection. The joint sections where the different panels meet are sealed with finishing tape and spackled over to provide a smooth transition. Sheetrock is relatively inexpensive and is easy to install. Fireproof sheetrock is 5/8 inch thick and has a better fire resistance than the 1/2 inch sheetrock. However, it's also heavier and more difficult to install than 1/2 inch sheetrock.

Check for any water stains on the walls or ceilings, or around any skylights. If you see water stains, it indicates that there's probably damage to the areas behind the walls and ceilings that isn't visible due to the finished covering. So be very careful about telling the client anything such as the water damage appears minor because the stain isn't very large. Water can do an *awful* lot of damage behind the finished coverings. So if you're not sure then just tell the client to have the stained area opened and evaluated further.

See if the house needs to be painted. Sometimes the client will ask you if there's lead paint in the house. The only way to identify lead paint is to have a sample taken to a lab for analysis. All linseed oil based paint prior to 1978 had lead in it. The reason for this is lead has a good wear quality and it is a strong "binder" for the paint. Therefore, if a house was built before 1978, then there will be lead in some of the paint. Latex based paint has never had a lead content in it and all paints today are non-toxic. When lead paint wears off it creates a dust. This lead dust causes soil contamination and health problems to anyone who breathes or drinks the lead. If the interior of the house has been painted after 1978, then the paint with the

> *All linseed oil based paint prior to 1978 had lead in it because the lead is a good "binder" for the paint. Therefore, if a house was built before 1978, then there will be lead in some of the paint.*

lead content will be encapsulated underneath the newer layers of non-lead paint. The main hazard of having lead in paint is if the paint is peeling and children can eat small sections of it. Also, if lead paint is sanded, then the dust created will have lead in it that will be breathed-in by the occupants of the house. Each State E.P.A. office has brochures with information about the hazards of lead in paint.

If there's wallpaper in the house, make sure it's not peeling off the walls. Tell the client that if they plan to remove the wallpaper, it is a time-consuming job that

can be expensive. They should get estimates if they are not going to remove it themselves. You have to be careful removing when wallpaper from sheetrock walls because you can pull the light cardboard paper off the

> *Check for the existence and operation of any smoke detectors. Smoke detectors are required on all levels of a house or condo. Heat detectors are recommended in the garage area.*

walls with the wallpaper. Some ceilings have acoustic tile coverings. These are also called *drop ceilings*. Try to lift some of these tiles to view underneath. Often these ceilings are installed to cover defects underneath.

Check for the existence and operation of any smoke detectors. Smoke detectors are **required** on all levels of a house or condo. Heat detectors are recommended in the garage area. If the smoke detectors are battery operated, they should have a small test button. Recommend that the client replace all batteries after moving in. Some smoke detectors have a *hard wired* installation. This simply means that they're electrically operated and not battery operated. Hard wired systems can't be evaluated during an inspection. Tell the client to get all instructions from the homeowner.

Windows and Doors

Spot check the windows and doors by opening and closing all doors and at least one window in each room. Sometimes they'll be difficult to open and close due to excess paint or settlement of the house. This is common, so just notify the client about it. Check for cracked or broken panes of glass. Make sure you move any drapes or blinds. Sometimes they're hiding broken windows.

Check for any *double key* door locks. These are the locks that require a key to exit and enter through the door. The purpose of these locks is so that if a burglar breaks a door window, they can't just turn a bolt and open the door. They'll need a key to open the lock. However, in some areas these locks are against the local fire codes because a key is needed to exit in case of an emergency. This can cause people to get trapped inside a house during a fire. Tell the client to check with the local fire and building department for

In some areas double key locks are against the local fire codes because a key is needed to exit in case of an emergency. This can cause people to get trapped inside a house during a fire.

their recommendation about door locks. Recommend that the client change all of the house locks after taking possession for security reasons.

Fireplaces

Check all fireplaces for any structural or backsmoking problems. Make sure the mortar joints are in satisfactory condition. Backsmoking is the result of downdrafts in the chimney flue that causes the smoke to come back into the house. Signs of backsmoking are black deposits, called *creosote*, on the front of the fireplace and mantel.

Sometimes the fireplace will have a metal firebox, a metal heat-a-lator, or a wood burning stove in it. You're limited in what you can evaluate with these because there's usually no access to view up the chimney flue.

Attic Inspection

Most houses will have an attic space that you <u>must</u> inspect if there's access to it due to the potential problems you can find. Just like crawl spaces, don't get lazy and just assume everything's OK in the attic area. Some houses won't have any accessible attic areas, so just do the best you can.

Sometimes the attic area has been finished and there are *knee wall* openings to the attic. These are small openings in the wall areas of the upper level that allow you to view a small portion of the attic and use it for storage. The access panels to most attics are located in the ceiling of the upper level hallway. Sometimes

I always recommend that a handrail be installed inside the attic area surrounding the access opening.
This will help prevent anyone in the attic area from falling through the access opening.

the access panel will be located in a bedroom closet. Ask the owner about this and don't assume there's no access panel because you didn't see one. It could be hidden.

I always recommend that a handrail be installed inside the attic area surrounding the access opening. This will help prevent anyone walking in the attic area from falling through the access opening. I have no idea why, but I haven't seen any building codes that require this handrail in new construction. What will happen is somebody is going to fall through the access panel and get killed someday and then the local building codes will add this safety precaution. Don't wait for that to happen, recommend they install a handrail now!

Usually you'll find most attics will have some wood board covering over the floor joists so the attic can be used to store lightweight items. If you see any very heavy objects, tell the client it's not recommended due to the excessive weight on the ceiling below. You have to be careful when you're in the attic area and not walk between any of the floor joists. If you do, then your foot will go right through the ceiling below!

Check the condition of the roof ridge beam, roof rafters and the roof sheathing while in the attic area. Look for any water stains that are due to water leaks or abnormal humidity in the attic area. Often there are old water stains from prior roof leaks that have been repaired. Just see if they look moist or recent. Check for any bowing in the wood members of the attic.

Attic Ventilation

It's very important that the attic area be properly ventilated to prevent excessive humidity or heat in this area. Even in cold winter months humidity can cause problems in attics. As a result, ventilation to the exterior is needed in the winter. In the summer months attics can reach 150 degrees Fahrenheit which adds a big heat load on the house.

Check for an adequate number of attic vents. Check the condition of the screens on these vents. They need to be kept clean. Screens help to keep birds and bees out of the attic. Any bathroom fans should discharge to the exterior. Sometimes you'll find them discharging in the attic. This isn't recommended because it promotes moisture problems.

Attic Insulation

Check to see if there is insulation in the floor joists of the attic area. The roof rafters don't need to be insulated because once heat has escaped through the upper level ceiling it's lost anyway. There's no sense trying to trap this heat in the attic. If you do, you'll only be trapping unwanted moisture in the attic by installing insulation between the roof rafters.

The benefit of having attic flooring is that you can use this area for storage. However, flooring prevents you from seeing if there's insulation throughout the attic area. Sometimes there's only insulation in the visible floor areas that aren't covered. The owner may have installed this insulation without bothering to remove the attic flooring that was there to insulate the entire attic.

Check to see how thick the insulation is. The insulation should be at least six inches thick. If it isn't just recommend that the client install an additional layer of insulation for better energy efficiency. Ask the owner if he/she has installed or knows of any prior owner's having installed insulation in the house. You want to warn you client about any *"blown-in"* type of insulation. In the past some houses had UFFI insulation blown-into the walls and floors. UFFI stands for *Urea Formaldehyde Foam Insulation* and the Environmental Protection Agency, *(EPA)*, has issued warnings about this type of insulation. If there's UFFI in the house, recommend that an air sample be taken to see if there are any health concerns.

Asbestos Insulation

Asbestos has been used for insulation as far back in time as ancient Greece. Almost all older houses have had asbestos insulation on the heating pipes. A thin layer of asbestos can sometimes be found on old hot air ducts if there is a furnace. Old cast iron boilers had asbestos on the interior insulating walls as well. Believe it or not, asbestos used to be required to be installed in all new construction. That's why so many buildings have asbestos in them. It was the miracle product when it was widely used. Asbestos has great insulating and fireproofing qualities, the only problem is the public wasn't made aware of the health problems associated with it until it was too late. This is one area you have to be careful about. Asbestos really scares potential home buyers because of the health concerns with it.

Asbestos causes lung cancer when it comes loose from the pipes and the fibers get into the air. The asbestos fibers are like tiny daggers and when you breathe them in, they stick into your lungs and stay there. The fibers cling to dust and can be stirred up off the floor when someone walks in a room where the fibers are located. There are about five different diseases related to exposure to asbestos. There are six different types of asbestos minerals.

> Asbestos causes lung cancer when it comes loose from the pipes and the fibers get into the air.
> The asbestos fibers are like tiny daggers and when you breathe them in, they stick into your lungs.

I did an inspection for an attorney who handled a lawsuit filed by the relatives of residents from a town in Australia. This attorney told me that **every** resident from that town was killed due to the *Blue Asbestos* mine that most of them worked at. Supposedly Blue Asbestos is the most dangerous type of asbestos to be exposed to. Just by getting <u>one</u> fiber in your lungs can be fatal!!! Just one fiber will not only create scar tissue in that section of the lung, but it will spread to cover the entire lung over time. This attorney told me that all of the workers in the mine were killed due to breathing the Blue Asbestos at work. Their families were all killed because the mine workers would bring home the fibers in their clothes which would spread in their homes. Also, the rest of the people in this town were killed due to the Blue Asbestos fibers being blown around town by the wind.

An asbestos lab technician told me that Steve

McQueen died of an asbestos related cancer. Supposedly Steve McQueen worked in the French Merchant Marine when he was younger and that's where he was overly exposed to asbestos. I'm not telling you these stories to try to scare you, I'm just letting you know about some potential health hazards you have to watch out for.

Asbestos pipe insulation usually has a white color and appears to have layers of ribbed cardboard in the middle sections. You'll probably see an off-white canvas covering over it. Old hot air heating ducts may have a very thin, white layer of asbestos around them. The only way to know for sure if any insulation is asbestos is to have a laboratory take a sample. You can charge an additional fee for this service if you'd like. I don't get involved in handling any asbestos myself and I don't recommend you do either.

Don't take any chances identifying asbestos in the house. Just tell the client when you see an asbestos type of insulation, and tell them the EPA recommendations. The Environmental Protection Agency has offices in every state that will provide

> *The EPA recommends that any asbestos insulation be professionally sealed or removed from the house by an EPA licensed asbestos contractor.*

anyone with free information and brochures. They provide information about Asbestos, Radon Gas, Oil Leaks, Lead in paint and water, and many other environmental and health concerns. Get the local number for your state office and obtain their brochures for more information. There are also classes you can take that are accredited by the EPA for more information about these items.

The Environmental Protection Agency recommends that any asbestos insulation be **professionally** sealed or removed from the house by an EPA licensed asbestos contractor. This means, the homeowner, the plumber or any other repair person should not touch any asbestos in the house!! Often you'll see a residue from asbestos insulation on the heating pipes. Evidence of this is small white particles on sections of the pipes, usually around the joints. This indicates that a non-EPA licensed person removed the asbestos and it should immediately raise a red flag for you to notify the client.

Many times the homeowner will have a new boiler put in and some foolish contractor will just rip asbestos off the pipes not knowing what he's doing. Or worse,

sometimes the contractor or the homeowner removes it intentionally just to get rid of it themselves. Big mistake on their part! When inspecting an older house you may not actually see the asbestos. If this were the case, you should assume that there was asbestos in the home at one time. It's better to be safe than sorry. Since asbestos was almost always used in older houses, it was probably unprofessionally removed and that's why you don't see it. I've found asbestos insulation on copper water supply pipes in houses that were built as late as 1960!!! When older houses have forced hot air heating systems, then there **really** is a problem if asbestos was used. I've found very thin layers of asbestos around forced hot air heating ducts and in the lining of furnaces. The furnace fan will circulate asbestos all over the house once it gets inside the air ducts. So not only will you have deadly fibers in the basement and behind the walls, you'll also have them in the livable rooms.

Tell your client to have a laboratory take an air sample to learn what the asbestos fiber content is in the house. There's no way for you to determine this during an inspection. Don't take any chances with this stuff. Asbestos lawsuits are big bucks. I've only heard of one home inspector getting sued for asbestos. But I have heard of many contractors getting sued for hundreds of thousands of dollars for improperly removing asbestos.

Don't let the clients be fooled by any Realtors or other third parties telling them not to worry about the asbestos in the house. A common line that I hear Realtors and other third parties say to my clients on inspections is: *"This asbestos is just fine, the Environmental Protection Agency says all you have to do is to wrap it in tape or plastic."* That really bothers me when I hear that. What gives that third party the right to sugarcoat a decision that concerns someone else's health? You can bet that if that Realtor or third party was the person buying that house, they'd insist that the asbestos be removed. They'd also make sure it was removed by a licensed EPA contractor prior to closing! Yet it's OK for them to let someone else buy the house and leave the asbestos there.

I'll never forget the time that I started inspecting a house for a client before they had arrived at the site. I was in the lower level of the house with a dishonest Realtor to the transaction who was getting a commission on the sale. I mentioned that there was asbestos on the heating pipes and that some of it appeared to have been removed unprofessionally or had fallen off sections of the pipes. This Realtor got worried and asked me what type of health concern there was with breathing in asbestos fibers. I told her, *"The fibers are like tiny daggers that stick in your lungs and create scar tissue."* She just turned and practically ran for the stairway and said, *"I'm getting out of this basement now, I'll be waiting upstairs."* When my client arrived, I told him about the asbestos. He then went upstairs and told this Realtor that he wanted it removed from the pipes prior to closing on the house. I could not believe it when I went back upstairs and the Realtor said to me, *"Why are you getting the client so scared about the asbestos?"* I felt like screaming at her! Just 15 minutes earlier this Realtor **ran** out of the basement because I told her about the asbestos on the pipes. Now suddenly she was worried because I might create problems with her deal by informing my client about the same health concern that she was so concerned about herself. I guess it's different when it's somebody else's lungs and not her own. Some people have an *amazing* ability to rationalize their actions. I'll talk more about this at the end of the book.

I tell my clients that they're better off having an EPA licensed contractor remove the asbestos from the house, as opposed to just having it wrapped professionally. The reason for this is that if the asbestos is left in the house and is only sealed, then when there's a pipe leak underneath the asbestos insulation, the covering will have to be removed. The asbestos will have to be exposed so that the pipe leak can be repaired. Once it's exposed, you have the problem all over again of fibers getting into the air of the house. Also, if the client has the asbestos removed from the house, as opposed to having it wrapped, then they don't have to worry about it bothering potential buyers when they sell the house.

When an Environmental Protection Agency licensed contractor removes asbestos, they seal the entire area where it's located. They work with completely sealed suits over their bodies. They then set up a vacuum to remove all of the dust from the area. When the asbestos is totally removed from the house, they take an air sample. The air sample is done to make sure the workers haven't left any fibers lying around that can be stirred up and breathed in later. Generally, any asbestos behind the walls is left alone. If there's no access to the asbestos and it can't be disturbed, there isn't that much of a health concern. Just let the EPA licensed asbestos contractor tell your client what to do. You only give recommendations from an appraiser's viewpoint.

Radon Gas

While we're on the lovely topic of lung cancer, let's talk about radon. A radon lab technician told me the story about how radon was discovered. I thought you might find it interesting. There was a man who lived in Reading, Pennsylvania that worked for some type of nuclear laboratory. When he used to go to work, he would set off the radiation detectors at the lab. The radiation detectors are installed so that the nuclear lab can monitor their employees to see if they're being exposed to radiation inside the lab. The lab employees couldn't figure out why the detectors were setting off, so they tested his house for radiation. While studying the problem, they stumbled upon radon gas. *(Fortunately or unfortunately for mankind. I guess it's just another way to develop cancer. Like there aren't enough already!)*

Radon gas testing is really becoming a daily part of all real estate sales transactions. It's a great additional source of income and you should consider providing this service as well. Radon is a radiation gas that's released naturally by rocks and soil in the earth. The radiation gas is created by the natural breakdown

> *Some houses will be left vacant while they're being sold. The point is, that if a house has a high radon reading, don't let anyone tell the client that it's only because the house was sealed up.*

or Uranium in the rocks and soil that leads to a by product called Radium. The radiation gas gradually seeps up from the ground and as long as it goes out into the open air it's not a problem. However, if the radon seeps through cracks in the foundation floor and walls it'll become trapped in the house and the levels will rise.

Some houses will be left vacant while they're being sold. Many people who think this will increase the radon level reading because no windows or doors are being opened. However, radon has a half life of only 3.825 days. Because of this fact, the maximum radon level that could build up would be a 3.825 day level. After that point, some radon will decay and then be replenished by new radon gas entering the house. The point is, that if a house has a high radon reading, ***don't let anyone tell the client that it's only because*** *the house was sealed up!* Don't let anyone make your client think that when he moves in, the radon level will be OK. If anyone says that, then tell that person to move into the house and call us in about 10 years after they have a chest X-ray.

As with asbestos and other environmental and health concerns, call your state Environmental Protection Agency office for their information, brochures and classes. The EPA considers radon to be the **number 2** leading cause of lung cancer behind smoking, so it's not something to take too lightly. Some experts feel that the EPA has over exaggerated the problem but I would let the client decide that for themselves. Don't try to make the decision for them.

The EPA uses a reading of 4 Pico Curies per liter to determine the maximum radon level in a house before mitigation is recommended. I'll give you some background so you have an idea of how Pico Curies are measured. The EPA office in my area says that one Pico Curie is the average indoor radon level and this is equal to getting about 100 chest X-rays per year. Now that may seem very high, but let me put it in the proper perspective. The EPA also informed me that the amount of radiation you receive from a normal chest

> *In some areas the radon levels tend to be higher than in other areas but all houses will get some radon gas reading!!! So don't let any Realtors, sellers, or other third parties talk your client out of getting an accurate radon test done.*

X-ray, usually isn't as high as most people think. For example, with a reading of one Pico Curie per liter, the Environmental Protection Agency estimates that 3-13 people out of 1,000 will die of lung cancer. This is similar to a nonsmoker's risk of dying of lung cancer.

With a reading of 4 Pico Curies per liter, it's estimated that 13-50 people out of 1,000 will die of lung cancer. This is similar to five times the nonsmoker's risk of dying of lung cancer. However, you still may want to inform your client about this so that *they* can decide for themselves if the radon levels found are acceptable to them or not. Don't take it upon yourself to make the decision for your client.

Mitigation is the term used for the treatment to remove the radon problem by reducing the levels in the house. When a house is mitigated, the radon contractor will seal all open cracks in the lower level walls and floors that they can find. They then drill a hole in the foundation floor which looks like a sump pump pit. Instead of installing a sump pump in this pit, the

contractor will install a fan with pipes leading to the outside of the house.

In some areas, the local codes require that these pipes discharge above the roof line. This will help prevent the radon from entering back into the house through an open window. The purpose of the mitigation is to vent all radon gas that builds up underneath the foundation, to the exterior of the house.

In some areas the radon levels tend to be higher than in other areas but all houses will get some radon gas reading!!! So don't let any Realtors, sellers, or other third parties talk your client out of getting an accurate radon test done. Sometimes they'll say to your client, *"Oh, you don't have to worry we don't have radon in this area."* HOGWASH!!!!! All houses will have a radon reading, even if it's minor trace element readings of 0.5 Pico Curie per liter. This is because radon is everywhere according to the EPA. There is always an average of 0.4 Pico Curie per liter reading in the air of the atmosphere. EPA has found that the average indoor radon level is 1.5 Pico Curies per liter.

It's also important to inform your client that you might not have a high radon reading today but you might have a high reading a month from now. Or you might have a high reading and your neighbor might not and vice versa. The reason for this is that radon is a radiation gas that's unstable and it fluctuates. There are many factors that affect the radon level in a house, some of which include:

1   The time of the year and the climate.

2   The type of soil and rocky terrain in the area around and under the house.

3   The type of construction of the house.

4   And there are other reasons as well.

Because of these factors the Environmental Protection Agency recommends that you retest for radon every six months to make sure that the levels are acceptable. It's also another source of income to retest all of your client's homes every six months. *Believe it or not, radon can even be found in water!* That's another reason to have a laboratory analyze well water samples. You're not misleading people or trying to milk them for money. You're simply showing them the EPA recommendations for retesting times because of the unpredictability of radon.

According to the Environmental Protection Agency there currently is no evidence that there is a health problem with drinking water with radon in it. This is because radon becomes soluble (dissolves) in

> *As with radon canisters and well water samples, you want to make sure that you deal with a reputable laboratory for radon water analysis.*
> *The radon reading accuracy will depend on the sophistication of the lab's analyzing equipment.*

water. The colder the temperature of the water then the more radon will dissolve in it. The health concern of having radon in your water is that the gas is released into the air. The water releases the radon gas whenever you run the faucet or dishwasher, take a shower, flush a toilet, use the washing machine, etc. Anytime you aerate the water you will be releasing the radon gas into the house and this is when it becomes a health concern.

The current standards that the EPA uses for the acceptable levels of radon in the water are 10,000 to 1. Meaning that for each 10,000 Pico Curies per liter of radon gas that you have in your water, you will be releasing about one Pico Curie per liter into the air in the house. For example, let's say you have a radon water reading of 40,000 Pico Curies per liter. Then you will have 4 Pico Curies per liter escaping into the air of the house and this is the level at which EPA recommends mitigation. Currently there is no evidence of a correlation between a high radon reading in the air in relation to the radon reading in the water of a house. For example, let's say that you have a high radon reading in the air of your house. Well this doesn't mean that you'll definitely have a high radon reading in the water of your house, and vice versa.

Air radon gas testing is usually done with a small, round metal canister that has charcoal inside. A canister is left in the house for about 3-5 days and then it's sealed and mailed back to the radon lab for analysis. Sometimes the seller or occupant of the house will ask you if there is a health risk of being in a house while a canister is there. Radon canisters don't emit anything hazardous. The charcoal inside the canisters merely absorbs the air in the room where they're placed so the lab can analyze them. Radon canisters do not present a health risk to the occupants of the house.

What makes a radon reading accurate is not the canister but the quality and sophistication of the lab's analyzing equipment. You could send the same canister to two different labs and get two different radon readings. That's another reason why you shouldn't let any third parties talk your client out of getting an accurate radon test done. Sometimes they'll say to your client: *"Oh, you don't have to test for radon, the seller already did that when they bought the house and he's willing to give you a copy of the test results for free!"* **(That sounds like the spider talking to the fly!)** How do you know how accurate the lab's equipment was that analyzed the seller's canister? How do you know the canister wasn't tampered with? Just because the seller had a low reading when he bought the house doesn't mean that there's a low reading in the house now. Remember, radon is always fluctuating.

Water radon gas testing is usually done with a special water bottle. The water sample ***must*** be obtained without letting any aeration of the water which would release as much as 99% of the radon in the water sample. The testing bottle has to seal the faucet so that it traps all of the radon gas as the bottle is filled with the water. Special hoses are usually included with the testing bottles. As with radon canisters and well water samples, you want to make sure that you deal with a reputable laboratory for radon water analysis. The radon reading accuracy will depend on the sophistication of the lab's analyzing equipment. So check the lab out and make sure that they know what they're doing.

As an appraiser and home inspector I wonder sometimes what my exposure is to asbestos fibers and radon. But I guess there's risk in everything, even crossing the street, so I don't worry about it. If it bothers you, just talk to your physician or a local asbestos and radon lab for their advice.

The Exterior Inspection

Roof

When you finish with the interior, take a walk around the outside of the house to get a quick look at the exterior. We'll start with the roof, but as I've said before, feel free to adapt the inspection process to any way you feel comfortable with. There shouldn't be any tree branches overhanging the roof. Overhanging branches can cause damage to the shingles. If you can, use a ladder to get a close look at the roof from the edge. While inside the house, you should view the roof close up from the interior windows if possible. This will enable you to make better conclusions and evaluations when you get to the exterior. If you can't view the roof closely, you should use a pair of strong binoculars to assist you.

Check for any bowing sections of the roof ridge beam, roof rafters or the roof sheathing which would indicate repairs being needed. Remember that if it's raining, the roof will look newer than it actually is because of the water on it. There is one benefit of doing an inspection on a rainy day. That is you'll have a better chance of finding any roof leaks or water problems in the lower level. If there's snow on the roof, just tell the client that you can only evaluate the visible portions.

The life expectancy of all roofs depends upon many factors. Some factors are: the quality of the shingles, the quality of the installation of the shingles and the roofing materials, the climate and exposure to the elements, and the maintenance given to the shingles. The vast majority of houses have five types of roofing shingles:

◊   Asphalt
◊   Wood Shingles and Wood Shakes
◊   Slate
◊   Tile
◊   Flat Roofing

Chimneys

Use your binoculars to view the chimney. Check to make sure that the chimney isn't leaning which would suggest a serious condition where it would have to be rebuilt. Make sure the mortar joints are in good condition and don't need to be repointed. The phrase *re-pointing* refers to patching any decayed areas of the mortar joints. This is a required maintenance item that needs to be done periodically. You may see the terra-cotta tile flue linings at the top of the chimney. Make sure they aren't cracked or broken.

Some chimneys are made of metal piping. Check these for any rust. Often on condominiums you'll find the metal chimneys are covered with a finished wood siding to match the exterior wall siding. You'll be limited in what you can see with this type of installation. Just do the best you can.

Siding

The siding on a house is used to provide weather protection. The siding doesn't support the house structurally. A load bearing wall is what provides the structural support of the house. If you find a building constructed of brick, stone or masonry, then these materials aren't considered the siding since they are load bearing walls. Check these types of structures for problems with bulging or leaning walls and deteriorated mortar joints. The different types of sidings that you'll generally encounter are:

◊   Wood Boards *(often called Clapboard Siding)*
◊   Wood Shingles and Wood Shakes
◊   Plywood Panels
◊   Aluminum Siding
◊   Vinyl Siding
◊   Asbestos-Cement Shingles
◊   Asphalt Siding
◊   Stucco
◊   Veneer Walls

All siding should be at least eight inches above the soil all around the structure. This will help prevent termite and rot problems. The moisture in the soil will rot out the siding. Also, when the siding is in contact with the ground, wood destroying insects can get behind the siding very easily

Check with the seller to see if they've replaced any siding or if there's an underlying layer of older siding on the house. You want to try to find out what's underneath the exterior layer. The exterior

> _All siding should be at least eight inches above the soil all around the structure._
> _This will help prevent termite and rot problems._

maintenance of condo units is usually paid for by a monthly charge assessed to all of the condo owners in the complex. Recommend that the client check with the Condo/Owner's Association to find out what the fees and responsibilities are for each owner in the complex. We will discuss this topic of condominium units further into the book.

Fascia, Soffits and Eaves

The _Fascia, Soffits_ and _Eaves_ are the molding areas at the bottom of the roof and the top of the siding. It's the small area where the roof overhangs the sides of the house. Check to see if the wood is rotted or if it needs to be painted or stained. Often you'll find there's an aluminum siding covering over the fascia, soffits and eaves. If you see vents at the bottom of the roof overhang area it indicates that the house may have soffit vents. _Soffit vents_ allow air to enter the bottom of the attic area and help remove heat and moisture from the house.

Gutters, Downs and Leade

Gutters are installed along the bottom edge of the roof to catch the rainwater running off the roof. _Downspouts_ are installed near the ends of the gutters and are used to drain the water from the gutters so they don't overflow. _Leaders_ are installed at the bottom of the downspouts to direct the rainwater away from the side of the structure.

The vast majority of gutters, downspouts and leaders are made of aluminum because it's lightweight, inexpensive and rust and rot resistant. Sometimes on older houses the gutters, downspouts and leaders will be made of copper. If copper gutters are painted, the only way to find out if they are copper is to look for the soldered joints. Wood gutters are not recommended since they have a short life expectancy due to rot.

There should be at least one downspout for every 30 feet of gutter to prevent any excessive weight from the rainwater from damaging the gutters. All downspouts should have leaders to pipe the rainwater five feet away from the foundation to help prevent any water problems in the lower level.

Some downspouts drain directly into the ground. These lead to dry-wells or underground drainage lines. They need to be checked periodically for clogging due to leaves and small animals getting stuck in them. In most areas, the local building codes prohibit sump pumps, gutters and downspouts from discharging water into the house plumbing drainage lines. This restriction is designed to prevent an excessive amount of water from entering the municipal sewer system.

Windows, Screens and Storms

Check the condition of the exterior window frames for any rot or if they need to be painted or stained. Check the condition of any storms and screens. If there are no storm windows you should recommend that they be installed in northern climates where the temperature gets cold. More heat is lost in a house through the windows than through any other area. Storm or thermal windows can reduce the heat loss by as much as 50%.

Entrances, Steps and Porches

Check all entrances, steps and porches for structural sturdiness and any tripping hazards. Make sure there are no cracks or uneven sections in any of the steps. The landing platform is the standing area in front of a door. Make sure there is a large enough space to safely open the exterior doors while someone is standing in front of them. You don't want anyone to be knocked down the steps when the door is opened. *(Unless of course it's an unwanted guest).*

There should be handrails for **all** stairs that are more than two steps in height. Make sure the handrails aren't loose or decayed. Recommend that they be

> *There should be handrails for all stairs that are more than two steps in height.*

installed when not noted. All steps should have an even and uniform height so that there's no tripping hazards. If there are any wood stairs, the base of the wood should be resting on concrete pads above the soil. This will prevent rot and termite infestation.

If there's an enclosed porch, tell the client to check with town hall to see if all valid permits and approvals have been filed. Sometimes people enclose an open porch area without knowing building permits are needed.

Walks

Check all walks for any tripping hazards. There shouldn't be any weeds growing between the walkway sections. If there are any uneven sections, recommend that they be repaired. Sometimes the sidewalk at the street will be uneven due to tree roots. Tell the client to check with the local building department to find out whose responsibility it is to repair the sidewalk. In most areas, the homeowner is responsible for repairing and shoveling the sidewalk in front of their house.

My brother and I received a building violation once for a sidewalk that was a tripping hazard. The sidewalk in front of one of our rental properties had some cracks due to the growth of roots from a large tree planted there. We had the sidewalk repaired by a contractor and then the violation was removed. Also, we received a summons for not shoveling the snow immediately after a snowfall in front of one of our rental properties. We paid someone to shovel the snow whenever it was necessary in front of the building. However, one time he didn't do it fast enough after the snowfall stopped. As a result, we were given a ticket for this.

Sometimes you'll appraise a house that's located on a private street. In this situation, both you and the client need to determine what rights and responsibilities they have as a homeowner on that road. Often homeowners who live on private streets have to pay for repaving and maintenance of the street. This will have an affect on the market value of the property and it must be evaluated.

Patios and Terraces

As with walks, check all patios and terraces for any tripping hazards. There shouldn't be any weeds growing between the joints of the sections. Any uneven sections need to be repaired. If the patio touches the side of the foundation, then it must be well caulked and sloped away to prevent water from draining toward the house. In most areas building permits and approvals are needed to build patios. You have to check this at town hall.

Decks

Decks _always_ require building department approvals because of the safety concern if they're improperly built. Check for any rotted sections of wood that need to be replaced. Some decks will be too low to the ground to view the structural members. Just do the best you can. The deck perimeter railings should be sturdy. The balusters under the railing must be spaced so that a maximum gap of four inches exists between them. This is to help prevent small children or dogs from falling through.

There should be lag bolts in the main beam, called the _header beam_, where the deck is attached to the side of the house. _Lag bolts_ are a **far superior** way to

> _Decks always require building department approvals because of the safety concern if they're improperly built._

support the deck as opposed to just using nails. Copper flashing should be installed between the header beam and the side of the house. This will prevent water from getting trapped and rotting the wood.

The floor joists of the deck should have steel support hangers. Steel support hangers give the floor joists more support then by just nailing them. All deck support posts and girders should have steel brackets at the top and the base for support. This will also keep the wood from being in contact with the soil. The base should be resting on a concrete support post.

Walls and Fences

Retaining walls are used to support the soil in areas, such as driveways or yards, which are dug into the earth. Check to see if any retaining walls are leaning. Any leaning conditions indicate that repairs **must** be made to prevent the wall from moving any further or collapsing. Some different types of retaining walls are:

◊ Stone and Cement Walls
◊ Dry Stone Walls
◊ Gabion Walls
◊ Concrete Block Walls
◊ Wood Timber Walls

All fences need to be checked for sturdiness. Tell the client to check with town hall to determine if the fence is within the subject property line. Often the homeowner or a neighbor will have a fence installed and the contractor will just guess where the property line is. This can lead to an _encroachment_ on someone else's property. This topic will be discussed further into the book.

Drainage and Grading

The soil next to the foundation should slope away from the house to prevent any rainwater from building up next to the foundation. Usually the soil only needs to slope 1/2 inch for every foot away from the house to properly drain the water accumulations. All bushes, shrubs and trees should be pruned away from the side of the house. This will allow enough sunlight and air next to the foundation to help prevent rot and wood destroying insect problems.

If the house is at the base of a hill there should be a _catch basin_ to prevent water problems. These are large concrete underground drains. Both you and the client must check with the local building department to figure out if the house is located in a designated flood hazard zone. If it is, then flood hazard insurance will be needed.

Driveways

Check all asphalt and concrete driveways for cracked and uneven sections. Asphalt driveways need to be sealed with a driveway sealer every two or three years to prevent them from drying out and cracking. Repaving an asphalt driveway can be expensive. If the driveway needs to be repaved, tell the client to get an estimate.

Some driveways don't have a finished surface and are made of gravel and dirt. Often they have holes which are tripping hazards that need to be repaired. Unfinished driveways lead to people tracking dirt into the house. These driveways also cannot be shoveled for snow removal in northern areas.

Garage

The different types of garages you'll encounter are Detached, Attached and Built-in or Tuckunder garages.

◊   *Detached* garages are separate structures from the main house.

◊   *Attached* garages are attached to the main house.

◊   *Built-in* or *Tuckunder* garages are set underneath the house and take up a section of the lower level.

A benefit of having an attached or built-in garage is that you can park the car and enter the house without worrying about the weather conditions. A detached garage is safer in the event that a car is left running by mistake, the exhaust fumes can't enter the house easily. A detached garage is also safer in the event of a fire, the flames and smoke can't spread to the house easily.

The inspection procedure for the garage is the same as with the exterior and interior aspects of the main house. Review those sections to find more comments and recommendations. Check the floor for any oil or gas drippings. Gas and oil must be cleaned to help prevent fires from starting. Garage walls and ceilings should be covered with fireproof sheetrock to help prevent the spread of any fires. Masonry walls and ceilings are an acceptable fireproof covering.

If the garage is attached or built-in there should be a fireproof entry door leading to the house. Also, this door should have a self-closing device to prevent it being left open. This will prevent car exhaust fumes or fires from spreading into the house easily.

Other Exterior Structures

Check all garden and tool sheds on the property for rot and wood destroying insect infestation. Make sure they're sturdy and there are no hazards. If there are any other exterior structures on the property, evaluate them just as you would the house itself. If there is anything you're unsure about, then just tell the client to have the structure evaluated further by a licensed contractor.

Swimming Pools

All swimming pools require local town approvals that need to be verified by you and your client. All swimming pools need to have fences surrounding them to prevent any unattended children from falling into the water and drowning. Also, special homeowners' insurance is needed with swimming pools. This is due to the increased liability of having a pool on the property.

Check the area around the pool for any tripping hazards. Check the pool walls for any leaks, cracks or bulging sections. If it's winter time and the outdoor air temperature gets below 32 degrees Fahrenheit, then the

All swimming pools require local town approvals. All pools need to have fences surrounding them to prevent any unattended children from falling into the water and drowning.

pool must be properly winterized. When water freezes it expands and this can crack the walls of a pool if proper winter maintenance has not been taken care of. If you have doubts about the pool, tell the client to call a swimming pool contractor for further evaluations.

Wood Destroying Insects

There are many different types of wood destroying insects, including 70 species of termites throughout the world. The wood destroying insects that you need to be the most concerned with are:

◊ *Subterranean Termites*
◊ *Dry Wood Termites*
◊ *Damp Wood Termites*
◊ *Powder Post Beetles*
◊ *Carpenter Ants*
◊ *Carpenter Bees*

This is another concern with buying a house that really scares people. So make sure you check thoroughly for wood destroying insects. If there was any aspect of performing home inspections that you would need X-ray vision, then this one takes the prize. If *Superman* really existed, he'd make a fortune as a Termite inspector. I've heard an awful lot of war stories about inspectors getting complaints from people because they didn't notice the termites that were behind

If there was any aspect of home inspections that you would need X-ray vision, then this one takes the prize. If Superman really existed, he'd make a fortune as a Termite inspector.

the sheetrock walls. Some people honestly believe that you should have told them that there were termites in areas that you couldn't even see. I have know idea where they get their logic from. If there are indications out in the open and you miss the signs, that's one thing. But don't expect someone to identify a problem that they can't even see!!

Occassionally you will have to rely on Lady Luck to help you find wood destroying insect damage. One time I was inspecting a house that was built on a concrete slab foundation. This type of construction doesn't have a basement area. As a result, termites can travel through cracks in the concrete slab. The wood beams and moldings of the livable rooms become an easy meal for the termites. I was just about finished with my inspection and only had one more closet to check. When I opened the closet door, there was termite damage all through the molding. The damaged wood was recently painted over and the termite tunnels were difficult to see. Had I cut corners by not checking that one last closet, I wouldn't have found the damaged wood. There were several times when I was in the lower level and Lady Luck was on my side. While looking around I radomnly probed some wood beams.

The screwdriver passed right through the beams due to wood destroying insect damage. I was lucky to find these damaged areas since there were no visible indications on the exterior of the wood.

Termites eat the wood and turn it into food. They have one-celled organisms in their digestive tracts that convert the cellulose of wood back into sugar which they can digest. In forests termites are beneficial since they help to decompose fallen trees and stumps. They help return the wood substances to the soil to be used again by other trees. Termite damaged wood will have channels in it and there won't be any sawdust around.

With *Subterranean Termites* you'll find mud in their tunnels. These termites bring mud into the wood channels since they can only survive in a warm, dark and moist environment. Probe wood with an awl or screwdriver, especially rotted or wet beams in dark areas, to check for termite infestation. You may see signs of mud on the outside sections of the wood indicating termite damage. What these termites do is they'll eat up to the very edge of the wood they are inside and leave a thin layer of wood on the exterior. This thin layer will prevent light or air from getting inside the channels and drying out the wood.

Dry Wood Termites are found in coastal warmer climate areas of the country. They have a caste system in their colonies similar to that of the Subterranean Termites. The difference is that they live and feed on sound, dry seasoned wood and they don't need to be in contact with the soil or a moisture source. As a result you won't see any mud tubes with these insects.

Damp Wood Termites are similar to subterranean termites but seldom live in the soil. They nest in damp wood and are associated with wood decay and don't construct tubing.

Powder Post Beetle larvae eat the wood and lay their eggs in it. They cannot convert the cellulose in the wood to sugar. Therefore, these insects must get their nourishment from the starch and sugar that the tree has stored in the wood cells. To these insects, the cellulose in the wood has no food value and is thus ejected from their bodies as wood powder or *frass*. They derive nourishment from the starch and sugar in the wood. Powder Post Beetle damaged wood will crumble like sawdust when you probe it. A common indication of these insects is the existence of tiny holes in the wood.

Carpenter Ants and *Carpenter Bees* merely excavate the wood to make nests. The damage they cause will leave sawdust outside the wood channels.

Often when you find damaged wood due to wood destroying insects, Realtors and other third party people will ask, *"Oh, is it active or inactive."* I just tell

> Often when you find damaged wood due to wood destroying insects, a Realtor, seller or other third party person will ask, "Oh, is it active or inactive."
> I just tell them that there's no way to know.

them that there's no way to know. The termites could just have moved to a different section of the house. There's just no way to know for sure. So **don't** let any Realtors or third parties tell your client that they don't have to worry about termites because you couldn't see them actually eating the wood. A lot of times dishonest Realtors and other third parties will do this to *"gloss over"* and underestimate the potential termite problem in the house.

The damage caused by termites is sometimes over exaggerated. There are very few houses on record that had to be knocked down due to serious structural problems due to termites. A full colony of termites can only eat about three feet of a wooden 2 x 4 beam in a

> They say there are two kinds of houses: Houses that have termites and Houses that will have termites. That's a fact. All houses will get termite damage of some sort eventually.

year. For them to do serious structural damage they would have to go unnoticed in the house for an awfully long time. I find minor termite damage in one out of every four houses that I inspect. Of these houses, I've only seen two or three of them that had very bad termite damage. But even those two or three houses could be repaired just be replacing some floor joists and treating the house with insecticide.

They say there are two kinds of houses: **Houses that have termites and Houses that will have termites**. That's a fact. All houses will get termite damage of some sort eventually. Sometimes builders will install a termite shield along the top of the foundation wall. *Termite shields* are similar to the cap plate used at the top of concrete block walls. A termite shield is a small metal guard. However, these shields do not prevent termites. The only benefit from them is that they might deter termites or make it a little more difficult for them to reach the wood.

There are certain houses that many Pest Control Operators, *(PCO)*, **will not** treat for wood destroying insects. Or else there will only be a few of them that will treat the houses with insecticide.

1   One case is houses with on-site well water systems. The PCO has to worry about contaminating the well water supply. If the well is less than 100 feet from the house, your chances of finding a PCO to treat will diminish even further.

2   Another case is houses that have brick foundation walls. The PCO has to worry about contaminating the house by seepage through the brick walls.

3   Another case is houses that have air ducts embedded in the lower level cement floor for the heating or air-conditioning systems. The PCO has to worry about contaminating the ducts.

4   Also, if the inspection is being conducted on a condominium, then the By-Laws or Prospectus of the Condo/Owner's Association may have limitations. There could be requirements that can restrict wood destroying insect treatments.

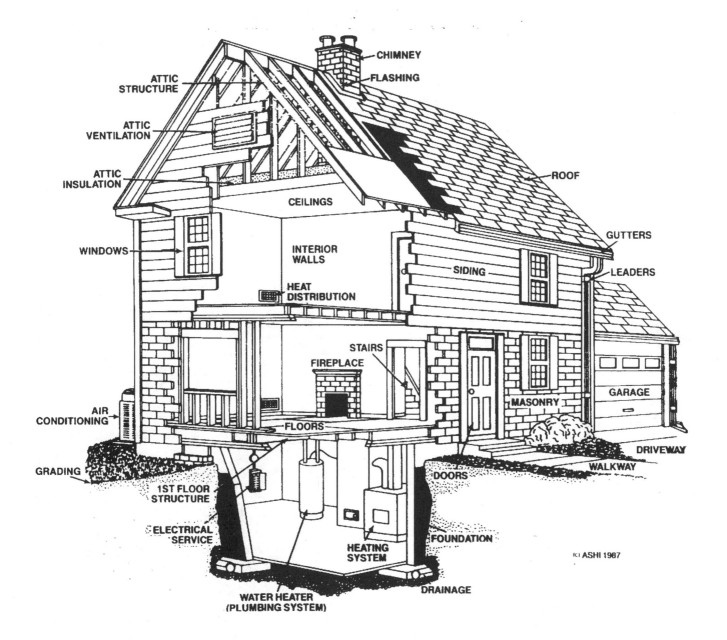

CHIMNEY

FLASHING

ATTIC
STRUCTURE

ATTIC
VENTILATION

ATTIC
INSULATION

ROOF

CEILINGS

WINDOWS

INTERIOR
WALLS

GUTTERS

SIDING

LEADERS

HEAT
DISTRIBUTION

STAIRS

FIREPLACE

MASONRY

GARAGE

AIR
CONDITIONING

FLOORS

DRIVEWAY

GRADING

DOORS

WALKWAY

1ST FLOOR
STRUCTURE

ELECTRICAL
SERVICE

FOUNDATION

HEATING
SYSTEM

(c) ASHI 1987

DRAINAGE

WATER HEATER
(PLUMBING SYSTEM)

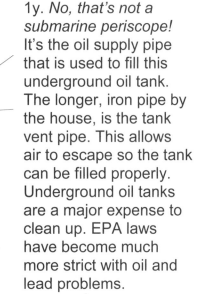

1y. *No, that's not a submarine periscope!* It's the oil supply pipe that is used to fill this underground oil tank. The longer, iron pipe by the house, is the tank vent pipe. This allows air to escape so the tank can be filled properly. Underground oil tanks are a major expense to clean up. EPA laws have become much more strict with oil and lead problems.

1z. There is a small fuel level gauge on the top of this interior oil tank. This interior oil tank has some signs of oil stains on the top. This can happen when the tank is overfilled.

Notice the patch on the bottom of this tank. Due to humidity, the bottom of these tanks often rust out over time. The patch is a temporary repair and replacing the tank is recommended.

The oil supply line has a firematic shut-off valve for safety.

The copper oil supply line is embedded in the concrete floor to protect it against damage.

4a. This is a properly installed water main line. The electrical grounding cable is clamped on both sides of the meter.
The bell shaped water pressure reducing valve indicates there is strong water pressure from the street main water line.
There are shut-off valves on each side of the meter for easy replacement of the meter. The lever shut-off valve *(upper right)* is more reliable than the knob type valve.
water meter

4d. This is called a disaster!! This water main has so many problems that I don't know where to begin.
The water meter is very old, outdated, and probably gives inaccurate readings.
There is no electrical ground cable on the main!
The water shut-off valve is ancient and corroded.
The main water pipe is lead and must be replaced *(wiped joint noted by valve)!*
The water lines need to be properly secured to the wall. The wood board is not an acceptable support.

7a. Electrical lines, conduits, and meters must be securely fastened to the side of the house. Tree branches need to be pruned away from the wires periodically. Three electrical lines at the service entrance head indicate 110/220 volts in this house. The "U" shape in the wires is called a drip loop. This is used to keep rainwater from entering the electrical conduit.

7b. Caulking the joint on the top of the electrical meter and where the wires enter the house will prevent water penetration problems. Over time this exterior caulk will dry and crack and needs to be repaired.

The shingles on this house are made of asbestos/cement and are in excellent condition. EPA precautions must be taken when removing or tampering with any type of asbestos.

7o. In the lower level of many homes, you'll find wiring installed through the floor joists. This is acceptable as long as it meets the NEC requirements. Also, the drill holes must be in the center of the wood and less than 1/4 of the height of the beam. This will preserve the structural integrity of the wood beam.

You can see Romex and Bx cables are installed through these floor joists.

7p. Using adapters when there is a lack of electrical outlets is a safety hazard. Too many appliances plugged into an outlet can create a fire or shock. The NEC recommends one outlet for every six feet of horizontal wall space. This will help prevent the use of usafe extension cord wiring and plug adapters.

To make matters even worse, this gas wall heater has a flexible supply line which is unsafe.

8h. Here's a quiz: *How many problem conditions do you see in this photograph?*
1. There are remnants of asbestos that was unprofessionally removed from the old steam heating pipes.
2. The heating pipes and also between the floor joists should be insulated for energy efficiency.
3. The heating system flue stack has a downward pitch after the elbow which will slow the exhaust gases from exiting.
4. There is no pipe extending the water heater pressure relief valve to within eight inches above the floor.
5. On the lower, left of the tree trunk, the flexible pipe material is unsafe for the gas supply to the water heater.
6. This tree trunk could be put to better use somewhere else. In very old homes, you may find tree trunks being used to support the main girder beam. A solid, metal support post should be used instead.

8i. A heating contractor took the easy route while installing this steam pipe. As a result, now there is a serious structural problem with the main girder beam. One-half of this beam was cut and removed which weakens the support. This pipe should have been routed around the girder. If that was not possible, then a hole, 1/4 of the height of the beam, could have been cut in the center of this girder.

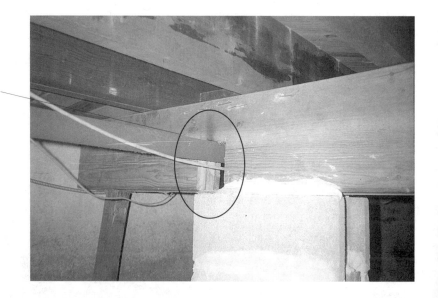

12a. When inspecting the kitchen, spot check appliances by briefly turning them on. *Just remember to turn them off when you're done - except for the refrigerator!* The countertop and cabinets should be securely fastened. All outlets by the kitchen sink must have GFCI protection. Remodeled kitchens and bathrooms are like any other changes made to a house - building department permits and final approvals are neeed from town hall.

12b. Bathroom tiles need to be evaluated for loose sections and open gaps. Loose areas can be detected by lightly banging on the tiles. The tiles in this bathroom are buckled and uneven. Prior water leaks behind the wall has caused this problem. To solve this problem, the tiles must be removed and the area behind must be repaired. Grout is used between ceramic tiles to prevent gaps that allow water penetration. Grout is a much harder material than caulk. Caulk is more flexible and used in areas where the joints will expand and contract more often.

12e. This window is too close to the floor level and is a safety hazard. Not only can a child fall through, but if an adult tripped, there is no window sill to stop their fall. Child guards should be installed on this window. In many areas the height of the window sill and the use of child guards are regulated by the local building and fire codes. *Don't wait for accidents to happen - take precautions ahead of time.*

While you're inspecting the interior rooms, jump on the floors to make sure they're structurally sound.

Check underneath the corner of the wall-to-wall carpeting. The only way to know what type of flooring is underneath is to check it. Don't assume there are hardwood floors under carpets just because you see hardwood in other rooms in the house.

If there are any pets in the house, you should have the carpets removed or fumigated prior to moving-in. You don't want any fleas as house guests.

12f. A vacuum seal is the air-tight space between the panes of glass in thermal windows and doors. Broken vacuum seals are indicated by dirt and condensation stains in between the two panes of glass, such as in this sliding glass door. Over time the moisture and dust stains will increase. Since this area can't be wiped clean, the window will become white and hazy. Repairing broken vacuum seals is expensive.

12g. Wood burning stoves can save a lot of money on heating fuel bills. These stoves can heat a large area of a home. However, safety precautions must be taken. Since these stoves radiate heat from the iron casing, they must not be touched while in use. A guardrail will help prevent accidental burns. Also, the flue stack for these stoves must be properly installed. A fireproof lining is needed and the flue should not be near any combustible materials, such as wood. Wood burning stoves, like forced hot air heating sytems, will dry out the air in the house. The metal pot on this stove is used to hold water. As the pot is heated, the water boils and turns to steam. This steam will add moisture back into the air so the occupants don't get sore throats or allergy problems from the dry air.

12h. *Creosote* is a black soot found in chimneys. Creosote is caused by the smoke from burning wood. You may find excess creosote stains on the face of a chimney and mantle, such as this one. This indicates a backsmoking problem. Backsmoking is caused by a firebox area that is too narrow and/or a flue stack that does not extend high enough above the roof to prevent downdrafts.

14d. *Here we are in asbestos heaven!* There are probably more asbestos fibers in this room than there are dust fibers. Almost always in older houses you'll find asbestos pipe insulation that is loose or has been removed unprofessionally. These conditions create very serious health hazards for the occupants of the house. Follow the EPA guidelines to resolve this.

15a. Radon gas is considered by EPA to be the number two leading cause of lung cancer behind smoking. Radon is everywhere since it's created by a natural breakdown of rocks and soil. Stone foundation walls and dirt floors in the lower level increase radon gas levels. The large rock embedded in this basement will add radon into the air. A cement floor covering will help reduce this problem.

The insulation vapor barrier is installed upside down!

16a. Asphalt/fiberglass shingles come in different weights. A heavier shingle has a 30 year life expectancy. Light weight shingles last about 20 years. These shingles are in good condition and there are no signs of old age or curling shingles.

With cable TV, antennas should be removed from roofs and chimneys. Antennas move in the wind and create water leaks. A cap and screen keep animals and water out of the chimney.

The small pipe in the roof is the vent stack for the plumbing drainage lines.

16d. A new roof will be needed on this house soon. These asphalt shingles are old and at the end of their life expectancy. When the shingles cup and curl and get frayed edges, it's a clear sign of old age. Get estimates prior to buying this house since a roof can be a major expense. If there are two layers of shingles on the roof, a third layer should not be installed on top. Three layers are too heavy for the roof. Remove the prior two layers of shingles and check the condition of the plywood sheathing before adding the new layer of roof shingles.

17f. All vines, ivy, shrubbery and trees must be pruned away from the house. This ivy clearly needs to be trimmed.

A minimum of at least eight inches above the soil is needed at the base of all siding. This clearance allows air and sunlight to help prevent rot and wood destroying insect problems.

Downspouts must be cleaned periodically. Clogged downspouts and gutters will create water problems around the foundation.

17g. *Here's an example of what can happen if you don't read my books!* The wood siding on this garage has rotted at the base. This decay was caused by the wood touching the soil. An eight inch clearance between the soil and the base of the siding would have prevented this problem.

18a. This welcome mat is resting on top of a safety hazard. Instead of "Welcome" this door mat should read: *"Stand here at your own risk!"*

A landing platforms is the standing area in front of a door. Landing platforms need to be large enough so the door can open safely. This storm door would knock someone down the steps if it was opened hastily.

The riser height is the vertical distance between each step. All risers should be evenly spaced about eight inches in height. This will help prevent tripping hazards from uneven stair heights.

18b. Do you know what's missing in this picture? *(No, it's not a matching gargoyle that's missing).* A handrail needs to be installed on these stairs. Whenever there are more than two steps in height, a handrail is needed for safety.

All stairways should have a light to prevent tripping hazards at night.

19a. There are several problems with this exterior deck support post.

1) The metal bracket is not sturdy enough to support the post where it meets the deck girder beam. Proper metal brackets need to be installed.

2) The base of this post is resting on a 2 x 6" wood board. This board will eventually rot and the deck will settle unevenly. Metal brackets are also needed at the base to properly secure the deck post to the concrete foundation.

19b. Clearly these deck support posts are unsafe! This is a high deck and if it collapses, **then someone is going to get hurt or killed!!** The posts have been installed improperly. The base of the wood is not resting evenly on the concrete foundation. The second post in the photo is off center on the concrete foundation. Metal brackets are needed to securely fasten deck supports to the concrete base.

23b. Here we have the exposed termite damage in a lower level floor joist. This is a common area for damage since the wood is close to the soil. The termite channels can be seen when the wood is probed and opens up. The mud and termite tunnels are mostly hidden from the light under a thin, outer layer of the wood. This is because termites need a dark, warm and moist environment at all times.

23a. On the exterior check the wood trim near the roofline. This area is prone to carpenter bee damage. The holes in this fascia board are an example of a carpenter bee nest. Carpenter bees and carpenter ants do not eat the wood for food, they merely excavate it to make a nest. Keeping a solid coat of stain or paint can reduce the chance of wood destroying insect damage.

Appraising Real Estate

Introduction To Appraising Real Estate

This is normally the first appraisal course that most people take if they are interested in becoming a licensed real estate appraiser. I will use my own notes from when I took the appraisal classes, along with my own comments and experience as a guideline for some of the following sections. The important items will be highlighted that I'm aware of from my experience as an appraiser and in the real estate business. I will try to keep these sections in a flowing format by including some additional comments and appraisal war stories. This will help explain anything that is new to you.

These courses have been renamed by state appraisal organizations to coincide with the Federal regulations of The Appraisal Foundation. Two of the class instructors that I had were some of the best teachers I've ever had. They were Anthony Fasanella and Dr. David Scribner. If you ever get a chance to

> Some readers of this book, such as home buyers or sellers, may not be interested in becoming licensed real estate appraisers. They may only be interested in getting a general working knowledge of appraisal concepts. For those readers, I would recommend you don't get too caught up in trying to memorize the in-depth math and appraisal concepts discussed in some sections of this book. Choose the sections you feel are most useful to you for now, and then you can learn the more in-depth topics later if needed.

take a class they're teaching, I suggest you do it. It'll be well worth your time and money. They are both true professionals with integrity and a sincere interest in improving the quality of real estate appraisers and the appraisal profession overall.

There's going to be appraisal math calculations in some of the following sections. If you're serious about real estate appraising then you're going to need to know this stuff so don't throw the book away or shut it for the day. I hate math as much as you do so I'll keep

it as simple as possible. I'm no rocket scientist myself, so if I can do the math then you certainly can too! I will round out the numbers when there are more than two decimal places. So please don't beat your head against the wall if the answers you get on your calculator have more than two decimal places or if they don't appear to *exactly* match the numbers in the book.

Some readers of this book, such as home buyers or sellers, may not be interested in becoming licensed real estate appraisers. They may only be interested in getting a general working knowledge of appraisal concepts. For those readers, I would recommend you don't get too caught up in trying to memorize the in-depth math and appraisal concepts discussed in some sections of this book. Choose the sections you feel are most useful to you for now, and then you can learn the more in-depth topics later if needed.

Real Estate Is Unique

There are at least four factors that make real estate unique and sophisticated as an investment:

1. It is *immobile* and therefore, external aspects around the building will affect the real estate. If an external aspect near the building turns away even **one** potential buyer, then it reduces the market value of the subject property. For example, if a house is located on a very busy street, then that will generally have a negative impact on market value. The reason for this is that the typical buyer will want to live in a quiet, residential area. A commercial property will have more appeal on a busy street because a business would generally want the exposure to the public and the traffic.

Because of the immobility of real estate we have a distinct market for it and that market is imperfect. Meaning that since you can't just pick up and move a house, *(not easily of course)*, that house is subject to the current market and area that it exists in. When prices rise and fall in that local market, then generally all of the real estate is affected by this. This is why the market is said to be imperfect because it is constantly changing. When you appraise a property, you estimate the market value *"As Of"* a particular date. That same property will generally be worth a different price at any given time, such as, a year before today or a year after today.

2. Real estate tends to be bought by an investment team. The investment team consists of the *Equity* investor, which is the owner, and the *Debt* investor, which is the mortgage lender.

Only the owner is listed on the deed for the property. The reason for this is that the lender or mortgage holder <u>does not</u> own the property. The lender has the owner sign a *note*. This note says that for a certain amount of interest and amortization period, the lender will let the owner borrow money to purchase or refinance the real estate. The lender also has the owner sign a *mortgage* which states that the real estate is the security for the loan. This way in the event that the borrower does not pay back the money as agreed to in the mortgage, then the lender can foreclose on the property. After foreclosing, the lender can sell the property to get their money back. The borrower generally cannot sell the property with a clear title until the loan is paid off.

3. Income property is only partially depreciable. Meaning that for tax depreciation purposes the land and the improvements are given two separate price values. *Improvement* means anything that is added to the land, such as the building.

Land cannot be depreciated for tax purposes, only improvements can be depreciated. *Depreciation* simply means that you are allowed to take a small tax deduction over a specified number of years. The yearly tax deductions attempt to adjust for the depreciating value of the asset due to normal wear and tear. These deductions will allow you to spend the funds that you save from the tax deduction. You can use the funds to make repairs and maintain the building.

4. Real estate is ubiquitous. This means that real estate is always around, everywhere simultaneously. It's not like a rare mineral or hard to find commodity.

The Bundle Of Rights

This section will cover some brief definitions concerning the rights of real estate. Land and anything attached to it is considered *Real Estate* because it is tangible and can be appraised for value. Real Estate refers to items that cannot be picked up and moved without dismantling anything. For example, when you appraise a home you don't evaluate the furniture which can be picked up and removed from the house. You evaluate the building itself which cannot be picked up and moved (unless you hire a house moving company that actually uses huge cranes, jacks, and equipment to lift a house up off the foundation and move it to another location). *Real Estate* and *Realty* refer to the same thing. Personal items, such as the furniture, are called *Personalty*.

Real Property refers to the rights of ownership of real estate which together are called the *Bundle of Rights*. When you sell real estate you're selling the **rights** of the real estate. The rights of real estate are:

1 The right to use. This refers to the owner's right to use his property as he wishes as long as it isn't for an illegal purpose.
2 The right to exclude. This refers to the owner's right to rent out his property to whoever he wants to.
3 The right to dispose. This refers to the owner's right to sell his property when he wants.

There are *Sub-Surface*, *Surface* and *Air* Rights of real estate. This refers to the fact that the ownership of real estate is considered to start at the center core of the earth. This ownership extends up to the heavens like a big "V" encompassing the property. Therefore, when you purchase real estate you also will own the sub-surface, surface and air rights of that property unless specified otherwise in the deed.

Fee Simple and *Fee Simple Absolute* refer to having full ownership rights of a property. Let's say for example, that someone has mineral rights (sub-surface) to your property. You or a prior owner may have purchased the property but later sold the mineral rights to someone else. For example, an oil speculator may have purchased the rights to any crude oil underneath your property. If that were the case then you would not have full Fee Simple ownership of your property. This must be taken into account when determining the market value of the real estate since it will affect the appraised value of the property.

The rights of real estate are severable and divisible. This means that the rights can be cut up and sold to other people. An example is a *life estate* which is the right granted to someone to use a property until they die. There was a house in my area that was sold by an elderly man to a builder. The agreement that they

> Real Estate refers to items that cannot be picked up and moved without dismantling anything.
> Personal items are called Personalty.

had was that the builder would subdivide the vacant parts of the property and build three new homes to sell for a profit. The elderly man not only got his purchase price for the property, but he also was given the right to stay in the house until he died. At the time of the elderly man's death, the property would revert to the builder to sell the last house on the lot. Both parties got what they wanted in the transaction.

A more common right granted with real estate is an *easement*. This is the right to provide access

> The rights of real estate are severable and divisible.
> This means that the rights can be cut up and sold.

through your property for someone else to run utility lines, install driveways, build a walkway on your property, etc.

All ownership of real estate comes from the sovereign. The *sovereign* in the United States is the individual states and the federal government.

Public Limits On Real Estate

There are some **Public** limits on the **Private** ownership rights of real estate:

1. *Condemnation*, also called *Eminent Domain* - This means that the State has the right to take your property from you for the benefit of the public. The State must compensate you by paying you the fair market value for the property that they condemn.

For example, let's say the State determined that a new airport was needed. They may have decided that the best place to build the airport was in a location where there were existing houses. The State would first have to condemn all of the houses in that location. This could be done on the basis that a new airport being built, in that particular location, was for the good of the public overall. They would then have appraisals done on all of the real estate in that area to figure out what the fair market value was for each property. Then the State would pay the owners of all of the condemned real estate the fair market value to compensate them.

Let's say an individual owner wanted to fight the State because they didn't want to sell. An owner might not want to move or may think that the condemnation sales price is too low. That owner would have to hire his own appraiser to find out if the State was paying him fair market value. If there was a large discrepancy between the two values, then the only recourse would be to go to court to settle the matter.

2. *Police Power* - This refers to the restrictions on real estate due to the zoning regulations, housing laws, building codes, etc.

I'll give you some appraisal trivia. *Zoning* laws started in 1916 when a building in New York City, located at 12 Broadway, was built so high that the adjacent property owners all complained to the city. The city then decided to impose restrictions on what property owners could do with their real estate. The purpose of zoning is to control the development of the land for the benefit of the general public. For example, if you live in a residential area you wouldn't want your neighbor building a warehouse. A warehouse next door would decrease your property value because buyers would not pay as much to live next to a warehouse.

It's the same thing with building codes. The State doesn't want people building unsafe housing, so they make sure that all construction is done to the minimum acceptable standards. Also, you wouldn't want your neighbor to be allowed to let his grass grow ten feet high would you? The building codes help protect the market value of your property. Building codes accomplish this by forcing a neighbor to maintain their property to conform with the other houses in the area.

3. *Escheat* - This refers to a situation when someone dies without a Last Will and Testament drawn up or any heirs to inherit their assets. If this were the case, then all of the deceased person's assets would go to the sovereign, (State). A friend of mine, named Mike Roe, is a CPA accountant who used to deal with settling estates that were in an escheat situation in New York City. He said that there were people who had died that were worth millions of dollars but they had no heirs to inherit their assets. *(How about giving it to me?)* The city would take over

Condemnation, also called Eminent Domain - This means that the State has the right to take your property from you for the benefit of the public.

the estate while they tried to locate an heir or relative of the deceased person. After a certain period of time, if there were any unclaimed assets then they would go to the State.

4. *Taxation* - We all know what this is! This restricts the rights of real estate in the sense that the State can assess a tax for the ownership of the property. You can dispute your property taxes and try to get them lowered by hiring an appraiser to determine if the tax assessment is too high.

Private Voluntary Limits On Real Estate

There are private **voluntary** limits that can be placed on the private ownership rights of real estate. This refers to restrictions that are voluntarily placed on the full rights of the real estate by the owner:

1. *Deed Restrictions* - This refers to something in the deed restricting the use of the property. For example, someone may sell a house with the restriction that it can never have an addition installed or no tress can be intentionally cut down. Years ago some people put deed restrictions on their properties when they sold that today would be illegal. These restrictions stated that any future owners of the property could not sell or rent the house to a person of a particular nationality or race. That type of deed restriction is against the federal discrimination laws and can't be enforced because it's no longer valid.

2. *Easements* - This allows someone to have access to your property, such as, running utility lines or installing a driveway.

3. *Leases* - This is simply granting the right to someone else to rent and use your property. Lease contracts can be written as simple or as detailed as both parties want. They outline specific rights and restrictions for the landlord and tenant.

4. *Mortgages* - This refers to a lender who secures their loan with the real estate property. The property cannot be sold with a clear title without the lender being paid off or permitting the new owner to assume the existing terms of the loan.

Private Involuntary Limits On Real Estate

There are private **involuntary** limits that can be placed on the private ownership rights of real estate. This refers to restrictions that are involuntarily placed on the full rights of the real estate by someone other than the owner. The involuntary limits are:

1. *Liens* - This refers to a legal claim against a property to secure the payment of a debt. A lien is a record listed with the deed at town hall. A lien says that someone has an interest in the property so that it cannot be sold without the lien being paid off or resolved. It's similar to a mortgage, only it usually involves: money owed from a court judgment, a repairman that was not paid for work done at the property, unpaid tax bills, etc.

2. *Encroachments* - This refers to something that is permanently located on someone else's property but it does not belong to the property

If this encroachment goes unnoticed and unchallenged for many years, then that part of your property becomes the ownership of your neighbor.

owner of the real estate it is on. For example, let's say your neighbor has a driveway or a fence installed and the contractor accidentally places part of it on your property. Part of the driveway or fence is then said to be encroaching on your property.

3. *Adverse Possession* - This refers to a person obtaining ownership of some real estate that was originally owned by you. However, that person did not pay you for this property. For example, let's say your neighbor has a fence or a garage built and the contractor accidentally places part of it on your property. The part of the fence or garage that crosses over your property line is an encroachment. If this encroachment goes unnoticed and unchallenged for many years, then that part of your property becomes the ownership of your neighbor. This change in ownership happens without any compensation or payment to you.

4. *Prescriptive Easement* - This refers to the fact that you must allow someone to have access to their property. For example, let's say someone purchased a lot behind your house. We'll assume that there was not an easement in your deed that granted

them the right to walk through your yard, or build a driveway on your property, to get to their yard. You would *have to* allow them access to get to their property. You couldn't stop them by saying they're trespassing on your yard. They have the right to gain access to their property, with or without your consent.

Basic Appraisal Concepts

The reason for an appraisal is to aid someone in making a decision. This could refer to: a mortgage lender, a potential home buyer or seller, an accountant who is trying to settle an estate, a homeowner disputing their property taxes, etc. An appraisal is an estimate of market value based upon the opinion of the appraiser.

The value of real estate is indeterminable due to the imperfect market. This means that real estate isn't like stocks and bonds where you can just look up its value in the newspaper. An appraisal is a supportable and defensible **estimate** of value based upon the **opinion** of the appraiser. It's not a *prediction* which is what a crystal ball is for, and it's not a *projection* which is a mathematical forecast. The difference between a forecast, a prediction and a projection:

◊ *Forecasting* is done with the best available information and facts that you have with reasonable conclusions to estimate the future.

◊ *Predictions* are less precise statements than forecasts. But a prediction has some basis, as opposed to something a fortune teller would tell you about the future.

◊ *Projections* are based on the past and it doesn't allow for contingencies to estimate the future. It's similar to statistics that uses projections of figures.

A forecast is an estimate. Appraisers forecast **not** predict because a forecast is based on whatever data is

An appraisal is a supportable and defensible estimate of value based upon the opinion of the appraiser. It's not a prediction which is what a crystal ball is for, and it's not a projection which is a mathematical forecast.

available and correct at the time of the report. Your appraised property value estimate is a forecast because it's the value in future benefits. The value of a property is the present value of future benefits from the ownership of that property.

The appraiser **measures** the value; he doesn't **determine** the value. The *market* determines the value. This means that potential buyers decide the value based upon recent, similar sales of comparable properties in the area. All the appraiser is trying to do is measure what the potential buyers are willing to pay for the real estate. Value is always measured through the eyes and aspects of the buyers and not the sellers. *People* make value and determine the sales prices of real estate, not a *property*.

The *Use* of a property leads to its *Productivity*, which leads to it's *Value*. For example, if you have a two-family house, it will generally be worth more

> *The appraiser measures the value; he doesn't determine the value. The market determines value.*

money than a one family house. The reason for this is that there is additional rental income from the second apartment. However, in some areas a single family house is worth more than a two-family house. That's because the single family fits-in with the other houses in the neighborhood, and there are no other two-family houses around. This is more common in a higher priced single family area.

Another example is in the case of a legal rooming house with many small apartments. As a rooming house the structure brings in a substantial amount of income. However, if you converted that rooming house to a one family dwelling, then you eliminate all the extra rental income. By doing this, it will generally reduce the property's market value.

43,560 square feet equals one acre.
There are 640 acres in one square mile.

DON'T FORGET THESE FIGURES!!! Often you will need to know these figures to make calculations for an appraisal. You may come across the terminology of *"chains"* concerning an acre. Just remember that one chain is equal to 66 feet. An acre is equal to one chain times ten chains or:

66 feet x 660 feet = 43,560 square feet.

Subjective And Objective Market Value

To have value, a property must have all of the following items:

1 *U* = Utility
2 *S* = Scarcity
3 *E* = Effective Demand
4 *T* = Transferable

An easier way to remember it is by the abbreviations: *USE + T*. *Utility* refers to the property being useful to a buyer. *Scarcity* refers to the property being unique enough that there aren't many other properties for sale in the area for a lot less money. *Effective Demand* refers to their being enough interest from potential buyers for the property. *Transferable* refers to the ability to transfer the ownership of the property to a buyer. If you cannot transfer a clear title and deed to a buyer, then no one is going to want to purchase your property.

The value of something depends upon people's desires. This changes from time to time since the market is imperfect and always fluctuating. It's just like the value of money which constantly fluctuates with inflation and the economy. Value is perceived from the eyes of a typical buyer for the item or property you estimate the value of. You have to understand the market of the real estate you are appraising. You have to identify your market very carefully. Try to figure out what type of tastes and income level a person would need for this property to be appealing to them. Remember that you look at value and the market through the eyes of the typical buyer.

The market *price* of a property can be equal to the market *value* of that property. However, this is not always the case. I'll clarify this statement by starting with some basic appraisal definitions.

The appraisal textbook definition of Market Value:

◊ *"Market Value is the most probable price in terms of money which a property should bring in a competitive and open market under all conditions requisite to a fair sale, the buyer and seller each acting prudently and knowledgeable, and assuming the price is not affected by undue stimulus."*

The appraisal textbook definition of Market Price:

◊   *"Market Price is an amount actually paid for a property in a particular transaction; an historic fact; and it may be forecast as most probable selling price."*

The market price is the actual sales price of a house. However, the sales prices can be different from market value because maybe the sale was not an *"arms length"* transaction. You value property as though it were an all cash deal and with normal loan financing. I'll talk more about all of this later, but for now I'll just give you a little info to "wet your appetite." Most mortgages are conventional because they're not insured or guaranteed by the government. Any "seller financing" with flexible terms on the subject property may affect the ***price*** but it doesn't affect the ***value*** of the property. It's the value of the property that you appraise. For example, let's say that a buyer is a relative of the seller. That buyer may be given a very low interest rate, purchase money mortgage loan by the seller. This low interest loan can be used to pay for part, or all, of the sales price for the property. Then that will affect the **sales price** of the property. However, it doesn't affect the **value** of the property.

> *The market price is the actual sales price of a house. However, the sales price can be different from market value if the sale was not an "arms length" transaction.*

The reason for this is that the value doesn't change just because a particular buyer was given good terms for his purchase of the property. This is why you only make an adjustment for favorable financing to the sales comparables that have nonconventional financing. By doing the adjustment, you'll make the comparables equal to an "arms length" transaction with conventional financing. Do you understand? If not, don't worry this is covered in detail later in the book.

You have to check to see what your State certification board gives as the definition of market value. Some States will have a slightly different definition to meet their particular needs. Also, there are different definitions for Condemnation Values, etc. that you should check on. Call your State Certification Board for any information they can provide you with.

If something affects value then you *HAVE TO* include it in the market value estimate of your appraisal report. I once did a foreclosure appraisal on a horse stable that had a **negative** market value!! How about them apples! The appraiser who originally did the mortgage loan appraisal report stated that a horse stable was the Highest and Best Use for the property. This stable was located in an area of million dollar homes! This guy must have been drunk when he did that report. To top it off, some local contractors had dumped some waste and toxic materials on the vacant site and contaminated the soil. The bank that foreclosed on the property had price estimates of over $1.5 million dollars just to clean up the soil. This clean up cost didn't even include the costs to knock down the stable, subdivide the lot, and then build new houses.

Market Value must be an **objective** value. Meaning, it must be an unbiased opinion of the value by the appraiser. The appraiser should not include their personal opinions if they are different from the opinions and judgments of the typical buyer in that

> *Market Value must be an objective value. Meaning, it must be an unbiased opinion of the value by the appraiser.*

market. For example, let's say you're appraising an older Tudor style house in a low income section of town. We'll assume that you personally don't like older houses, Tudor style houses, and/or the low income section of town. If this were the case, then you do not estimate the market value to be unrealistically low just because <u>you</u> don't like the house or because <u>you</u> wouldn't want to buy it and/or live in that neighborhood. You only measure the potential value from the eyes and opinions of the typical purchaser that would consider buying that house. The reason for this is that just because you don't like that house and you wouldn't want to buy it, doesn't mean that no one else would buy it. There are many buyers that love older, Tudor style houses and maybe they can only afford to buy a house in a low income area. That's the estimated value you're determining because there are people who will pay a certain price for that house. Your job is to estimate what that price is.

Value in Use is a **subjective** value. Meaning, it is a biased opinion of the value by the buyer or the seller. One example is a person who doesn't want to sell their house or will only sell at a very high price. This may be because the property has more importance and value to him than it does to a typical purchaser. Possibly the house has been in his family for years and it has sentimental value, or any number of other reasons. This unrealistically high market value in that person's eyes is called Value in Use.

Another example of a subjective value is a person

who is willing to buy a house at a much higher price than the typical buyer. This can occur because the property has more importance and value to him than it does to a typical purchaser. Possibly the house is located next door to his mother's house and he needs to live near there to watch over her, or any number of other reasons.

> *This is another reason why you want to get more than the minimum number of three sales comps for ALL of your appraisal reports.*

Let's say you were using a sales comparable that sold for an unusually high price due to the *Value in Use* of the buyer or seller. You must make an adjustment to the sales comp to reflect the personal opinions of the buyer or seller; if they paid a much higher price than the typical buyer would have in that market. Your adjustment amount should bring the total sales price of the comparable down to what it would have been if it were sold in an "arms length" transaction. This is another reason why you want to get more than the minimum number of three sales comps for **all** of your appraisal reports. When you're writing up the report, there will be times when you will find a problem with a comparable sale. Or you just get the feeling that a sales comp doesn't accurately reflect the local market and that something is wrong. If you have additional sales, then you can finish the report with the other sales comps that you have. Another option is that you can just apply less weight on that one comparable that's abnormal.

Amenity value is not really measurable in terms of money. This is similar to Value In Use, which was explained earlier. Amenity value is the value of something to a person due to their own tastes and desires. For example, someone may be willing to pay a very high price for a house that's located next to their mother-in-law's home. *(Well, maybe this example is a little far reaching, but it'll get my point across.)* This value of the property in their eyes is an amenity value because it doesn't reflect the opinion of the typical buyer. The amenity value to a particular person may not accurately reflect the value in the eyes of the typical buyer in the local market. Therefore, you can't really put a value on it because it's a subjective value and it's not tangible.

The Principles Of Property Valuation

1. **Supply and Demand** - Physical, Economic, Government and Social are the four forces that influence demand. The abbreviations make it easier to remember as *P E G S*.

a   *P* = Physical
b   *E* = Economic
c   *G* = Government
d   *S* = Social

Physical refers to the actual physical property for sale and how appealing it is to potential buyers. The more appealing, the more potential buyers there are. *Economic* refers to the economic conditions in the area where the property is located. *Government* refers to the federal, state and local government situation in that area. For example, perhaps the city politicians are planning to build an airport, or a huge garbage dump or waste disposal facility next to the subject property. Obviously this will have a negative affect on the demand to buy that real estate. If the property is located in an excellent school district this will increase demand from potential buyers. *Social* refers to the social conditions of the area around the subject property. For example, is the house located in a desirable community?

Effective Demand is the desire for new housing plus the income potential to buy the new housing. For example, there are millions of people who would like to buy a large house overlooking the ocean. You could therefore conclude that the demand for large houses overlooking the ocean is extremely high. However, this doesn't mean that the market value of these houses shoots sky high because it is not an *effective* demand for these houses. Meaning that even though there are millions of people who have the desire to buy these houses, effective demand is measured **only** by the people who actually can afford these houses and who want to live in that particular area.

The supply and demand are very important principles in estimating the market value of real estate. You relate it to the supply of houses for sale that the subject property is competing with. If there are many houses for sale in the area, then the market values will drop because there is too much supply. Supply is also called *standing stock* and is inelastic. This phrase "inelastic" is used because you can't build houses very quickly to meet a sudden increase in demand for them. Demand analysis can refer to whether people are moving into or out of the area. If an area has become undesirable, then the market values and sales prices of the homes will decrease due to a lack of buyers. Also, is it Effective Demand where the potential buyers have enough money and the desire to purchase the houses.

2. **Highest and Best Use** - there are four forces that influence H&B Use, which in turn have an affect on the market value of real estate. These four are discussed in more detail in the Highest and Best Use section of this book.

a   Physically Permissible
b   Legally Permissible
c   Appropriately Supported *(access to it)*
d   Economically Feasible

3. **Substitution** - the opportunity cost of making one investment decision over another has an affect on the market value of real estate. It's the choice someone has to make between different investment options.   The *Principle of Substitution* is an alternative course of action open to a purchaser. The purchaser's alternative is to buy another property or investment with the same utility and depreciation as the subject property. This is the basis for the Direct Sales and Cost Approaches to estimate market value. It can also apply to the Income Approach to estimate market value as well. For example, let's say there's an area that has very similar designs of houses that are relatively all the same age. What if all of the houses in the area are on the market for sale at $200,000, and one house is on the market for $250,000. Then the chances of that seller getting the higher price of $250,000 is unrealistic. The reason for this is that the typical buyer would purchase a similar and competitive house in the area for the $200,000 sales price.

4. **Marginal Productivity** - the different contributions made to an investment by its aspects. In terms of real estate, adjustment amounts are made for the pluses and minuses of a property to account for the marginal productivity. For example, there may be something about the subject property that is more appealing to buyers than other properties for sale in the area, such as a swimming pool.   The appraiser will need to make a plus adjustment in their report for this to increase the estimated market value of the house.

5. **Variable Proportions** - the increasing and decreasing rate of returns. This refers to the law of

diminishing returns for any improvements made to a property. For example, let's say you have to spend $15,000 in repairs to a house. Then how much will the value of the house increase when the work is finished? From an appraisal standpoint the normal rate of return for repairs should be at least one-to-one. This means that for each $1.00 you spend in repairs and improvements; you should increase the value of the property by at least $1.00. So using our example, if you spent the $15,000 then the market value of the property should increase by at least $15,000. If it doesn't than your rate of return on your invested money will diminish or decrease. This will lower the estimated market value of the property.

6. **Change** - the real estate market is always fluctuating due to the physical, economic, government, and social conditions (*PEGS*). This change is reflected in the four stages which make up the lifecycle of a neighborhood.

a   Growth
b   Stability
c   Decline
d   Renewal

The *Principle of Change* is reflected in the lifecycle of a neighborhood.   This means neighborhoods can change over time. The area may go through a period of *growth* during good economic times. Then the area will be *stable* for several or many years. Then the conditions could change and the area may start to *decline*. When the conditions change again, the area may begin a *renewal* process to complete the cycle.

The neighborhood where a property is located is **crucial** to the appraisal report. This is important because of the effect the external aspects have on the market value of a property. Every property takes on the characteristics of its neighborhood. As a result, if the neighborhood is in decline, then the property values will decline as well.

7. **Anticipation** - the value of an investment at the end of a certain period of time is what an investor is interested in. This is also known as *appreciation* which is the gradual increase in market value of a house or asset. This is mainly more important for income producing properties. However, all homeowners want their properties to appreciate in value over time. The *Principle of Anticipation* is the basis for the Income Approach to estimate market

value. It's the present value of future benefits for an investment. For example, if an investor is purchasing an income producing property, he's going to determine his purchase price based upon anticipated future profits in the deal.

The Analysis Of A City

As was noted in the Principles of Property Valuation section for supply and demand: Physical, Economic, Government and Social (*PEGS*) are the four forces that will influence demand. Just like *PEGS* effects the value of a particular property, it also effects the value and appeal of a city or neighborhood.

1 *P* = Physical Boundaries
2 *E* = Economic Activity
3 *G* = Government
4 *S* = Sociological Characteristics

1. **Physical Boundaries** - this refers to lakes, rivers, mountains, etc. that are some type of divider between cities and/or neighborhoods. This <u>does not</u> mean that you just use the city boundaries listed on a map for an appraisal report. The boundaries that are on a map may be different from the actual physical boundaries of the area. Also, just because a street has heavy traffic, it doesn't make it a boundary for the neighborhood. When you do use a street as a boundary, you technically use the properties up to 1/2 of one side of the street, on either side, as the boundary for the neighborhood. Look at price ranges and incomes as possible boundaries to use for your appraisal reports.

2. **Economic Activity** - this refers to the dominant economic activity of a city and/or neighborhood. Some examples of the different types found are: the nice areas of the city with the expensive homes and/or apartments, the expensive retail areas, the low income residential areas, the heavy industrial areas, transportation that's available in an area, such as, airports, bus terminals, railroad, etc.

Linkages refer to easy access to highways, job opportunities and employment centers, etc. of a neighborhood. Driving time is important for linkage with the supporting facilities for the subject property. *Supporting Facilities and Services* refers to hospitals, shopping centers, schools, recreational facilities, etc. to service the neighborhood. All of these will have an affect on the values of real estate in an area.

3. **Government** - this refers to the jurisdiction and stability of the government, tax structure, building department regulations, zoning, etc. that is found in cities. Are the building department regulations and zoning very strict? This could limit a buyer of a home from building an addition to a house or garage, etc. All of which must be considered in estimating market values of homes in that area.

4. **Sociological Characteristics** - this refers to the quality of the schools and recreational facilities, diversity of the churches, culture, arts and theaters, etc. that are found in cities. The more diversity and appealing these are, then the higher the property values will be due to increased buyer demand.

The Economic Base Of A City

You need to know the market and the economic conditions to be a good, thorough appraiser. To a certain degree you have to be an economist to really know what you're doing. The *Economic Base* of a community is the economic activity in that community which enables it to attract income from other areas outside its borders. It's not just referring to the job someone holds, but the type of industry their job comprises. For example, employment in areas of Texas is predominantly in the oil industry. Just like employment in Silicon Valley in California is predominantly in the computer related industries.

From an appraisal standpoint you're interested in the *Location Quotient*. The Location Quotient refers to the percentage of employment in a particular industry of an area as it compares to the national percentage in that industry for all areas. If the location quotient is greater than one, using the following math equations, then that industry is considered the base industry for the area. This means that in our examples above, Texas has a much higher Location Quotient percentage of employment in the oil industry, as compared to the national average of the oil industry employment for all areas of the country. Silicon Valley has a much higher Location Quotient percentage of employment in the computer industry, as compared to the national average of the computer industry nationwide. *(I know it can be confusing, but if you read it a few times over than it will begin to make sense to you.)*

Remember that if the Location Quotient > 1 (greater than one) then it is a basic industry or service for that city. If the economic activity is being exported, then it's the Economic Base of a city.

Now let's see how all of this relates to an actual appraisal example. Let's say there was going to be an increase in the local population due to new jobs that opened in a particular industry. You have been hired by the company offering the new jobs to find out what amount of housing is needed for the new employees. Through you're research and knowledge of the local market; you have the following data to work with:

◊ LQ = Location Quotient
◊ LEi = Local Employment in an Industry
◊ LEt = Local Employment Total in all industries
◊ NEi = National Employment in an Industry
◊ NEt = National Employment Total in all industries
◊ LQ = (LEi/LEt)/(NEi/NEt)

◊ Et = Total Employment
◊ Eb = Base Employment
◊ Es = Service Employment
◊ Et = Eb - Es

◊ Ke = Employment Multiplier
◊ Ke = Et/Eb
◊ Pt = Total Population
◊ Kp = Population Multiplier
◊ Kp = Pt/Et

1   The total population, Pt, for the area is currently 60,000 people.

2   The increase in the population of the area created by the new job openings will be 857 people.

3   The current density of the population has been averaged out to determine there are 2.5 people for each apartment unit and 3.5 people for each single family house in the area.

4   The housing accommodations for the current population is averaged out to estimate that 40% of the people in the area live in apartments and 60% of the people live in single family houses.

To start we'll determine how many of the 857 people hired will live in apartments and how many will live in single family houses. To find this, simply use the percentages that currently exist in the area. We know that currently 40% of the people live in apartments and 60% of the people live in single family houses.

857 x 40% = 343 will live in apartments

857 x 60% = 514 will live in single family houses

Next, using these figures, we need to figure out how many apartments and how many single family houses are needed for the new employees. This is found by using the numbers that currently exist in the area. We know that currently there are 2.5 people for each apartment unit and 3.5 people for each single family house in the area. Simply divide the new employees for each type of dwelling unit by these amounts.

343/2.5 = 137 apartments will be needed

514/3.5 = 147 single family houses will be needed

137 + 147 = 284 total housing units will be needed

Add the total apartments needed to the total single family houses needed. The result is, that 284 units would be the increase in the total housing needed for the increased employment and population growth in the area, due to the new job openings.

The "As Of" Date Of Valuation

An appraisal is a supportable and defensible estimate of value of a property "as of" a certain date. The *"As Of"* date sets up the conditions at the time of the value estimate, such as, physical conditions, economic conditions, etc. The date of sale is important due to the market condition "as of" the date of the sale.

The "As Of" date is **critical** in every appraisal report. It's critical because the house you're appraising is most likely worth a different price today than it was one year ago. The house will also be worth a different price one year after today. Changes in the market value are created by the fluctuating market. Therefore, you have to account for this fact. You decide what the typical buyer would pay in an "arms length" transaction, "as of" the date you are estimating the market value of the subject property. For example, let's say you're doing a house appraisal for an estate. Estate appraisals are always needed for tax purposes after someone dies. However, often the people overseeing the estate will order the appraisal many months or even years after the owner of the property has died. Let's say the person died four years ago. Then you would have to go back and find records of sales comparables from four years ago. You would also have to find the information needed for the cost and income approaches at the time of the owner's death. If the person died 20 years ago, then you would have to go back 20 years to estimate the market value! The reason for this is due to the "As Of" date of your appraisal which in this example is 20 years ago.

One of my instructors for the appraisal courses told us that he has a friend who had to do an appraisal for a particular group of American Indians. They were trying to decide how much money the government owed these Indians, in today's dollar value, due to land that was taken from them many years ago. The "As Of" date of the appraisal wasn't just 20 years ago; it was 200 years ago!!! Imagine trying to find data from 200 years ago to do all three approaches to estimate market value of vacant land? To make it even more difficult, the appraiser had to figure out the value of the land in today's prices. Two hundred years ago many things were purchased with bartering instead of money. So instead of paying someone a $10 bill, you paid them with some food, or tools, or cattle, or anything else you could exchange with them. *(Can you could handle an appraisal assignment like that?)*

The Highest And Best Use

You value property in relation to its *Highest and Best Use.* This may not always be its present use and the property's H&B Use can change over time. The H&B Use is based upon all factors, such as, the neighborhood data, market data, zoning, etc.

Market Value is always estimated by the **Highest and Best Use** for the subject property and the **Date** of the appraisal. Highest and Best Use is one of the most *critical* factors in all appraisals. The "As Of" date of the appraisal is the other critical factor. H&B Use and the "As Of" date, are the two factors that the entire appraisal is based upon. In the H&B Use, land is always residual. The type of improvement that you put on that site must yield the most value for it to be the H&B Use. For example, if you build a single family house in an area mostly of four family buildings, then the single family house is probably not the H&B Use of that site. The type of improvement must conform to

> Highest and Best Use is one of the most CRITICAL factors in all appraisals. The "As Of" date of the appraisal is the other critical factor.

the approved zoning for the site, in order for it to be the H&B Use. Let's say you converted a single family home into a two family house by separating the first and second floors to create two apartments. If the local zoning does not allow a two family house on that site, then it cannot be the H&B Use of the property. Potential buyers will not want to purchase a property if it violates the zoning laws.

The Highest and Best Use of a property is the most profitable, likely use to which a property can be put. Consider it as the use in which a property is put which will give the highest value to the site. To determine the highest and best use, you need to have *all* of the following factors:

1. It must be a **legally permitted** use for the property. For example, let's say you're appraising a single family house. What if the zoning on the property states it can be used for a one-family or a two-family dwelling. If two-family houses are worth more money in that area, then you may determine that the highest and best use is a two-family. That is, if it is feasible for

the house to be converted to a two-family. However, if the zoning is for a single family house only, then you cannot estimate the value based upon the possible conversion to a two-family house. That is, unless the conversion could be done without any extensive zoning changes.

2.   It must be a **physically possible** use for the property. For example, let's say you're appraising a two-family house that has a frame construction. *Frame* construction means that the walls of the house are made of wood materials and not masonry materials, like brick or stone. The zoning on the property may state that it can be used for a two-family *frame* dwelling or a four-family *masonry* dwelling. What if four-family houses are worth more money in that area. If this were the case, then you cannot decide that the highest and best use is a four-family. That is, unless you calculate into your analysis the cost of knocking down the existing frame house, and building a new masonry structure.

3.   It must be an **appropriately supported** use for the property. For example, let's say you're appraising a vacant lot in a forest area. We'll assume that you want to determine if the H&B Use is a single family house as opposed to the current vacant lot. You would have to be able to get utility lines to the property and have some roadways providing access to it, in order to decide that the highest and best use is a single family house.

4.   It must be an **economically feasible** use of the property. For example, let's say you're appraising a one family house and you want to find out if the highest and best use is a three-family house. You would need to evaluate the following:

a   You must learn if a three-family house is marketable in the subject area. Marketability is determined by: the quality of the space *(demand for the real estate)*; the quantity of the space *(supply of other houses on the market for sale)*; the location of the real estate; and any special conditions that will enhance the marketability.

b   You must also find out if a three-family house meets a typical investor's criteria. One requirement it would have to meet would be an adequate rent roll or appreciation to provide a good return on their money invested in the property.

Highest And Best Use Example

Let's say, you're hired by an investor to find out the H&B Use of a property he's considering purchasing. The investor wants to know that if he buys this single family house, and then knocks down the house to build a four-family building; will a four-family be the H&B Use of the subject property?

From your field work and the data you have obtained, you make the following conclusions:

Under The Current Use:
◊ $40,000 = Site Value with the zoning for a single family house
◊ $150,000 = Building + Site Value

Under The Proposed Use:
◊ $10,000 = Demolition Cost of the single family house
◊ $180,000 = New Construction Cost of the four family house
◊ $75,000 = New Site Value with the zoning for a four family house
◊ $240,000 = New Construction Value of the four family house

The first step is to figure out the total loss in value for demolishing the existing improvements on the site. This is found by subtracting the current value of the building plus the site, from the current site value.

$$150,000 - $40,000 = $110,000$$

The next step, is to figure out what the costs will be for everything from the demolition of the single family house, to the construction of the four-family house. We find this by adding the current value of the site, plus the loss in value for demolishing the single family house, plus the cost of this demolition, plus the cost to construct the four-family house.

$$40,000 + $110,000 + $10,000 + $180,000 = $340,000$$

Then we determine what the new value will be for the building plus the site, with the four-family house on it. We find this by adding the new construction value plus the new site value with these improvements.

$240,000 + $75,000 = $315,000$

We then subtract the value of the current site plus the current building, from the value of the new site plus the new building. The purpose of this is to learn what the added value will be with the four-family house built.

$315,000 - $150,000 = $165,000$

The value added by this change in use is only $165,000. We have now found, that the cost to change the use of the site from a single family to a four-family is $340,000. The new total value of the site plus building will only be $315,000. This will give the investor a $25,000 loss if the change is made. Therefore, we can conclude that it's *not* the Highest and Best Use to change from the single family house to the four-family house. By making this change, it will cost the investor more money than he will gain in increased value, when the conversion is all finished.

Property Analysis

You must know the property you're appraising and the facts about it, the measurements, the negative and positive aspects, etc. It's important that you look at **all** areas of the house, top to bottom, and not the furniture. You look at the *building* when doing an appraisal. The exterior shell and roof, and the integrity of the interior must be maintained. These items have a lot to do with the remaining economic life of the building. The furniture and decorations may make the house more appealing on the inside, but they're not part of the real estate that you're appraising. Therefore, you have to picture the house for your value estimate as though the furniture and decorations weren't even there.

Only include the aspects that affect the *value* in your report, not your own personal biases. The role of an appraiser is to reflect the *market* and not their own bias. When you walk around, notice what has to be repaired in and around the house. See how the rooms flow and the layout of the floor plan. Meaning that you should make sure you don't have to go through a bedroom to get to the only bathroom on a floor. This type of floor layout is similar to those found in the old railroad style apartments and will negatively affect the market value. See if the kitchen is located on the third floor, or if there are no bathrooms on the floor with the

bedrooms. If this is the case, then it is a functional drawback because this is an abnormal room layout and will lower a potential buyer's purchase price.

Check the site to decide if it's too large or too small as compared to other houses in the area. Does the site have a very steep slope that makes most of the vacant land unusable? Is it located on a busy street that

> It's important that you look at all areas of the house, top to bottom, and not the furniture. You look at the building when doing an appraisal.

would decrease the market value? Is it located on a private street that has a positive or negative affect on value? Does the landscaping conform with the overall appearance of the other houses in the area? Etc. I think you get the picture here. Just open your eyes and use your common sense when you're doing appraisals.

One of the things that really helps me out on an appraisal is: *I try to look at the property the same way a typical purchaser for that house would look at it.* Try not to get too involved in the mathematical equations, the exact square footage, the adequacy and type of insulation in the house, if every faucet is working properly, etc. Not that these items shouldn't be accounted for; it's just that you don't want to forget to take a step back and look at the house as though you were a typical buyer. A typical buyer will look at the general appeal of the house and the area. They wouldn't go through the home with a microscope and nitpick with the seller about a stain in the carpet, or a peeling section of wallpaper, or other trivial items.

Land And Site Valuation

In valuing vacant land, the best approach is generally the Direct Sales Comparison approach. When you have improvements on the site, you have to consider what effect a building has on the land value. The improvements could have a positive or negative affect on the land value, as opposed to if the site were left vacant.

As always, the Highest and Best Use and the "As Of" Date of Valuation are critical factors for your appraisal. Sub-soil conditions are also important. Such as, is the land part of a wetland or conservation area that can't be built upon? Or are there minerals in the soil that are worth money? Has the soil been contaminated with toxic substances or oil leaking from an underground tank? Or are there any other factors that affect the value? A site is valued from an appraisal standpoint as if it is vacant and available to be put to its Highest and Best Use. A *Site* is a buildable lot derived from taking vacant land and improving it so that it's ready to be built upon. For example, knocking down some trees, leveling the lot, running utility lines underground, etc. are all examples of improving vacant land. Location is important in H&B Use, and particularly important in land value.

You value land on a physical basis or by its productivity. The productivity of the land refers to how many houses or apartments or the maximum building square footage amount that can be built upon it.

Plottage refers to two or more adjoining lots that when combined, they produce a higher utility and value. *Assemblage* refers to two or more lots that when combined, they do not produce a higher utility and value. Meaning that just because you buy two lots that are next to each other, it doesn't necessarily mean that you increase their market value by combining them. Perhaps there are zoning restrictions that wouldn't make it beneficial to be the sole owner of the two combined lots. You may get the same market value if the lots were owned by two different people.

There are many different ways of estimating land values. Some of these include:

1   *Front Foot Basis*
2   *Gross Area Basis*
3   *Price Per Acre Basis*

I'll give you some examples on how these work.

We'll assume we have found a lot that sold for $56,000 and the dimensions are 40 feet wide by 128 feet long. *Front Foot Basis* is calculated by the sales price of the lot divided by the total amount of frontage feet of the property. *Frontage Feet* simply refers to the length of the lot that is touching or facing the street. The larger the frontage feet the more property you have on the street. This is often more desirable than just having a narrow property by the street which widens as it goes

> *In valuing vacant land, the best approach is generally the direct sales comparison approach.*

inward more. This is especially true for commercial properties. Commercial businesses want as much exposure as possible to attract more customers off the street. Anyway, the estimated value of our example on a *Front Foot Basis* is:

$$\$56,000/40 = \$1,400 \text{ per } \textbf{frontage} \text{ foot}$$

Gross Area Basis is calculated by the sales price of the lot divided by the total square feet of the property. *Square Feet* simply refers to the length of the lot multiplied by the width of the lot. The estimated value of our example on a Gross Area Basis is:

$$40 \times 128 = 5,120 \text{ square feet}$$

$$\$56,000/5,120 = \$10.94 \text{ per } \textbf{square} \text{ foot}$$

Price Per Acre Basis is calculated by the sales price of the lot divided by the percentage of acres of the property. The first thing we need to do is to find out what the actual acreage is of the subject lot. To do this, we divide the square feet of the lot, by the number of square feet in an acre. You do remember that there are 43,560 square feet in an acre, don't you? *(I'll be disappointed if you forget that!)*

$$40 \times 128 = 5,120 \text{ square feet}$$

$$5,120/43,560 = .12 \quad \text{or} \quad 12\% \text{ of an acre}$$

We then take the sales price and divide it by the actual acreage. This will give us the estimated value of the property on a Per Acre Basis.

$$56,000/.12 = \$466,667 \text{ per } \textbf{acre}$$

The Direct Sales Comparison Approach

The three approaches used to estimate market value of real estate are shown in the sample appraisals included in this book. Please review those appraisals as you read the sections outlining the following three approaches for estimating market value:

1   The Direct Sales Comparison Approach
(also called the Market Data Approach)

2   The Cost Approach

3   The Income Approach

The *Direct Sales Comparison Approach (DSCA)* is based on the assumption that by using recent, closed sales in the local market, the appraiser can estimate market value of the subject property. "Closed sales" refers to properties that have sold and the deal was done (closed) on a date very close to the "as of" date for your appraisal. For example, let's say you were hired to appraise a condominium with an "as of" valuation date of two years ago for your report. You cannot choose condo sales comparables that sold two months ago because they won't accurately reflect the real estate market conditions two years ago. Using

> *The DSCA is usually the most effective and accurate technique in appraising single family houses and condos.*

the DSCA, the appraiser evaluates and compares houses that have recently sold which are located very close to and are very similar to the subject property to estimate market value of the subject property. This is usually the most effective and accurate technique in appraising single family houses and condominiums. The DSCA is the method that you will use most often for your appraisal reports. Basically, in order to estimate market value of the subject property using the DSCA, you analyze recent sales of <u>competitive</u> and <u>comparable</u> properties. You then make adjustments in

your appraisal report to try to "equalize" the comparable sales as though they had the exact same characteristics as the subject property. Closed sales comparables for an appraisal report are chosen based upon many factors. Since no two properties are identical, cost adjustments must be made to **estimate what the sales comparable would have sold for if it was identical to the subject property.** You have to remember that with the DSCA technique you're always comparing the sales comps to the subject property, not vice versa. Don't get confused while writing up a report. For example, don't make a plus adjustment to a sales comp that has a two-car garage when the subject only has a one-car garage. I'm going to describe the appraisal adjustment process and more details about this in the following sections.

The units of sales comparison to use when evaluating sales comparable properties include:

◊   *Physical* - compare acre to acre, square feet to square feet, etc.

◊   *Economic* - compare rental income to rental income, etc.

For the Direct Sales Comparison Approach you need to consult all data sources that accurately list recent sales in the area. An appraiser's own files should always be the primary source of data for an

> *Basically, in order to estimate market value of the subject property using the DSCA, you analyze recent sales of competitive and comparable properties.*

assignment. This means that you should have enough information, about the local market and recent sales, in your files to assist you on your appraisals. Obviously, the longer you're in business, the larger and more helpful your files will become in obtaining data. Some other helpful sources that you should use are: the local town hall, the real estate *Multiple Listing Service* (MLS), *REDI Data*, and any other sources that are available to you.

Just be careful when you're obtaining your data. If you find discrepancies between two different data sources, then you should always use the public record at town hall as the most reliable source. For example, let's say the local MLS has a sales comparable listed that sold for $135,000 four months ago. Well since you're an **"A to Z Appraiser"** who does good, thorough appraisals, you will try to verify this information at the local town hall. You then find out that the public record for this sales comparable states that it sold for $127,000 five months ago. If this were the case then you should always use the public record as the final say in the matter.

I'm letting you know ahead of time that there will be many times that you'll find discrepancies in the data sources. Some discrepancies will involve what the data source has listed, and what is actually at the site for the

> *I'm letting you know ahead of time that there will be many times that you'll find discrepancies in the data sources.*

subject property and sales comps. For example, you'll often find a data source that says the property has a two-car garage. However, when you view the property personally, you find it only has a one-car garage. Or it says the house is in good condition and when you look at it, it's clearly a mess that needs work on the exterior. So you see, don't get lazy and cut corners or else you may end up in a very uncomfortable situation, where you can't defend your actions.

If you read the MLS and other data sources, they clearly state in the books that *"The information is believed accurate but not warranted."* This simply means that the data source company is not guaranteeing that the information from their books is 100% accurate. There are many times that you will find discrepancies in different data sources. You have to be very careful about using data sources that can be unreliable. Sometimes you have no choice, but that's why you always verify *all* information at the town hall. You should make copies of everything about the subject property, all sales comparables and any pertinent data that you can obtain. These copies should be kept with your own records in case you need them in the future to answer questions or refer back to an old appraisal report you did. This includes the deeds, tax information, zoning information, flood hazard zones, lot sizes, house square footage, age of the house, building department violations, etc.

You have to personally go out and look at all subject properties and all sales comparables if you're going to sign your name to the appraisal report. Don't just take it for granted that the site and building are OK and still standing. Remember that it's your neck on the line if you sign off on that appraisal. If you're the review appraiser, you don't have to go out and view the properties. However, you do have to at least see recent photographs taken for the appraisal report. You're probably wondering why I'm telling you that. Well, I'll give you a few war stories so you realize why.

One of my appraisal instructors told our class about a court case that he was working on. This case involved a lawsuit against an appraiser who never went out to view the comparable sales he used for a single family appraisal report. Apparently this appraiser had used sales comps that were abnormally low for his appraisal report. Upon reviewing this appraisal for the court case, the instructor found that the sales comps were vacant land sales and not single family house sales! Even if the appraiser's data source incorrectly listed them as single family sales, the appraiser is still in trouble. He's in trouble because he did not go out to verify this information with his own eyes. All he had to do, was drive to those addresses and he would have found that there were no houses at the site. Then he would have known that these sales were incorrectly listed in his data source. He must have gotten too lazy over the years and now he's going to pay for it.

> *You have to personally go out and look at all subject properties and all sales comparables if you're going to sign your name to the appraisal report.*

Another one of my instructors told our class about an appraiser who never went out to view the subject property. When this appraiser turned in his report, the client called him up to ask if he looked at the house on the "as of" date listed on his report. The appraiser was awfully surprised when the client informed him that the house had burned down the day before the "as of" date in which he apparently inspected the subject property!! This is another reason why the "as of" date is so crucial to an appraisal report. The day after that fire the subject property obviously was not worth as much as it was the day before. So learn a lesson from these two examples and make sure you personally view the subject property and all sales comps for all of your appraisal reports.

You can save a lot of time viewing and photographing the sales comps for an appraisal report by planning ahead. Map out your route to photograph and view the comparable sales for your reports before you leave your office. Purchase a good map of your area and photocopy the pages that have the subject property and the sales comparables on them. You can then use a highlighting marker to map out the best route to take. This will save you a lot of time and it will help prevent you from getting lost and driving around in circles. You should also purchase a good, reliable car compass. You'll be very surprised to find out how helpful an accurate compass is while you're driving around for your appraisal reports.

There will be times when you can't get inside the subject property or there will be any inaccessible areas during some appraisals. For example, if you're doing a foreclosure appraisal for a bank it's possible that the current tenant/occupant of the house doesn't allow you to come inside the home. Perhaps the basement or garage is sealed up and you don't have access. When you encounter a situation like this, just tell the client

You should exceed the form requirements on all of your appraisals. This is how you do quality work that is far better than 90% of the appraisers in the business.

about it and make sure you mention this in your written report. If you have any doubts about the subject property or the sales comps, make sure you put that in the report as well. This way everything is up front and nobody can accuse you of being lazy or hiding something that you should have told them about.

Get extra sales comparables for all your appraisals. Don't just stick to the minimum three sales to fill out the form reports. Don't just do the minimum requirements of the items listed on the standard appraisal forms. You should **exceed** the form requirements on all of your appraisals. This is how you do quality work that is far better than 90% of the appraisers in the business. You should also include additional data in the addendum's, extra photos, etc.

There will be many times when you're writing up an appraisal report, when you'll have a sales comparable that doesn't accurately reflect the local market. Possibly it has sold for an unusually high or low sales price. Maybe you will find some other problem with the comparable sale. You might just get the feeling that this sale doesn't accurately reflect the local market and that something is wrong. If you have additional sales, then you can finish the report with the other sales comps that you have. You'll also have the

option of just applying less weight in your evaluation to that particular sales comp. This is another reason why you want to get more than the minimum number of three sales comps for **all** of your reports.

Narrowing Down The Search For Good Comps

There are many ways to narrow down your search for good sales comparables to use for an appraisal report. Some things to look for to narrow down your search for good comps are:

a   Sales that are an *"arms length"* transaction.

b   The most recent sales possible based upon the *"as of"* date of your appraisal report.

c   Sales that are located as close as possible to the subject property.

d   Sales that are as similar as possible to the subject property.

I'll elaborate on items A, B, C and D so they're easier to understand.

A: Sales that are an "arms length" transaction refers to sales that have conventional financing terms for the purchase of the property. There also must be no known factors that abnormally affected the buyer's or seller's decisions in the deal. If the buyer obtained a mortgage loan at the market interest rate without any

Sales that are an "arms length" transaction refers to sales that have conventional financing terms for the purchase of the property.

seller financing or lower than normal interest rates, then it can be assumed that the financing is *conventional* Also, if there are no known factors that led to a *motivated* buyer or seller, then it can be considered an "arms length" transaction.

A motivated person could be someone who has to sell or buy the property for an important and urgent reason. For example, let's say the seller can't afford to make the mortgage payments anymore. We'll assume he cannot make the payments because his business is unfortunately going bankrupt. As a result, he will be motivated to sell the property for a lower price. The seller will be forced to sell the house before the bank can foreclose on his mortgage. Another possibility is that the seller is getting divorced and has to sell the house as part of the divorce settlement. In this case also, he will be motivated to sell the property for a lower price just to get rid of the house. Another example is if the buyer has to purchase a house next to a sick relative or family member. If he needs to be close enough to care for that person, then he'll be motivated to pay a higher price just because of the location of the house.

You adjust the sales comparables for *Sales and Financing Concessions* first and then time, locational, physical, etc. adjustments are made. The reason for this is that you first adjust the sales comps, if needed, to be "arms length" transactions on the date that they sold. The purpose of the adjustment process is to estimate what the sales comp would have sold for if it had possessed all the market recognized characteristics of the subject property. Market recognized characteristics refers to all items that affect value.

When you make financing adjustments in appraisal reports, it's generally required for seller financing on the comparable sales and not with bank financing. Seller financing is adjusted for if the financing was provided at a lower interest rate then the market lending rate, at the time of the sale of the **comparable**, not for the sale of the subject property. Meaning, that if the **subject property** is being sold with seller financing and good terms, then you *don't* adjust the sales comps downward if they were sold with conventional bank financing. The reason for this is that the flexible terms for the sale of the subject property will affect the market price. However, flexible terms don't affect the market value of the property. If that's confusing for you, then go back to the section in this book that defines and explains market value and market price. Any bank financing generally doesn't need to be adjusted for with the sales comparables. This is because bank loan financing is usually lent at the market interest rate at the time of the sale of that sales comparable property.

B: When you're looking for good sales comps, start checking the data sources for sales that have occurred within the last six months. You want to try to find the sales that have occurred within six months prior to the "as of" date of the appraisal. Hopefully you can find enough sales within the past six months for

your report. The reason for this is that the more recent the sales are, the more accurately they reflect the market conditions "as of" the date of your appraisal.

It's not uncommon that you have to go back further than six months, so just do the best you can. If you can't find sufficient sales that have closed within the past six months, then go back up to one year. If you still can't find enough sales that have closed within the past year, then keep moving backwards until you find them. Just remember that you **have to make time adjustments** if necessary for the different market conditions at the time the sales comps closed. These time adjustments are made to reflect the market conditions at the time the comparables sold, as opposed to the "as of" date for the appraisal of the subject property. Also, many lenders will not accept

> *The reason for this is that the more recent the sales are, the more accurately they reflect the market conditions "as of" the date of your appraisal report.*

sales comps that are over one year old. That's why you have to make an extra effort to find sales that have sold within a six month period prior to the "as of" date. You don't want to finish a report and have a client bounce it back in your lap. They might do this if the sales are too old and they refuse to accept them as accurate comps.

Time adjustments in the appraisal report are also known as *Market-to-Market Comparisons*. The reason for this is that the time adjustments are used to factor in any changes in the local real estate market. Changes from the time that the sales comps sold, to the time of the "as of" date for the subject property valuation. The negative aspect of the Direct Sales Comparison Approach is that a closed sale is history and the market is constantly changing. This is why you need to use sales comparables that are no more than six months old. This way the comparables should accurately reflect the most recent market conditions "as of" the date of the appraisal.

Don't use the date the title of the property is recorded in the public record for the closing date of any sales comparables unless you have no other choice. The reason for this is that the title may not be recorded until long after the house was sold. One of my instructors gave our class an example of someone he met once that worked at a bank or a title company. This person had accidentally found a bunch of property titles in his desk drawer. The houses had sold a long time before that and this bank or title company employee had forgotten to record these property titles at town hall! If you used the title date for these properties as the actual closing date on your appraisal report, then you would be way off base. You'd be off because the market will be different from the actual date of the sale which was much earlier in time then the title recording date.

You can use the contract date for sales comparables because that is when the *meeting of the minds* between the buyer and the seller took place. Just make sure that if you do this, then you must use the contract date for all of your other sales comparables as well. Remember you have to compare the actual market conditions at the time of each sale. The contract date is generally at least several months before the actual closing date on the property. This is because there are mortgage applications that have to be approved, title searches and other legal work needs to be done, an appraisal must be ordered and then reviewed, etc.

C: Sales that are located as close as possible to the subject property is another factor to look for to narrow down your search for good comps. The closer a sale is to the subject property, the more it is similar to the subject, as far as how any external advantages or disadvantages affect it. Some items you have to consider when evaluating the subject and any sales

> The closer a sale is to the subject property, the more it is similar to the subject, as far as how any external advantages or disadvantages affect it.

comps are: the school district it's in; tax structure of the area; the town it's located in; proximity to highways, shopping, employment, and entertainment; the income level of the area; is it located on a private road; etc.

For example, if the subject property is located near an airport, there will probably be some negative affect on market value. Negative impact on value is caused by the noise from the airplanes flying over the houses in the area. If you pick a sales comparable from an area that isn't affected by the airport noise, then you <u>must</u> adjust for this factor. You have to adjust for the superior location because the airport didn't affect the sales price of the comp. Another example could be a different school district or the amount of taxes between the subject property and sales comparable. You have to try to compare apples to apples all the time. If the subject is located in an area that has a lower quality educational system or lower taxes than a sales comparable, then you <u>must</u> adjust for these factors. An

adjustment is needed because these factors would have affected the sales price of the comparable property if it was located in the same area as the subject property.

It's often said that in real estate the three most important factors are *Location, Location, Location.* The reason for this is that you can take two identical houses and place them in two different locations and have a big difference in their market values. For example, let's say you took an average house for your area and placed it onto a vacant lot that was overlooking the ocean. Does the market value suddenly increase? You bet it does! That's why location is so important in real estate.

D: Sales that are as similar as possible to the subject property is something to look for to help you find good comps. The form appraisal reports list many different aspects you have to evaluate to determine how similar the comps are to the subject property. I'll go through the items listed on the back of the single family appraisal form and give you some descriptions to explain them in more detail. We have already discussed the first three items that are adjusted on the form: **A:** *Sales or Financing Concessions,* **B:** *Date of Sale/Time* and **C:** *Location.*

1. **Site/View** - This refers to the topography and size of the site and the type of view there is from the site. Is the lot very hilly or is it relatively flat and does it have usable space? A very hilly lot will not be as usable to the homeowner as a flat lot. What size is the lot? If the lot sizes are different, then determine what adjustment is needed to compensate for this in the eyes of the typical buyer. If the lots are only slightly different in size, then an adjustment may not be needed. The reason for this is that the typical buyer may not lower or higher the purchase price due to a slight difference in two lots. What type of view does the property owner have? If one house overlooks a nice forest area and the other house overlooks a busy street, then an adjustment is needed.

2. **Design and Appeal** - This refers to the style and appeal of the house. Is the house a Ranch style in an area of mostly Colonial style homes? The typical buyer will generally be looking for a house that conforms with the other homes in the area. What type of appeal does the house have? Is the overall design and appeal something that the typical buyer would find a nice home to live in or not?

3. **Quality of Construction** - This refers to the type and quality of the construction of the house. Is the house built of brick construction in an area of mostly wood frame constructed homes? The typical buyer will generally be willing to pay more for a house made of brick or stone, as opposed to a wood frame structure. What is the quality of the construction? Is it something that the typical buyer would find to be an overall well made home to live in or not?

4. **Age** - This refers to the age of the house. Is there a significant difference between the age of the subject property and that of the comparable sales? The typical buyer will generally be willing to pay more for a house that is newer. If the ages are significantly different, then decide what adjustment is needed to compensate for this in the eyes of the typical buyer. If the ages are only slightly different, then an adjustment may not be needed. An adjustment may not be needed because the typical buyer may not lower or higher the purchase price due to a slight difference in age of the two houses. You can also account for a slight age difference by making an adjustment in the *Condition* section on the appraisal form, instead of in this section.

5. **Condition** - This refers to the overall interior and exterior condition of the house. Is there a significant difference between the condition of the subject property and that of the comparable sales? The typical buyer will generally be willing to pay more for a house that is in "move-in" condition where no significant work is needed. If the conditions are significantly different, then determine what adjustment is needed to compensate for this in the eyes of the typical buyer. You won't have access to the interiors of the comparable sales because the owners of the sales comps don't have any interest in the appraisal of the subject property. They obviously don't want strangers knocking on their doors asking them to go inside, inspect their homes, take photos, measurements, etc. Just do the best you can with the data sources and information you have concerning the interior condition of the sales comps. You must at least view the sales comps on the outside from the street and take photos to evaluate the overall condition of the property.

6. **Above Grade Room Count** - This refers to the room count of the house. The total number of rooms in a house refers to the rooms in the *livable* areas that are *above grade*. The total number of rooms <u>does not</u> include the bathrooms nor any rooms in the basement or attic. Bathrooms are counted and listed separately. Although the bedrooms are listed separately

on the form, they are included in the total room count number. Is there a significant difference between the number of total rooms, bedrooms and bathrooms of the subject property, in relation to the comparable sales? The typical buyer will be willing to pay more for a house that has more total rooms, bedrooms and baths.

If the room numbers are significantly different, then decide what adjustment is needed to compensate for this in the eyes of the typical buyer. If the room counts are only slightly different, an adjustment may

> *The total number of rooms in a house refers to the rooms in the livable areas that are "above grade."*

not be needed. The reason for this is the typical buyer may not lower or higher the purchase price due to a slight difference in the room count of two houses. You can also account for a slight room count difference by making an adjustment in the *Gross Living Area* section on the appraisal form, instead of in this section. Generally, the difference in the number of bathrooms is adjusted for in this section. The difference in the total room count and the number of bedrooms is adjusted for in the *Gross Living Area* section.

7. **Gross Living Area** - *(No, this doesn't refer to a dirty, disgusting living area!)* This refers to the total livable square feet of space inside the house. The gross living area, (GLA), in a house refers to the square footage in the *livable* areas that are *above grade,* which doesn't include the basement or attic areas. Is there a significant difference between the GLA of the subject property and that of the comparable sales? The typical buyer will generally be

> *The gross living area, (GLA), in a house refers to the square footage in the livable areas that are "above grade," which doesn't include the basement or attic areas.*

willing to pay more for a house that is larger. If the GLA's are significantly different, then determine what adjustment is needed to compensate for this in the eyes of the typical buyer. If the GLA's are only slightly different then an adjustment may not be needed. This is because the typical buyer may not lower or higher the purchase price due to a slight difference in the size of the two houses.

You need to estimate what standard GLA multiplier would be good to use for the local market. You can obtain this information from other more experienced appraisers that do appraisals in the local market area of the subject property and sales comps.

You then multiply this figure by the difference between the GLA for each sales comparable as opposed to the subject property. This simplifies the adjustment process for the Gross Living Area in your comps. For example, let's say Sale #1 was 235 square feet larger than the subject and Sale #4 was 140 square feet smaller than the subject. Let's say you estimated that the GLA multiplier is $35 per square foot for the local market. Then the adjustment for Sale #1 would be $35 x (-235) = -$8,225 and the adjustment for Sale #4 would be $35 x (+140) = +$4,900.

8. Basement and Finished Rooms Below Grade - This refers to whether there is a basement and/or finished lower level rooms in the house. These are areas that are *below grade.* This means that these rooms are 3/4 or more below the soil line on the exterior of the house. Is there a full or a partial basement? Is it completely finished, partly finished or unfinished? By saying "finished" it means that there are wall, ceiling and floor coverings in this room so that it can be used as livable space. The typical buyer will generally be willing to pay more for a full basement because they can use that area for a playroom, laundry room, etc. Also, if the lower level is finished with carpeting, sheetrock, outlets, etc. it will increase the market value of the house.

9. Functional Utility - This refers to the overall flow of the interior rooms of the house or other functional items. Is there a significant problem with the functional layout of the subject property or with any of the comparable sales? The typical buyer will generally be willing to pay more for a house that has a typical room layout where no significant changes are needed. If there are functional problems with the house, then determine what adjustment is needed to compensate for this in the eyes of the typical buyer.

For example, a house that has a kitchen on the third floor can be considered to have a functional problem. The house has a functional problem because this type of floor plan is very uncommon and can be inconvenient for the occupants. Other examples of functional problems that you might encounter are: having no bathrooms on a floor where the bedrooms are located, or a floor of the home that has only one bathroom that can only be reached by going through someone's bedroom.

10. Heating/Cooling - This refers to the type, age and condition of the heating and/or air-conditioning systems in the house. Is the house lacking a central air-conditioning system in an area where most homes have central A/C? The typical buyer will generally pay more for a house with central A/C and a newer heating system.

11. Garage/Carport - This refers to the type, size and condition of the garage or carport of the house. A *carport* is just a small roof covering over the driveway area, it's not enclosed on the sides. Is the house lacking an enclosed garage in an area where most homes have them? The typical buyer will generally pay more for a house with an enclosed garage than one with just a carport. Also, a two-car garage is more desirable than a one-car garage due to the extra car and/or storage capacity for the owner.

12. Porches, Patio, Pools, etc. - This refers to any porches, patios, swimming pools, decks, etc. on the property. Is the house lacking a pool or a deck in an area where most homes have them? The typical buyer will generally pay more for a house with a pool, porch or a nice deck, etc.

13. Special Energy Efficient Items - This refers to any extra insulation installed, thermal windows, etc. in the house. Is the house lacking thermal windows in an area where most homes have these items? The typical buyer will generally pay more for an energy efficient house because it will save them money on utility bills. Newer houses have better insulation. Older houses sometimes have no insulation in the exterior walls.

14. Fireplace(s) - This refers to the number of fireplaces. Is the house lacking a fireplace in an area where most homes have them? Is there only one fireplace instead of several? The typical buyer will generally pay more for a house with a fireplace.

15. Other (e.g., remodeling, kitchen equip.) - This refers to any other aspects about the house that have an effect on value that weren't covered in the other adjustment areas on the appraisal form. Is there a burglar/fire alarm system, a central vacuum system, etc.? Is the kitchen of the house modern or is it outdated? Are the fixtures and appliances modern or very old? The typical buyer will generally pay more for a house with a nice kitchen, bath, fixtures, etc. that have been upgraded. Kitchens and bathrooms can have a BIG effect on many home buyers when they're looking at a house as a potential purchase.

The Adjustment Process

The adjustment process refers to the price changes that you make to the comparable sales to equalize them to have the same characteristics as the subject property. For example, let's say the subject property has a full, finished basement and the sales comp has a partial, unfinished basement. The sales comp would have sold for a higher price if it had a full, finished basement like the subject property. Therefore, you have to adjust the actual sales price of the sales comparable <u>upward</u> to equalize it to the subject. And it's the same thing if it were vice versa, with the sales comparable having the more appealing aspect than the subject property. Then the sales comps actual selling price would be adjusted <u>downward</u> to equalize it to the subject. This is how you accurately estimate market value.

> *The first point is you have to be very careful not to double dip your comparable sales adjustments.*
> *The second point I want to make is that you don't have to stick to the standard appraisal form layout!!*

There are two important points you need to be aware of when writing up your appraisal reports:

1   The first point is that you have to be very careful not to **_double dip_** your comparable sales adjustments. Meaning, you don't want to adjust for the same item in two different places on the appraisal form. If you do this, then you'll be making an exaggerated cost adjustment. An exaggerated adjustment will throw off your final adjusted sales price for that comp. For example, often you will need to make an adjustment due to the difference in the condition between the subject property and a sales comp. Sometimes the condition of the sales comparable is inferior to the condition of the subject property because the comp is an older house. If this were the case, then you could pick up the condition difference in the *Age* section adjustment, instead of in the *Condition* section, or vice versa. You don't want to make two adjustments for the same thing in this type of situation by making an adjustment in <u>both</u> sections of the form. If you did that, then you would be "double dipping" the adjustment.

2   The second point I want to make is that you **_don't_** have to stick to the standard appraisal form layout! You can add items, comments, sections, etc. to the form by using addendums and other explanatory comments. This will help you clarify something that affects the value that isn't found on the form. Too many appraisers restrict themselves by only sticking to the exact layout of the standard appraisal form. Remember that you should adapt the appraisal forms to meet the particular needs of the appraisal assignment that you're working on!

The adjustment process for the Direct Sales Comparison Approach can be done on a dollar basis or on a percentage basis. You can use a dollar amount to adjust the sales comparable for a particular item. You also can use a percentage amount of the sales price to adjust a sales comp. There is a sequence on the appraisal forms that follow the adjustment process.

There are four aspects to adjust first:

1   *Real Property Rights Conveyed* - this refers to whether the rights sold with the real estate are fee simple, leasehold, etc.

2   *Financing Terms* - this refers to what type of financing terms were given with the sale, such as, a conventional loan, an FHA or VA loan, a purchase money mortgage, etc.

3   *Conditions of the Sale* - this refers to what type of terms were given with the sale other than financing, such as, was the deal an "arms length" transaction, was the house sold to a family member for an abnormally low price, was there a motivated seller or buyer involved in the deal, etc.

4   *Date of the Sale* - this refers to what the conditions of the market were "as of" the date of the sale, any time adjustments needed for changes in the local market, etc.

You should find an experienced appraiser in your area to assist you with learning how to make the proper adjustments for the local market. This will help you get a feel for the adjustment process. I want to make that point clear because your local real estate market will have different adjustment amounts needed than the identical item on/in a property located in a different market. For example, the adjustment amount for a 500 square foot difference in size for a sales comparable located in New York City will be *very* different then a 500 square foot adjustment made to a property in Tulsa, Oklahoma. **There's no set**

amounts that are used nationwide because each local market in the country is different. You also have to remember to round out your adjustment amounts because appraising is not an exact science. For example, you shouldn't use adjustments like $8,739.24 in your report. You should just round out to the nearest $50 or $100 mark, or some other figure, that's used in the local area. So instead of using $8,739.24 in your report, you would use $8,750. Remember, an appraisal is an *estimate* of market value. Appraising is not an exact science and that's why you round out the adjustment figures.

Don't expect to find identical comparable sales on your appraisals. It just doesn't happen, or at least it's a *very* rare occurrence. This is why there are appraisers! If there were identical sales all the time, then the client wouldn't need to hire an appraiser, he could estimate the market value himself. You're the professional. You're the expert with the knowledge of how to compare different houses and make the proper adjustments to estimate market value. Just try to find the best comps you can. By doing this you won't have to exceed the adjustment guidelines to "make a sale work" as a comparable for the subject property. If you send a client an appraisal report with comps that have an abnormally high number of adjustments, then the client is going to wonder if you really took the time to do the field work. If this were the case, don't be

When you make adjustments to the comp sales, remember to look at the difference between the subject property and the sale through the eyes of the typical buyer!!

surprised if the client sends the report back to you and asks you to find them better comps for the appraisal. There will be times when you can't find very good sales to use as comparables and you'll want to pull your hair out trying to find good comps. Just make that the exception and not the norm by taking the time to know the local market and get all of the pertinent data.

When you make your adjustments to the comparable sales, just remember to look at the difference between the subject property and the sale **through the eyes of the typical buyer!!** I want to stress that point. Sometimes appraisers get carried away doing all of the field work, photographs, and math calculations, etc. By doing this, they forget to look at the subject and the sales comps the way a typical buyer would. A *typical buyer* refers to someone who has enough income and would be looking to purchase a competitive or similar property in the area, under "arms length" transaction conditions. Just ask

yourself before you make any adjustment: *"How would the typical buyer in this local market compensate his purchase price for the difference between these two competing and similar properties?"* Significant differences need to be adjusted for, but very minor items don't really have an affect on market value and

When making adjustments remember that you're comparing the sales to the subject property so don't forget to use the proper plus and minus signs!!!

don't need to be adjusted for. So be thorough, but don't get carried away and go overboard in your adjustments. If you go too far by making unnecessary or exaggerated adjustments, then you may end up opening a can of worms. This means that the client might bounce the appraisal back in your lap asking for it to be rewritten.

Use your common sense and think about your adjustments. For example, let's say the subject property had a septic system and a well water system. We'll assume that the sales comparables you're using, along with most of the houses in the area, are connected to the municipal water and sewer systems. Since they do not have their own septic and well water systems, you should make an adjustment for this. The logic behind this adjustment would be, that the typical buyer is willing to pay more for a house that is connected to the municipal water and sewer systems. An identical house in the area that has a septic and well system, would not be as appealing as having the home hooked up to the city water and sewer lines. The reason is if a house is connected to the municipal water and sewer systems, then the homeowner will not have to worry about the costs of maintaining a well water and septic system.

When making adjustments remember that you're comparing the sales to the subject property so **don't forget to use the proper plus and minus signs!!!** I want to stress that point as well. Sometimes appraisers get carried away with all of the field work, the photos, math calculations, etc. When appraisers do this, they forget to properly use the proper plus and minus signs in their adjustment figures for the comparable sales. You have to adjust the sales comparable as though it had the same exact characteristics as the subject property. For example, let's say you're appraising a house that does not have central air-conditioning and does have a two-car garage. One of the sales comparables you're evaluating **does** have central air-conditioning and only has a **one**-car garage. Well, when you make your adjustments next to the sales comp on the appropriate line, you have to remember that the adjustment for the central A/C will have a <u>minus</u> sign. Also, the adjustment for the one-car garage will have a <u>plus</u> sign. The reason for this is that the sales price of the comparable would have been lower if it didn't have central A/C and the price would have been higher if the comparable had a two-car garage.

You'll be doing a thorough interior and exterior inspection of the subject property; you'll have photographs; you'll be getting information about the house from the seller, Realtor, or another third party; and you'll also be checking things out at town hall. Therefore, you obviously will have more information and knowledge about the subject property than you will for the comparable sales. You're going to have to make some assumptions about the sales comps when you're evaluating them and making your adjustments. For example, you'll be viewing the operating systems and the interior of the subject property with your own eyes. As a result, you'll know exactly what to write in the report about the condition. Obviously you can't get access to the interior of the comparable sales. As a result, you have to go by whatever information you have on the sales comps and use your own judgment. Just do the best you can with the information you have and always use your common sense. If you have the opportunity to call one of the real estate agents or the owner involved in the sale of the comp, then great! Give them a call and ask them some questions. Just make notes of your conversation and the information you obtained and put it in the written appraisal report.

Please review the sample appraisals included in this book to view examples of the Direct Sales Comparison Approach adjustment process for an actual written appraisal report.

Guidelines For The Adjustments

I'll go through the basic guidelines for making adjustments to the sales comps. These guidelines are used to assist the appraiser in evaluating comparable sales for an appraisal report.

10% is the maximum adjustment that should be made on the appraisal form for an <u>individual</u> item as compared to the selling price of the sales comparable. This is a **horizontal** adjustment on the form. The 10% does not account for the plus or minus signs in the dollar amount for an adjustment on the form. This means it is the absolute value of the number that is considered. The *absolute value* of a number disregards the plus or minus sign of that number.

15% is the maximum adjustment that should be made on the appraisal form for all <u>combined</u> items as compared to the selling price of the sales comparable. This is a **vertical** adjustment on the form. The 15% maximum adjustment for all of the combined items does account for the plus or minus signs in the total *dollar* amount. However, the 15% does not account for the plus or minus signs in the total *percentage* amount. This means it is the absolute value of that number.

25% is the maximum overall adjustment that should be made on the appraisal form for all <u>combined</u> items as compared to the selling price of the sales comparable. This is a **vertical** adjustment on the form. However, this differs from the 15% maximum adjustment for all of the combined items. It differs because this adjustment *does not* account for the plus or minus signs in the total dollar adjustment *dollar* amount, as well as in the total *percentage* amount. Meaning that you take the absolute value and disregard all of the plus and minus signs in your adjustment amounts and just add up the numerical amounts.

For example, let's say you had the following six adjustments for a sales comparable that had a recorded selling price of $170,000:

-11,500, +6,250, +3,000, +5,750, -2,750, -9,000

The largest horizontal adjustment would fall below the 10% maximum amount. Remember that this is an absolute value we're considering that does not account for any plus or minus signs:

$$\$11,500/\$170,000 = .07 \quad \text{or} \quad 7\%$$

The combined vertical adjustment, accounting for the *individual* dollar amount plus or minus sign but disregarding the *total* dollar amount plus or minus sign, would fall below the 15% maximum amount:

$$-11,500 +6,250 +3,000 +5,750 -2,750 -9,000 = -\$8,250$$

$$\$8,250/\$170,000 = .05 \quad \text{or} \quad 5\%$$

The combined vertical adjustment, disregarding the *individual* and the *total* dollar amount plus or minus signs, would fall below the 25% maximum amount of the appraisal guidelines:

$$11,500 + 6,250 + 3,000 + 5,750 + 2,750 + 9,000 = \$38,250$$

$$\$38,250/\$170,000 = .23 \quad \text{or} \quad 23\%$$

Therefore, we can conclude that this sales comparable may be used on the appraisal form. The reason it can be used is that the adjustments that we deemed necessary for the sales comparison approach, all fall within the recommended percentage guidelines.

Let's take another example of a sales comparable that has adjustments that do not fall within the guidelines of the appraisal form. We'll use the same six adjustments as in our example above for our new sales comparable, but it has a selling price of only $95,000:

$$-11,500, +6,250, +3,000, +5,750, -2,750, -9,000$$

The largest horizontal adjustment would fall above the 10% maximum amount. Remember that this is an absolute value we're considering that does not account for any plus or minus signs:

$$\$11,500/\$95,000 = .12 \quad \text{or} \quad 12\%$$

The combined vertical adjustment, accounting for the *individual* dollar amount plus or minus sign but disregarding the *total* dollar amount plus or minus sign, would fall below the 15% maximum amount:

$$-11,500 +6,250 +3,000 +5,750 -2,750 -9,000 = -\$8,250$$

$$\$8,250/\$95,000 = .09 \quad \text{or} \quad 9\%$$

The combined vertical adjustment, disregarding the *individual* and the *total* dollar amount plus or minus signs, would fall above the 25% maximum amount of the appraisal guidelines:

$$11,500 + 6,250 + 3,000 + 5,750 + 2,750 + 9,000 = \$38,250$$

$$\$38,250/\$95,000 = .40 \quad \text{or} \quad 40\%$$

Therefore, we can conclude that this sales comparable **should not** be used on the appraisal form. It should not be used because the adjustments that we deemed to be necessary for the sales comparison approach, do not all fall within the recommended percentage guidelines. The 15% maximum adjustment does fall within the guidelines, but the other two adjustments do not. The purpose for these guidelines is to try to help the appraiser to obtain only good comparable sales for the appraisal report. If you have a sales comparable that does not fall within the recommended guidelines, then it should immediately raise a red flag in your mind. The guidelines help you identify sales comparables that should not be used. Some sales should not be used because there may be factors involved in the deal that you can't determine in your adjustments and/or that you're not aware of.

For example, maybe the house was sold to a friend of the family. Another possibility could be that there was some type of tradeoff of services or personal items. A tradeoff of services or other items could lead to a reduction in the sales price between the buyer and seller, etc. Sales with terms and agreements such as these cannot necessarily be detected by the appraiser from the public record. Sometimes you'll find that you have a sales comparable that just doesn't seem right. After you make your adjustments and are reviewing the appraisal, you can see that something's wrong. You may conclude that there may be more to the deal than meets the eye. Therefore, you should not use that sales comparable in your appraisal report. If you don't have extra sales comparables, you will have to wait until you do some more field work to dig-up additional comps to finish writing the appraisal report.

Please review the sample appraisals included in this book to view examples of the Direct Sales Comparison Approach guidelines for the adjustment process for an actual written appraisal report.

APPRAISAL OF

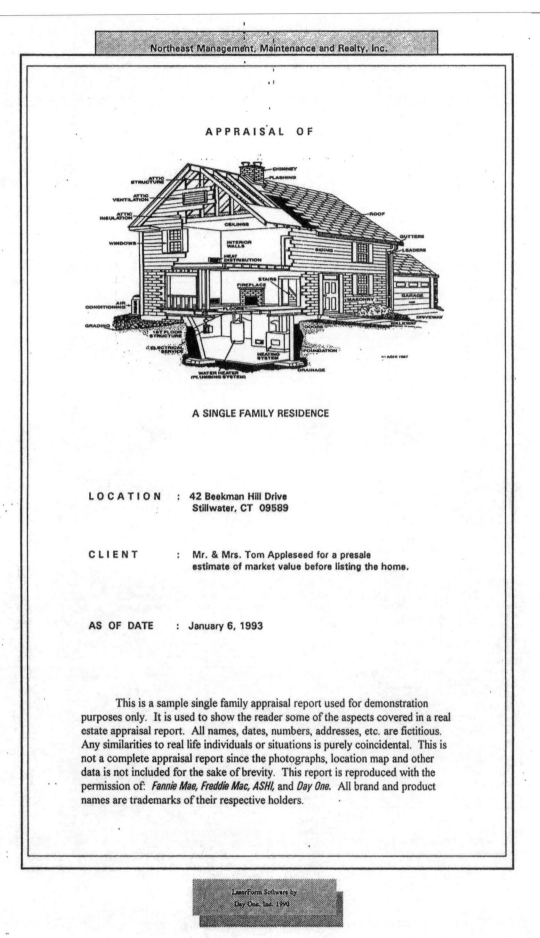

A SINGLE FAMILY RESIDENCE

LOCATION : 42 Beekman Hill Drive
Stillwater, CT 09589

CLIENT : Mr. & Mrs. Tom Appleseed for a presale
estimate of market value before listing the home.

AS OF DATE : January 6, 1993

This is a sample single family appraisal report used for demonstration purposes only. It is used to show the reader some of the aspects covered in a real estate appraisal report. All names, dates, numbers, addresses, etc. are fictitious. Any similarities to real life individuals or situations is purely coincidental. This is not a complete appraisal report since the photographs, location map and other data is not included for the sake of brevity. This report is reproduced with the permission of: *Fannie Mae, Freddie Mac, ASHI,* and *Day One.* All brand and product names are trademarks of their respective holders.

Northeast Management, Maintenance and Realty, Inc.

UNIFORM RESIDENTIAL APPRAISAL REPORT

Property Description & Analysis   File No. A9834D92

SUBJECT

Property Address	42 Beekman Hill Drive	Census Tract	
City	Stillwater	County	Rockland	State CT	Zip Code 09589
Legal Description	District C, Lot 24, Map 286-247, Block 402
Owner/Occupant	Mr. & Mrs. Tom Appleseed	Map Reference Hagstrom
Sale Price $	N/A	Date of Sale 01/06/93
Loan charges/concessions to be paid by seller $	N/A	Presale
R.E. Taxes $	+/- 5,860	Tax Year 1992	HOA $/Mo. N/A
Lender/Client	Mr. & Mrs. Tom Appleseed for a presale estimate of market value before listing the home.

LENDER DISCRETIONARY USE
Sale Price $ _____
Date _____
Mortgage Amount $ _____
Mortgage Type _____
Discount Points and Other Concessions
Paid by Seller $ _____
Source _____

PROPERTY RIGHTS APPRAISED
[X] Fee Simple
[ ] Leasehold
[ ] Condominium (HUD/VA)
[ ] De Minimis PUD

NEIGHBORHOOD

	Urban	Suburban	Rural
LOCATION	[ ] Urban	[X] Suburban	[ ] Rural
BUILT UP	[X] Over 75%	[ ] 25-75%	[ ] Under 25%
GROWTH RATE	[ ] Rapid	[X] Stable	[ ] Slow
PROPERTY VALUES	[ ] Increasing	[X] Stable	[ ] Declining
DEMAND/SUPPLY	[ ] Shortage	[X] In Balance	[ ] Over Supply
MARKETING TIME	[ ] Under 3 Mos.	[X] 3-6 Mos.	[X] Over 6 Mos.

NEIGHBORHOOD ANALYSIS	Good	Avg.	Fair	Poor
Employment Stability		[X]		
Convenience to Employment		[X]		
Convenience to Shopping		[X]		
Convenience to Schools		[X]		
Adequacy of Public Transportation		[X]		
Recreation Facilities		[X]		
Adequacy of Utilities		[X]		
Property Compatibility	[X]			
Protection from Detrimental Cond.		[X]		
Police & Fire Protection		[X]		
General Appearance of Properties	[X]			
Appeal to Market		[X]		

PRESENT LAND USE %
Single Family 80
2-4 Family ___
Multi-family ___
Commercial ___
Industrial ___
Vacant 20

LAND USE CHANGE
Not Likely [X]
Likely [ ]
In process [ ]
To: ___

PREDOMINANT OCCUPANCY
Owner [X]
Tenant [ ]
Vacant (0-5%) [X]
Vacant (over 5%) [ ]

SINGLE FAMILY HOUSING
PRICE $(000) / AGE (yrs)
350 Low New
550 High 35
Predominant 475 - 10

Note: Race or the racial composition of the neighborhood are not considered reliable appraisal factors.

COMMENTS: The subject neighborhood is located by the Westchester County line about 3 miles north of the Merritt Parkway. The area consists of mostly Colonial & Contemporary style dwellings. The subject neighborhood maintenance level is judged to be good. Most of the homes are newer construction.

SITE

Dimensions	+/- 296.8 X 175-195 feet
Site Area	+/- 1.2 Acres	Corner Lot No
Zoning Classification	R A-1, 1 Acre Single Fam	Zoning Compliance Yes
HIGHEST & BEST USE: Present Use	Yes	Other Use No

Topography Gently Rolling
Size Typical For Area
Shape Irregular
Drainage Fair, pond next to home
View Average
Landscaping Good
Driveway Gravel/Fair
Apparent Easements Yes, for pond maint
FEMA Flood Hazard Yes* ___ No XX
FEMA* Map/Zone 090015 0002 B, Zn C

UTILITIES	Public	Other	SITE IMPROVEMENTS	Type	Public	Private
Electricity	[X]	200 Amp CB	Street	Asphalt Paved	[X]	[ ]
Gas	[ ]	None	Curb/Gutter	Asphalt	[X]	[ ]
Water	[ ]	Privat Well	Sidewalk	None	[ ]	[ ]
Sanitary Sewer	[ ]	Septic Sys.	Street Lights	None	[ ]	[ ]
Storm Sewer	[ ]		Alley	None	[ ]	[ ]

COMMENTS (Apparent adverse easements, encroachments, special assessments, slide areas, etc.): Flood Map dated 01/16/81. Site is a typical suburban lot for this neighborhood. No known encroachments. There is an easement listed on the deed for repairs and maintenance to the pond and retaining walls.

IMPROVEMENTS

GENERAL DESCRIPTION
Units 1
Stories 2.5
Type (Det./Att.) Detached
Design (Style) Contemporary
Existing Yes
Proposed No
Under Construction No
Age (Yrs.) +/- 10
Effective Age (Yrs.) 2

EXTERIOR DESCRIPTION
Foundation Concrete Block
Exterior Walls Wood Clapboard
Roof Surface Asphalt Shingl
Gutters & Dwnspts. Aluminum
Windows Type Alum/Thermal
Storm Sash Thermal Units
Screens Yes
Manufactured House No

FOUNDATION
Slab No
Crawl Space Part
Basement Part
Sump Pump None Noted
Dampness Not in home
Settlement Normal
Infestation None Noted

BASEMENT
Area Sq.Ft. 400
% Finished 100
Ceiling Sheetrock
Walls Sheetrock
Floor Carpeting
Outside Entry Yes, Permits and approvals are needed for finish

INSULATION
Roof None [ ]
Ceiling Good [X]
Walls Good [X]
Floor Good [X]
None [ ]
Adequacy Good [X]
Energy Efficient Items: Thermal Windows

ROOM LIST

ROOMS	Foyer	Living	Dining	Kitchen	Den	Family Rm.	Rec. Rm.	Bedroom	# Baths	Laundry	Other	Area Sq. Ft.
Basement					1							+/- 400
Level 1	1	1	1	1					.5			1,438
Level 2								2	1	1		468
3rd								1	1			1,078

Finished area above grade contains: 8 Rooms; 3 Bedroom(s); 2.5 Bath(s); 2,984 Square Feet of Gross Living Area.

INTERIOR

SURFACES Materials/Condition
Floors Carpet/Good
Walls Drywall/Good
Trim/Finish Softwood/Good
Bath Floor Marble/Good
Bath Wainscot Marble/Good
Doors Hollow Wood/Average
Fireplace(s) Brick # 1

HEATING
Type F Hot Air
Fuel Oil
Condition Good
Adequacy Good
COOLING
Central Yes
Other None
Condition Good
Adequacy N/Test

KITCHEN EQUIP.
Refrigerator [X]
Range/Oven [X]
Disposal [X]
Dishwasher [X]
Fan/Hood [ ]
Compactor [X]
Washer/Dryer [X]
Microwave [X]
Intercom [ ]

ATTIC
None [ ]
Stairs [ ]
Drop Stair [X]
Scuttle [ ]
Floor [ ]
Heated [ ]
Finished [ ]
Storage [X]

IMPROVEMENT ANALYSIS	Good	Avg.	Fair	Poor
Quality of Construction	[X]			
Condition of Improvements	[X]			
Room Sizes/Layout	[X]			
Closets and Storage	[X]			
Energy Efficiency	[X]			
Plumbing-Adequacy & Condition	[X]			
Electrical-Adequacy & Condition	[X]			
Kitchen Cabinets-Adequacy & Cond.	[X]			
Compatibility to Neighborhood	[X]			
Appeal & Marketability	[X]			
Estimated Remaining Economic Life				95 Yrs.
Estimated Remaining Physical Life				N/A Yrs.

CAR STORAGE: Garage [X] No. Cars 2 Carport [ ] Condition Good None [ ]
Attached [X] Detached [ ] Built-In [ ]
Adequate [X] Inadequate [ ] Electric Door [X]
House Entry [X] Outside Entry [ ] Basement Entry [X]

COMMENTS

Additional features: Marble in baths and new fixtures installed, flagstone patio, new carpeting, finished lower level, driveway lighting, water softener, central vacuum, cedar closet, security system, sump pump alarm, jacuzzi with large master bathroom, 2 decks.

Depreciation (Physical, functional and external inadequacies, repairs needed, modernization, etc.): Physical: Subject is judged to be about 2% depreciated using the Age/Life Method. There are no significant functional or external inadequacies noted. Large living room windows need child guards for safety, upper deck has rotted boards, handrails needed for exterior walks, metal brackets needed for deck supports.

General market conditions and prevalence and impact in subject/market area regarding loan discounts, interest buydowns and concessions: Market Values have begun to stabiliz in some areas after a long period of decline. Buydowns and concessions are not common in pre-owned homes. Many lenders are being very conservative with their lending policies.

Freddie Mac Form 70 10/86 12 CPI   Fannie Mae Form 1004 10/86

Valuation Section

UNIFORM RESIDENTIAL APPRAISAL REPORT

File No. A9834D92

Purpose of Appraisal is to estimate Market Value as defined in Certification & Statement of Limiting Conditions.

BUILDING SKETCH (SHOW GROSS LIVING AREA ABOVE GRADE)
If for Freddie Mac/Fannie Mae, show only square foot calculations & cost approach comments.

```
        X           X           =
        X           X           =
        X           X           =
        X           X           =
        X           X           =
        X·          X           =
```

The site value represents 42% of the total value

ESTIMATED REPRODUCTION COST - NEW - OF IMPROVEMENTS:

Dwelling 2,584 Sq. Ft. @ $ 90.00	= $	232,560
Bsmnt 400 Sq. Ft. @ $ 70.00	=	28,000
Extras Jacuzzi, Marble baths	=	15,000
Alarm Sys, Central Vac, etc	=	12,500
Special Energy Efficient Items	=	
Porches, Patios, etc. 2 Decks	=	10,000
Garage/Carport 530 Sq. Ft. @ $ 25.00	=	13,250
Total Estimated Cost New	= $	311,310

	Physical	Functional	External
Less 2%			
Depreciation 6,300			= $ 6,300
Depreciated Value of Improvements			= $ 305,010
Site Imp. "as is" (driveway, landscaping, etc.)			= $
ESTIMATED SITE VALUE			= $ 205,000
(If leasehold, show only leasehold value.)			
INDICATED VALUE BY COST APPROACH			= $ 510,010

(Not Required by Freddie Mac and Fannie Mae)

Does property conform to applicable HUD/VA property standards? ☐ Yes ☐ No

If No, explain: _____

Construction Warranty ☐ Yes ☐ No _____

Name of Warranty Program _____

Warranty Coverage Expires _____

The undersigned has recited three recent sales of properties most similar and proximate to subject and has considered these in the market analysis. The description includes a dollar adjustment, reflecting market reaction to those items of significant variation between the subject and comparable properties. If a significant item in the comparable property is superior to, or more favorable than, the subject property, a minus (-) adjustment is made, thus reducing the indicated value of subject; if a significant item in the comparable is inferior to, or less favorable than, the subject property, a plus (+) adjustment is made, thus increasing the indicated value of the subject.

ITEM	SUBJECT	COMPARABLE NO. 1	+(-)$ Adjustment	COMPARABLE NO. 2	+(-)$ Adjustment	COMPARABLE NO. 3	+(-)$ Adjustment
Address	42 Beekman Hill D Stillwater, CT	280 Beekman Hill Dr. Stillwater, CT		98 Beekman Hill Dr. Stillwater, CT		30 Beekman Hill Dr. Stillwater, CT	
Proximity to Subject		1 block		1 block		250 feet	
Sales Price	$ N/A	$ 545,000		$ 475,000		$ 515,000	
Price/Gross Liv. Area	$ 0.00	$ 136.25		$ 143.94		$ 180.70	
Data Source	Inspection	MLS / RE Broker		MLS / RE Broker		MLS / RE Broker	
VALUE ADJUSTMENTS	DESCRIPTION	DESCRIPTION		DESCRIPTION		DESCRIPTION	
Sales or Financing Concessions		None Known		None Known		None Known	
Date of Sale/Time	01/06/93	07/24/92		05/01/92		04/30/92	
Location	Average	Average		Average		Average	
Site/View	+/- 1.2/Aver	+/- 1.0 A/Av		+/- 1.2 A/Av		+/- 1.2 A/Av	
Design and Appeal	Contemp/Good	Contemp/Good		Colonial/Avg	10,000	Contemp/Good	
Quality of Construction	Frame/Good	Frame/Good		Frame/Good		Frame/Good	
Age	1983	1979		1980		1986	
Condition	Good	Good		Good		Good	
Above Grade Room Count	Total 8 Bdrms 3 Baths 2.5	Total 8 Bdrms 4 Baths 3	-1,500	Total 9 Bdrms 3 Baths 4	-3,000	Total 8 Bdrms 3 Baths 3.5	-2,000
Gross Living Area	2,984 Sq. Ft.	4,000 Sq. Ft.	-30,480	3,300 Sq. Ft.	-9,480	2,850 Sq. Ft.	4,020
Basement & Finished Rooms Below Grade	Part Finished	Part Finished		Full Finished		Full Unfinished	3,000
Functional Utility	Average	Share Drvway	15,000	Average		Share Drvway	8,000
Heating/Cooling	FHA/Central	FHA/Central		FHA/Central		FHA/Central	
Garage/Carport	2 Car Attach	2 Car Attach		2 Car Attach		2 Car Attach	
Porches, Patio, Pools, etc.	2 Deck, Alrm Marble, HTub	Patio, Deck Alarm System	5,000	Deck, Terrac Alarm System	5,000	Deck, Patio Alarm System	5,000
Special Energy Efficient Items	Good Efficiency	Good Efficiency		Good Efficiency		Good Efficiency	
Fireplace(s)	One	Two	-1,500	One		One	
Other (e.g. kitchen equip., remodeling)	Modern Kitchen	Modern Kitchen		Modern Kitchen		Modern Kitchen	
Net Adj. (total)		☐ + ☒ - $ -13,480		☒ + ☐ - $ 2,520		☒ + ☐ - $ 18,020	
Indicated Value of Subject		-2 %Net 10 %Gr $ 531,520		.53 %Net 6 %Gr $ 477,520		3.5 %Net 4 %Gr $ 533,020	

Comments on Sales Comparison: See attached sheet.

INDICATED VALUE BY SALES COMPARISON APPROACH	$	485,000
INDICATED VALUE BY INCOME APPROACH (If Applicable) Estimated Market Rent $ N/A /Mo. x Gross Rent Multiplier N/A	= $	0

This appraisal is made ☒ "as is" ☐ subject to the repairs, alterations, inspections or conditions listed below ☐ completion per plans and specifications.

Comments and Conditions of Appraisal: The income approach is not applicable due to the lack of sales/rental data.

Final Reconciliation: The sales comparison analysis is the most reliable approach as it reflects the actions of buyers and sellers in the marketplace.

This appraisal is based upon the above requirements, the certification, contingent and limiting conditions, and Market Value definition that are stated in

☐ FmHA, HUD &/or VA instructions.

☒ Freddie Mac Form 439 (Rev.7/86) / Fannie Mae Form 1004B (Rev.7/86) filed with client _____ 19___ ☒ attached.

I (WE) ESTIMATE THE MARKET VALUE, AS DEFINED, OF THE SUBJECT PROPERTY AS OF January 6 19 93 to be $ 485,000

I (We) certify: that to the best of my (our) knowledge and belief the facts and data used herein are true and correct; that I (we) personally inspected the subject property, both inside and out, and have made an exterior inspection of all comparable sales cited in this report; and that I (we) have no undisclosed interest, present or prospective therein.

APPRAISER(S)	REVIEW APPRAISER
Signature	(If applicable) Signature _____ ☐ Did ☐ Did Not
Name Harry Simpson	Name _____ Inspect Property

Freddie Mac Form 70 10/86 12 CPI | LaserForm Software by DAY ONE, Inc. 1987 | Fannie Mae Form 1004 10/86

MARKET DATA ANALYSIS

File No. A9834D92

These recent sales of properties most similar and proximate to subject have been considered in the market analysis. The description includes a dollar adjustment, reflecting market reaction to those items of significant variation between the subject and comparable properties. If a significant item in the comparable property is superior to, or more favorable than, the subject property, a minus(-) adjustment is made, thus reducing the indicated value of subject; if a significant item in the comparable is inferior to, or less favorable than, the subject property, a plus(+) adjustment is made, thus increasing the indicated value of the subject.

ITEM	SUBJECT	COMPARABLE NO. 4	+(-)$ Adjustment	COMPARABLE NO. 5	+(-)$ Adjustment	COMPARABLE NO. 6	+(-)$ Adjustment
Address	42 Beekman Hill D Stillwater, CT	66 Beekman Hill Dr. Stillwater, CT		102 Spring Lane Stillwater, CT		723 Milton Avenue Stillwater, CT	
Proximity to Subject		250 feet		2 blocks		3 blocks	
Sale Price	$ N/A	$ 412,500		$ 421,000		$ 483,000	
Price/Gross Liv. Area	$ 0.00 /□	$ 165.00 /□		$ 120.29 /□		$ 182.26 /□	
Data Source	Inspection	MLS / RE Broker		MLS / RE Broker		MLS / RE Broker	
VALUE ADJUSTMENTS	DESCRIPTION	DESCRIPTION	+(-)$ Adjustment	DESCRIPTION	+(-)$ Adjustment	DESCRIPTION	+(-)$ Adjustment
Sales or Financing Concessions		None Known		None Known		None Known	
Date of Sale / Time	01/06/93	12/21/92		12/18/92		09/18/92	
Location	Average	Average		Average		Average	
Site / View	+/- 1.2/Aver	+/- 1.1 A/Av		+/- 1.2 A/Av		+/- 1.0 A/Av	
Design and Appeal	Contemp/Good	Ranch/Avg	10,000	Colonial/Avg	8,000	Contemp/Good	
Quality of Construction	Frame/Good	Frame/Good		Frame/Good		Frame/Good	
Age	1983	1968	25,000	1964	25,000	+/- 1980	
Condition	Good	Good		Good		Good	
Above Grade	Total / Bdrms / Baths	Total / Bdrms / Baths		Total / Bdrms / Baths		Total / Bdrms / Baths	
Room Count	8 / 3 / 2.5	8 / 3 / 2.5		8 / 3 / 3.5	-2,000	7 / 3 / 2.5	
Gross Living Area	2,984 Sq.Ft.	2,500 Sq.Ft.	14,520	3,500 Sq.Ft.	-15,480	2,650 Sq.Ft.	10,020
Basement & Finished Rooms Below Grade	Part Finished	Full Finished		Full Unfinished	3,000	Full Unfinished	3,000
Functional Utility	Average	Average		Average		Average	
Heating / Cooling	FHA/Central	HW/Central		FHA/Central		FHA/Central	
Garage / Carport	2 Car Attach	2 Car Attach		1 Car	4,000	2 Car Attach	
Porches, Patio, Pools, etc.	2 Deck, Alrm Marble, HTub	Porch, Patio Alarm System	5,000	Patio, Alarm System	10,000	Similar to subject prop	
Special Energy Efficient Items	Good Efficiency	Average Efficiency	3,500	Average Efficiency	3,500	Good Efficiency	
Fireplace(s)	One	One		Two	-1,500	One	
Other (e.g. kitchen equip., remodeling)	Modern Kitchen	Modern Kitchen		Modern Kitchen		Modern Kitchen	
Net Adj. (total)		☒+ □- $	58,020	☒+ □- $	34,520	☒+ □- $	13,020
Indicated Value of Subject		14 %Net / 14 %Grs	$ 470,520	8.2 %Net / 17 %Grs	$ 455,520	2.7 %Net / 3 %Grs	$ 496,020

Comments on Market Data

Sales 2, 4 & 5 were judged to be slightly less appealing and adjusted accordingly. Age adjustments were deemed necessary for sales 4 & 5. The condition for these older houses was accounted for in the age adjustment.

Sales 1 & 3 were adjusted for having a common driveway with one and two neighbors. The gross living area adjustments are based upon about $30.00 per square foot.

In this appraisal assignment, the existence of potentially hazardous material used in the construction or maintenance of the building, such as the presence of Urea-formaldehyde foam insulation, asbestos, underground oil tanks and/or the existence of toxic waster or radon gas, which may or may not be present on the subject property, was not observed by the appraiser, nor do I have any knowledge of the existence of such materials on or in the property. The appraiser is not hired, required and/or qualified to detect such substances. The existence of Urea-formaldehyde insulation, asbestos, underground oil tanks, radon gas or other potentially hazardous waste mterial may have an effect on the value of the property. It is our opinion, that the client should retain an expert in this field if desired or any doubts exist.

SUBJECT PHOTOGRAPH ADDENDUM

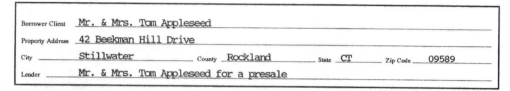

Borrower Client	Mr. & Mrs. Tom Appleseed
Property Address	42 Beekman Hill Drive
City	Stillwater County Rockland State CT Zip Code 09589
Lender	Mr. & Mrs. Tom Appleseed for a presale

**FRONT OF
SUBJECT PROPERTY**

**REAR OF
SUBJECT PROPERTY**

STREET SCENE

COMPARABLES PHOTOGRAPH ADDENDUM

Borrower Client	Mr. & Mrs. Tom Appleseed
Property Address	42 Beekman Hill Drive
City	Stillwater County Rockland State CT Zip Code 09589
Lender	Mr. & Mrs. Tom Appleseed for a presale

COMPARABLE SALE # 1

280 Beekman Hill Dr.
Date of Sale: 07/24/92
Sale Price : 545,000
Sq. Ft.   : 4,000
$ / Sq. Ft. : 136.25

COMPARABLE SALE # 2

98 Beekman Hill Dr.
Date of Sale: 05/01/92
Sale Price : 475,000
Sq. Ft.   : 3,300
$ / Sq. Ft. : 143.94

COMPARABLE SALE # 3

30 Beekman Hill Dr.
Date of Sale: 04/30/92
Sale Price : 515,000
Sq. Ft.   : 2,850
$ / Sq. Ft. : 180.70

COMPARABLES 4 5 6 PHOTOGRAPH ADDENDUM

Borrower Client **Mr. & Mrs. Tom Appleseed**

Property Address **42 Beekman Hill Drive**

City **Stillwater**   County **Rockland**   State **CT**   Zip Code **09589**

Lender **Mr. & Mrs. Tom Appleseed for a presale**

COMPARABLE SALE # 4

66 Beekman Hill Dr.
Date of Sale: 12/21/92
Sale Price : 412,500
Sq. Ft.   : 2,500
$ / Sq. Ft. : 165.00

COMPARABLE SALE # 5

102 Spring Lane
Date of Sale: 12/18/92
Sale Price : 421,000
Sq. Ft.   : 3,500
$ / Sq. Ft. : 120.29

COMPARABLE SALE # 6

723 Milton Avenue
Date of Sale: 09/18/92
Sale Price : 483,000
Sq. Ft.   : 2,650
$ / Sq. Ft. : 182.26

Location Map

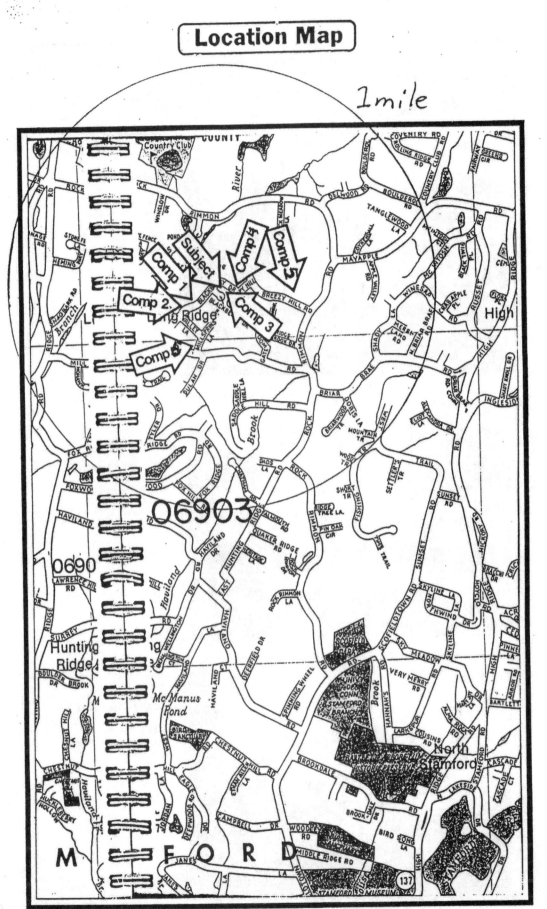

Borrower Name : **Mr. & Mrs. Tom Appleseed**   File No. **A9834D92**

DEFINITION OF MARKET VALUE :   The most probable price which a property should bring in a competitive and open market under all conditions requisite to a fair sale, the buyer and seller, each acting prudently, knowledgeably and assuming the price is not affected by undue stimulus. Implicit in this definition is the consummation of a sale as of a specified date and the passing of title from seller to buyer under conditions whereby: (1) buyer and seller are typically motivated; (2) both parties are well informed or well advised, and each acting in what he considers his own best interest; (3) a reasonable time is allowed for exposure in the open market; (4) payment is made in terms of U.S. dollars or in terms of financial arrangements comparable thereto; and (5) the price represents the normal consideration for the property sold unaffected by special or creative financing or sales concessions* granted by anyone associated with the sale.

*Adjustments to the comparables must be made for special or creative financing or sales concessions. No adjustments are necessary for those costs which are normally paid by sellers as a result of tradition or law in a market area; these costs are readily identifiable since the seller pays these costs in virtually all sales transactions. Special or creative financing adjustments can be made to the comparable property by comparisons to financing terms offered by a third party institutional lender that is not already involved in the property or transaction. Any adjustment should not be calculated on a mechanical dollar for dollar cost of the financing or concession, but the dollar amount of any adjustment should approximate the market's reaction to the financing or concessions based on the appraiser's judgment.

CERTIFICATION AND STATEMENT OF LIMITING CONDITIONS

CERTIFICATION: The Appraiser certifies and agrees that:

1. The Appraiser has no present or contemplated future interest in the property appraised; and neither the employment to make the appraisal, nor the compensation for it, is contingent upon the appraised value of the property.

2. The Appraiser has no personal interest in or bias with respect to the subject matter of the appraisal report or the participants to the sale. The "Estimate of Market Value" in the appraisal report is not based in whole or in part upon the race, color, or national origin of the prospective owners or occupants of the property appraised, or upon the race, color or national origin of the present owners or occupants of the properties in the vicinity of the property appraised.

3. The Appraiser has personally inspected the property, both inside and out, and has made an exterior inspection of all comparable sales listed in the report. To the best of the Appraiser's knowledge and belief, all statements and information in this report are true and correct, and the Appraiser has not knowingly withheld any significant information.

4. All contingent and limiting conditions are contained herein (imposed by the terms of the assignment or by the undersigned affecting the analyses, opinions, and conclusions contained in the report).

5. This appraisal report has been made in conformity with and is subject to the requirements of the Code of Professional Ethics and Standards of Professional Conduct of the appraisal organizations with which the Appraiser is affiliated.

6. All conclusions and opinions concerning the real estate that are set forth in the appraisal report were prepared by the Appraiser whose signature appears on the appraisal report, unless indicated as "Review Appraiser." No change of any item in the appraisal report shall be made by anyone other than the Appraiser, and the Appraiser shall have no responsibility for any such unauthorized change.

CONTINGENT AND LIMITING CONDITIONS: The certification of the Appraiser appearing in the appraisal report is subject to the following conditions and to such other specific and limiting conditions as are set forth by the Appraiser in the report.

1. The Appraiser assumes no responsibility for matters of a legal nature affecting the property appraised or the title thereto, nor does the Appraiser render any opinion as to the title, which is assumed to be good and marketable. The property is appraised as though under responsible ownership.

2. Any sketch in the report may show approximate dimensions and is included to assist the reader in visualizing the property. The Appraiser has made no survey of the property.

3. The Appraiser is not required to give testimony or appear in court because of having made the appraisal with reference to the property in question, unless arrangements have been previously made therefor.

4. Any distribution of the valuation in the report between land and improvements applies only under the existing program of utilization. The separate valuation for land and building must not be used in conjunction with any other appraisal and are invalid if so used.

5. The Appraiser assumes that there are no hidden or unapparent conditions of the property, subsoil, or structures, which would render it more or less valuable. The Appraiser assumes no responsibility for such conditions, or for engineering which might be required to discover such factors.

6. Information, estimates, and opinions furnished to the Appraiser, and contained in the report, were obtained from sources considered reliable and believed to be true and correct. However, no responsibility for accuracy of such items furnished the Appraiser can be assumed by the Appraiser.

7. Disclosure of the contents of the appraisal report is governed by the Bylaws and Regulations of the professional appraisal organizations with which the Appraiser is affiliated.

8. Neither all, nor any part of the content of the report, or copy thereof (including conclusions as to the property value, the identity of the Appraiser, professional designations, reference to any professional appraisal organizations, or the firm with which the Appraiser is connected), shall be used for any purpose by anyone but the client specified in the report , the borrower if appraisal fee paid by same, the mortgagee or its successors and assigns, mortgage insurers, consultants, professional appraisal organizations, any state or federally approved financial institution, any department, agency, or instrumentality of the United States of any state or the District of Columbia, without the previous written consent of the Appraiser; nor shall it be conveyed by anyone to the public through advertising, public relations, news, sales, or other media, without the written consent and approval of the Appraiser.

9. On all appraisals, subject to satisfactory completion, repairs, or alterations, the appraisal report and value conclusion are contingent upon completion of the improvements in a workmanlike manner.

ENVIRONMENTAL DISCLAIMER: The value estimated in this report is based on the assumption that the property is not negatively affected by the existence of hazardous substances or detrimental environmental conditions. The Appraiser is not an expert in the identification of hazardous substances or detrimental environmental conditions. The Appraiser's routine inspection of and inquiries about the subject property did not develop any information that indicated any apparent significant hazardous substances or detrimental environmental conditions which would affect the property negatively unless otherwise stated in this report. It is possible that tests and inspections made by a qualified hazardous substance and environmental expert would reveal the existence of hazardous substances or detrimental environmental conditions on or around the property that would negatively affect its value. The Appraiser assumes no responsibility for the presence of radon gas, as the Appraiser has no expertise in this area.

Date **January 6, 1993**   Signature: _____

                                                                        Harry Simpson

Northeast Management, Maintenance and Realty, Inc.

APPRAISAL OF

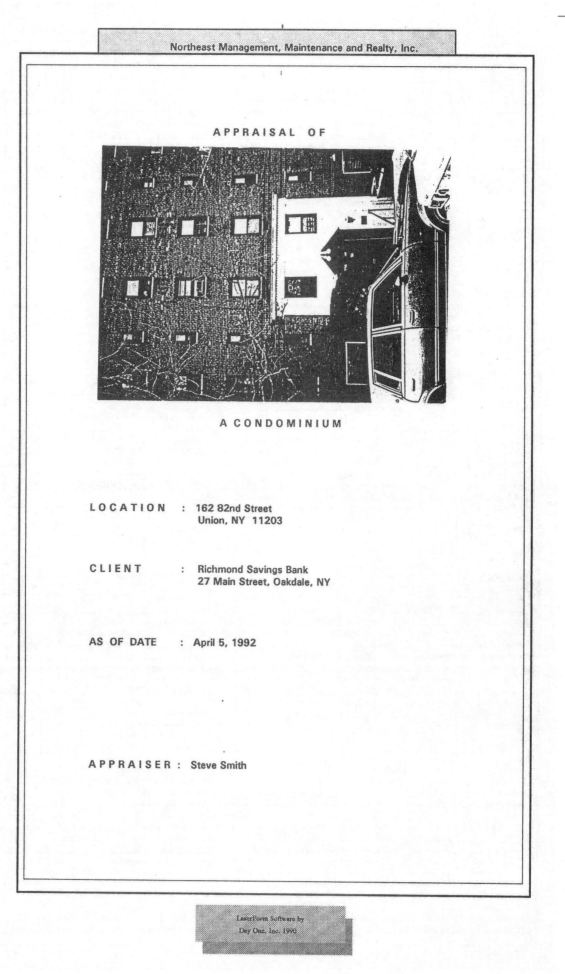

A CONDOMINIUM

LOCATION : **162 82nd Street**
Union, NY 11203

CLIENT : Richmond Savings Bank
27 Main Street, Oakdale, NY

AS OF DATE : April 5, 1992

APPRAISER : Steve Smith

Northeast Management, Maintenance and Realty, Inc.

APPRAISAL REPORT - INDIVIDUAL ☐ CONDOMINIUM OR ☐ PUD UNIT   File No. A0238D92

Borrower **Stephen Jones**	Census Tract **0036** Map Reference **HAG22A16**
Unit No. **E-27** Address **162 82nd Street**	Project Name/Phase No. **Ridge Hill**
City **Union** County **Oakdale**	State **NY** Zip Code **11203**

Actual Real Estate Taxes $ **Incl in maint.** (yr.) Sale Price $ **58,000** Property Rights Appraised ☐ Fee ☒ Leasehold

Loan charges to be paid by seller $ **N/A** Other sales concessions **N/A**

Lender/Client **Richmond Savings Bank** Lender's Address **27 Main Street, Oakdale, NY**

Occupant **Occupied** Appraiser ____ Instructions to Appraiser **Estimate market value**

☐ FNMA 1073A required   ☐ FHLMC 465 Addendum A required   ☐ FHLMC 465 Addendum B required

NEIGHBORHOOD

		NEIGHBORHOOD RATING	Good	Avg.	Fair	Poor
Location	☒ Urban ☐ Suburban ☐ Rural	Adequacy of Shopping		☒		
Built up	☒ Over 75% ☐ 25% to 75% ☐ Under 25%	Employment Opportunities		☒		
Growth Rate	☒ Fully Developed ☐ Rapid ☐ Steady ☐ Slow	Recreational Facilities	☒			
Property Values	☐ Increasing ☒ Stable ☒ Declining	Adequacy of Utilities		☒		
Demand/Supply	☐ Shortage ☒ In Balance ☒ Oversupply	Property Compatibility	☒			
Marketing Time	☐ Under 3 Mos. ☒ 4-6 Mos. ☒ Over 6 Mos.	Protection from Detrimental Conditions	☒			

Present Land Use **25** % 1 Family **40** % 2-4 Family **15** % Apts **15** % Condo ... Police and Fire Protection | | ☒ | |
5 % Commercial ___ % Industrial ___ % Vacant ... General Appearance of Properties | ☒ | | |

Change in Present Land Use ☒ Not Likely ☐ Likely ☐ Taking Place* ... Appeal to Market ☒

*From ____ To ____

			Distance	Access or Convenience
Predominant Occupancy	☒ Owner ☐ Tenant ____ %Vacant			Good Avg Fair Poor
Condominium: Price Range $ **35,000** to $ **125,000** Predominant $ **60,000**	Public Transportation	**1 blk**	☒
Age **25** yrs. to **75** yrs. Predominant **50** yrs.	Employment Centers	**NYC**	☒
Single Family: Price Range $ **125,000** to $ **325,000** Predominant $ **200,000**	Neighborhood Shopping	**3 blks**	☒
Age **50** yrs. to **100** yrs. Predominant **65** yrs.	Grammar Schools	**.25 mi**	☒
	Freeway Access	**6 blks**	☒

Describe potential for additional Condo/PUD units in nearby area **Additional Co-Ops may** not be feasible at this time due to the poor Co-Operative market. The area appears to be fully developed.

Note: FHLMC/FNMA do not consider race or the racial composition of the neighborhood to be reliable appraisal factors.

Describe those factors, favorable or unfavorable, affecting marketability (e.g. public parks, schools, noise, view, mkt. area, population size, financial ability). **The subject neighborhood is located along the Narrows Lower Bay shoreline, one mile north of the Fort Hamilton Army Base. Neighborhood maintenance level is judged to be good.**

SITE

Lot Dimensions (if PUD) **N/A** = ____ Sq. Ft. ☐ Corner Lot   Project Density When Completed as Planned ____ Units/Acre

Zoning Classification **Residential**   Present improvements ☒ do ☐ do not conform to zoning regulations

Highest and best use: ☒ Present use ☐ Other (specify) ____

	Public	Other (Describe)	OFF-SITE IMPROVEMENTS	
Elec.	☒	**No Access**	Street Access: ☒ Public ☐ Private	Project Ingress/Egress (adequacy) **Average/Average**
Gas	☒		Surface **Asphalt paved**	Topo **Rolling**
Water	☒		Maintenance: ☒ Public ☐ Private	Size/Shape **Average For Area/Mostly Rectangular**
San. Sewer	☒		☒ Storm Sewer ☒ Curb/Gutter	View Amenity **Average - Residential**
			☒ Underground Elec. & Tel. ☒ Sidewalk ☒ Street Lights	Drainage/Flood Conditions **Minimal Flood Hazard**

Is the property in a HUD identified Special Flood Hazard Area? ☒ No ☐ Yes

Comments (including any easements, encroachments or other adverse conditions) **Flood Map 360497-63. Site is lightly tree shaded and well landscaped and maintained. No known adverse conditions.**

PROJECT IMPROVEMENTS

TYPE PROJECT			PROJECT RATING	Good	Avg.	Fair	Poor
☒ Existing	Approx. Year Built 19 **56**	Original Use **Rentals**	Location		☒		
☐ Condo ☐ PUD	☒ Converted (19 **83**)		General Appearance		☒		
☐ Proposed	☐ Under Construction		Amenities and Recreational Facilities		☒		
☐ Elevator	☒ Walk-up No. of Stories **6**		Density (units per acre)		☒		
☐ Row or Town House	☒ Other (specify) **Mid Rise Building**		Unit Mix		☒		
☒ Primary Residence	☐ Second Home or Recreational		Quality of Constr. (mat'l & finish)		☒		

If Completed: No. Phases **1** No. Units **178** No. Sold **167** ... Condition of Exterior | | ☒ | |
If Incompleted: Planned No. Phases **N/A** No. Units **N/A** No. Sold **N/A** ... Condition of Interior | | ☒ | |
Units in Subject Phase: Total **178** Completed **178** Sold **167** Rented **11** ... Appeal to Market | | ☒ | |

Approx. No. Units for Sale: Subject Project **N/A** Subject Phase **N/A**

Exterior Wall **Brick** Roof Covering **Built-Up Roof** Security Features **Deadbolts, intercom**

Elevator: No. **2** Adequacy & Condition **Average** Soundproofing: Vertical **Average** Horizontal **Average**

Parking: Total No. Spaces **Street** Ratio **N/A** Spaces/Unit ____ Type **Street** No. Spaces of Guest Parking **Average**

Describe common elements or recreational facilities **Hall, laundry room**

Are any common elements, rec. facilities or parking leased to Owners Assoc.? **None known** If yes, attach addendum describing rental, terms and options.

SUBJECT UNIT

☒ Existing ☐ Proposed ☐ Under Constr. Floor No. **5** Unit Livable Area **629** ☐ Basement **0** % Finished **N/A**

Parking for Unit: No. **0** Type **Street** ☐ Assigned ☐ Owned Convenience to Unit **Average**

Room List	Foyer	Liv	Din	Kit	Bdrm	Bath	Fam	Rec	Lndry	Other
Basement										
1st Level										
2nd Level										
5th Level	x	1		1	1	1				

		UNIT RATING	Good	Avg.	Fair	Poor
Floors:	☒ Hardwood ☐ Carpet over ____	Condition of Improvement		☒		
Int. Walls	☐ Drywall ☒ Plaster	Room Sizes and Layout		☒		
Trim/Finish:	☐ Good ☒ Average ☐ Fair ☐ Poor	Adequacy of Closets and Storage		☒		
Bath Floor:	☒ Ceramic ____ Wainscot ☒ Ceramic	Kit. Equip., Cabinets & Workspace		☒		
Windows (type):	**Aluminum Double Hung** ☒ Storm Sash ☒ Screens ☒ Combo	Plumbing - Adequacy and Condition		☒		
Kitchen Equip:	☒ Refrig. ☒ Range/Oven ☐ Fan/Hood ☐ Washer ☐ Dryer	Electrical - Adequacy and Condition		☒		
	☒ Intercom ☐ Disposal ☐ Dishwasher ☐ Microwave ☐ Compactor	Adequacy of Soundproofing		☒		
		Adequacy of Insulation		☒		
		Location within Project or View		☒		
HEAT:	Type **Steam** Fuel **Oil** Cond. **No Access**	Overall Livability		☒		
AIR COND:	☐ Central ☒ Other **Window** ☒ Adequate ☐ Inadequate	Appeal and Marketability	☐	☒		

Est. Effective Age ____ to **5** yrs.
Est. Remaining Economic Life ____ to **55** yrs.

☐ Earth sheltered Housing Design	☐ Solar Design/Landscape	☐ Solar Space Heat/Air Cond.	☐ Solar Hot Water
☐ Flue Damper	☐ Elec./Mech. Gas Furn. Ignition	☐ Auto Setback Thermostat	☒ Dble/Triple Glazed Windows ☒ Caulk/Weatherstrip

INSULATION (state R-Factor if known) ☐ Walls **U/K** ☐ Ceiling **U/K** ☐ Floor **U/K** ☐ Roof/Attic **U/K** ☐ Water Heater **No Access**

If rehab proposed, do plans and specs provide for adequate energy conservation? ____ If no, attach description of modification needed.

ENERGY EFFICIENCY APPEARS: ☐ High ☒ Adequate ☐ Low   Energy Audit: ☐ Yes (attach, if available) ☒ No

COMMENTS (special features, functional or physical inadequacies, modernization or repair needed, etc.) **Subject unit is judged to be about 9% physically depreciated. There appears to be no significant functional or external inadequacies.**

BUDGET ANALYSIS

Unit Charge $ 290 /Mo. x 12 = $ 3,480 /Yr. ($ 5.53 /Sq. Ft./year of livable area) Ground Rent (if any) $ N/A /yr.

Utilities included in unit charge: ☐ None ☒ Heat ☐ Air Cond. ☐ Electricity ☐ Gas ☒ Water ☒ Sewer

Note any fees, other than regular Condo/PUD charges, for use of facilities None known.

To properly maintain the project and provide the services anticipated, the budget appears ☐ High ☒ Adequate ☐ Inadequate

Compared to other competitive projects of similar quality and design subject unit charge appears: ☐ High ☒ Reasonable ☐ Low

Management Group: ☐ Owners Association ☐ Developer ☒ Management Agent (identify) J.C. Kemper 347-9248

Quality of Management and its enforcement of Rules and Regulations appears: ☐ Superior ☐ Good ☒ Adequate ☐ Inadequate

Special or unusual characteristics in the Condo/PUD Documents or otherwise known to the appraiser, that would affect marketability (if none, so state) Lisa in the sales office provided information. Could not get any further data from a Mr. Benson.

Comments None.

NOTE: FHLMC does not require the cost approach in the appraisal of condominium or PUD units.

COST APPROACH

Cost Approach (to be used only for detached, semi-detached, and town house units):

Reproduction Cost New	____ Sq. Ft. @ $ ____ per Sq. Ft. =	$	0
Less Depreciation: Physical $ ____ Functional $ ____ Economic $ ____		(	0)
Depreciated Value of Improvements:			0
Add Land Value (if leasehold, show only leasehold value - attach calculations)			
Pro-rata Share of Value of Amenities		$	
Total Indicated Value: ☐ FEE SIMPLE ☐ LEASEHOLD		$	0

Comments regarding estimate of depreciation and value of land and amenity package The Cost Approach is not applicable to this report.

The appraiser, whenever possible, should analyze two comparable sales from within the subject project. However, when appraising a unit in a new or newly converted project, at least two comparables should be selected from outside the subject project. In the following analysis, the comparable should always be adjusted to the subject unit and not vice versa. If a significant feature of the comparable is superior to the subject unit, a minus (-) adjustment should be made to the comparable; if such a feature of the comparable is inferior to the subject, a plus (+) adjustment should be made to the comparable.

LIST ONLY THOSE ITEMS THAT REQUIRE ADJUSTMENT

ITEM	Subject Property	COMPARABLE NO. 1	+ (-) $ Adjustment	COMPARABLE NO. 2	+ (-) $ Adjustment	COMPARABLE NO. 3	+ (-) $ Adjustment
Address-Unit	162 82nd Street Unit E-27	28 Tree Lane Unit 4B		971 Overton Street Unit 3N		7290 Ridge Drive Unit 5A	
Project Name							
Proximity to Subj.		22 Blocks		3 Blocks		5 Blocks	
Sales Price	$ 58,000	$ 67,000		$ 54,000		$ 50,000	
Price/Living Area	$ 92.21	$ 100.90		$ 99.63		$ 72.99	
Data Source	Inspection	SREA Data		SREA Data		SREA Data	
Date of Sale and Time Adjustment	04/05/92	06/10/91	-1,650	07/15/91	-1,175	12/16/91	-450
Location	Average	Average		Inferior	2,500	Average	
Site/View	5thLevel/Avg	4thLevel/Avg	500	3rdLevel/Avg	1,000	5thLevel/Avg	
Design and Appeal	MidRise/Avg	MidRise/Avg		MidRise/Avg		MidRise/Avg	
Quality of Constr.	Average	Average		Average		Average	
Age	1956	+/- 1954		+/- 1931		+/- 1950	
Condition	Average	Average		Average		Average	
Living Area, Room Count & Total	Total 3 B-rms 1 Baths 1	Total 3 B-rms 1 Baths 1		Total 3 B-rms 1 Baths 1		Total 3 B-rms 1 Baths 1	
Gross Living Area	629 Sq. Ft.	664 Sq. Ft.	-1,050	542 Sq. Ft.	2,610	685 Sq. Ft.	-1,680
Basement & Bsmt. Finished Rooms	N/A	N/A		N/A		N/A	
Functional Utility	Average	Average		Average		Average	
Air Conditioning	Window Units	Central AC	-2,500	WindowUnits		Wall Units	
Storage	Average	Average		Average		Average	
Parking Facilities	Street	Street		Street		Street	
Common Elements and Recreation Facilities	Hall, Laundry Room	Hall, Laundry Room		Hall, Laundry Room		Hall, Laundry Room	
Mo. Assessment	+/- 290.00	+/- 385.00	1,000	+/- 524.00	4,250	+/- 589.00	4,750
Leasehold/Fee	Leasehold	Leasehold		Leasehold		Leasehold	
Special Energy Efficient Items	Average Efficiency	Average Efficiency		Average Efficiency		Average Efficiency	
Other (e.g. fireplaces, kitchen equip., remodeling)	No Fireplace Std. Kitchen Appliances	No Fireplace Std. Kitchen Appliances		No Fireplace Renovated Appliances	-2,000	No Fireplace Std. Kitchen Appliances	
Sales or Financing Concessions	None Known	None Known		None Known		None Known	
Net Adj. (total)		☐ Plus ☒ Minus $	-3,700	☒ Plus ☐ Minus $	7,185	☒ Plus ☐ Minus $	2,620
Indicated value of Subject		-6 %Net 10 %Gr $	63,300	13 %Net 25 %Gr $	61,185	5.2 %Net 14 %Gr $	52,620

Comments on Market Data Analysis SEE ATTACHED ADDENDUM

INDICATED VALUE BY MARKET DATA APPROACH $ 58,000

INDICATED VALUE BY INCOME APPROACH (If applicable) Economic Market Rent $ N/A /Mo. x Gross Rent Multiplier N/A = $ 0

This appraisal is made ☒ "as is" ☐ subject to repairs, alterations, or conditions listed below ☐ subject to completion per plans and specifications.

Comments and Conditions of Appraisal: The cost and income approaches are not applicable to this report.

Final Reconciliation: The market data analysis is the only reliable approach as it reflects the behavior of buyers and sellers in the marketplace. No repairs or modernization were deemed necessary at this time.

Construction Warranty ☐ Yes ☐ No Name of Warranty Program ____ Warranty Coverage Expires ____

This appraisal is based upon the above requirements, the certification, contingent and limiting conditions, and Market Value definition that are stated in

☒ FHLMC Form 439 (Rev. 7/86)/FNMA Form 1004B (Rev. 7/86) filed with client ____ ,19 ___ ☒ attached.

I ESTIMATE THE MARKET VALUE, AS DEFINED, OF SUBJECT PROPERTY AS OF April 5 ,19 92 to be $ 58,000

Appraiser(s) Steve Smith Review Appraiser (if applicable) Harry Jones

Date Report Signed May 6 ,19 92 ☐ Did ☒ Did Not Physically Inspect Property

FHLMC Form 465 Rev. 9/80   LaserForm Software by DAY ONE, Inc. 1987   FNMA Form 1073 Rev. 9/80

MARKET DATA ANALYSIS

File no. A0238D92

The appraiser, whenever possible, should analyze two comparable sales from within the subject project. However, when appraising a unit in a new or newly converted project, at least two comparable should be selected from outside the subject project. In the following analysis, the comparable should be adjusted to the subject unit and not vice versa. If a significant feature of the comparable is superior to the subject unit, a minus (-) adjustment should be made to the comparable; if such a feature of the comparable is inferior to the subject, a plus (+) adjustment should be made to the comparable.

LIST ONLY THOSE ITEMS THAT REQUIRE ADJUSTMENT

ITEM	Subject Property	COMPARABLE NO. 4	+(-) $ Adjustment	COMPARABLE NO. 5	+(-) $ Adjustment	COMPARABLE NO. 6	+(-) $ Adjustment
Address-Unit	162 82nd Street	255 Baybowl Place		255 Baybowl Place			
Project Name	Unit E-27	Unit 4H		Unit 8S			
Proximity to Subj.		7 Blocks		7 Blocks			
Sale Price	$ 58,000	$ 60,000		$ 63,000		$	
Price/Living Area	$ 92.21	$ 81.30		$ 90.00		$	
Data Source	Inspection	SREA Data		SREA Data			
Date of Sale and Time Adjustment	04/05/92	07/26/91	-1,250	07/27/91	-1,325		
Location	Average	Inferior	2,500	Inferior	2,500		
Site / View	5thLevel/Avg	3rdLevel/Avg	1,000	4thLevel/Avg	500		
Design and Appeal	MidRise/Avg	MidRise/Avg		MidRise/Avg			
Quality of Construction	Average	Average		Average			
Age	1956	+/- 1963		+/- 1963			
Condition	Average	Average		Average			
Living Area, Room Count & Total	Total 3 / B-rms 1 / Baths 1	Total 3 / B-rms 1 / Baths 1		Total 3 / B-rms 1 / Baths 1		Total / B-rms / Baths	
Gross Living Area	629 Sq.Ft.	738 Sq.Ft.	-3,270	700 Sq.Ft.	-2,130	Sq.Ft.	
Basement & Bsmt. Finished Rooms	N/A	N/A		N/A			
Functional Utility	Average	Average		Average			
Air Conditioning	Window Units	WindowUnits		WindowUnits			
Storage	Average	Average		Average			
Parking Facilities	Street	Street		Street			
Common Elements and Recreation Facilities	Hall,Laundry Room	Hall, Laundry Room		Hall, Laundry Room			
Mo. Assessment	+/- 290.00	+/- 263.00		+/- 327.00			
Leasehold/Fee	Leasehold	Leasehold		Leasehold			
Special Energy Efficient Items	Average Efficiency	Average Efficiency		Average Efficiency			
Other (e.g. fireplaces, kitchen equip., remodeling)	No Fireplace Std. Kitchen Appliances	No Fireplace Std. Kitchen Appliances		No Fireplace Std. Kitchen Appliances			
Sales or Financing Concessions	None Known	None Known		None Known			
Net Adj. (total)		☐ Plus ☒ Minus $	-1,020	☐ Plus ☒ Minus $	-455	☐ Plus ☐ Minus $	0
Indicated Value of Subject		-2 %Net / 13 %Grs	$ 58,980	-1 %Net / 10 %Grs	$ 62,545	%Net / %Grs	$ 0

Comments on Market Data All sales were adjusted .25% per month due to the declining Co-Op market.
   Sales 2, 4, & 5 were judged to be inferior in location due to their being on busier streets and being closer to commercial activities.
   All sales, except 3, were adjusted for the view.
   The gross living area adjustments are based on $30.00 per square foot.
   Sales 1, 2 & 3 were adjusted for the monthly maintenance charge in relation to their square footage, as compared to the subject.

   No evaluations are made as to the existence or potential effects on market value for any environmental conditions or substances on or near the subject property. Any environmental concerns must be analyzed and reported by a professional in that field of expertise. The appraiser is not qualified and makes no evaluations or determinations of these matters in the estimated market value of the subject property or in evaluating the comparable sales.

SUBJECT PHOTOGRAPH ADDENDUM

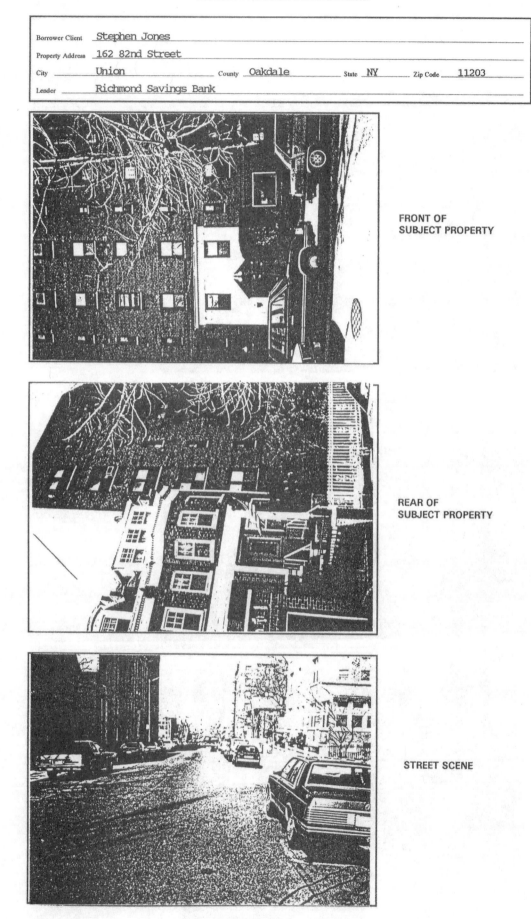

Borrower Client — Stephen Jones

Property Address — 162 82nd Street

City — Union   County — Oakdale   State — NY   Zip Code — 11203

Lender — Richmond Savings Bank

FRONT OF
SUBJECT PROPERTY

REAR OF
SUBJECT PROPERTY

STREET SCENE

COMPARABLES PHOTOGRAPH ADDENDUM

Borrower Client Stephen Jones

Property Address 162 82nd Street

City Union   County Oakdale   State NY   Zip Code 11203

Lender Richmond Savings Bank

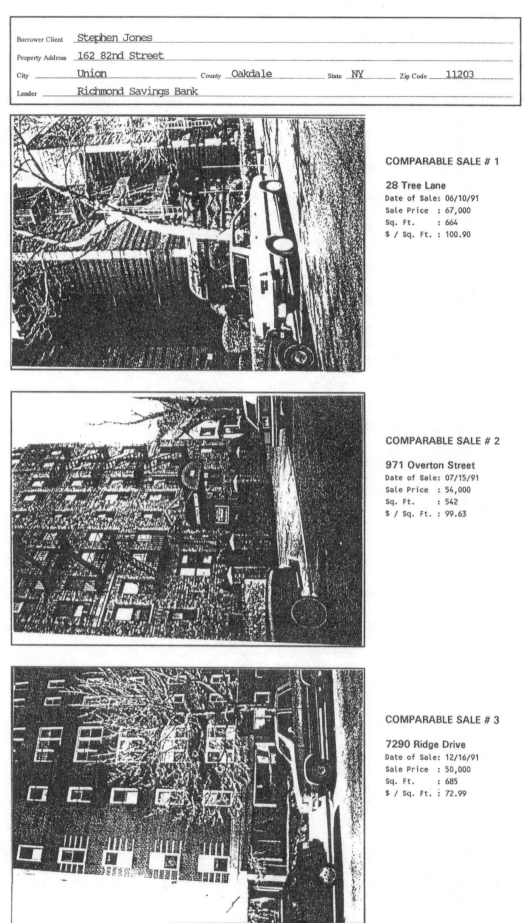

COMPARABLE SALE # 1

28 Tree Lane
Date of Sale: 06/10/91
Sale Price : 67,000
Sq. Ft.   : 664
$ / Sq. Ft. : 100.90

COMPARABLE SALE # 2

971 Overton Street
Date of Sale: 07/15/91
Sale Price : 54,000
Sq. Ft.   : 542
$ / Sq. Ft. : 99.63

COMPARABLE SALE # 3

7290 Ridge Drive
Date of Sale: 12/16/91
Sale Price : 50,000
Sq. Ft.   : 685
$ / Sq. Ft. : 72.99

COMPARABLES 4 5 6 PHOTOGRAPH ADDENDUM

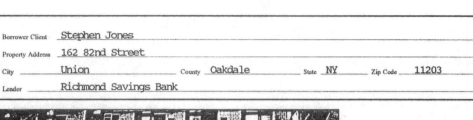

Borrower Client **Stephen Jones**

Property Address **162 82nd Street**

City **Union** County **Oakdale** State **NY** Zip Code **11203**

Lender **Richmond Savings Bank**

COMPARABLE SALE # 4

255 Baybowl Place
Date of Sale: 07/26/91
Sale Price : 60,000
Sq. Ft.   : 738
$ / Sq. Ft. : 81.30

COMPARABLE SALE # 5

255 Baybowl Place
Date of Sale: 07/27/91
Sale Price : 63,000
Sq. Ft.   : 700
$ / Sq. Ft. : 90.00

COMPARABLE SALE # 6

Date of Sale:
Sale Price :
Sq. Ft.   :
$ / Sq. Ft. :

Location·Map

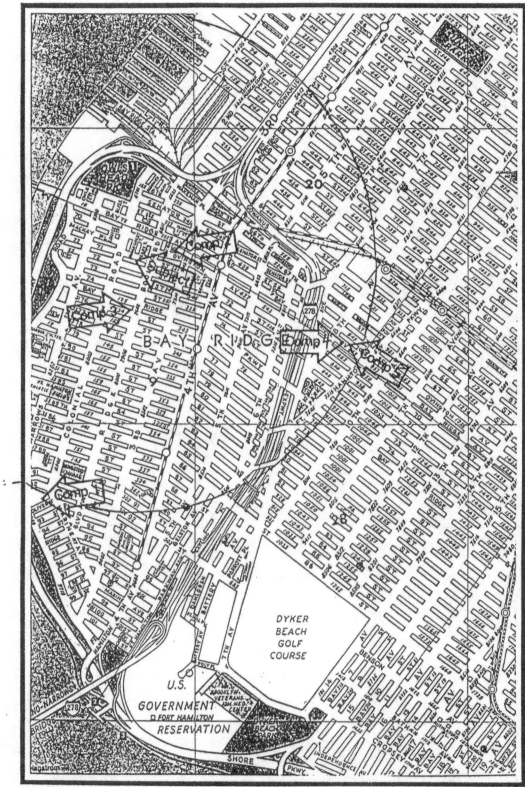

Borrower Name : **Stephen Jones**   File No. **A0238D92**

DEFINITION OF MARKET VALUE :   The most probable price which a property should bring in a competitive and open market under all conditions requisite to a fair sale, the buyer and seller, each acting prudently, knowledgeably and assuming the price is not affected by undue stimulus. Implicit in this definition is the consummation of a sale as of a specified date and the passing of title from seller to buyer under conditions whereby: (1) buyer and seller are typically motivated; (2) both parties are well informed or well advised, and each acting in what he considers his own best interest; (3) a reasonable time is allowed for exposure in the open market; (4) payment is made in terms of cash in U.S. dollars or in terms of financial arrangements comparable thereto; and (5) the price represents the normal consideration for the property sold unaffected by special or creative financing or sales concessions* granted by anyone associated with the sale.

*Adjustments to the comparables must be made for special or creative financing or sales concessions. No adjustments are necessary for those costs which are normally paid by sellers as a result of tradition or law in a market area; these costs are readily identifiable since the seller pays these costs in virtually all sales transactions. Special or creative financing adjustments can be made to the comparable property by comparisons to financing terms offered by a third party institutional lender that is not already involved in the property or transaction. Any adjustment should not be calculated on a mechanical dollar for dollar cost of the financing or concession but the dollar amount of any adjustment should approximate the market's reaction to the financing or concessions based on the appraiser's judgment.

CERTIFICATION AND STATEMENT OF LIMITING CONDITIONS

CERTIFICATION: The Appraiser certifies and agrees that:

1. The Appraiser has no present or contemplated future interest in the property appraised; and neither the employment to make the appraisal, nor the compensation for it, is contingent upon the appraised value of the property.

2. The Appraiser has no personal interest in or bias with respect to the subject matter of the appraisal report of the participants to the sale. The "Estimate of Market Value" in the appraisal report is not based in whole or in part upon the race, color, or national origin of the prospective owners for occupants of the property appraised, or upon the race, color or national origin of the present owners or occupants of the properties in the vicinity of the property appraised.

3. The appraiser has personally inspected the property, both inside and out, and has made an exterior inspection of all comparable sales listed in the report. To the best of the Appraiser's knowledge and belief, all statements and information in this report are true and correct, and the Appraiser has not knowingly withheld any significant information.

4. All contingent and limiting conditions are contained herein (imposed by the terms of the assignment or by the undersigned affecting the analyses, opinions, and conclusions contained in the report).

5. This appraisal report has been made in conformity with and is subject to the to the requirements of the Code of Professional Ethics and Standards of Professional Conduct of the appraisal organizations with which the Appraiser is affiliated.

6. All conclusions and opinions concerning the real estate that are set forth in the appraisal report were prepared by the Appraiser whose signature appears on the appraisal report, unless indicated as "Review Appraiser." No change of any item in the appraisal report shall be made by anyone other than the Appraiser, and the Appraiser shall have no responsibility for any such unauthorized change.

CONTINGENT AND LIMITING CONDITIONS:

The certification of the Appraiser appearing in the appraisal report is subject to the following conditions and to such other specific and limiting conditions as are set forth by the Appraiser in the report.

1. The Appraiser assumes no responsibility for matters of a legal nature affecting the property appraised or the title thereto, nor does the Appraiser render any opinion as to the title, which is assumed to be good and marketable. The property is appraised as though under responsible ownership.

2. Any sketch in the report may show approximate dimensions and is included to assist the reader in visualizing the property. The Appraiser has made no survey of the property.

3. The Appraiser is not required to give testimony or appear in court because of having made the appraisal with reference to the property in question, unless arrangements have been previously made therefor.

4. Any distribution of the valuation in the report between land and improvements applies only under the existing program or utilization. The separate valuations for land and building must not be used in conjunction with any other appraisal and are invalid if so used.

5. The Appraiser assumes that there are no hidden or unapparent conditions of the property, subsoil, or structures, which would render it more or less valuable. The Appraiser assumes no responsibility for such conditions, or for engineering which might be required to discover such factors.

6. Information, estimates, and opinions furnished to the Appraiser, and contained in the report, were obtained from sources considered reliable and believed to be true and correct. However, no responsibility for accuracy of such items furnished the Appraiser can be assumed by the Appraiser.

7. Disclosure of the contents of the appraisal report is governed by the Bylaws and Regulations of the professional appraisal organizations with which the Appraiser is affiliated.

8. Neither all, nor any part of the content of the report, or copy thereof (including conclusions as to the property value, the identity of the Appraiser, professional designations, reference to any professional appraisal organizations, or the firm with which the Appraiser is connected), shall be used for any purposes by anyone but the client specified in the report , the borrower if appraisal fee paid by same, the mortgagee or its successors and assigns, mortgage insurers, consultants, professional appraisal organizations, any state or federally approved financial institution, any department, agency, or instrumentality of the United States or any state or the District of Columbia, without the previous written consent of the Appraiser; nor shall it be conveyed by anyone to the public through advertising, public relations, news, sales, or other media, without the written consent and approval of the Appraiser.

9. On all appraisals, subject to satisfactory completion, repairs, or alterations, the appraisal report and value conclusion are contingent upon completion of the improvements in a workmanship like manner.

Date **April 5, 1992**   Signature _____

Steve Smith

Freddie Mac   Fannie Mac
Form 439 JUL 86   Form 1004B Jul 86

APPRAISAL OF

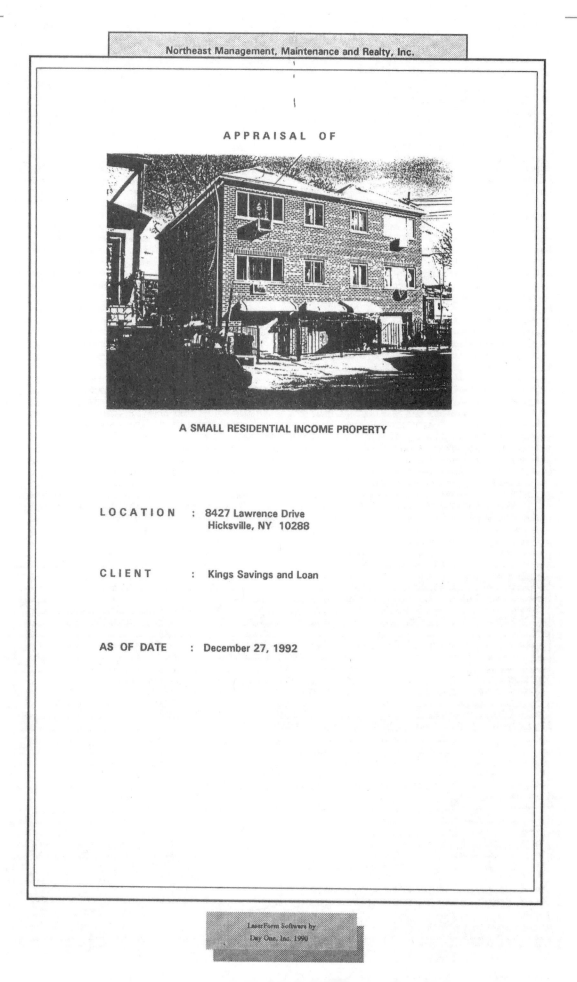

A SMALL RESIDENTIAL INCOME PROPERTY

LOCATION : 8427 Lawrence Drive
Hicksville, NY 10288

CLIENT : Kings Savings and Loan

AS OF DATE : December 27, 1992

PROPERTY DESCRIPTION
& ANALYSIS

Northeast Management, Maintenance and Realty, Inc.
SMALL RESIDENTIAL INCOME PROPERTY APPRAISAL REPORT   File no. A0451H92

Subject

Property address 8427 Lawrence Drive	Lender discretionary use
City Hicksville County Kings State NY Zip Code 10288	Sale price $
Legal description Block 5441, Lot 6	Gross monthly rent $
Owner/occupant Unknown/3 tenants Tax Year 1992 R.E. taxes $ +/- 2,350	Closing date
Sale price $ 220,000 Date of Sale 12/27/92 Census tract 158 Map Reference Hagstrom	Mortgage amount $
Property rights appraised [X] Fee Simple [ ] Leaschold [ ] Condominium or [ ] PUD HOA$ N/A /Mo.	Mortgage type
Borrower N/A Project Name N/A	Discount points and other concessions
Loan charges/concessions to be paid by seller $ N/A	Paid by seller $
Lender/client Kings Savings and Loan	Source
Appraiser Harry Richmond	

Neighborhood

Location	[X] Urban	[ ] Suburban	[ ] Rural	Predominant Occupancy	Single family housing		Neighborhood Analysis	Good	Avg.	Fair	Poor
					PRICE $ (000)	AGE (yrs)					
Built up	[X] Over 75%	[ ] 25-75%	[ ] Under 25%		180 Low	10	Employment stability		[X]		
Growth rate	[ ] Rapid	[ ] Stable	[X] Slow	[X] Owner	240 High	75	Convenience to employment		[X]		
Property values	[ ] Increasing	[X] Stable	[ ] Declining	[ ] Tenant	Predominant		Convenience to shopping	[X]			
Demand/supply	[ ] Shortage	[X] In balance	[ ] Over supply	[X] Vacant (0-5%)	200	55	Convenience to schools	[X]			
Marketing time	[ ] Under 3 mos.	[X] 3 - 6 mos.	[X] Over 6 mos.	[ ] Vacant(over5%)			Adequacy of public transportation	[X]	[X]		

Typical 2-4 family bldg. Type Detachd	Present land use %	Land use change	2-4 family housing					
No. stories. 2 No. units 2	One family 30	[X] Not likely	PRICE $ (000)	AGE (yrs)	Recreation facilities		[X]	
Age 55 yrs. Condition Average	2-4 family 50	[ ] Likely	200 Low	12	Adequacy of utilities		[X]	
Typical rents $ 550 to $ 875	Multifamily	[ ] In process	270 High	75	Property compatibility	[X]		
[ ] Increasing [X] Stable [ ] Declining	Commercial 20	To:	Predominant		Protection from detrimental cond.		[X]	
Est neighborhood apt vacancy 2 %	Industrial		240	55	Police & fire protection		[X]	
[ ] Increasing [X] Stable [ ] Declining	Vacant	Rent controls [X] Yes [ ] No [ ] Likely	General appearance of properties		[X]		
			Appeal to market	[X]	[X]		

Note: Race and the racial composition of the neighborhood are not considered reliable appraisal factors.

Description of neighborhood boundaries: North and East to I-295 Throggs Neck Expwy, West to East Tremont Avenue, South to Cross Bronx Expwy. See location map

Description of those factors, favorable or unfavorable, that affect marketability (including neighborhood stability, appeal, property conditions, vacancies, *rent control*, etc.):
The subject neighborhood is located in the Schuylerville section of the east portion of the Bronx, 3 blocks from the Throggs Neck Expwy, the Cross Bronx Expwy, Intermediate School #192, the NY Public Library Throggs Neck branch, and a nursing home. The area is comprised of mostly attached and detached two family dwellings. There are commercial businesses on East Tremont Avenue. The vast majority of the houses are of the same style, Brick Row houses, and the same approximate age. The neighborhood maintenance level is judged to be average.

The following available listings represent the most current, similar, and proximate competitive properties to the subject property in the subject neighborhood. This analysis is intended to evaluate the inventory currently on the market competing with the subject property in the subject neighborhood and recent price and marketing time trends affecting the subject property.
(Listings outside the subject neighborhood are not considered applicable).

ITEM	SUBJECT	COMPARABLE LISTING NO. 1	COMPARABLE LISTING NO. 2	COMPARABLE LISTING NO. 3
Address	8427 Lawrence Dri Hicksville, NY	2290 Prospect Ave. Hicksville, NY	2986 Kenneth Ave. Hicksville, NY	982 Marytill Drive Hicksville, NY
Proximity to subject		2 blocks	9 blocks	5 blocks
Listing price $	245,000	[X] Unf. [ ] Furn. $ 295,000	[X] Unf. [ ] Furn. $ 275,000	[X] Unf. [ ] Furn. $ 250,000
Approximate GBA	+/- 2,330	+/- 2300	+/- 2300	+/- 2300
Data Source	Inspection	MLS / REDI Data	MLS / REDI Data	MLS / REDI Data
#Units/Tot. rms/BR/BA	3 14 6 4	2 12 4 2	2 13 5 2	2 13 4 2
Approximate year built	+/- 1971	+/- 65 years	+/- 65 years	+/- 60 years
Approx. days on market	N/A	+/- 2 years	+/- 4 months	+/- 4 months

Comparison of listings to subject property. All listings are located in similar neighborhoods to the subject neighborhood. All listings are reported to be similar in quality to the subject.

Reconciliation: Description and analysis of the general market conditions that affect 2-4 family properties in the subject neighborhood (including the above neighborhood indicators of growth rate, property values, demand/supply, and marketing time) and the prevalence and impact in the subject/market area regarding loan discounts, interest buydowns, and concessions; and identify trends in listing prices, average days on market and any change over past year, etc.: There does not appear to be an oversupply of multi-family dwellings in the area due to a number of recent sales. However, it is a buyer's market in some areas with real estate prices "bottoming out" after a long period of decline. Sales concessions have been offered recently by some developers of new homes to stimulate sales. These concessions usually consist of a partial or full payment of the closing costs by the developer. Fixed and adjustable rate mortgages are typical.

Site

Dimensions +/- 100 x 28 x 26 = 2,700 SF	Topography Gently Sloping
Site Area +/- .6 A Corner lot [X] No [ ] Yes	Size Typical For Area
Specific zoning classification and description Tax Class Residential Dwelling 2 fam	Shape Irregular
Zoning Compliance [X] Legal [ ] Legal nonconforming (Grandfather use) [ ] Illegal [ ] No zoning	Drainage Appears Adequate
Highest & best use as improved [X] Present Use [X] Other use(explain) First floor apartmnt	View Average
was added by the owner and is an illegal dwelling.	Landscaping Fair
	Driveway Concrete

Utilities	Public	Other	Off-site Improvements	Type	Public	Private	
Electricity	[X]	3 meters	Street	Asphalt Paved	[X]		Apparent easements Noted in deed and client was notified. Reel 155, Page 531.
Gas	[X]	2 meters	Curb/gutter	Concrete	[X]		
Water	[X]		Sidewalk	Concrete	[X]		FEMA Special flood hazard area [ ] Yes* [X] No
Sanitary sewer	[X]		Street lights	Yes	[X]		*FEMA Zone/Map Date Map N/A at town hall
Storm sewer	[X]		Alley	None			*FEMA Map No.

Comments (apparent adverse easements, encroachments, special assessments, slide areas, illegal or legal nonconforming zoning, use, etc.): There is a third kitchen located in the finished area of the first level. This apartment is an illegal dwelling. This is a safety and health hazard that MUST be resolved prior to closing. NO evaluations are made of the restrictions in the deed for this appraisal report. The client was notified.

Freddie Mac Form 72 10/89 2-4 units 12CH   PAGE 1 OF 4   LaserForm software by DAY ONE,INC.   Fannie Mae Form 1025 2-4 units 10/89

PROPERTY DESCRIPTION & ANALYSIS, continued

SMALL RESIDENTIAL INCOME PROPERTY APPRAISAL REPORT

Description of improvements

General description		Exterior description	(Materials/condition)	Foundation		Insulation	(R-value if known)
Units/bldgs.	3 / 1	Foundation	P Concrete/Average	Slab	Yes	☐ Roof	Concealed
Stories	2	Exterior walls	Brick/Average	Crawl space	No	☐ Ceiling	Concealed
Type (det./att..)	Semi-Attachd	Roof surface	Ashpalt Shing/Avg	Sump Pump	None Noted	☐ Walls	Concealed
Design	Row House	Gutters & downspouts	Aluminum/Average	Dampness	None Noted	☐ Floor	Concealed
Existing/proposed	Yes / No	Window type	Metal Slider/Avg	Settlement	Normal	☐ None	
Under construction	No	Storm sash/Screens	Poor Condition	Infestation	None Noted	Adequacy	Average
Year Built	+/- 1971	Manufactured housing	☐ Yes ☒ No	Basement	0 % of 1st floor area	Energy efficient items	Average
Effective age(yrs.)	6	(Complies with the HUD Manufactured Housing Construction and Safety Standards)		Basement finish	N/A	Efficiency	

Units	Level(s)	Foyer	Living	Dining	Kitchen	Den	Family rm.	# Bedrooms	# Baths	Laundry	Other	Sq. ft./unit	Total ☑
1 N/	1	1	1		1			1	1			570	570
1	2		1	1	1			3	2			880	880
1	3		1	1	1			3	2			880	880

Improvements contain: 14   Rooms;   7   Bedroom(s);   5   Bath(s);   2,330   Square feet of GROSS BUILDING AREA*

*GROSS BUILDING AREA(GBA) IS DEFINED AS THE TOTAL FINISHED AREA(INCLUDING COMMON AREAS) OF THE IMPROVEMENTS BASED UPON EXTERIOR MEASUREMENTS.

SURFACES	(Materials/condition)	HEATING		Kitchen equip. (#/unit-cond.)		Attic		Improvement Analysis	Good	Avg.	Fair	Poor
Floors	Wood/Carpet/Avg	Type	FH Air	Refrigerator	3/Avg	☒	None	Quality of construction		X		
Walls	Drywall/Average	Fuel	Gas	Range/oven	3/Poor		Stairs	Condition of improvements		X		
Trim/finish	Softwood/Average	Condition	Good	Disposal			Drop stair	Room sizes/layout		X		
Bath floor	Ceramic/Average	Adequacy	Good	Dishwasher			Scuttle	Closets and storage			X	
Bath wainscot	Ceramic/Average	COOLING		Fan/hood			Floor	Energy efficiency		X		
Doors	Hollow Wood/Fair	Central	None	Compactor			Heated	Plumbing - adequacy & condition		X		
		Other	None	Washer/dryer			Finished	Electrical - adequacy & condition		X	X	
		Condition	N/A	Microwave			Unfinished	Kitchen cabinets - adequacy & cond.		X		
Fireplace(s)	None # 0	Adequacy	N/A	Intercom				Compatibility to neighborhood	X	X		
Car storage:		☒ Garage	☒ Attached	☒ Adequate		☐ None		Appeal & marketability	X	X		
No. cars	1	☐ Carport	☐ Detached	☐ Inadequate		☐ Offstreet		Estimated remaining economic life		95		yrs.

Comments on repairs needed, additional features, modernization, etc.: Client commissioned a home inspection along with the appraisal. Review the written home inspection report for details on the repairs and upgrading needed.

Additional comments on neighborhood, site & description of improvements

Depreciation (physical, functional, and external inadequacies, etc): The subject is judged to be approximately 6% physically depreciated using the Age/Life Method. No functional or external inadequacies were noted.

Environmental conditions observed by or known to the appraiser: No environmental factors were noted or known to the appraiser. The value estimated in this report is based on the assumption that the property is not negatively affected by the existence of hazardous substances or detrimental environmental conditions. The appraiser is not an expert in the identification of hazardous substances or detrimental environmental conditions. The appraiser's routine inspection of and inquiries about the subject property did not develop any information that indicated any significant hazardous substances or detrimental conditions which would negatively affect property value.

VALUATION ANALYSIS

Purpose of Appraisal is to estimate Market Value as defined in the Certification & Statement of Limiting Conditions

Cost approach

Comments on cost approach, accrued depreciation, and estimated site value:

The site value is about 40% of the total value.

ESTIMATED REPRODUCTION COST-NEW-OF IMPROVEMENTS:		
570 Sq. Ft. @ $ 75.00 = $		42,750
880 Sq. Ft. @ $ 75.00 =		66,000
880 Sq. Ft. @ $ 75.00 =		66,000
Sq. Ft. @ $ =		
Extras (Garage = 250 SF) =		12,000
=		
=		
Special Energy Efficient Items =		
Porches, Patios, etc. =		
Total Estimated Cost New .... = $		186,750

Less (Physical / Functional / External)

Depreciation 11,205	=$	11,205
Depreciated Value of Improvements .... =$		175,545
Site Imp. "as is" (driveway, landscaping, etc.) ..... =$		
ESTIMATED SITE VALUE .... =$		95,000
(If leasehold, show only leasehold value.)		
INDICATED VALUE BY COST APPROACH..... =$		270,545

Freddie Mac Form 72 10/89 2-4 units 12CH   PAGE 2 OF 4   LaserForm software by DAY ONE, INC.   Fannie Mae Form 1025 2-4 units 10/89

VALUATION
ANALYSIS, continued   SMALL RESIDENTIAL INCOME PROPERTY APPRAISAL REPORT

Sales comparison analysis

The undersigned has recited three recent sales of properties most similar and proximate to the subject property and has described and analyzed these in this analysis. If there is a significant variation between the subject and the comparable properties, the analysis includes a dollar adjustment reflecting the market reaction to the items or an explanation supported by the market data. If a significant item in the comparable property is superior to, or more favorable than, the subject property, a minus(-) adjustment is made, thus reducing the indicated value of the subject; if a significant item in the comparable is inferior to, or less favorable than, the subject property, a plus (+) adjustment is made, thus increasing the indicated value of the subject.
[(1) Sales Price / Gross Monthly Rent)]

ITEM	SUBJECT	COMPARABLE SALE NO. 1	+(-) $ Adjustment	COMPARABLE SALE NO. 2	+(-) $ Adjustment	COMPARABLE SALE NO. 3	+(-) $Adjustment
Address	8427 Lawrence Drive Hicksville, NY	943 Porch Avenue Hicksville, NY		3387 Victory Lane Hicksville, NY		23 Lucastone Drive Hicksville, NY	
Proximity to subject		1 block		1.5 blocks		3 blocks	
Sales price	$ 220,000	X Unf. Furn. $ 230,000		X Unf. Furn. $ 232,000		X Unf. Furn. $ 220,000	
Sales price/GBA	$ 94.42	$ 95.83		$ 116		$ 88	
Gross monthly rent	$ 1,775	$ 1,700		$ 1,750		$ 2,000	
Gross mo. rent mult.(1)	123.93	135.29		132.57		110	
Sales price per unit	$ 110,000	$ 115,000		$ 116,000		$ 110,000	
Sales price per room	$ 18,333	$ 19,170		$ 19,330		$ 15,710	
Data Source		MLS/REDI D/Town Hal		MLS/REDI D/Town Hal		MLS/REDI D/Town Hal	
ADJUSTMENTS	DESCRIPTION	DESCRIPTION	+(-) $ Adjustment	DESCRIPTION	+(-) $ Adjustment	DESCRIPTION	+(-) $Adjustment
Sales or financing concessions		None Known		None Known		None Known	
Date or sale/time	12/27/92	02/19/92		10/19/92		07/30/92	
Location	Average	Average		Average		Average	
Site/View	+/- .6 A/Avera	+/- .10 A/A	-11,000	+/- .05 A/A		+/- .13 A/A	-12,000
Design and appeal	2 Fam/Semi-Att	2 Fam/Detac	-10,000	2 Fam/Attac	10,000	2 Fam/Detac	-10,000
Quality of construction	Brick/Avg	Brick/Avg		Brick/Avg		Frame/F-Avg	20,000
Year built	+/- 1971	+/- 1930	22,500	+/- 1960	3,500	+/- 1960	3,500
Condition	Average	Average		Average		Average	
Gross Building Area	2,330 Sq. ft.	2,400 Sq. ft.	-1,750	2,000 Sq. ft.	8,250	2,500 Sq. ft.	-4,250
UNIT BREAKDOWN	No. of units / Room count Tot Br. Baths / No. Vac — 1 6 3 2 0 ; 1 6 3 2 1	No. of units / Room count Tot Br. Baths / No. Vac — 1 6 3 1 0 ; 1 6 3 1 0	1,750 ; 1,750	No. of units / Room count Tot Br. Baths / No. Vac — 1 6 2 2 0 ; 1 6 2 2 0		No. of units / Room count Tot Br. Baths / No. Vac — 1 7 3 2 0 ; 1 7 3 2 0	
Basement description	N/A	None		None		None	
Functional utility	Average	Average		Average		Average	
Heating/cooling	FH Water/None	Steam/None		Hot W/None		FH W/None	
Parking on/off site	1 Car Garage	1 Car Garag		None	4,000	1 Car Garag	
Project amenities and fee (If applicable)	Additional apartment	Additional apartment		None	6,000	None	6,000
Other	N/A	N/A		N/A		N/A	
Net Adj. (total)		X + ☐ - $	3,250	X + ☐ - $	31,750	X + ☐ - $	3,250
Adj. sales price of comparables		1.4 Net% 21 Gross % $	233,250	14 Net % 14 Gross % $	263,750	1.5 Net % 25 Gross % $	223,250

Comments on sales comparison (including reconciliation of all indicators of value as to consistency and relative strength and evaluation of the typical investors'/purchasers' motivation in the market): No time adjustments were deemed necessary. Condition adjustments were accounted for in the age adjustments. The gross living area adjustments are based on about $25.00 per square foot. The appraiser is not taking into account any deed easements, restrictions, etc. The client was notified of this. Any problems in the deed WILL affect the market value of the property. Investigate this condition fully!

INDICATED VALUE BY SALES COMPARISON APPROACH $ 235,000

Prior sales of subject and comparables within one year of the date of this appraisal : None Known

Income Approach

Total gross estimated rent $ 1,720 /month x gross rent multiplier 123.93 = $ 213,159.6 INDICATED VALUE BY INCOME APPROACH

Comments on income approach (including expense ratios, if available, and reconciliation of the GRM) The total gross monthly estimated rent was arrived at from the comparable rents listed above. However, the first level apartment rental of $600 per month was not calculated into the income approach because it is an illegal apartment.

Reconciliation

INDICATED VALUE BY SALES COMPARISON APPROACH .... $ 235,000
INDICATED VALUE BY INCOME APPROACH .... $ 213,159.6
INDICATED VALUE BY COST APPROACH .... $ 270,545

This appraisal is made X "as is" ☐ subject to repairs, alterations, inspections or conditions listed below ☐ subject to completion per plans and specifications.

Comments and conditions of appraisal: This appraisal is subject to a free and clear title report and a deed with no adverse easements, encroachments, violations, etc.

Final reconciliation: The sales comparison analysis is the most reliable indicator of value as it reflects the actions of typical buyers and sellers in the marketplace.

This appraisal is based upon the above conditions and the certification, contingent and limiting conditions, and Market Value definition that are stated in Freddie Mac Form 439/Fannie Mae Form 1004B (Rev. 07/86) X attached or ☐ filed with client _____ or ☐ other attached.

I (WE) ESTIMATE THE MARKET VALUE, AS DEFINED, OF THE SUBJECT PROPERTY AS OF December 27, 1992 to be $ 235,000

I (We) certify that to the best of my (our) knowledge and belief the facts and data used herein are true and correct; that I (we) personally inspected the subject property, both inside and out, and have personally made an exterior inspection of all comparables cited in this report; and that I (we) have no undisclosed interest, present or prospective therein.

APPRAISER(S)
SIGNATURE _____   REVIEW APPRAISER (if applicable) SIGNATURE _____   ☐ Did ☐ Did not
NAME Harry Richmond   NAME _____   inspect property

Freddie Mac Form 72 10/89 2-4 units 12CH   PAGE 4 OF 4   LaserForm software by DAY ONE, INC.   Fannie Mae Form 1025 2-4 units 10/89

VALUATION
ANALYSIS, continued   SMALL RESIDENTIAL INCOME PROPERTY APPRAISAL REPORT

Comparable rental data

At least three rental comparables should be reported and analyzed in this section. The rental comparables should represent the most current rental information on properties as similar and proximate to the subject property as possible. (This comparison is based on current rental data, therefore, the rental comparables typically are not the same comparables used in the sales comparison analysis.) The appraisal report should assure the reader that the units and properties selected as comparables are comparable to the subject property (both the units and the overall property) and accurately represent the rental market for the subject property (unless otherwise stated within the report).

ITEM	SUBJECT	COMPARABLE RENTAL NO. 1	COMPARABLE RENTAL NO.2	COMPARABLE RENTAL NO. 3
Address	8427 Lawrence Drive Hicksville, NY	3982 Uptown Road Hicksville, NY	198 Downhill Ave. Hicksville, NY	9037 Procall Lane Hicksville, NY
Proximity to subject		2 blocks	9 blocks	5 blocks
Lease Dates (if available)	N/A	N/A	N/A	N/A
Rent survey date	12/92	09/92	08/92	08/92
Data source		MLS / REDI Data	MLS / REDI Data	MLS / REDI Data
Rent concessions	N/A	None Known	None Known	None Known
Description of property-units, design, appeal, age, vacancies, and conditions	No. Units 2 No. Vac. 0 Yr. Blt.: +/- 1971 Location/Avg Quality/Avg Condition/Avg	#Units 2 No.Vac. 0 Yr.Blt: 1927 Location/Average Quality/Average Condition/Average	#Units 2 No.Vac. 0 Yr.Blt: 1927 Location/Average Quality/Average Condition/Average	#Units 2 No.Vac. 0 Yr.Blt: 1933 Location/Average Quality/Average Condition/Average

	Rm. Count Tot Br Bath	Size Sq. Ft.	Total Monthly Rent	Rm. Count Tot Br Bath	Size Sq. Ft.	Total Monthly Rent	Rm. Count Tot Br Bath	Size Sq. Ft.	Total Monthly Rent	Rm. Count Tot Br Bath	Size Sq. Ft.	Total Monthly Rent
Individual unit breakdown	6 3 2	880		4 1 1	700	$ 550	5 2 1	900	$ Owner	5 2 1	900	$ Owner
	6 3 2	880		6 3 1	1,000	725	6 3 1	1,000	775	4 2 1	850	Family

Utilities, furniture and amenities included in rent	N/A	Heat & Hot W includ in the rent payment	Heat & Hot W includ in the rent payment	Heat & Hot W includ in the rent payment
Functional utility, basement, heating/cooling, project amenities, etc.	Functional/Avg Extra apartmnt FH Water/None	Functional/Avg Extra apartment Hot Water/None	Functional/Average Extra apartment Steam heat/None	Functional/Average Extra apartment Steam heat/None

Reconciliation of rental data and support for estimated market rents for the individual subject units (including the adjustments used, the adequacy of comparables, rental concessions, etc.)

All rentals are located in the subject neighborhood. Quality and condition of all of the rentals are reprted to be similar to the subject. All monthly rent figures are based on comparable market rent.

Subject's rent schedule

The rent schedule reconciles the applicable indicated monthly market rents to the appropriate subject unit, and provides the estimated rents for the subject property. The appraiser must review the rent characteristics of the comparable sales to determine whether estimated rents should reflect actual or market rents. For example, if actual rents were available on the sales comparables and used to derive the gross rent multiplier (GRM), actual rents for the subject should be used. If market rents were used to construct the comparables' rents and derive the GRM, market rents should be used. The total gross estimated rent must represent rent characteristics consistent with the sales comparable data used to derive the GRM. The total gross estimated rent is not adjusted for vacancy.

Unit	Lease Date Begin	End	No. Units Vacant	ACTUAL RENTS Per Unit Unfurnished	Furnished	Total Rents	ESTIMATED RENTS Per Unit Unfurnished	Furnished	Total Rents
N/A	No lease		0	$ 600	$	$ 0	$	$	$ 0
1	No lease		0	875		875			0
1	No lease		0	900		900			0
						0			
2			0			$ 1,775			$ 0

Other monthly income (itemize) N/A $

Vacancy: Actual last yr U/K % Previous year U/K % Estimated: 3 % $ 640 Annually   TOTAL GROSS ESTIMATED RENT $ 1,720

Utilities included in estimated rents: [ ] Electric [X] Water [X] Sewer [X] Gas [ ] Oil [X] Trash collection [X] Hot Water and Heat

Comments on the rent schedule, actual rents, estimated rents (especially regarding differences between actual and estimated rents), utilities, etc.: The rent schedule is based on the appraiser's research and analysis of market rent in the subject area. Data sources include: REDI Data, Multiple Listing Service, and local real estate offices. Utilities included in the projections are considered typical. The total gross estimated rent is adjusted for vacancy.

SUBJECT PHOTOGRAPH ADDENDUM

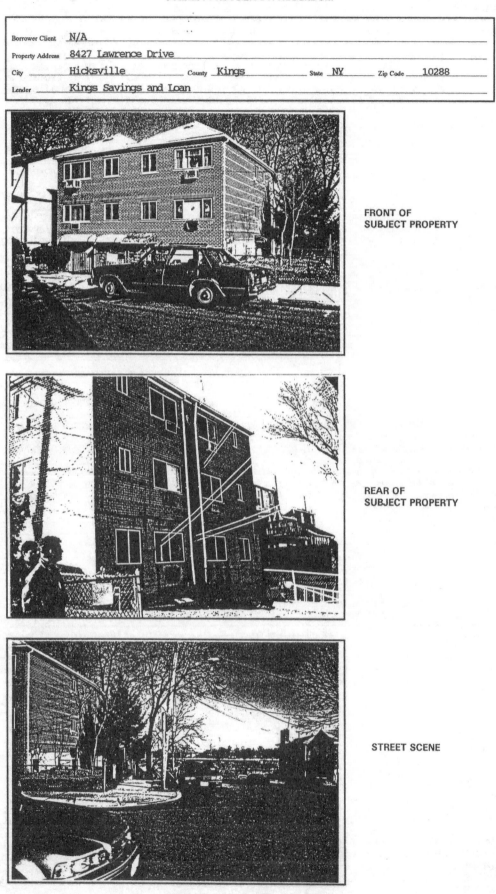

Borrower Client   N/A

Property Address   8427 Lawrence Drive

City   Hicksville   County   Kings   State   NY   Zip Code   10288

Lender   Kings Savings and Loan

FRONT OF
SUBJECT PROPERTY

REAR OF
SUBJECT PROPERTY

STREET SCENE

COMPARABLES PHOTOGRAPH ADDENDUM

Borrower Client __N/A__

Property Address __8427 Lawrence Drive__

City __Hicksville__ County __Kings__ State __NY__ Zip Code __10288__

Lender __Kings Savings and Loan__

COMPARABLE SALE # 1

943 Porch Avenue
Date of Sale: 02/19/92
Sale Price : 230,000
Sq. Ft. : 2,400
$ / Sq. Ft. : 95.83

COMPARABLE SALE # 2

3387 Victory Lane
Date of Sale: 10/19/92
Sale Price : 232,000
Sq. Ft. : 2,000
$ / Sq. Ft. : 116

COMPARABLE SALE # 3

23 Lucastone Drive
Date of Sale: 07/30/92
Sale Price : 220,000
Sq. Ft. : 2,500
$ / Sq. Ft. : 88

Location Map

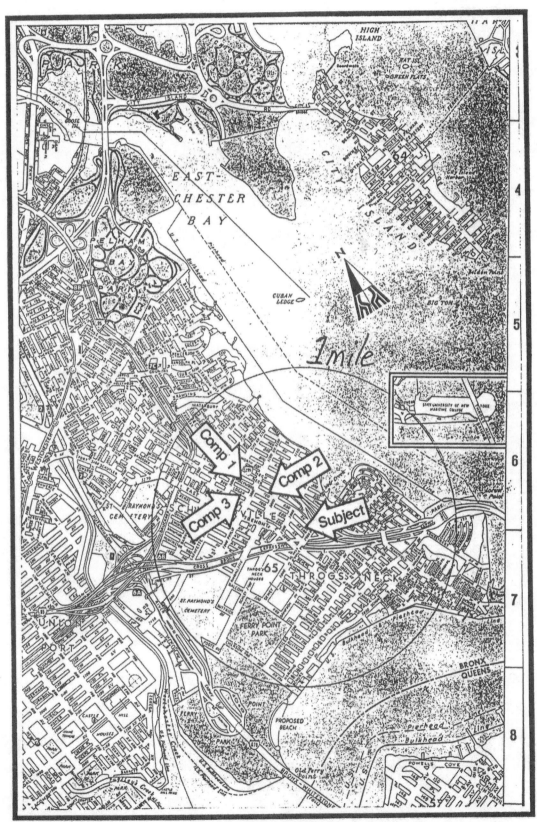

Borrower Name : N/A   File No. A0451H92

DEFINITION OF MARKET VALUE :   The most probable price which a property should bring in a competitive and open market under all conditions requisite to a fair sale, the buyer and seller, each acting prudently, knowledgeably and assuming the price is not affected by undue stimulus. Implicit in this definition is the consummation of a sale as of a specified date and the passing of title from seller to buyer under conditions whereby: (1) buyer and seller are typically motivated; (2) both parties are well informed or well advised, and each acting in what he considers his own best interest; (3) a reasonable time is allowed for exposure in the open market; (4) payment is made in terms of cash in U.S. dollars or in terms of financial arrangements comparable thereto; and (5) the price represents the normal consideration for the property sold unaffected by special or creative financing or sales concessions* granted by anyone associated with the sale.

*Adjustments to the comparables must be made for special or creative financing or sales concessions. No adjustments are necessary for those costs which are normally paid by sellers as a result of tradition or law in a market area; these costs are readily identifiable since the seller pays these costs in virtually all sales transactions. Special or creative financing adjustments can be made to the comparable property by comparisons to financing terms offered by a third party institutional lender that is not already involved in the property or transaction. Any adjustment should not be calculated on a mechanical dollar for dollar cost of the financing or concession but the dollar amount of any adjustment should approximate the market's reaction to the financing or concessions based on the appraiser's judgment.

CERTIFICATION AND STATEMENT OF LIMITING CONDITIONS

CERTIFICATION: The Appraiser certifies and agrees that:

1. The Appraiser has no present or contemplated future interest in the property appraised; and neither the employment to make the appraisal, nor the compensation for it, is contingent upon the appraised value of the property.

2. The Appraiser has no personal interest in or bias with respect to the subject matter of the appraisal report of the participants to the sale. The "Estimate of Market Value" in the appraisal report is not based in whole or in part upon the race, color, or national origin of the prospective owners for occupants of the property appraised, or upon the race, color or national origin of the present owners or occupants of the properties in the vicinity of the property appraised.

3. The appraiser has personally inspected the property, both inside and out, and has made an exterior inspection of all comparable sales listed in the report. To the best of the Appraiser's knowledge and belief, all statements and information in this report are true and correct, and the Appraiser has not knowingly withheld any significant information.

4. All contingent and limiting conditions are contained herein (imposed by the terms of the assignment or by the undersigned affecting the analyses, opinions, and conclusions contained in the report).

5. This appraisal report has been made in conformity with and is subject to the to the requirements of the Code of Professional Ethics and Standards of Professional Conduct of the appraisal organizations with which the Appraiser is affiliated.

6. All conclusions and opinions concerning the real estate that are set forth in the appraisal report were prepared by the Appraiser whose signature appears on the appraisal report, unless indicated as "Review Appraiser." No change of any item in the appraisal report shall be made by anyone other than the Appraiser, and the Appraiser shall have no responsibility for any such unauthorized change.

CONTINGENT AND LIMITING CONDITIONS: The certification of the Appraiser appearing in the appraisal report is subject to the following conditions and to such other specific and limiting conditions as are set forth by the Appraiser in the report.

1. The Appraiser assumes no responsibility for matters of a legal nature affecting the property appraised or the title thereto, nor does the Appraiser render any opinion as to the title, which is assumed to be good and marketable. The property is appraised as though under responsible ownership.

2. Any sketch in the report may show approximate dimensions and is included to assist the reader in visualizing the property. The Appraiser has made no survey of the property.

3. The Appraiser is not required to give testimony or appear in court because of having made the appraisal with reference to the property in question, unless arrangements have been previously made therefor.

4. Any distribution of the valuation in the report between land and improvements applies only under the existing program or utilization. The separate valuations for land and building must not be used in conjunction with any other appraisal and are invalid if so used.

5. The Appraiser assumes that there are no hidden or unapparent conditions of the property, subsoil, or structures, which would render it more or less valuable. The Appraiser assumes no responsibility for such conditions, or for engineering which might be required to discover such factors.

6. Information, estimates, and opinions furnished to the Appraiser, and contained in the report, were obtained from sources considered reliable and believed to be true and correct. However, no responsibility for accuracy of such items furnished the Appraiser can be assumed by the Appraiser.

7. Disclosure of the contents of the appraisal report is governed by the Bylaws and Regulations of the professional appraisal organizations with which the Appraiser is affiliated.

8. Neither all, nor any part of the content of the report, or copy thereof (including conclusions as to the property value, the identity of the Appraiser, professional designations, reference to any professional appraisal organizations, or the firm with which the Appraiser is connected), shall be used for any purposes by anyone but the client specified in the report , the borrower if appraisal fee paid by same, the mortgagee or its successors and assigns, mortgage insurers, consultants, professional appraisal organizations, any state or federally approved financial institution, any department, agency, or instrumentality of the United States or any state or the District of Columbia, without the previous written consent of the Appraiser; nor shall it be conveyed by anyone to the public through advertising, public relations, news, sales, or other media, without the written consent and approval of the Appraiser.

9. On all appraisals, subject to satisfactory completion, repairs, or alterations, the appraisal report and value conclusion are contingent upon completion of the improvements in a workmanship like manner.

Date December 27, 1992   Signature _____

                                           Harry Richmond

Freddie Mac   Fannie Mae
Form 439 JUL 86   Form 1004B Jul 86

The style/design of
this house is:

Split Level

The style/design of
this house is:

Ranch

The style/design of
this house is:

Colonial

The style/design of
this house is:

English Tudor

The style/design of
this house is:

Contemporary

The style/design of
this house is:

BIG!!

Above: This is what you'll see on most appraisal assignments -
a home filled with furniture and personal items.

Below: *So why did I include two photos of an empty home?*
Because this is how you have to picture the interior of a house,
condo or building in your mind when doing your appraisals.
Remember, you're appraising the **building** - not the appeal
and value of the furniture and personal items!

A private tennis court can increase the market value and appeal of a house.

You have to take this into account when writing up your appraisal reports. Remember to make adjustments for this when evaluating the sales comparables in your appraisals.

This is a very appealing finished basement area. This adds usable space for the occupants of a home. Finished basements can increase the market value of a house or condo.

I encountered this on one of the foreclosure appraisals and inspections I did for a bank. The prior owner had spent his money on building an indoor basketball court, indoor swimming pool, sauna and Jacuzzi room, along with some other luxurious and expensive additions to the house and site. The problem was, that after he spent all this money he couldn't pay his mortgage payments and the bank had to foreclose on the property! I guess you could say that it wasn't "money well spent" *(or should I say it was "money spent down the well")*.

Can you see what I outlined in this photo? The picture is dark because it was overcast on the day of the appraisal so you might not be able to see the image clearly. It's a metal statue of a very large eagle standing on a globe with it's wings spread out wide (side view). The frontal view photo of this statue is below. This is one of the eagle statues from Grand Central Station in New York City. I don't know how the homeowner of the property got a hold of this statue, but I'm sure you won't find many of these during your appraisals! This thing was about 20 feet high.

No, it's not a junkyard or auto salvage site. It's actually the yard of a home I had to appraise and inspect for a client. I doubt you'll ever encounter a situation like this one. However, if you do just remember to make adjustments in your report based upon how all of this junk would affect the purchase price offered by potential buyers of this property. *(You better make it a BIG negative adjustment!)*

Jack and Jill went up the hill, to fetch a pail of water,

But because the homeowner didn't properly seal up the well,

Jack fell down and broke his crown, and Jill came tumbling after!

So you see what happens when you don't take the advice in my *Home Inspection From A to Z* book? Jack and Jill ended up getting hurt because of the negligence of the property owner.
(I wonder if Jack and Jill got an "ambulance chaser" attorney to file a lawsuit against the homeowner?)

All unused wells must be properly sealed for safety. This well has a sealed cover over it.

Sample Business Card, Brochures, Stationery, & Price Quote Card

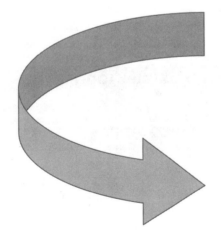

Sample Business Stationery

Sample Business Card

Sample Envelope

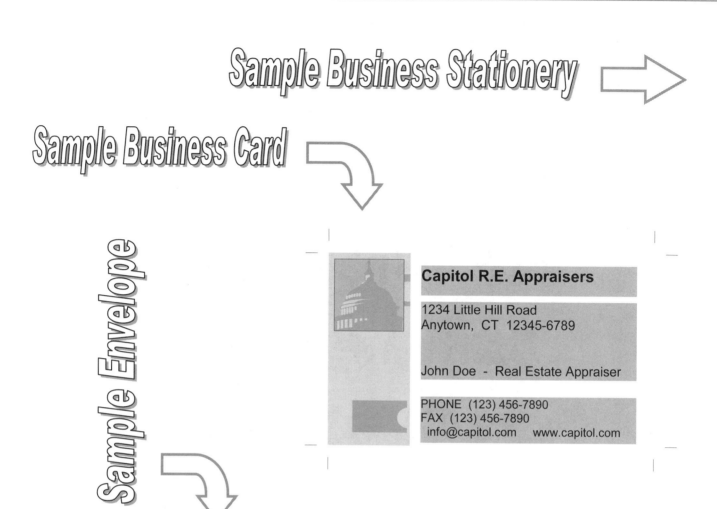

Capitol R.E. Appraisers

1234 Little Hill Road
Anytown, CT 12345-6789

John Doe - Real Estate Appraiser

PHONE (123) 456-7890
FAX (123) 456-7890
info@capitol.com   www.capitol.com

Capitol Real Estate Appraisers
John Doe
1234 Little Hill Road
Anytown, CT 12345-6789

Capitol Real Estate Appraisers

John Doe
1234 Little Hill Road
Anytown, CT 12345-6789

PHONE (123) 456-7890   FAX (123) 456-7890
Email: info@capitol.com   Web: www.capitol.com

Capitol Real Estate Appraisers

1234 Little Hill Road
Anytown, CT 12345

Phone (123) 456-7890
Fax (123) 456-7890
Emai: info@capitol.com
Web: www.capitol.com

Capitol Real Estate Appraisers
1234 Little Hill Road
Anytown, CT 12345-6789

Recipient Name
Address Line 1
Address Line 2
Address Line 3

Our Real Estate Appraisals Include:

◇ Subject Property Analysis for overall condition and appeal

◇ Appraisal Depreciation Aspects

◇ Land and Site Valuation

◇ Highest and Best Use Analysis

◇ Town Hall Records Search

◇ Neighborhood Evaluation

◇ Numerous Comparable Sales evaluated to estimate market value of the property

Price Quote Card

Report Number		Date of Inspection/Appraisal
Bldg. Address	Zip	Day of Week & Time
Inspector/Appraiser	Present Owner	Phone

Client	Comments, Directions, etc.
Address	
Zip	
Home Phone	
Work Phone	
Attorney	
Address	
Zip	
R.E. Agent	
	(c) 1992 Guy Cozzi

Price Quote Card

Report Number		Date of Inspection/Appraisal
Bldg. Address	Zip	Day of Week & Time
Inspector/Appraiser	Present Owner	Phone

Client	Comments, Directions, etc.
Address	
Zip	
Home Phone	
Work Phone	
Attorney	
Address	
Zip	
R.E. Agent	
	(c) 1992 Guy Cozzi

Inspection   Appraisal

Item		
Date Price Quoted		
How You Heard of Us		
Type of Property	Condo	1 Family
Square Footage		
Bedrooms / Bathrooms / Garage		
Reported Age of Bldg.		
Overall Condition	Very Good Good	Average Fair Poor
Basement / Crawl Space		
Air Conditioning		
Septic System Test		
Well System Test		
Water Lab Test		
Termite Inspection		
Radon Test		
Location Factor		
Selling Price		
TOTAL FEE $		

Inspection   Appraisal

Item		
Date Price Quoted		
How You Heard of Us		
Type of Property	Condo	1 Family
Square Footage		
Bedrooms / Bathrooms / Garage		
Reported Age of Bldg.		
Overall Condition	Very Good Good	Average Fair Poor
Basement / Crawl Space		
Air Conditioning		
Septic System Test		
Well System Test		
Water Lab Test		
Termite Inspection		
Radon Test		
Location Factor		
Selling Price		
TOTAL FEE $		

Email nemmar@hotmail.com for prices

Narrative Report Generator and *On-Site Checklist*

Includes: CD-Rom with the *best* Narrative Report Generator and On-Site Checklist on the market! These documents will enable you to *easily* do 30 page narrative, professional home inspection reports to send to your clients. The On-Site Checklist will assist you at the inspection site to be sure that you properly evaluate the subject property. Designed to walk you through the entire inspection process with very detailed instructions on how to properly evaluate the condition and status of **all** aspects of a home in a fool-proof, step-by-step system. The most thorough and professional Report Generator in the business!

Home Buyer's Survival Kit

Includes: One video tape plus one audio cassette tape which are over 2 hours long. The video and audio tapes will assist you with the biggest investment of your life - your own home! Learn how to determine the true market value and condition of any home. Whether you are buying selling or renovating a home, identifying the hidden problem conditions can save you thousands of dollars! As an added bonus, you get the *Video Companion Guide* plus a sample real estate appraisal report to help you evaluate a house.

Complete Real Estate Appraising From A to Z Kit

Includes the in-depth book + four audio CD's + two video tapes: Textbook Manual that tells you the truth and covers *every* aspect of the Real Estate Appraisal Business from A to Z. *"The **real facts** the other appraisal books don't tell you!"* Starter Kit with a large assortment of appraisal supplies. This will get you up and running with your new appraisal business. The appraisal supplies you receive include: Single family URAR forms, a variety of appraisal photo forms, sketch addendum forms, certification and limiting condition forms, and a variety of property stencils.

Complete Home Inspection Business From A to Z Kit

Includes the in-depth book + four audio CD's + two video tapes + inspection report and checklist: Textbook Manual that tells you the truth and covers *every* aspect of the Home Inspection Business from A to Z. *"The **real facts** the other home inspection books don't tell you!"* Report Writing Document (condensed version) that enables you to *easily* do narrative, professional inspection reports to send to your clients. On-Site Checklist booklet (condensed version) to assist you at the inspection site to be sure that you properly evaluate the subject property.

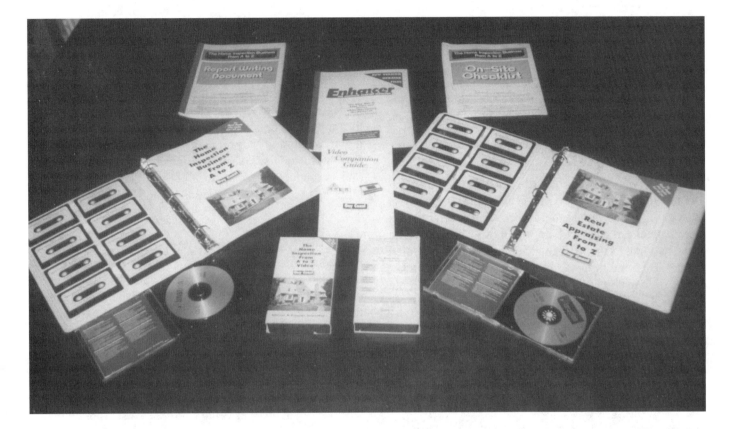

**Just some of our books, video and audio
tapes, CD's, and much more!
Email nemmar@hotmail.com for prices
Visit us at www.nemmar.com**

The Cost Approach

The Cost Approach

The *Cost Approach* uses the reproduction cost to estimate the market value of the subject property. This approach takes into account the cost to build an identical house to the subject property. The cost of the identical house is determined at today's prices, minus the three forms of depreciation, *(physical, functional and external)*. I will describe the three forms of depreciation a little later. The result of the cost analysis at today's prices minus the depreciation will give you the depreciated value of the building. The site value with its improvements is then added to the depreciated value of the building to get the final estimated market value of the subject property. Please review the sample appraisals in this book to view examples of the Cost Approach for an actual written appraisal report.

The Cost Approach is based on the assumption that a typically informed buyer would not pay more money for the subject property then it would cost him

> The Cost Approach is based on the assumption that a typically informed buyer would not pay more for the subject property then it would cost him to build a similar property.

to build a similar property. The similar property being considered would have the same utility and depreciation as the subject property. Meaning, that if a house was selling for $215,000 and the typical buyer could have a similar house built for about $190,000, then the buyer would probably build a similar house. The buyer might want to build a similar house, rather than pay more money for the existing subject property. Now you have to remember that the cost of the similar house the buyer would be pricing to have built for himself, must take into account all of the three forms of depreciation that the subject property currently has.

The Cost Approach uses the *Replacement Cost* and the *Reproduction Cost*. The Replacement Cost estimates the cost of replacing the **utility** of the subject property. This takes into account the three types of depreciation of the subject property: physical,

functional and external. The Reproduction Cost is the cost to **reproduce** the subject property by building it with all new construction, from the ground up. The construction will be in the identical style, square footage, room layouts, construction materials, etc. as the subject property. The Reproduction Cost is the dollar amount of reproducing the building with it's current materials, (plaster, stone, sheetrock, etc.). In this reproduction cost, it also includes all of the building's current depreciation, (physical, functional and external).

Basically, the Cost Approach takes the Reproduction Cost New of the building, minus the depreciated items, plus the site value. The result is used as an estimate of current market value. There are four methods used to estimate the market value by the Cost Approach.

1   Quantity Survey Method - *A method of cost estimation that replicates the contractor's original procedure in detail.* This is the most detailed way to estimate market value using the Cost Approach.

2   Unit In Place Method - *A method of cost estimation that includes materials and labor in the unit cost of component sections of the structure "in place."*

3   Trade Breakdown or Segregated Cost Method - *A method of cost estimation that breaks the major functional parts of the structure into an installed unit cost.* It's the breakdown to cost out the structure as though you were building it new.

4   Comparable Unit Method - *A method of cost estimation that lumps together all components of the structure and converts the lump sum amount to a unit basis (e.g., per square ft, per cubic foot).* This is the method that is most often used to fill out the form appraisal reports. Cost estimate books are used to assist the appraiser. Unfortunately, it's also the least accurate method to use for the Cost Approach to estimate market value.

The cost estimate that you arrive at in the Cost Approach <u>does not</u> have to equal the value of the property. This means that the estimate of value in the

> *The Cost Approach also DOES NOT have to be the highest estimate of value for all three approaches to value.*

Direct Sales Comparison or Income Approaches, doesn't have to equal the value you estimate in the Cost Approach. The Cost Approach also ***DOES NOT*** have to be the highest estimate of value for all three approaches to value, (Direct Sales, Income and Cost Approaches). I'll elaborate on that again so you don't forget it. Don't use the assumption that the Cost Approach should always be the highest value for the subject property. This is an old myth that some appraisers are led to believe is always true. Because of

> *Many appraisers will try to tell you that the Cost Approach has to be the highest estimated value in a report. Baloney!!*

this myth, all of their appraisal reports intentionally show the Cost Approach as the highest estimate of value. You have to keep an open mind about this. Many appraisers, and some third parties, will try to tell you that the Cost Approach has to be the highest estimated value in a report. Baloney!! Anyone who tells you that doesn't know what they're talking about.

It's true that often the Cost Approach will be the highest estimate of value. However, let's say you're appraising a house and you do the cost analysis of the construction materials to duplicate the site and improvements. After you do this cost analysis, you find that it costs less money to build the subject property than it's estimated value using the Direct Sales Comparison Approach. The difference between the <u>cost</u> of the site and improvements and the <u>value</u> of the site and improvements, could be due to the builders profit! This has to be figured into the calculations of the cost to reproduce the property. The Cost Approach doesn't have to always be higher than the other approaches to value. The reason for this is: why would someone go through all the problems and risks of building a house just to have a small profit, or no profit at all. The builder will want to make a profit on the deal for all of his time and effort. If the <u>cost</u> of the site and improvements is greater than the <u>value</u> of the site and improvements, then the builder will lose money on the deal! How long could you stay in business if you lost money on every house you built? Not very long. If you want, you can include a figure in your cost analysis amounts to account for the builder's profit.

The Cost Approach is only really effective when used for relatively new buildings that are the Highest and Best Use of the site. This approach isn't very effective for older houses. It's not effective due to the margin for error with an older house in estimating the three types of depreciation. Also, with older houses there is a large margin for error in estimating the cost of using the same construction materials today. The Cost Approach is used more effectively when there are no good comparable properties available to assist the appraiser. A reason for a lack of sales could be due to unique or unusual improvements on the subject site.

For buildings in crowded urban areas there are probably very few vacant land sales to analyze and so the Cost Approach isn't very effective. If you have no vacant land sales, then you have to estimate the land value by using a residual technique. This simply means that you have to take sales and estimate the cost of only constructing the building. After that, you must take out for any depreciation that affected the sale. What you are left with is a *residual* value for the vacant land which is an estimate of the land value.

There are three types of residuals used for appraisal purposes:

1 Land
2 Building
3 Property

Land doesn't depreciate from wear and tear over the years. It can lose or gain value, but it doesn't depreciate from a tax deduction standpoint. You can use the residual values to help you in estimating the depreciation of a site or the improvements. For example, let's say you were doing the Cost Approach for a single family appraisal. We'll assume that you were trying to estimate the value of the lot for a sales

> *The Cost Approach is only really effective when used for relatively new buildings that are the Highest and Best Use of the site. This approach isn't very effective for older houses.*

comparable. However, you can't find any vacant land sales because the area is too built-up and/or there are no recent vacant lot sales to use as comparables. You could estimate the Reproduction Cost New of the building, and then subtract the depreciation amount. Then take this figure, plus the site improvements, and subtract it from the value of the property. You're left with an estimated value of the vacant lot.

You can also use the *Assessed Value Ratio* for the area to help you figure out the vacant land value. Do this if there are no vacant land sales in the subject neighborhood. I'll talk more about the Assessed Value Ratio in the **Tax Assessments** section of the book. There are various other techniques you can use. However, they're much more involved and you would be better off learning them while taking the state appraisal courses. They're too involved to teach properly outside a classroom atmosphere.

The Basics Of Appraisal Depreciation

There are three types of depreciation that you have to consider for an appraisal report. These depreciation items are also evaluated for the Cost Approach. (*Obsolescence* is also used to describe *Depreciation*). This section covers some definitions and explanations that you will need to know for the depreciation and Cost Approach examples later in this book:

1   **Physical Depreciation**
2   **Functional Depreciation**
3   **External Depreciation**

Let's say you want to repair, change, update, and/or add something to a house. We'll assume that the repairs will have a neutral or positive impact on the market value of the house. Well if this were the case, then from an appraisal standpoint you should make the repairs and/or additions to the house. To determine if something is a curable item, simply ask yourself whether it's worth it to repair the problem. If the repair costs equal or exceed the value that the repaired item will add to the property, then you should go ahead and repair the item and/or make the changes. In order to make it a **curable** problem, you should at least break even with the money you spend to repair the problem. The break-even point we're referring to, is in relation to what the increased value of the property will be when you're finished.

To determine if something is an incurable item, simply use the same logic. Ask yourself whether or not it's worth it to repair the problem. From an appraisal standpoint, if the repair costs do not equal or exceed the value that the repaired item will add to the property, then you should not repair the item and/or make the change. It's an **incurable** problem if you will not at least break even with the money you spend to repair the problem. The break-even point is in relation to what the increased value of the property will be when you're finished with the repairs.

Physical Depreciation:
1.   **Physical Curable** - refers to physical items that are worth paying the expense to repair the problem because of the neutral or positive impact on market value it will have for the subject property.

2.   **Physical Incurable** - refers to physical items that are not worth paying the expense to repair the problem because they will not have a neutral or positive market value impact for the subject property.

3.   **Physical Short-Lived Items** - refers to physical items and operating systems of a house that have normal depreciation and wear and tear on them over time. Such items can be the roof, heating system, air-conditioning system, appliances, etc.

4.   **Physical Long-Lived Items** - refers to the basic structure of the building, such as, the foundation, the walls, etc.

Functional Depreciation:
1.   **Functional Curable** - refers to functional items that are worth paying the expense to repair and/or change the problem because of the neutral or positive impact on market value it will have for the property.

2.   **Functional Incurable** - refers to functional items that are not worth paying the expense to repair and/or change the problem because they will not have a neutral or positive impact on market value for the subject property.

External Depreciation:
1.   **External Incurable** - refers to external items that negatively influence the market value of the subject property. External items are very rarely curable because resolving the problem is out of the hands of the owner of the subject property. Some examples of external depreciation items are: locational problems with the area; environmental problems; economic problems in the economy and the local market; etc.

I'll briefly define and give you examples of some aspects for estimating depreciation from an appraisal standpoint: Physical and Functional depreciation in the Cost Approach should be the same, or compatible, with the like adjustments that you make in the Direct Sales Comparison Approach. This means that, let's say you make an adjustment in the Direct Sales Comparison Approach for a physical or functional depreciation item. Then you should make an adjustment that's equal to or accurately reflects, the same depreciation adjustment for this item which you make in the Cost Approach. For example, let's say you determine that an adjustment of $3,250 is needed in the Cost Approach to account for a large wood deck on the house. If this were the case, then you would have to make the same or a compatible adjustment in the Direct Sales Comparison Approach to accurately reflect the wood deck. You can't make adjustments in each approach that contradict one another. Remember that you have to be consistent throughout the entire appraisal report!

An example of *Functional Obsolescence* is a property that has been over-improved **(obsolescence is the same thing as saying depreciation).** An *over-improvement* occurs when a homeowner makes an improvement or change to a property that costs more money than the increased value it brings to the property (see the *functional incurable depreciation* definition).

An example of *External Obsolescence* is a property that is located next to a highway or on a very busy street. External Obsolescence items have to be allocated proportionately to the land and the building for depreciation purposes. For example, let's say a house is located on a busy street and this has a negative impact on market value. Well even if the house was knocked down, the vacant lot would still be negatively affected by the busy street. That's why you have to figure out the dollar or percentage amount of the negative impact that is allocated separately to the land and to the building. External, location and economic obsolescence are all synonyms and they're measured in the neighborhood.

Economic Obsolescence *(External)* depreciation refers to: high interest rates, high labor costs, high taxes, drop in the employment in the base industry, etc. You can use economic obsolescence for an external depreciation adjustment in the Cost Approach, if there's a poor real estate market in the area. You must apply the percentage to the building and the percentage to the site, as separate amounts for economic obsolescence.

Accrued Depreciation and *Diminished Utility* are interchangeable because they essentially are the same. The appraisal course definition for Accrued Depreciation *(diminished utility)* is:

"Total depreciation from all sources, measured as the difference between reproduction cost new of the improvements and the present worth of those improvements as of the date of the appraisal."

Total or *Remaining Economic Life* refers to how long the improvements (the house itself) will add value to the land. Meaning, that for how many more years do you feel that the property will be worth more with the existing house still standing. As opposed to, knocking down the house to build a new one or just knocking down the house and leaving the land vacant.

Physical Age refers to how old the improvements (the house) actually are. In simple terms, what is the actual age of the house listed at town hall in the public record. *(Don't just use the age the owner tells you or what is stated in the real estate listing. Often they're wrong, so use the public record).*

Effective Age refers to how old the improvements (the house) appear to be. This means that if you didn't know what the actual age of the house was, then when would you estimate the house last had any major repairs and upgrading. Effective Age is often different from the actual age of the house. The cause of this difference is due to the normal maintenance and upgrading done over the years, or the lack of it not being done over the years. For example, let's say you're appraising a house that's 85 years old. Chances are very good that the house has gone through several major upgradings over the years by different owners to keep up with the changing times. The Effective Age you estimate would be the last time you felt that the house has had some significant repairs and upgrading done to it. Pay particular attention to the kitchens, bathrooms, windows and doors. These areas really can show the age of a house that is outdated due to the lack of any significant upgrading over the years.

Cost Approach
Example #1

Let's use a depreciation example to walk you through the Cost Approach process. We'll assume the following figures were obtained during our appraisal field work and inspection of the subject property.

◊   Actual Age = 10 years
◊   Effective Age = 5 years
◊   Total Economic Life = 50 years
◊   Reproduction Cost New = $75,000

Physical Curable:
◊   Painting needed = $750
◊   Gutters needed = $450
◊ $750 + $450 = $1,200 is the total Physical Curable depreciation

Short Lived Items:

	Cost	Effect-ive Age	Useful Life	% of Deprec	$ of Deprec
Roof	$2,000	10	20	50	$1,000
Heat System	1,500	10	25	40	600
Carpets	600	2	6	33	200
Kitch. Appl.	1,800	10	15	67	1,206

Total Cost of Items:	**$5,900**		Actual Depre-ciation Cost:	**$3,006**

There's a point to remember when estimating the Total Physical depreciation amount for the structure. That is, to use the **Actual Depreciation Cost,** and not the total cost new of the items, as your *Short Lived Items* depreciation amount. This means that the Short Lived Items are still in operating order but they have aged and won't last as long as a similar new item. For example, the roof is 10 years old but it has a life expectancy of 20 years. This gives the roof another 10 years before it will need to be replaced. If it costs $2,000 to install a new roof and it's 50% depreciated now, then the current depreciated dollar amount value of the roof is $1,000. It's similar to buying a used car. A used car may still be operating properly but you wouldn't buy it for the same price you could get a new one for, would you?

The percentage of depreciation for the value of the *Long Lived items* (the structure) is estimated by dividing the *Effective Age* by the *Total Economic Life* of the subject property. This is also referred to as the

Age/Life Method for estimating the physical depreciation of a building. The Total Economic Life is also called the Remaining Economic Life. Therefore, in our example it would be:

Effective Age/Total Economic Life = % of Depreciation

$$5/50 = .10 \quad or \quad 10\%$$

We will use the 10% depreciation figure to estimate the depreciation dollar amount for the Long Lived Items. But first we must subtract the Physical and Short Lived Items from the Reproduction Cost New, before estimating the depreciation for the Long Lived Items. We do this by taking the depreciation cost of the Physical Curable depreciation items, and then adding this amount to the total cost *new* of the Short Lived Items. We then subtract this amount from the Reproduction Cost New. In our example we end up with the following formula.

$$\$75,000 - (\$1,200 + \$5,900) = \$67,900$$

Therefore, $67,900 is the amount left to be depreciated by the percentage amount we derived earlier. This is needed to estimate the depreciation dollar amount for the Long Lived Items.

$$\$67,900 \times .10 = \$6,790$$

Therefore, we are left with the following dollar amounts of depreciation:

Physical	=	$1,200
Short Lived Items	=	$3,006
Long Lived Items	=	$6,790

We add these to get our Total Physical Depreciation for the building.

$$\$1,200 + \$3,006 + \$6,790 = \$10,996$$

You **have to** remember, that you must subtract the Physical Curable depreciation and the *total cost new* of the Short Lived Items, from the Reproduction Cost New before estimating the depreciation for the Long Lived Items. The reason for this is that if you don't, you'll be "double dipping" when you estimate your depreciation amounts. Meaning that the depreciation amount that you subtract for the Long Lived Items, will be incorrectly increased by the inclusion of the depreciation amounts for the Physical Curable and

Short Lived Items. You would then be taking out more depreciation then you should be. We'll use our example to show you the **incorrect** way of doing this so you can see what I mean by "double dipping."

$$\$75,000 \times .10 = \$7,500$$

The increase would be $7,500 - $6,790 = $710. This would incorrectly increase the amount of Total Physical Depreciation for the subject property by $710.

Now we'll take an example of *Functional Obsolescence*. Remember that *obsolescence* is the same as saying depreciation. Let's say that the vast majority of houses in the area that are similar to the subject property have central air-conditioning. Therefore, we can conclude that the typical buyer would expect the house to have central A/C. If it didn't, then the buyer would pay a little bit less for the house to compensate for the air-conditioning not being installed. This is considered a Functional Depreciated item, as opposed to a Physical Depreciated item. The reason for that is the central air-conditioning <u>is not</u> installed in the house, so there's no physical depreciation on it to account for.

We have to first estimate what the cost would be to install a central air-conditioning system "as of" the date of the appraisal. Let's say we asked a local A/C contractor, or checked the published cost manuals, and get an estimate. We'll assume that the estimate is $1,750 to correct the problem by installing the central air-conditioning. We then must estimate what it would have cost to install the central air-conditioning at the time the house was built. Our research tells us that during construction of the property it would have cost $1,500 to install the central air-conditioning.

We can now conclude the *Accrued Functional Depreciation* for the subject property. We do this by subtracting the two figures.

$$\$1,750 - \$1,500 = \$250$$

From our research we have found that a comparable house to the subject property would sell for an additional $2,800 if central air-conditioning was installed. We have already estimated that it would cost $1,750 to install. Therefore, the central air-conditioning is a *Functional Curable Item* because the value added to the subject property by installing it, is equal to or greater than the cost of installing the A/C.

Now we'll take an example of *Locational Obsolescence*. This is also called External or Economic Obsolescence. Let's say, there's a gas station next to the subject property. From our knowledge of the area, we conclude that the typical buyer would pay less for the house to compensate for the location next to a gas station. The typical buyer would rather have a house with only other residential properties around it and not any commercial properties in view.

You **have to** apply any Locational Obsolescence values *separately* to the building and the land of the subject property. This is because the land is not a depreciable item. However, site improvements do have depreciated values, such as, driveways, landscaping, etc. The land will be affected by a Locational Obsolescence and you have to take that into account in your site value estimate.

In order to estimate the total Locational Obsolescence depreciation amount, we need to make some evaluations. We must first decide what percentage of the value of the subject property is allocated to land, and what percentage is allocated to the building. This is called the *Land Value to Building Value Ratio*. This technique is also used for tax purposes. The technique is used to figure out the depreciation amount on your tax returns for real estate. Let's say our research of the area has shown that typically the estimate of value is 20% allocated to the land and 80% allocated to the building. Another way of saying this is that the *Land Value to Building Value Ratio* is 1:4. Meaning the ratio is one part land plus four parts building. This tells us that 1/5 (or 20%) of the value is allocated to the land.

From our research, we have found that a comparable house to the subject property would sell for an additional $4,200 if it was not located next to the gas station. We simply multiply this figure by the percentage of value allocated to the building, to get our Locational Obsolescence amount.

$$\$4,200 \times .80 = \$3,360$$

Now we will add up all of the three depreciation amounts we have estimated. We do this to obtain the depreciated value of the Reproduction Cost New of the subject property.

Total Physical Depreciation = $10,996
Total Functional Depreciation = $250
Total Locational Depreciation = $3,360

We add these to get our *Total Depreciation* for the building.

$$\$10,996 + \$250 + \$3,360 = \$14,606$$

Now we simply subtract the total depreciation amount from the Reproduction Cost New.

$$\$75,000 - \$14,606 = \$60,394$$

Therefore, the *depreciated value* of the Reproduction Cost New of the subject property is estimated to be **$60,394**.

Cost Approach Example #2

I know how much you liked the first one, so let's try another depreciation example to walk you through the Cost Approach process again! I'll make this one a little more narrative so you think I'm telling you a bedtime story, but don't fall asleep on me. Let's say, you've been hired to appraise a single family house that's 20 years old. It's similar to the other houses in the neighborhood and it has an effective age of 20 years.

◊ The estimated cost of the items which you decided need to be repaired is: Painting of the trim work $1,000, a broken door $200, and a hole in the kitchen wall $100.

◊ During your inspection and field work you noted some depreciated short-lived items and have made the following calculations:

Short Lived Items:

	Cost	Effect-ive Age	Useful Life	% of Deprec	$ of Deprec
Refrigerator	$800	5	20	25	$200
Furnace	2,500	15	30	50	1,250
Oven	400	5	20	25	100
Roof	5,000	10	20	50	2,500

Total Cost of Items:	**$8,700**		Actual Depre-ciation Cost:	**$4,050**

◊ The estimated reproduction cost new of the structure is $100,000. The site improvements have a depreciated value of $5,000. After analyzing the market you estimate that the value of the vacant site is $20,000.

◊ After curing all forms of physical depreciation the remaining structure has an effective age of 15 years. An analysis of the market has shown that similar houses have an economic life of 50 years.

◊ The subject property has a one-car garage and most homes in the area have a two-car garage. The subject property is currently rented for $1,000 per month. (This is also known as the *contract rent*.) An analysis of the market shows that comparable homes which are rented with two car garages, bring in $1,075 per month in rental income. You have analyzed many recent sales, and a gross rent multiplier of 100 is determined to be a good estimate for the area. A local contractor has estimated that the cost of enlarging the garage now to have a two-car capacity would be $6,000. If the second car capacity was included during the original construction it would have cost $4,000.

◊ You have not found any external factors that negatively affect the market value of the subject property. Therefore, there is no external obsolescence depreciation amount.

What is the estimated market value of the subject property using the Cost Approach to value?

Reproduction Cost New = $100,000

Physical Curable Deferred Maintenance:

Trim Painting	=	$1,000
Broken Door	=	$ 200
Kitchen Wall Hole	=	$ 100

Total Physical Curable = $1,300

Physical Incurable Short Lived Items:

	Cost	Effect-ive Age	Useful Life	% of Deprec	$ of Deprec
Refrigerator	$800	5	20	25	$200
Furnace	2,500	15	30	50	1,250
Oven	400	5	20	25	100
Roof	5,000	10	20	50	2,500

Total Cost
of Items: **$8,700**

Actual Depre-
ciation Cost: **$4,050**

Physical Incurable Long Lived Items:

Reproduction Cost New	=	$100,000
Minus Physical Curable	=	$1,300
Minus Cost New Physical	=	$8,700
Incurable Short Lived Items	=	- $10,000
Cost of Bone Structure	=	$90,000

Percent of Depreciation = Effective Age
(after curing)
Economic Life

$$30\% = 15/50$$
$$\$90,000 \times .30 = \$27,000$$

Summation of Physical Depreciation:

Physical Curable Deferred Maintenance	=	$ 1,300
Physical Incurable Short Lived	=	$ 4,050
Physical Incurable Long Lived	=	$27,000
Total Physical Depreciation	=	$32,350

Functional Obsolescence:

For a one-car garage as opposed to a two-car garage.

Market Rent minus Contract Rent = Rent Differential
$$\$1,075 - \$1,000 = \$75$$

Loss in Value = Rent Differential x Gross Rent Multiplier
$$\$7,500 = \$75 \times 100$$

If the increase in value to the subject property for installing a two-car garage is equal to or greater than the Cost to Cure then it is a Curable item.
$$\$7,500 \geq \$6,000 \text{ Cost to Cure}$$

If the item is curable then the depreciated Functional Obsolescence value is: Cost New minus

Cost if it was included during the original construction = the depreciated value amount.

$$\$6,000 - \$4,000 = \$2,000$$

External Obsolescence:

There were no external obsolescence items noted that affected the subject property.

Estimated Market Value Using The Cost Approach:

Reproduction Cost New	=	$100,000
Physical Depreciation	=	$32,350
Functional Obsolescence	=	$ 2,000
External Obsolescence	=	$ 0
Total Depreciation	=	- $34,350
Depreciated Reproduction Cost	=	$65,650
Depreciated Site Improvements	=	$ 5,000
Depreciated Improvements Value	=	$70,650
Plus Land Value	=	$20,000

Total Indicated Value By The Cost Approach =

$90,650

Cost Approach Example #3 & 4

There are two additional examples of the Cost Approach method in the sample Singe Family appraisal report and the sample Multi-Family appraisal report included in this book. Please review those sample appraisals.

The Income Approach

The following sections will cover the Income Approach and other income related methods used by real estate appraisers. Today, any computer can do all the math calculations for you which greatly simplifies the process, unlike years ago. There is an additional example of the Income Approach method in the sample Multi-Family appraisal report included in this book. Please review that sample appraisal.

The *Income Approach* uses the potential income generated by the property to estimate the market value of the subject property. The Income Approach is based on the assumption that a typically informed buyer would estimate the value of a property based upon the anticipated future benefits of purchasing it. Future benefits could be in dollar amounts or in amenities of

> *The Income Approach is more effective in appraising income producing properties in which the typical buyer would be an investor.*

ownership. The Income Approach is more effective in appraising income producing properties in which the typical buyer would be an investor. The anticipated future income is discounted to what the present value is worth today. For example, a dollar earned by someone today is worth more money than a dollar earned five years from now. The reason for this is inflation, which is the cause of rising prices over the years. Also, if you have a dollar today, you can invest it or put it in the bank to earn interest. Therefore, in five years you can end up with much more money than the original dollar you started with. Whether you're talking about one dollar or a million dollars, the concept is the same.

The Income Approach is not very effective for appraising a single family house or condominium. The reason for this is that single family homes and condos are generally not purchased based on the net rental income that they earn. Single family houses and condos tend to be purchased as a residence for the owner, as opposed to being purchased to rent out.

Basic Algebra

Now here's the part that you've all been waiting for. Let's get into some **heavy duty** math formulas and calculations! I tried to include the more serious math sections as far back in the book as I could to "break it to you gently". **When you read the *Cash Equivalency Example #3* you'll see how all the following math sections relate to an actual appraisal report.** So don't get bored and put this book on the shelf to collect dust. Instead of looking at the math with a negative attitude, try to be like Dorothy from the *Wizard Of Oz* and keep repeating to yourself over and over: *"There's no place like math class. There's no place like math class. There's no place like math class."* If you do it with your eyes closed while you click your heels, then you might start to believe what you're saying! Just use your computer to handle most of the math calculations which takes the tedious work out of the process. I will round out the numbers when there are more than two decimal places. So please don't worry if you get answers with more than two decimal places and they don't appear to *exactly* match the numbers in the book.

We'll start off with some simple algebra. In algebra you always multiply and divide before you do any other calculations in a formula, unless there are

> *When you read the Cash Equivalency Example #3 you'll see how all the following math sections relate to an actual appraisal report. Instead of looking at the math with a negative attitude, try to be like Dorothy from the Wizard Of Oz and keep repeating to yourself over and over: "There's no place like math class..."*

parentheses around part of the formula. Anything inside the parenthesis is always calculated first. To solve the equation $5/7 + 6/11$ you have to first make the *denominator* (lower figure) equal for both sets of numbers. You do this by multiplying each number by the opposite number's denominator. For example, the *numerator* (top figure) and the denominator in 5/7 would be multiplied by 11 to give you:

$$5/7 \times 11 = 55/77$$

The numerator and the denominator in 6/11 would then be multiplied by 7:

$$6/11 \times 7 = 42/77$$

This leaves us with:

$$55/77 + 42/77 = 97/77$$

The *reciprocal* of a number is that number turned upside down. For example:
The reciprocal of X = 1/X
The reciprocal of 4 = 1/4
The reciprocal of 6/11 = 11/6

The *complement* of a number is 1 minus that number. For example:
The complement of X = 1 - X
The complement of 4 = 1 - 4
The complement of 75% = 1 - .75

Let's try to solve the equation:

$$(8X - 4) 2 = 3 (14 - 3X)$$

First we'll multiply the numbers that are located inside the parenthesis:

$$16X - 8 = 42 - 9X$$

Then we'll add 8 to each side of the equation to eliminate the non-X number on one side:

$$16X = 50 - 9X$$

Then we'll add 9X to each side of the equation to eliminate the X number on one side:

$$25X = 50$$

Then we'll divide each side of the equation by 25 to find the X value. This will give us our answer:

$$X = 2$$

Leverage Example

There are three types of leverage:

1. *Negative Leverage* - This is also called unsuccessful leverage because the investor or lender ends up losing on their money invested in the deal.

2. *Neutral Leverage* - This is called neutral leverage because the investor or lender ends up breaking even on their money invested in the deal.

3. *Positive Leverage* - This is also called successful leverage because the investor or lender ends up making a profit on their money invested in the deal.

◊ Vo or Price = $100,000
◊ Ym = 10%
◊ Rate = Income/Value
◊ ADS = $100,000 x 10% which equals $10,000. *ADS* stands for the Annual Debt Service. Meaning that the total mortgage payments for the year on this loan will be $10,000.

Let's say you were buying an investment property for $100,000 and your mortgage interest rate was 10%. If your rate of return on this investment is greater than 10%, than you have positive leverage. You have positive leverage because the return on investment exceeds the interest rate you pay as the borrower of the money needed to purchase the property.

Let's say this property has a $15,000 total positive cash flow for the year. A *positive cash flow* simply means that the rental income from the apartments can pay all of the bills on the property each month, and there will still be extra money left over.

$$\$15,000/\$100,000 \ = \ .15$$
or
15% rate of return

The 15% rate of return on investment is greater than the 10% you're being charged by the bank for the mortgage funds. Therefore, you have positive leverage on this deal. That's the way to go!

Effective Interest Rate Example

◊ Vm = The Value of the Mortgage
◊ Rm = The Rate of the Mortgage *(also called the mortgage constant)*
◊ Ym = Yield of the Mortgage *(also called the interest rate or the return on investment)*
◊ Vo = Value of the Property
◊ ADS = Annual Debt Service *(the amount of the total yearly payments on the mortgage)*
◊ n = Term of the loan *(the length of time that the mortgage is amortized)*
◊ b = balloon payment or loan balance due. A balloon refers to the remaining balance amount of a loan that comes due in one large sum at a specified time in the future.
◊ M = Loan-to-Value ratio *(amount of money lent divided by total value of property,* Vm/Vo)
◊ Ve = Value of the Equity *(the amount of equity in the property which is the total value of the property minus any existing mortgage loans)*
◊ Points = Points on a loan refers to the extra charge assessed by the lender to process the loan application and provide the funds. This is in addition to the interest payments made on the loan. One point is equal to 1% of the total amount of the loan given. For example, a $50,000 mortgage loan that has 3 points. The total amount the borrower has to pay for the points is $50,000 x 3% = $1,500
◊ Amortization = The monthly payment schedule to gradually pay off the loan balance of principal plus interest over a specified period of time.

Let's take an example so we can put all these abbreviations to work:

◊ Vm = $100,000
◊ Ym = 12%
◊ n = 20 years
◊ Points = 6

Six points are equal to 6 x 1% = .06

.06 x $100,000 = $6,000

$100,000 - $6,000 = $94,000

This tells us that the borrower has to pay back $100,000 but he actually only receives $94,000 from the lender. The $6,000 is kept by the lender to pay for the points on the loan.

◊ ADS = Vm x Ym which in this equation would be $100,000 x 12% = $12,000

$12,000/$100,000 = .12 or 12%

$12,000/$94,000 = .1277 or 12.77%

Therefore, the *contract* interest rate for this loan is 12% but the *effective* interest rate for this loan is 12.77%. This simply means, that due to the additional cost for the loan points, the actual interest rate that the borrower is being charged for the money is 12.77% and not just 12%. This is why all loan agreements state the effective interest rate at the top of the loan document. By doing this, the borrower can see the full amount of interest, and the total of all of the payments, that they are being held responsible for.

Nominal interest rate is the <u>annual</u> rate charged for a loan and it's the same thing as the contract interest rate. It's just another phrase used to describe what the interest rate is that's stated in the loan contract.

The monthly *effective* interest rate charged for the loan is the effective rate divided by 12.

.1277/12 = .0106 or 1%

ITAO Example #1

Let's try another example and we'll use the ITAO tables. ITAO stands for the *Installment To Amortize One* dollar. You purchase ITAO tables at a bookstore that sells loan amortization tables as well. If you look at the ITAO tables, you'll see two column headings listed for each different interest rate listed. The first column heading, *ITAO*, is used to figure out the monthly loan payment on a particular loan. The second column heading, *Rm*, is used to figure out 12 of the loan payments or 1 full year of the annual debt service, ADS, to amortize a particular loan. If you multiply the ITAO figure by 12 you'll get the Rm figure, and if you divide the Rm figure by 12 you'll get the ITAO figure. The row headings on the left side of the tables correspond to the remaining term of the loan.

Let's say that you wanted to determine the monthly payment for a $50,000 loan that had a term of 30 years and an interest rate of 10%. First you would go to the

ITAO table with the 10.00% interest rate. Next you would go down the list until you reached the 30 year column heading, giving you an ITAO figure of 0.008776. You would then multiply $50,000 x 0.008776 = $438.80 which is the monthly loan payment to amortize that loan over a 30 year period.

If you wanted to figure out the total loan payments for 1 year, or the ADS, you could multiply the $438.80 x 12 = $5,265.60. Or you could go down the Rm list until you get to the 30 year figure of 0.105312. Multiply the loan amount of $50,000 x 0.105312 = $5,265.60 which is the same yearly amount. Either way you arrive at the same answer.

◊   Vo or Price = $125,000
◊   Vm or Mortgage = $100,000
◊   Ym or Interest Rate = 10%
◊   n or Term = 30 year payment term *(amortization)* with a balloon payment for the remaining balance due in 10 years.
◊   b or balloon payment due date = 30 - 10 = 20 years will be left on the loan balance amount at the time the balloon payment will be due.
◊   Rate = Income/Value *(Mortgage Rate = Mortgage Income/Mortgage Value)*
◊   Value = Income/Rate
◊   Income = Value x Rate
◊   CRRT = Contract rate for the remaining term of the loan
◊   ADS = Vm x CRRT x 12

◊ $100,000 x 0.008776 = $877.60 is the monthly loan payment as determined by the ITAO tables. The ADS is $877.60 x 12 = $10,531.20.

Now in this example the loan has a balloon payment due in 10 years. This means that the remaining 20 year balance of the loan is due after only 10 years of loan payments have been made. A balloon payment enables a borrower to have lower monthly payments before the balloon amount comes due. For example, let's say this loan was fully amortized over a 10 year period. This would mean that it would be totally paid off after 10 years including the loan principal and the loan interest amounts. If this were the case then we take the ITAO for 10 years and multiply it by the loan amount to get $100,000 x 0.013215 = $1,321.50. The loan payment to fully amortize this loan over 10 years instead of 30 years would be $1,321.50 instead of the $877.60.

So what we want to do now is figure out what the balloon payment amount will be for the loan in our example. We do this by dividing the original loan term ITAO for 30 years, by the ITAO for the balloon payment date of 20 years. *(There is another way of doing this: by dividing the monthly payment by the new ITAO, or by dividing the yearly ADS by the new Rm figure to get the same result. This will be covered in the next section.)*

$$0.008776/0.009650 = 0.90943$$

To figure out the balloon payment, just multiply this new number by the original loan amount.

$$0.90943 \times \$100,000 = \$90,943$$

Therefore, our balloon payment is $90,943. You might be wondering why the balloon payment is so close to the original $100,000 loan amount borrowed. The reason is that in the first 15 years of a 30 year loan, the vast majority of your monthly loan payments go toward paying off the interest amount. In the first half of the loan, the monthly payments barely pay off any of the loan principal amount. Each monthly loan payment gradually reduces your loan principal amount. When you get to the last 7 years of the loan, you begin to reduce more principal with each payment, as opposed to reducing the interest payment.

Another way to figure out the balloon payment is to divide the Rm figure for 30 years by the Rm figure for 20 years.

$$0.105312/0.115800 = 0.90943$$

$$0.90943 \times \$100,000 = \$90,943$$

Either way you get the same result. Just remember that you have to use the same column heading for your calculations on this. Don't take the 30 year *ITAO* figure and divide it by the 20 year *Rm* figure or vice versa. If you do, your calculations will be **wrong!!** You have to compare apples to apples and not apples to oranges.

◊   DSCR = Debt Service Coverage Ratio. This is what a property will generate in net operating income and the amount of the debt service that the property income could pay. Net income refers to the amount of money left over after all of the bills *(operating expenses)* are paid. It's also called cash flow and it can be positive, neutral *(break even)* or negative. Banks like to see a positive cash flow when they're lending money on a rental property.

◊ GI = Gross Income. Gross income refers to the total amount of income received before the bills have been paid.
◊ OE = Operating Expenses
◊ NOI = Net Operating Income

For this example we'll assume:

◊ GI = $20,000
◊ OE = $5,960

$$GI - OE = NOI$$
or
$$\$20,000 - \$5,960 = \$14,040$$

Now let's take this a step further. Remember we found out that $100,000 x 0.008776 = $877.60 is the monthly loan payment as determined by the ITAO tables for our sample mortgage.
The ADS is $877.60 x 12 = $10,531.20.

$$DSCR = NOI/ADS$$

The property in our example has a NOI of $14,040 per year. We want to find the DSCR.

$$\$14,040/\$10,531.20 = 1.33$$

Our answer of 1.33 is a positive number. It's a number that the bankers would like to see if they were lending money on this property. Bankers like to see a positive cash flow balance to make their mortgage loan more secure.

Let's take it a step further and try to figure out the Loan-to-Value ratio.

$$M = Vm/Vo$$
or
$$\$100,000/\$125,000 = 0.8$$

Our answer of 0.8 is the same as an 80% loan-to-value ratio

In our example, we'll now try to determine the rate of the mortgage, Rm, *without* looking at the ITAO tables. Remember that Rate = Income/Value which is the same as Rm = ADS/Vm.

◊ ADS = $10,531.20

◊ Vm = $100,000

$$\$10,531.20/\$100,000 = 0.105312$$

If you check the ITAO tables for a 10% loan that has a 30 year amortization period, you will see it matches our answer.

ITAO Example #2

Let's try to solve another ITAO problem:

◊ Vm or Mortgage = $80,000
◊ Ym or Interest Rate = 12%
◊ n or Term = 30 year payment term *(amortization)*
◊ b or balloon payment due date = 20 years
◊ CRRT = Contract rate for the remaining term of the loan
◊ ADS = Vm x CRRT x 12

To figure out the ADS, annual debt service, we find that the Rm in the ITAO tables for a 12% interest rate loan, with a 30 year amortization term, is 0.123432.

$$\$80,000 \times 0.123432 = \$9,874.56$$

Another way to find the ADS, is to take the figure under the ITAO column, which is the monthly loan payment figure, and multiply it by 12. The result will give you one full year's loan payment amount.

$$\$80,000 \times 0.010286 = \$822.88$$

$$\$822.88 \times 12 = \$9,874.56$$

Now we'll figure out the remaining loan balance when the balloon payment is due after 20 years of loan payments. We can do this two ways, using either the ITAO column figure or the Rm column figure. *(There is another way of doing this: by dividing the original ITAO figure by the new ITAO figure, or by dividing the yearly Rm figure by the new Rm figure to get the same result. This was covered in the prior section.)*

First we find that the ITAO figure for a 12% interest loan at the 10 year term is 0.014347. Since we are using the *monthly* ITAO then we must use the *monthly* loan payment to figure out the balloon payment.

$822.88/0.014347 = $57,355.54

Or we can find that the Rm figure for a 12% interest loan at the 10 year term is 0.172164. Since we are using the *yearly* Rm then we must use the *yearly* loan payment to determine the balloon payment.

$9,874.56/0.172164 = $57,355.54

Using both methods we come up with the same answer. The balloon payment due after 20 years of loan payments in our example will be $57,355.54.

Cash Equivalency Example #1

Cash equivalencies will make the market price higher than the market value due to flexible terms given to the buyer by the seller. The market *price* can be equal to the market *value* but this is not always the case. If necessary, you have to make the adjustment with the sales comparables for flexible terms given. This is done to bring the market value of the sales comparable down to what an all cash deal would have brought the seller. If the market interest rate at the time of the sale is the same as the interest rate paid by the buyer for a seller financed purchase money mortgage to buy the property, then no cash equivalency adjustment is needed. For example, let's say the market interest rate was 13% and the buyer paid only 10% for his interest on the mortgage. Then an adjustment for cash equivalency has to be made because the buyer might actually be paying about $110,000. However, due to the favorable financing, the adjusted sales price may be around $95,000 after you make the proper ITAO calculations.

You could even take this a step further, if you wanted to figure out the *Present Value* of flexible financing terms. You can purchase Present Value tables that are used in a similar manner to the ITAO tables. Present Value calculations and adjustments are used to estimate what a future amount of money would be worth in today's market. For example, let's say you had a mortgage loan that was due in 25 years. You would use these tables to estimate what the mortgage loan balance would be worth to a lender **today.** The value of the loan to the lender today, would be compared to the lender waiting 25 years to fully amortize the loan and get their money.

Now before you get angry at me for including all these math formulas, let me show you an actual *Cash Equivalency* example. By showing you an actual example, you can see how this relates to doing real estate appraisals. We'll use the same loan as we did in the prior example.

◊   Vm or Mortgage = $80,000
◊   Ym or Interest Rate = 12%
◊   n or Term = 30 year payment term *(amortization)*

We already found out that the monthly mortgage payment is $822.88. Let's assume that after you have been making payments on this loan for 4 years, the loan interest rates that the banks are charging goes up from 12% to 15%. The 15% is now the *market* interest rate. We need to now determine what the *book value* of this loan is in today's market.

◊   Book Value = Monthly Loan Payment/ITAO at CRRT
◊   ITAO at CRRT = The Installment To Amortize One dollar at the *Contract* Rate for the Remaining Term of the loan.

You've been making payments on the loan for 4 full years. So we need to figure out the remaining term of this loan at that point in time.

30 - 4 = 26 years remaining

If you check the tables, the ITAO for a loan term of 26 years at 12% interest is 0.010470. Now we'll find out the remaining loan balance with 26 years remaining on this loan. Remember we can do this two ways, using either the ITAO column figure or the Rm column figure. We'll use the ITAO column figure.

Since we are using the *monthly* ITAO, then we must use the *monthly* loan payment to determine the remaining loan balance at 26 years.

$822.88/0.010470 = $78,594.08

Now we'll figure out what this loan is worth at the *market* interest rate, which is 15% in our example. You have to compare apples to apples, so we use the same ITAO remaining loan term. The remaining loan term is 26 years in our example.

◊ ITAO at MRRT = The Installment To Amortize One dollar at the *Market* Rate for the Remaining Term of the loan.

If you check the tables, the ITAO for a loan term of 26 years at 15% interest is 0.012765. Now we'll figure out the remaining loan balance with 26 years remaining on this loan, at the *market* interest rate and the *contract* monthly loan payment. Remember we can do this two ways, using either the ITAO column figure or the Rm column figure. We'll use the ITAO figure.

Since we are using the *monthly* ITAO, then we must use the *monthly* loan payment to find out the remaining loan balance at 26 years.

$$\$822.88/0.012765 = \$64,463.77$$

We now have determined what our current loan balance is at the contract interest rate of 12%. We have also figured out what the loan balance would be with the contract monthly loan payment at the market interest rate of 15%. Now we will determine what our loan is worth to the lender *today*. We do this by dividing the market rate by the contract rate figure.

$$\$64,463.77/\$78,594.08 = 0.82$$

Our answer is 0.82 which is the same as 82%. This indicates that the existing loan at a 12% interest rate, is only worth 82% of what the exact same loan would be worth in today's market of 15% interest. That is a discount of 18% (100% - 82% = 18%). This simply means that if your banker lent the equivalent of your unpaid loan balance to someone in today's market, he would get an additional 18% profit over what he is getting from you for the same loan amount. So the $78,594.08 outstanding loan balance at the contract interest rate of 12% is only worth $64,463.77 in today's market at current market interest rates of 15%. This is why an adjustment is often needed to a sales comparable that has seller financing and flexible terms.

Using the above example, let's say a seller decided to finance part of the sales price of his house. The seller did this by giving the buyer a 12% purchase money mortgage. If the banks were lending money to everyone else at 15%, then that buyer would be getting the seller financed loan at an 18% discount! This means that an adjustment would have to be made to this sale if you were using it as a comparable for a house that you were appraising. The flexible terms with the low interest rate can cause a buyer to pay more than someone else would normally pay for that same house at that particular time.

Cash Equivalency Example #2

We'll use our prior ITAO example for another problem. Let's say we wanted to find out what the separate loan principal and interest amounts were for the **first** monthly payment.

◊ Vm or Mortgage = $80,000
◊ Ym or Interest Rate = 12%
◊ n or Term = 30 year payment term *(amortization)*

Using the ITAO tables for the 30 year term we found the correct monthly loan payment amount:

$$\$80,000 \times 0.010286 = \$822.88$$

We need to figure what amount of the $822.88 first monthly payment is applied toward loan principal and what amount is toward loan interest. To do this we first need to find the monthly interest rate. The *nominal* interest rate is given to us as 12%. The monthly interest rate is simply the nominal rate divided by 12.

$$.12/12 = .01 \text{ or } 1\% \text{ interest per month}$$

The total loan principal amount for the first monthly payment is given to us as $80,000. If the monthly interest rate is 1%, we then multiply this by the outstanding loan principal amount to determine what the interest payment is, for that particular monthly payment.

$$\$80,000 \times .01 = \$800.00$$

Now we have found the interest payment for the first month to be $800.00. All we need to do is subtract this amount from the total monthly loan payment to figure out the loan principal amount for that month.

$$\$822.88 - \$800.00 = \$22.88$$

The amortization of the loan principal or the *recapture of capital* for the first monthly loan payment is $22.88. This may seem surprisingly low, but I noted the reason for this earlier. The vast majority of the loan

---

payments made in the early years are applied toward paying down the loan **interest** balance, instead of the loan **principal** balance.

We'll use this same example for another problem. Let's say we wanted to find what the remaining loan principal balance is after the first **year** of loan payments. As shown in prior examples, we can do this two ways, using either the ITAO column figure or the Rm column figure. First we find the ITAO figure for a 12% interest loan at the 29 year term is 0.010324. Since we are using the *monthly* ITAO, then we must use the *monthly* loan payment to find the remaining loan principal amount.

$$\$822.88/0.010324 = \$79,705.54$$

Or we can find that the Rm figure for a 12% interest loan at the 29 year term is 0.123888. Since we are using the *yearly* Rm, then we must use the *yearly* loan payment to determine the loan principal amount.

$$\$9,874.56/0.123888 = \$79,705.54$$

Using both methods, we come up with the same answer. The loan principal balance that is outstanding after 1 year of loan payments will be $79,705.54.

We can figure out the amount of loan principal paid during the first year of loan payments. To do this, we simply subtract the original loan principal amount from the remaining amount after 1 year of payments.

$$\$80,000 - \$79,705.54 = \$294.46$$

The amortization of the loan principal, or the *recapture of capital,* after the first year of loan payments is $294.46.

We'll use this same example to see how the loan amortizes over 5 year intervals. Let's say we wanted to determine what the remaining loan principal balance is after **10** years of loan payments. As shown in prior examples, we can do this two ways, using either the ITAO column figure or the Rm column figure.

First we find that the ITAO figure for a 12% interest loan at the 20 year term is 0.011011. Since we are using the *monthly* ITAO, then we must use the *monthly* loan payment to find out the remaining loan principal amount.

$$\$822.88/0.011011 = \$74,732.54$$

Or we can find that the Rm figure for a 12% interest loan at the 20 year term is 0.132132. Since we are using the *yearly* Rm, then we must use the *yearly* loan payment to determine the loan principal amount.

$$\$9,874.56/0.132132 = \$74,732.54$$

Using both methods, we come up with the same answer. The loan principal balance that is outstanding after 10 years of loan payments will be $74,732.54.

We can determine the amount of loan principal paid during the first 10 years of loan payments. Simply subtract the original loan principal amount from the remaining amount after 10 years of payments.

$$\$80,000 - \$74,732.54 = \$5,267.46$$

(Yes, we're going to keep practicing it until you can do this in your sleep!) Now we'll learn what the remaining loan principal balance is after **15** years of loan payments.

First we find that the ITAO figure for a 12% interest loan at the 15 year term is 0.012002.

$$\$822.88/0.012002 = \$68,561.91$$

Or we can find that the Rm figure for a 12% interest loan at the 15 year term is 0.144024.

$$\$9,874.56/0.144024 = \$68,561.91$$

Using both methods, we come up with the same answer. The loan principal balance that is outstanding after 15 years of loan payments will be $68,561.91.

Now we'll find out what the remaining loan principal balance is after **20** years of loan payments.

First we find that the ITAO figure for a 12% interest loan at the 10 year term is 0.014347.

$$\$822.88/0.014347 = \$57,355.54$$

Or we can find that the Rm figure for a 12% interest loan at the 10 year term is 0.172164.

$9,874.56/0.172164 = $57,355.54

Using both methods, we come up with the same answer. The loan principal balance that is outstanding after 20 years of loan payments will be $57,355.54.

(OK, this is the last one - practice makes perfect!) Now we'll learn what the remaining loan principal balance is after **25** years of loan payments.

First we find that the ITAO figure for a 12% interest loan at the 5 year term is 0.022244.

$822.88/0.022244 = $36,993.35

Or we can find that the Rm figure for a 12% interest loan at the 5 year term is 0.266928.

$9,874.56/0.266928 = $36,993.35

Using both methods, we come up with the same answer. The loan principal balance that is outstanding after 25 years of loan payments will be $36,993.35.

Cash Equivalency Example #3

Now we'll use some of this information to put together another *Cash Equivalency* example to see how it would relate to an actual appraisal report. Let's say, you were appraising a house and you found a sales comparable that was sold with an assumable mortgage loan. As assumable mortgage means that a buyer can "assume" or take over the mortgage loan when buying the house instead of having to get a new loan to pay off the existing mortgage. Basically, the buyer just makes the remaining payments on the existing mortgage. This makes the sale of the house more flexible and easier to find potential buyers who may be willing to pay a higher price for the convenience of being able to assume the existing loan. The buyer will not have to go through the hassle and expense of getting a new mortgage and pay the points, bank fees, and maybe even a higher interest rate. Assumable loans were easy to find years ago. Now back to our example: The recorded sales price of the house was $100,000. The mortgage loan that was assumed by the buyer was the same loan and terms that we've used in our examples;

$80,000 loan at a 12% interest rate for a 30 year term. The seller of the house has been making loan payments for 10 years on this mortgage loan before the buyer assumes it. We already found out, (from our prior examples), that the monthly mortgage payment is $822.88. However, at the time of the sale when the buyer assumed this loan, the *market* interest rates were 16.5% for conventional financing mortgages.

We first need to determine what the remaining loan principal balance is at the time the new buyer assumes the mortgage. This loan in our example has a principal balance remaining after 10 years of making loan payments of:

$822.88/0.011011 = $74,732.54
or
$9,874.56/0.132132 = $74,732.54

Using both methods, we come up with the same answer. The loan principal balance that is outstanding after 10 years of loan payments will be $74,732.54.

Next we need to figure out what the down payment amount was that the buyer had to pay to purchase this house. We find this by simply subtracting the balance of the assumable loan from the total sales price.

$100,000 - $74,732.54 = $25,267.46

The amount of the buyer's down payment is determined to be $25,267.46.

As I said, the seller has been making payments on this loan for 10 years. The loan interest rates that the banks are charging at the time of the sale, have gone up from 12% to 16.5%. The 16.5% is now the *market* interest rate. We need to now determine what the *book value* of this loan was at the time that the loan was assumed by the buyer.

◊   Book Value = Monthly Loan Payment/ITAO at CRRT
◊   ITAO at CRRT = The Installment To Amortize One dollar at the *Contract Rate for the Remaining Term* of the loan.

The seller has been making payments on the loan for 10 full years. So we need to find out the remaining term of this loan.

30 - 10 = 20 years remaining

Now we'll figure out what this loan is worth at the *market* interest rate which is 16.5% in our example. You have to compare apples to apples, so we use the same ITAO remaining loan term, which is 20 years in our example.

◊ ITAO at MRRT = The Installment To Amortize One dollar at the *Market Rate for the Remaining Term* of the loan.

If you check the tables, the ITAO for a loan term of 20 years at 16.5% interest is 0.014289. Now we'll find what the remaining loan balance is with 20 years remaining on this loan, at the *market* interest rate and the contract monthly loan payment. Remember we can do this two ways, using either the ITAO column figure or the Rm column figure. We'll use the ITAO column figure. Since we are using the *monthly* ITAO, then we must use the *monthly* loan payment to find the remaining loan balance at 20 years.

$$\$822.88 / 0.014289 = \$57,588.35$$

We now have determined what the current loan balance is at the contract interest rate of 12%. We've also found what the loan balance would be with the contract monthly loan payment, at the market interest rate of 16.5%. Now we will figure out what the loan is worth to the lender today. We do this by dividing the market rate figure by the contract rate figure.

$$\$57,588.35 / \$74,732.54 = 0.77$$

Our answer is 0.77 which is the same as 77%. This indicates that the existing loan, at a 12% interest rate, is only worth 77% of what the exact same loan would be worth in today's market of 16.5% interest. That's a discount of 23% (100% - 77% = 23%). This simply means, that if the seller's banker lent the equivalent of the unpaid loan balance to someone in today's market, **the bank would get an additional 23% profit** over what they are getting from the seller for the same loan amount! So the $74,732.54 outstanding loan balance at the contract interest rate of 12%, is only worth $57,588.35 in today's market at the current market interest rate of 16.5%.

Now since we are using this sale as a comparable for one of our appraisals, we **have to** make a cash equivalency adjustment to the sales price of the comp. We do this because the loan that was assumed by the buyer has a lower interest rate than a loan that a typical buyer would obtain, at the time that the sale of the

comparable took place. An adjustment is needed because the recorded sales price does not reflect an "arms length" transaction. This is because the buyer had received a lower than normal interest rate loan to buy the house which probably caused them to pay a higher sales price due to the favorable terms.

We can figure out the adjustment to make by subtracting the *recorded* sales price of the comparable, from the *adjusted* sales price. The adjusted sales price takes into account the low interest rate loan. To do this,

Now do you see why I had to teach you all of this math? I hope so. Believe me, I wouldn't have included all of these math examples in the book unless it was a necessary part of teaching the techniques and methods of real estate appraising. The math calculations can get boring but there will be times when you need to know this stuff for an appraisal report.

we first need to decide what the adjusted sales price is. This is calculated by adding the buyer's down payment to the *market* rate of the loan balance assumed.

$$\$57,588.35 + \$25,267.46 = \$82,855.81$$

The adjusted sales price of the comparable in our example is $82,855.81. Meaning that this is what the house actually sold for because of the low interest rate of the loan assumed by the buyer. The $100,000 recorded sales price of that sales comparable then is not an "arms length" transaction.

Now we need to determine the adjustment to make in the appraisal report. We do this by simply subtracting the adjusted sales price of the comparable from the recorded sales price. Remember that you have to round out your adjustment amounts because appraising is not an exact science.

$$\$82,855.81 - \$100,000 = -\$17,144.19$$

The rounded adjustment in the appraisal report that we would make to the recorded sales price of the comparable in our example is -$17,150.

Now do you see why I had to teach you all of this math? I hope so. Believe me, I wouldn't have included all of these math examples in the book unless it was a necessary part of teaching the techniques and methods of real estate appraising. The math calculations can get boring but there will be times when you need to know this stuff for an appraisal report.

How To Make Big Money With The ITAO Tables

Now I'll really try to get you interested in all this math by showing you how you can use it to save yourself tens of thousands of dollars!! And I'll even give you a real life example. One of my instructors told our class this story while he was teaching the appraisal course. His friend had a 12% *contract* interest rate loan with a bank. The current *market* interest rates were 16.5% at the time his friend was selling his house. The remaining loan balance on the mortgage was $75,000 at the 12% interest rate. Using the ITAO tables, his friend showed the banker that the *book value* of the bank's loan was worth less than $65,000 with the market interest rates at 16.5%. He told the banker that if they would accept $65,000 as **full** payment for the loan, instead of the $75,000 that was the actual balance due, he would pay them off in a few months. He would pay off the loan early, rather than the bank having to wait many more years of just getting monthly loan payments. Believe it or not, the banker accepted the guy's offer and he put an additional $10,000 in his pocket when he sold his house!

This guy must have been an appraiser or an economist to figure this technique out. But either way, I think it's a brilliant idea to try to save a lot of money when you pay off any of your loans. However, it's like

> *Now I'll really try to get you interested in all this math by showing you how you can use it to save yourself tens of thousands of dollars!!*

negotiating anything else, some lenders will say "yes" to the idea, and some lenders will say "no". If you have the courage and smarts to ask for a discount, you can only get two answers and one of them is great!

Obviously, my class instructor's friend didn't tell the banker that he was selling his house. I think he just said that he had gotten some extra money to pay them off with. If you're going to do this and you don't tell the lender that you're selling the house, then it becomes a business decision for the bank to make. The bank has to decide if it would be more profitable for them to take a discount on the loan and receive a lump sum now. This would enable them to lend that money out again at a higher interest rate. If they do this, then they won't have to wait for their monthly payments to fully

amortize the loan. The banker may say "no" to the discount if he feels that you're going to sell the house anyway. In order to sell your house, and give the buyer a "clear" title, you'll have to pay off all of the existing mortgages and liens on the house. If the lender knows you're getting the money to pay off the loan from the sale proceeds, he also knows that you have no choice if he insists on getting the full loan balance from you. However, if the lender thinks that he's going to have to wait many more years of only receiving monthly loan payments to fully amortize his loan, then he has some incentive to give you the discount. Try it out on your own mortgage and see what your bank says. Hey, you never know, if they say yes you'll profit big time!

Income Capitalization Example

When you buy a property, you buy either the amenities it offers or the income it offers. It's sometimes assumed that the income property market behaves rationally, whereas, the residential market doesn't. Meaning, that the income properties are purchased by investors who look at the deal as a business decision. Residential properties are generally purchased by people looking for the amenities in the deal and they can get too emotionally involved in the purchase to act rationally and may pay too much.

Here's some abbreviations you'll need for the following sections concerning the Income Approach:

◊   GI = Gross Income
◊   PGI = Potential Gross Income
◊   GI = PGI = Rent Roll
◊   V = Vacancy
◊   EGI = Effective Gross Income
◊   NOI = Net Operating Income
◊   OE = Operating Expenses
◊   (GI or PGI) - (V + Collection Losses) = Effective Gross Income
◊   Effective Gross Income - Operating Expenses = Net Operating Income
◊   Operating Expense Ratio = OE/EGI
◊   ADS = Annual Debt Service
◊   CTO = Cash Throw Off
◊   NOI - ADS = CTO

Capital costs, such as, depreciable items, do not appear in the equation. Capital costs or depreciable items refer to items whose cost to purchase and install cannot be totally deducted in the year the expense is incurred. The expense deduction for these items must be depreciated over a specified number of years according to the tax laws. Any payments to the debt or equity investors, (mortgage lender and owner), as well as income taxes paid do not appear in the equation.

Income property is always treated on an <u>annual</u> basis. This accounts for the winter and summer expenses in the calculations. Income property is always treated on a cash method of accounting and not an accrual method of accounting. A *cash method* of accounting simply means that any income is reported as "earned" when it's *actually* received. Any expenses are reported as "paid" when the money is *actually* spent to pay the bills. An *accrual method* of accounting simply means that any income is reported as "earned" at the time the work or service is performed. The income **is not** reported as earned at the time it's *actually* received. Any expenses are reported as "paid" at the time the bills are *supposed* to be paid and not when they're *actually* paid. According to a friend of mine who is a CPA, the accrual method of accounting is a "truer" method to use.

Let's try an income capitalization example:

The GI or PGI or Rent Roll includes 20 apartments at $200 per month rental income.

(20 x $200) x 12 = $48,000 rental income per year

The Vacancy and Collection Losses are estimated to be 5% per year.

$48,000 x .05 = $2,400 lost income per year

There is additional income that is estimated to be $100 for each occupied apartment unit. This additional income is from the coin operated laundry and soda machines plus rented garage spaces. However, there is a vacancy factor to account for in this calculation.

20 x .05 = 1 vacant unit per year

20 - 1 = 19 occupied units per year

19 x $100 = $1,900 additional income per year

Therefore, we add these calculations to determine the *Effective Gross Income* for the property.

$48,000 + $1,900 = $49,900

$49,900 - $2,400 = $47,500 in Effective Gross Income

Next we need to figure out the *Operating Expenses* for the building. This simply refers to the expenses to operate the building for one full year. *Fixed Expenses* refers to expenses that **don't** really fluctuate depending upon the occupancy of the building, such as, real estate taxes and insurance. *Variable Expenses* refers to expenses that **do** fluctuate depending upon the occupancy of the building, such as, management fees, electricity, heating fuel, etc.

Fixed Expenses:

Real Estate Taxes		$6,600
Insurance		600
	Total	*$7,200*

Variable Expenses:

Management Fees are 3% of EGI		$1,425
Electricity		250
Water + Sewer Fees		190
Heating Fuel		4,560
Miscellaneous		240
	Total	*$6,665*

Repairs and Maintenance	$8,635

Total Operating Expenses = *$22,500*

Operating Expense Ratio is then determined to be:

$22,500/$47,500 = 47%

To figure out the *Net Operating Income,* we subtract the total *Operating Expenses* from the *Effective Gross Income.* The *Debt Service* amount is not added to the expenses to figure out the Net Operating Income.

$47,500 - $22,500 = $25,000

Now we'll assume that this property has a $187,500 mortgage at 8% interest for a 20 year term. No payments have been made yet on the mortgage since it's a new loan. So we will find out the monthly payment from the ITAO tables for 8% interest.

$187,500 x 0.008364 = $1,568.25

Now we'll determine the ADS or *Annual Debt*

Service from the monthly payment calculation.

$$12 \times \$1,568.25 = \$18,819$$

To figure out the CTO or *Cash Throw Off,* (the positive cash flow on the property), we need to do the following calculations:

$$\$25,000 - \$18,819 = \$6,181$$

> The <u>most important</u> criteria in analyzing an income producing property is where Capital Recapture, also called Recapture or Capital Recovery, will come from.

The **most important** criteria in analyzing an **income producing property is where** *Capital Recapture,* **also called** *Recapture or Capital Recovery,* **will come from.** Recapture or Capital Recovery refer to someone receiving back the initial amount of money that they have invested in the deal. This is determined by the following equations:

◊   Ro = Capitalization Rate
◊   NOI = Net Operating Income
◊   Vo = Value of the Property
◊   Ro = NOI/Vo
◊   NOI/Ro = Vo

We can find the equity in this building using these equations with our example. We'll assume the subject property is worth $250,000 in the current market.

$$25,000/250,000 = .10$$
$$\text{or}$$
$$10\% \text{ Capitalization Rate}$$

Let's assume that we didn't know what the value of the property was. But we knew that the investor in the deal was looking for a *Capitalization Rate* of at least 10%. The investor then asks you during your appraisal process, what the subject property would have to be worth in order for him to obtain his 10% Capitalization Rate. This is found by dividing the *Net Operating Income* by the *Capitalization Rate.*

$$\$25,000/.10 = \$250,000$$

The answer is that the subject property would have to be worth $250,000 in order for the investor to obtain his 10% Capitalization Rate.

The return **of the initial investment** made by an

investor in a deal is called *Capital Recapture.* The return **on the initial investment** made by an investor in a deal is called *Interest Rate* or *Risk Rate.* If you wanted to use a straight line method (equal yearly amounts) to determine the Capital Recapture, then the following equation would apply:

◊   ARR = Annual Recapture Rate
◊   YUL = Years of Useful Life
◊   ARR = 100%/YUL
◊   YUL = 100%/ARR

Using the figures in our example, let's say the investor asks you to determine the number of *Years of Useful Life* of the investment for him to obtain his 10% Capitalization Rate. The following equation applies:

$$100\%/10\% = 10$$
$$\text{or}$$
$$10 \text{ Years of Useful Life}$$

For an investor, the return amount **of** or **on** their initial investment that they will require before making the deal will depend upon the amount of risk they are assuming with the investment. The more risk, then the higher the returns need to be to make the deal worthwhile. A **low risk** investment will generally have a **low** Capitalization Rate and the price of the subject property will be **high**. A **high risk** investment will generally have a **high** Capitalization Rate and the price of the subject property will be **low**.

Income Approach and Statistics Example

You will encounter situations where knowledge of statistics is needed for real estate appraising and the Income Approach. For example, you will need to analyze the sales comparables for the Income Approach on an appraisal assignment. Using statistics will enable you to determine if the sales comps you have are what is considered a "tight fit". When you have a "tight fit" then you can assume that your data is an acceptable descriptive representation of the market. Meaning that the values you're analyzing are probably good comparables to use and accurately reflect the local market. A tight fit from an appraisal standpoint is generally one in which the Percentage Deviation is 10% or less.

When someone refers to *population* in statistics, it doesn't have to mean that they are talking about "people". It refers to whatever units of measurement or values you're analyzing. For example, it could refer to cars, houses, rents, dollar amounts, etc. In statistics an *absolute* number is the number without any negative or positive signs before it. If you're analyzing a set of numbers, your first step should always be to set them up in an ascending or descending order. This order is based on the values of the numbers. For example, let's say you're analyzing some recent comparable sales of houses for an appraisal assignment. You're analyzing the sales prices *(SP)* of the houses; their gross monthly rents *(GMR)* for unfurnished apartments; and their gross rent multipliers *(GRM)* in your area; to assist you on the appraisal. GRM or Gross Rent Multiplier is equal to the SP or Sales Price divided by the monthly rent of unfurnished units. The *Gross Rent Multiplier* is used for the Direct Sales Comparison Approach for small residential income properties. You use unfurnished apartment rental figures for this.

Your field work for this appraisal assignment has found the following information:

1. The **Sales Prices** of the houses are: $125,000, $92,000, $87,000, $116,000, $147,000, $138,000.

2. The **GMR** of the houses are: $370, $290, $285, $355, $405, $390.

3. The **GRM** of the houses are: 337.84, 317.24, 305.26, 326.76, 362.96, 353.85.

Your first step is to place this information in an order that makes it easier to analyze the data statistically.

Sale No.	Sales Price	G.M.R.	G.R.M.
1	$147,000	$405	362.96
2	$138,000	$390	353.85
3	$125,000	$370	337.84
4	$116,000	$355	326.76
5	$92,000	$290	317.24
6	$87,000	$285	305.26
	$705,000	**$2,095**	**2,003.91**

Mean - refers to the number that is the **average** of all of the values. We find the Mean by dividing the total *amount* of the values, by the total *number* of values we are analyzing. In our example the Mean for the Sales Prices, the GMR, and the GRM would be calculated with the following equations:

$$\$705,000/6 = \$117,500 \text{ is the}$$
Mean or average Sales Price

$$\$2,095/6 = \$349.17 \text{ is the}$$
Mean or average GMR

$$2,003.91/6 = 333.99 \text{ is the}$$
Mean or average GRM

Median - refers to the number that is the **midpoint** of all of the values. When you have an even number of figures, for example the six that we are using, you have to add the two middle figures and then divide them by two. Think of the Median as a *position* on the scale of values that you're dealing with. In our example the Median for the Sales Prices, the GMR, and GRM would be calculated with these equations:

$$(\$125,000 + \$116,000)/2 = \$120,500 \text{ is the}$$
Median or midpoint Sales Price

$$(\$370 + \$355)/2 = \$362.50 \text{ is the}$$
Median or midpoint GMR

$$(337.84 + 326.76)/2 = 332.3 \text{ is the}$$
Median or midpoint GRM

Mode - refers to the number that is **repeated** most often in all of the values. For example, let's say sale #1 and sale #2 both sold for $138,000. Since the two sales prices are identical then the Mode would be $138,000 for the Sales Prices. It's the same thing for the GMR and the GRM, or any other values your analyzing. If you have values that have several different numbers that are identical, then the Mode would be the number that is found the most frequently. For example, let's say sale #1 and sale #2 both sold for $138,000 but sales #4, #5, and #6 all sold for $92,000. The Mode in this situation would be $92,000 because there are 3 values with that identical number. In our example there is no Mode because none of the values are repeated.

Range - refers to the number that is the **difference** of all of the values. You simply subtract the lowest value from the highest value to get the Range. In our example the Range for the Sales Prices, the GMR, and the GRM would be calculated with the following equations:

$$\$147,000 - \$87,000 = \$60,000 \text{ is the}$$
Range or difference of Sales Prices

$$\$405 - \$285 = \$120 \text{ is the}$$
Range or difference of GMR

$$362.96 - 305.26 = 57.7 \text{ is the}$$
Range or difference of GRM

Absolute Deviation - refers to the number that is the difference from the **Mean** for each of the individual values. Remember that an absolute number disregards any plus or minus signs for the values. First we have to set up another table to be able to analyze the values clearly. Then you simply subtract each value from the Mean number, and then add those amounts together to get the Absolute Deviation. This would be calculated as follows:

Sale No.	Sales Price	Mean	Absolute Deviation
1	$147,000	$117,500	$29,500
2	$138,000	$117,500	$20,500
3	$125,000	$117,500	$7,500
4	$116,000	$117,500	$1,500
5	$92,000	$117,500	$25,500
6	$87,000	$117,500	$30,500
	$705,000		**$115,000**

The total of the Absolute Deviation from the Mean of the Sales Prices is determined to be $115,000.

Now we'll find the Absolute Deviation from the Mean of the Gross Monthly Rent values:

Sale No.	G.M.R.	Mean	Absolute Deviation
1	$405	$349.17	$55.83
2	$390	$349.17	$40.83
3	$370	$349.17	$20.83
4	$355	$349.17	$5.83
5	$290	$349.17	$59.17
6	$285	$349.17	$64.17
	$2,095		**$246.66**

The total of the Absolute Deviation from the Mean of the Gross Monthly Rent values in our example is determined to be $246.66.

Now we'll find the Absolute Deviation from the Mean of the Gross Rent Multiplier values:

Sale No.	G.R.M.	Mean	Absolute Deviation
1	362.96	333.99	28.97
2	353.85	333.99	19.86
3	337.84	333.99	3.85
4	326.76	333.99	7.23
5	317.24	333.99	16.75
6	305.26	333.99	28.73
	2,003.91		**105.39**

The total of the Absolute Deviation from the Mean of the Gross Rent Multiplier values in our example is determined to be 105.39.

Now we'll find the *Arithmetic Deviation* for all three sets of values that we're analyzing:

Arithmetic Deviation - refers to the number that is the **average** of the **total** of the Absolute Deviation values. You simply divide the total Absolute Deviation value by the number of values to get the Arithmetic Deviation. In our example the Arithmetic Deviation for the Sales Prices, the GMR, and the GRM would be calculated with the following equations:

$$\$115,000/6 = \$19,166.67 \text{ is the}$$
Arithmetic Deviation for the Sales Prices

$$\$246.66/6 = \$41.11 \text{ is the}$$
Arithmetic Deviation for the GMR

$$105.39/6 = 17.57 \text{ is the}$$
Arithmetic Deviation for the GRM

Now we'll use all these calculations, to show you how statistics math equations can help you to do an actual appraisal report. As we said earlier, we'll assume that you're analyzing these recent sales prices *(SP)* of houses; their gross monthly rents *(GMR)* for unfurnished apartments; and their gross rent multipliers *(GRM)* in your area; to assist you on an appraisal assignment.

We've found the Arithmetic Deviation for all three sets of values. Now we will use this data to decide whether these sales are good comparables which accurately reflect the local market. We learn this by finding out the percentage difference of the Arithmetic Deviation from the Mean of each set of values. We calculate this percentage by dividing to Arithmetic Deviation by the Mean of each set of values. Therefore, in our example the percentage difference for the Sales Prices, the GMR, and the GRM would be calculated with the following equations:

$$\$19,166.67/\$117,500 = .16 \text{ or } 16\% \text{ is the}$$
Percentage Deviation of the Sales Prices

$$\$41.11/\$349.17 = .12 \text{ or } 12\% \text{ is the}$$
Percentage Deviation of the GMR

$$17.57/333.99 = .05 \text{ or } 5\% \text{ is the}$$
Percentage Deviation of the GRM

Now, I'll repeat what I said earlier in this section so you see why we had to go through all these statistics examples for an Income Approach appraisal. When you have what is considered a "tight fit" then you can assume that your data is an acceptable descriptive representation of the market. Meaning that the values you're analyzing are probably good comparables to use and accurately reflect the local market. A tight fit from an appraisal standpoint is generally one in which the Percentage Deviation is 10% or less. Using the example sales, we have learned that the only "tight fit"

for the three different sets of values we're analyzing is in the Gross Rent Multiplier amounts. The Gross Rent Multiplier amounts only deviate from the Mean by 5%. One way to estimate market value using the Income Approach is to multiply the Monthly Total Gross Estimated Rent *(GMR)* by the Gross Rent Multiplier amount *(GRM)*. An example is shown in the sample Multi-Family appraisal report in this book.

Income Approach GRM Example

We'll use the same data and sales comparables from the prior example for another Income Approach appraisal. For this assignment you have to use the Gross Rent Multiplier *(GRM)* of the sales comparables to estimate the market value of the subject property. Let's say that you've analyzed the Sales Prices of the houses; their Gross Monthly Rents for unfurnished apartments; and their Gross Rent Multipliers. You use unfurnished apartment rental figures for this. The following equations are needed:

◊ SP = Sales Price
◊ GMR = Gross Monthly Rents
◊ GRM = Gross Rent Multiplier
◊ GRM = SP/GMR

Your field work for this appraisal assignment has found the following information:

1 The **Sales Prices** of the houses are: $125,000, $92,000, $87,000, $116,000, $147,000, $138,000.

2 The **GMR** of the houses are: $370, $290, $285, $355, $405, $390.

3 The **GRM** of the houses are: 337.84, 317.24, 305.26, 326.76, 362.96, 353.85.

4 The **GMR** of the **Subject Property** is: $380.

Your first step is to place this information in an order that makes it easier to analyze.

Sale No.	Sales Price	G.M.R.	G.R.M.
1	$147,000	$405	362.96
2	$138,000	$390	353.85
3	$125,000	$370	337.84
4	$116,000	$355	326.76
5	$92,000	$290	317.24
6	$87,000	$285	305.26
Subject	**$?**	**$380**	**?**

We need to determine the GRM for the subject property. We do this by taking the **average** of the GRM figures for the sales comparables.

$$362.96 + 353.85 + 337.84 + 326.76 + 317.24 + 305.26 = 2003.91$$

$$2003.91 / 6 = 333.99$$

334 is the rounded out GRM amount

Next we need to use this figure to estimate the market value of the subject property. We do this by multiplying the GRM amount by the GMR amount for the subject property.

$$334 \times \$380 = \$126,920$$

$127,000 is the rounded out estimated market value of the subject property.

You would use these Income Approach figures to fill out the appraisal form for this report. You can estimate market value by multiplying the Monthly Total Gross Estimated Rent *(GMR)* by the Gross Rent Multiplier amount *(GRM)*. An example is shown in the sample Multi-Family appraisal report in this book.

Income Approach GIM Example

We'll use the same data and sales comps from the prior example for another Income Approach appraisal on a different subject property. For this appraisal you have to use the Gross Income Multiplier *(GIM)* of the sales comparables to estimate the market value of the subject property. Let's say you've analyzed the Sales Prices of the houses; their Gross Annual Income *(GAI)* for unfurnished apartments; and their Gross Income Multipliers *(GIM)*. You will use unfurnished apartment rental figures. The following equations are needed:

◊ SP = Sales Price
◊ GAI = Gross Annual Income
◊ GIM = Gross Income Multiplier
◊ GIM = SP/GAI

Your field work for this appraisal assignment has found the following information:

1 The **Sales Prices** of the houses are: $125,000, $92,000, $87,000, $116,000, $147,000, $138,000.

2 The **GAI** of the houses are: $4,440, $3,480, $3,420, $4,260, $4,860, $4,680.

3 The **GIM** of the houses are: 28.15, 26.44, 25.44, 27.23, 30.25, 29.49.

4 The **GAI** of the **Subject Property** is: $4,200.

Your first step is to place this information in an order that makes it easier to analyze.

Sale No.	Sales Price	G.A.I.	G.I.M.
1	$147,000	$4,860	30.25
2	$138,000	$4,680	29.49
3	$125,000	$4,440	28.15
4	$116,000	$4,260	27.23
5	$92,000	$3,480	26.44
6	$87,000	$3,420	25.44
Subject	**$?**	**$4,200**	**?**

We need to determine the GIM for the subject property. We do this by taking the **average** of the GIM figures for the sales comparables.

28.15, 26.44, 25.44, 27.23, 30.25, 29.49 = 167

167 / 6 = 27.83

28 is the rounded out GIM amount

Next we need to use this figure to estimate the market value of the subject property. We do this by multiplying the GIM amount by the GAI amount for the subject property.

28 x $4,200 = $117,600

$117,600 is the rounded out estimated market value of the subject property.

Tax Assessments

Tax assessments are based upon the *Assessed Value*, which should be the Highest and Best Use, though it may not be the present use of the subject property. A residential house can be taxed as a commercial property if it's located in an area of businesses. By being in a business location, this could make the H&B Use of the subject property a commercial use. An apartment building can be taxed as a condominium building because it's located in an area of condo buildings. Also, depth tables are used by tax assessors. They're not accurate enough to estimate market value for an appraiser to use them.

I've seen many cases where single family, or small multi-family dwellings, have a higher tax rate than they should. This is because these buildings have illegal apartment units. For example, let's say you had a single family house and you made an apartment in the basement and rented it out. Even though the property doesn't have the legal zoning for two apartments, your property can still be taxed as a two-family building. A two-family tax base will generally be a higher tax rate than a single family. And to make matters even worse, the building department will give you a building code violation for having the illegal, second apartment! Just because you're taxed as a two-

> The building department is a separate entity from the tax department. As a result, the building department doesn't care how your property is taxed, they only care that it meets all of the local building code requirements.

family, it doesn't mean that the apartment suddenly becomes a legal rental unit. You don't have the right to go ahead and rent this extra apartment out to someone. It's still an illegal apartment until you have a building inspector sign-off on it as a safe and acceptable living area that meets all of the local regulations. The building department is a separate entity from the tax department. As a result, the building department doesn't care how your property is taxed, they only care that it meets all the local building code requirements.

The *Effective Tax Rate* is the rate based upon the full amount of the estimated market value of the property. This rate is **not** based on the Assessed Value of the property. It's similar to the Effective Interest Rate example that we discussed earlier. It's the actual amount the owner is paying in taxes, in relation to the market value of his property. The assessed value of a property is usually less than the actual market value of the property. To calculate the effective tax, divide the taxes paid for the property, by the market value of the property. For example, let's say a house is worth $185,000 and the current taxes on the property were $6,750 per year. The effective tax rate would be:

$$\$6,750/\$185,000 = 0.04 \quad or \quad 4\%$$

The *actual* real estate taxes that a property owner pays are usually based on the *assessed value* of the house. Actual real estate taxes are **not** based on the actual *market value*. To calculate the actual tax rate, multiply the assessed value for the property, by the tax "mill rate" for the property. For example, let's say a house is assessed for $147,000 and the current mill rate for the yearly tax on the property is $53 per $1,000 of assessed value. The actual tax rate per year would be:

$$\$147,000/\$1,000 = 147$$

$$147 \times \$53 = \$7,791$$

The *Assessed Value Ratio* is the ratio between the assessed value amount of the subject property and the current market value amount. It's the *percentage* that the owner is paying in taxes, as compared to the market value of his property. To calculate the assessed value ratio, divide the assessed value of the property by the current market value of the property. In our example above the assessed value is $147,000 and the current market value for the property is $185,000. The assessed value ratio would be:

$$\$147,000/\$185,000 = .79 \quad or \quad 79\%$$

Obtaining Information At Town Hall

You have to make a trip to town hall to check **all** of the records pertaining to the subject property. You also need to verify the pertinent information concerning the sales comparables that you'll be using for the appraisal report. There will be times when you'll find discrepancies between some data sources. A real estate listing, for example, may have different information from what is recorded at town hall for the subject property and sales comps. When you encounter a situation like this, you may not be able to accurately determine which data source is correct. When this happens, you should always use the public record at town hall as the final say in the matter. You'll be much better off "Covering Your Assets" with the information from the public record than you will from any other data source.

In most areas you can purchase copies of the flood maps, tax maps, zoning maps and other information

> *You have to make a trip to town hall to check all of the records pertaining to the subject property.*
> *You also need to verify the pertinent information concerning the sales comparables you'll be using for the appraisal.*

from the local municipality. If you purchase these maps you can do some of the appraisal field work at your office. This can save you time at town hall. You'll also be able to get some appraisal information before you even go out to view the subject property.

When you get to town hall you usually have to visit several different departments to obtain all of the information that you need. Ask the employees in each department to assist you. You can save **a lot** of time by having them help you out. They know exactly where the information will be and they can help you with any questions you might have about it. As long as you're polite and friendly, they're usually willing to assist you. Don't go in there with an attitude like you're something special and they have to cater to your needs. If you have a nasty attitude or if you talk down to them, then you're not going to get much help from them. *Sounds basic doesn't it?* Well believe me, I've seen people go into town hall with an attitude toward the workers there like they were saying, *"gimme, gimme, gimme."* They have no consideration for the

town employees. People with an attitude like that end up wasting a lot of time because they have to find everything out for themselves. I have found that if you're friendly to the town hall employees they can help you tremendously in finding information. This will save you time and money.

Not all local town halls are the same. Some have more information than others and some have a filing and recording system that makes it easier to find the

> *Check to make sure that all necessary building dept. permits have been filed and all building department approvals have been obtained.*

information. Just do the best you can with what you have to work with in your area. Here's a list of some of the information you need to check at town hall but don't limit yourself to this list. Always get as much as data and information as you can for your appraisals:

1. Check the **field card or building papers** that describe the house and/or site. This should tell you the square footage of the house; type of construction materials used; the size of any decks, pools, garages; the age of the house; number of rooms; the site acreage etc. Determine if there is/was an underground septic system, well water system, and/or an underground oil tank on the site. Also, find out if all valid permits and approvals have been obtained for the installation and/ or the discontinued use of these underground items.

2. Check to make sure that all necessary **building department permits** have been filed and that all building department approvals have been obtained. This is required for any changes to the house and/or site from the time of the original construction or inspection by the local building department. Any decks, pools, garages, additions, updated kitchens and baths, etc. that have been added *must* have building department permits and approvals. Don't just take it for granted that they were filed. Check it out yourself!

3. Check to see if there are any **building code violations** against the subject property. This is something that the client and the title company will need to know. A building code violation is generally a safety hazard item found at the subject property that was recorded at town hall by the building inspector. Violations can be for any number of items that do not meet the standards and regulations of the local town. A violation must be repaired and then reinspected by the town building department inspectors to be removed from the record against the house.

4. Check to make sure that there is an up-to-date **Certificate of Occupancy** (C of O) for the subject property. Check the **zoning** for the subject property. You have to make sure that there are no zoning violations against the property. You also need to see what the conversion potential is for the property to decide what the Highest and Best Use will be. For

> *Check to see what the current taxes are on the property. Also, see when the next assessment is due so that you can find out if the taxes are going to go up soon.*

example, let's say the property has the zoning potential of being converted to a two-family house from the current single family house. Then you have to decide if a two-family house would be the H&B Use for the subject property, as opposed to a single family.

5. Check the **deed** for the subject property and all sales comps. This will list the legal description of the property, what the sales price was for the last sale, and sometimes for prior sales of the property, when these sale(s) took place, if there are any easements on the property, etc.

6. Check to see what the **current taxes** are on the property. Also, see when the **next assessment** is due so that you can find out if the taxes are going to go up soon. For example, the property taxes might not be high now. However, what if there's going to be a new tax assessment in the area that will greatly increase the yearly tax bill. This is something that the client will need to know and it will also have an effect on market value. There was a town in my area where the real estate taxes had not been reassessed for 10 years. When the city finally got around to reassessing property taxes, they raised the property taxes by as much as 60% for many homeowners! So many homeowners complained that the town had to roll-back part of that property tax increase.

7. Check the **flood hazard map** for the subject property. These are maps that the government publishes to figure out if a property is located in a designated flood hazard zone. A *flood hazard zone* is an area that is determined to have some potential for flooding from time to time. The cause of the flooding could be a river, lake, stream, etc. that is close to the subject property. A high groundwater table in the area could also cause the flooding. If a property is located in a designated flood hazard zone, then special flood hazard insurance will be needed.

8. Check the **survey** for the property. Surveys are very difficult to read so just do the best you can. Surveys are used to find the property line boundaries of real estate. The United States government survey applies in the whole country except the original 13 states: Texas, Tennessee, Kentucky and the New England area states. *Mete* is the name referring to a distance on a survey. *Bound* is the name referring to a direction on a survey. The direction can be a compass direction or the name of an adjacent property owner. If you ever see a surveyor at work you'll be amazed to find how precise their measurements are. I had a survey done on one of my rental properties before I sold it and the surveyor's were taking down measurements up to 1/1000 of an inch! I couldn't believe how precise they were about it.

Condominium and Co-Operative Units

Appraising Condos and Co-Ops is the same as appraising single family houses. There are a few additional factors that you have to consider on Condos and Co-Ops. Most areas of the country have Condominium units. Co-Operatives are only found in very few areas. Many people have never even heard of Co-Ops because they don't have any in their area.

Condominiums are usually owned with *Fee Simple* ownership rights. The idea of condominium complexes is that it provides the purchaser with a less expensive form of home ownership. A condo owner will not have to spend as much money as is needed to buy a single family house. Also, many people like having the exterior of their home, as well as the grounds, maintained by someone else for a relatively

> *Condos are attached units with common areas that all of the owners in the whole complex have the right to use. The common areas usually have a Tenancy in Common ownership.*

inexpensive fee. Condos are attached units with common areas that all of the owners in the whole complex have the right to use. The common areas usually have a *Tenancy in Common* ownership. This ownership is spread between all the individual unit owners in the complex. There are *monthly assessment fees* that all of the individual unit owners have to pay to maintain the exterior of the complex and the common areas. The individual owners cannot paint, change or alter the exterior of their units in any way unless the Condo Board approves the changes.

There is a Board of some elected Condo owners as well as a *Prospectus* that outlines the rules and regulations of owning a condominium in the complex. The reason for this is to keep the exterior and common areas looking very uniform and well kept. You wouldn't want your neighbor to paint the outside of his Condo fluorescent pink would you? The regulations have guidelines on how the common areas can be used. Sometimes there are rules of whether the individual Condo units can be rented out to tenants or whether you can have pets. The whole intent of the rules and regulations in the Prospectus of each complex is to try to keep a uniform and pleasant environment. This is for the benefit of all the unit owners, as opposed to catering to each person's individual needs and tastes.

Co-Operatives are owned with *Leasehold* ownership rights. The idea of Co-Ops is that it provides the owner with an alternative to renting. It is a less expensive form of home ownership than having to spend more money to buy a single family house. Again, many people like the idea of having the exterior of their home, as well as the grounds, maintained by someone else for a relatively inexpensive fee. Co-Operatives are similar to Condos, however, Co-Ops are generally only found in converted apartment buildings in urban areas, like New York City. Often an apartment building will be converted to a Co-Op building just by selling off the individual apartments. The first step is that the current owner of the building, called the *Sponsor*, will set up a corporation with shares of stock. Rather than selling the buyer Fee Simple ownership, they purchase shares of stock from the corporation. The larger your apartment, or Co-Op unit, then the more shares of stock you obtain. But, the sales price is higher when you buy more shares of the stock. The owner of a Co-Operative unit in a building is legally a renter. By owning that particular share of the stock, which is *Personalty*, it gives him the right to rent a certain apartment from the corporation. The important document is the *Proprietary Lease*.

It's important that you understand that with a Co-Op you're legally still a renter. However, as a shareholder you have the right to live in one of the apartments. The reason behind the whole concept of Co-Operatives is that in a large, built-up urban city, like New York City, there are no single family houses.

The only option is to sell off individual units in an existing apartment building which gives people an opportunity to buy their home as opposed to renting an apartment.

As with Condos, Co-Ops have common areas that all of the owners in the whole building have the right to use. There are *monthly assessment fees* that all of the individual unit owners have to pay to maintain the exterior of the building and the common areas. The individual owners cannot paint, change or alter the exterior of their units in any way unless the Co-Op

> *The individual owners cannot paint, change or alter the exterior of their units in any way unless the Condo/Co-Op board approves the changes.*

board approves the changes. Co-Ops have elected Board members but instead of a Prospectus they have *By-Laws*. The *By-Laws* outline the rules and regulations of owning a Co-Op unit, (shares of stock), in the building, (corporation). The reason for this is to keep the exterior and common areas looking very uniform and well kept. Co-Op By-Law regulations are usually **very** strict. Much more strict than many Condo rules. The By-Laws regulate how the common areas can be used and whether the individual Co-Op units can be rented out to tenants or whether you can have pets. As with Condos, the whole intent of the rules and regulations in the By-Laws is to try to keep a uniform and pleasant environment. This is for the benefit of *all* the unit owners as opposed to catering to each person's individual needs and tastes.

With Co-Ops there is a Co-Op board that has to approve any potential tenants that you can rent your unit to, if the rules allow tenants. The board also has to approve any potential buyers that you have for your unit when you try to sell it. This is the strict part of the By-Laws that can really bother some people. It's similar to having someone "approve" you to become a member of a private country club. One possible reason for this is that Co-Op corporations have an underlying mortgage for the purchase of the building. The *underlying mortgage* is the mortgage that is taken out by the corporation to originally purchase the entire building from the current owner, (sponsor). The unit owners purchase the building when the individual shares of stock are sold to them. Each buyer or stockholder has a monthly assessment charge to pay their portion of the underlying mortgage payment. It's similar to the monthly assessment for Condos. However, with Co-Ops you not only have the underlying mortgage but you also have the monthly assessment fee. The monthly assessment fee pays for the maintenance of the exterior of the building and the common areas.

Some things you have to watch out for when appraising Condos and Co-Ops are the rules and regulations of the Prospectus and By-Laws. Sometimes you'll find that a particular complex has unusually strict rules that can affect the market value of the individual units. Remember that even if just **one** buyer

> *Sometimes you'll find that a particular complex has unusually strict rules that can affect the market value of the individual units.*

is turned away because of something about the subject property; then that is something that must be considered in the appraisal report. This is because that aspect has a negative influence on market value.

I've done quite a few foreclosure appraisals on Co-Ops where the bank had taken the property back from the defaulting mortgagee. The bank would often find potential buyers at lower than normal sales prices just because they wanted to sell the Co-Op quickly. However, the sale wouldn't go through. The Board members of the complex would come up with all sorts of reasons why they wouldn't approve the sale to this potential buyer. One bank in particular had to actually get to the point of threatening some of the Co-Op Boards with a lawsuit. The bank did this because the Co-Op Boards kept denying approval for the sale to all interested buyers that the bank could find. Some bank employees told me that the reason the Co-Op Boards did this is that the sales prices were lower than normal. The low sales prices were the result of the property being a foreclosure. These Co-Ops generally needed a lot of work on the interior of the unit. If the Board approved a low-priced sale, then it would bring down the market value of all the other units in the complex. Market values would drop because that low sale could be used as a sales comparable for an appraisal that involved other units in the complex. This would hurt the market value of **all** of the units in the building.

Some banks will often find potential buyers at lower than normal prices because the bank is not concerned with trying to wait to get top dollar for the unit. They merely want to sell the unit for a lower than normal price just to get rid of it quickly. The reason for this is that banks do not want to be in the property management business. They make their profits by lending money out, not by selling houses, Condos or Co-Ops. If they tried to get top dollar for a foreclosure

property on their books, then they might have to wait a long time before a qualified buyer came along. The longer a bank keeps a property on their books, then the more money it costs the bank in monthly fees for the property management, maintenance, taxes, etc. These fees can become extremely costly, especially when the bank has already paid extensive legal fees to go through the entire foreclosure process.

Another aspect you need to consider with Co-Ops is the underlying mortgage balance and the due date of this mortgage. Many underlying mortgages have *balloon* payments. This refers to a set date in the future when the remaining balance of the loan becomes due and payable to the lender. When the mortgage comes due, then the Co-Op corporation has to secure new financing to pay off the balance. If they cannot obtain financing then the whole building and corporation will go into foreclosure for the loan! If the underlying mortgage is due in the near future, then a typical buyer will be a little leery about buying stock, (apartment), in that building. This will have an effect on market value. The reason for this is that I've seen a number of cases where the underlying mortgage loan was in foreclosure proceedings started by the lender. This means that if you were a stockholder, and you had been making all of your monthly mortgage and monthly assessment payments, you could still lose your equity position. Your equity would be lost because the lender was foreclosing on the underlying mortgage. That will definitely affect the market value of all of the Co-Ops in the building. A foreclosure proceeding on the underlying mortgage will make a typical buyer alter their purchase price drastically and they will probably back out of the deal altogether.

The monthly assessments have to be considered when you're appraising Condos and Co-Ops. Two units in two separate complexes can have the same asking price and be very similar in construction. However, if

> *The reason for this is that banks do not want to be in the property management business.*
> *They make their profits by lending money out, not by selling houses, Condos or Co-Ops.*

the monthly assessment fees are different, then the typical buyer will take this into account. Remember that the monthly assessment *is not* a mortgage payment that benefits the individual unit owners. It's merely used to pay for the maintenance of the exterior and the common areas. This monthly fee will increase with inflation as prices go up in the economy and the costs of maintaining and managing the complex increase. It's no different from paying a small rent payment each month. That payment <u>does not</u> increase the equity for the individual unit owner. You should find out what the rules in the complex are for increases in monthly assessment charges. Can they double overnight? If so, then it's going to have an effect on market value.

You have to check all Condo´ and Co-Op complexes for the number of individual units that have been sold and how many are rented or owned by the builder or sponsor of the complex. The reason for this is that when most or all of the units are sold, then the complex generally has a steady cash flow from the

> *Remember that the monthly assessment is not a mortgage payment that benefits the individual unit owners.*
> *It's merely used to pay for the maintenance of the exterior and common areas*

monthly assessments to pay all of the common area charges. But when the builder or sponsor own most of the complex, then you have many vacancies and the cash flow may not be enough to pay the monthly bills. This can lead to the common areas being neglected and/or the underlying mortgage not being paid. To offset a cash flow problem or large bills, most complexes will have a "special assessment" fee. This is an increased monthly payment that all the current unit owners have to pay. The payment is in addition to their regular payments and it's needed to compensate for the poor cash flow. This will have an effect on market value so make sure you do your homework and check these things out completely.

Over Improvements

Be wary of houses that have over improvements. A homeowner creates an "over improvement" when they spend more money in repairs and/or upgrading than they gain in increased market value for the property. For example, I once did an appraisal on a house located in a neighborhood of homes that ranged from $475,000 - $700,000. The homeowner had purchased the house for about $525,000 and then a year later they spent another **$430,000** to do more improvements to the house. They didn't just remodel the kitchens and baths for $430,000. They added a new floor on the house, they built an addition on the side of the house, they remodeled the entire interior, etc. When the work was completed the house was beautiful. The only

problem was that they spent about *$250,000* too much!! That's what you call an *over improvement*.

Since this house was located in an area where all of the houses ranged in value from $475,000 - $700,000, then this homeowner could not expect to sell the house for more money than the area could demand. If a typical buyer wanted to spend $955,000 on a house, ($525,000 + $430,000), that potential buyer wouldn't purchase this subject property because the market values of the other houses weren't even close to that price. The potential buyer would spend $955,000 in an area where the value of the other houses all fell within that range. Therefore, the additional work the homeowner in this example had done, was not well-spent money from an investment standpoint. Now that doesn't mean that the homeowner isn't happy with the work they did. There is an **amenity** value for the property owner by living in a remodeled house that they're in love with. However, this is a *subjective* opinion of that particular homeowner. If the typical buyer would not agree with that same reasoning, then the excess renovation funds were not well spent from an investment standpoint.

Some people don't realize that just because they spend $1.00 in repairs and/or upgrading to their house, it doesn't guarantee that they're going to increase the market value by at least $1.00. That's why homeowners need to properly evaluate any extensive work they're planning on doing *before* they spend the money to have it done. One of the best things for a

> *Some people don't realize that just because they spend $1.00 in repairs and/or upgrading to their house, it doesn't guarantee that they're going to increase the market value by at least $1.00.*

homeowner to do is to hire a good appraiser to give them an *As Repaired* market value estimate. This is simply an estimate based upon certain conditions and/ or repairs being completed. An "as repaired" appraisal will be like telling the client, *"Well, if you make the renovations and build the addition according to the building plans your architect has shown me, then the estimate of market value for your house when it's all completed will be $...."*

Other Types Of Housing

A *Planned Unit Development*, (PUD), is <u>not</u> a form of ownership like a condominium or a co-operative unit. A PUD is just a land plan and it usually centers around manufactured housing, such as a trailer park. Manufactured Housing and Mobile Homes can be well made housing with today's technology. Many people think you only get junk when you buy a prefabricated house, but that's not true. I know contractors that build houses from scratch that have considered putting up prefabricated houses. The reason for this is that all of the essential construction parts of the house are built in large warehouses that are like an assembly line. Since the sections are put together in a controlled environment, they can be very well made because the weather doesn't affect the workers or the materials. The different parts are then shipped to the vacant site and put together to form a finished house.

Row Houses generally all look the same as units that are next to them. Row houses are mostly found in older cities. *Town Houses* generally all look a little different from the units that are next to them.

Mortgages, Mortgages And More Mortgages

Some states have *Deeds of Trust* as opposed to *Mortgages*. One difference between the two is that a Deed of Trust generally takes less time to foreclose on someone than a mortgage does. The mortgage or deed of trust is the collateral for the money lent. A *mortgagee* is the lender of a loan. A *mortgagor* is the borrower of a loan. A *Deed* is a document to transfer title of a property. Title passes on real estate when the buyer accepts the deed. The deed **does not** require the buyer's signature in order to pass title.

A **First Mortgage** refers to the mortgage that is paid off first in case of a foreclosure or sale of the property. All mortgages and liens should <u>always</u> be recorded at the local town hall to notify the public that someone has a lien or collateral against the property. This is done to make sure that nobody else records a new mortgage against the subject property before any existing mortgages are recorded. For example, let's say a bank lent you money to refinance your house. Well if the bank's attorney or the title company forgot to

record that mortgage at town hall, then you could take out another mortgage against your house and the second lender wouldn't even know the first mortgage existed! A properly recorded second mortgage on a property is called a *Junior Mortgage* because it's recorded after the existing first mortgage.

Mortgages take priority in the order in which they are recorded at the town hall. For example, let's say there are five mortgages on a house and the house is sold. At the closing, the seller must pay off all of the mortgage holders to give the buyer a "clear" title. A clear title simply means that the new buyer will obtain the deed for the property without any encumbrances against it. The only encumbrances will be those that

> All mortgages and liens should be recorded at the local town hall to notify the public that someone has a lien or collateral against the property

the new buyer incurs to purchase the property, such as his own bank financing mortgage. The mortgage holders that are paid off at the closing will sign a *Satisfaction of Mortgage*. This is a document stating the lenders have removed any claims or liens they have against the subject property.

If a house has five mortgages against it and the house is foreclosed on by one of those mortgage holders, then the person with the first mortgage is paid off first. Then the second mortgage holder is paid off next, etc. so on down the line. However, if there isn't enough money to pay off any or all of the mortgage holders, then they get stuck holding the bag and end up losing money. In some states an unpaid mortgage holder can then sue the property owner to be paid through the personal funds or assets of that person. Because of the order in which the mortgage holders are

> The fifth mortgage holder can still foreclose on the property even though everyone else is getting paid on time.

paid off, it's more desirable for a lender to have a first mortgage as opposed to a second or third mortgage. The lower on down the line you get, the less secure the mortgage loan becomes in case of a foreclosure sale. That's why many junior mortgages have higher interest rates and lower loan-to-value ratios. The lender is at a greater risk with their loan so they have a higher interest rate and a lower loan-to-value ratio to try to compensate for this additional risk.

The **Loan-To-Value Ratio** simply refers to the amount of money lent against the property as opposed to what is the actual market value of the property. For example, let's say a house is appraised at $275,000 and the lender is willing to give the borrower a 75% loan-to-value ratio loan for a first mortgage. That means that if the loan application is approved, then the lender will lend the borrower $275,000 x 75% = $206,250. Let's say that same lender is asked by the borrower to lend him money secured by a *second* mortgage on his house. In this case the lender may only have a 50% loan-to-value ratio for a second mortgage because it's a riskier loan to grant someone. That means that if the loan application is approved, then the lender will lend the borrower $275,000 x 50% = $137,500.

Any of the mortgage holders can foreclose on the property owner for not living up to the terms of the mortgage note agreement. For example, let's say the owner of the property makes all of his loan payments on time to the first four mortgage holders but doesn't pay the fifth mortgage holder. The fifth mortgage holder can still foreclose on the property even though everyone else is getting paid on time. However, the fifth mortgage holder will only get paid from the money that's left over from paying off the first four mortgages from the foreclosure sale proceeds. As a result, this lender's chances of getting all of their money back can be greatly reduced by a foreclosure sale on the property. This generally will give the lender some incentive to "work out" a new loan payment agreement with the borrower instead of rushing into a foreclosure proceeding.

Now I don't want to give you the wrong impression by making you think that there are a lot of houses out there that have four or five mortgages on them. The vast majority of houses have only one mortgage on them and sometimes you'll find a second mortgage lien as well.

A **Purchase Money Mortgage** is given in lieu of receiving cash. It's often called *seller financing*. This is what happens when you buy a house and the seller takes part of the sales price amount in a mortgage. No cash changes hands for the amount of the purchase money mortgage. For example, let's say you agreed to buy the house for $115,000 and you obtained a mortgage from the bank for $75,000 and you paid $25,000 of your own money to the seller. That only totals $100,000. To make up the difference, the seller agreed to accept $15,000 in a second mortgage behind your bank's first mortgage position. That $15,000 is called a *purchase money mortgage* or *seller financing*. A real estate deal structured in a

manner, such as the one in this example, can be said to have "creative financing." This means that the type of financing arrangements in the deal are different from a typical real estate transaction in the area. From an appraisal standpoint you have to be careful when you find out that a comparable sale has had a purchase money mortgage involved in the financing. The reason

> *From an appraisal standpoint you have to be careful when you find out that a comparable sale has had a purchase money mortgage involved in the financing.*

for this is that the total sales price in this deal may not indicate the value for the property in an all cash equivalent sale. The seller generally can get a higher sales price for his property by offering the buyer better terms, such as a purchase money mortgage agreement.

As we have seen by the ITAO table examples, the reason the seller can get a higher sales price is that often the seller will offer the buyer a lower interest rate for the purchase money mortgage than the buyer could obtain from a conventional mortgage lender. Also, if a buyer doesn't have a sufficient income to qualify for a large enough mortgage to pay the asking price of the house, the seller can offer a purchase money mortgage to help the buyer. This is known as giving the buyer "good terms" on the sale. When a buyer gets good terms then they're more willing to pay a higher price for the property. As a result, the sales price for a deal with good terms can be inflated over what a typical buyer would have paid for that same house under a conventional mortgage loan and terms.

Insured or **Guaranteed Mortgages** help to protect the lender in the event of a foreclosure. However, the lender generally is not fully insured for their loan. There are Federal Housing Authority, *(FHA)*, and Veterans Administration, *(VA)*, loans that are 95% guaranteed for the mortgage lender. This means that if the lender gives the buyer the loan on a property that meets the FHA or VA loan qualifications, then that loan will be insured for 95% of its value. For example, let's say the buyer stopped making the monthly loan payments. Well, if the bank foreclosed and didn't receive all of its money, then the FHA or VA would pay the lender up to 95% of the remaining balance of the loan until the lender was paid off completely.

Open End Mortgages allow the borrower to add to the loan principal balance by borrowing more money without have to reapply for a new loan. These loans are commonly used for construction of buildings. The builder gets additional funds in stages as the work progresses to complete the construction of the building. This gives the lender some type of security by not giving one large sum of money up front. The builder gets the funds as they are needed to complete the different stages of the construction process.

Participation Mortgages refer to more than one lender loaning money on the deal. For example, it's when several different banks put in a portion of the total loan funds for the transaction. This provides the lenders with some additional security and lowers the risk of the loan. If the loan is for many millions of dollars, then it would be a severe loss to just one lender if they had to foreclose on the loan. However, if many different banks are involved in lending the money, then the losses are spread out. Since spreading out the losses reduces the risk, the income also reduces because the different banks involved in the transaction have to share the profits of the loan. Many insurance companies do this when they write very large insurance policies. If there was a claim against a multimillion dollar policy, then the losses are spread out over many different insurance companies who took part in writing the policy. They have to share the income from the yearly premiums but the tradeoff is that they don't have to pay any losses alone.

ARM refers to **Adjustable Rate Mortgages**. These mortgages have an interest rate that is adjusted at specified intervals. The adjustments are based upon a certain index that must be available for the public to monitor. Some of the indexes they are linked to are the Prime lending rate, Treasury bills, etc. With these loans your monthly loan payment will change with each adjustment made. Often an ARM will have an adjustment cap and a lifetime cap. This means that the loan payment adjustment can only go up or down a certain percentage for each specified period and over the life of the loan.

You have to be very careful if you ever get an adjustable rate mortgage. Statistics that show that as many as 25% of adjustable rate mortgage loans are improperly calculated.

You have to be <u>very careful</u> if you ever get an adjustable rate mortgage. There have been statistics that have shown that as many as 25% of the adjustable rate mortgage loans are improperly calculated. When this happens, the borrower ends up paying the bank more money than they're owed. There are companies that provide a service that will properly calculate what your ARM loan payments and remaining loan balance

should be. The fee for this service is usually inexpensive. If you have any doubts about an ARM loan, and you should due to the record of poor monitoring by the banks, then hire these services to make sure you're not overpaying on your loan.

GPM refers to **Graduated Payment Mortgages**. *(Some people jokingly call these "jip-um" mortgages)*. With these mortgages the payments are lower than the actual amortized loan payment would normally be. For example, let's say you have a 20 year amortized loan and the normal loan payment for the loan would be $1,000 a month. With a GPM the loan payment might only be $750 per month. However, the additional $250 that is needed to fully amortize the loan over the 20 year term is added to the outstanding loan principal balance. This results in negative amortization and the principal balance of the loan <u>increases</u> instead of decreasing over time. This growth continues until the loan payments are adjusted high enough to start to amortize the loan principal balance. The purpose of this type of loan is it enables the borrower to take out a loan with lower monthly payments in the early years. This will help someone get an approval for a higher mortgage loan than they would if the loan had a normal amortization loan.

Negative Amortization refers to the type of loan payment schedule where the monthly loan payments do not fully amortize the loan. As a result, the loan principal does not get reduced with each payment. The interest is reduced with the payments as the principal balance increases.

A **Land Contract** is a document representing an installment sale. A *Land Contract* is also called an *Installment Sales Contract*. This refers to a sale of a property that does not pass the title to the buyer until all payments are made and the full purchase price is paid. For example, let's say you were selling your house and the buyer wanted to "assume" your existing mortgage loan. If your loan was not an assumable loan, then your lender would make you pay off the loan at the closing before you could pass clear title to the buyer. However, you could sell your property on a land contract and not tell the bank about it. The way it would work would be the buyer would take possession of the house but he wouldn't receive the deed or title until your mortgage loan was paid off and you had received the full purchase price for the house. You can agree to almost anything as far as the terms of any payments go.

However, it must be noted that a land contract is usually against the rules and agreements of any existing mortgages on a property and it should not be used to sell or buy a property. The current mortgage holders usually have signed mortgage note saying that they will be paid off in full when the property is sold. Even though the deed or title does not pass to the new buyer at the new closing on the property, it's still considered a sale. If the existing mortgage holders ever found out about such an agreement, then they can call the mortgage due and payable immediately! If you didn't have the funds to pay them in full, they could begin a foreclosure proceeding.

Another drawback to a land contract is that the buyer of the property may have no way of knowing if the current deed or title holder puts a new mortgage on the property. The buyer also will not know if any liens are recorded against the property **after** the original closing and before the deed or title is eventually passed to the new buyer. So you see, it's a very risky way of trying to sell a house and I wouldn't recommend that you get involved with a transaction like that.

Loan Principal is the balance or amount of the outstanding loan that is left to pay off. This does not include the interest amount on the loan.

Loan Interest is the balance or amount of the outstanding interest left to pay off. This does not include the principal amount on the loan. Paying loan interest is basically paying rent for the use of borrowed money.

An **Assumable Loan** is an outstanding loan balance that can be "assumed" or taken over by someone else other than the person who originally borrowed the money. For example, let's say you took out an assumable mortgage loan on your house. If you

> *You have to be careful though with assumable loans. Sometimes the original borrower is still held accountable for the repayment on the loan after someone else assumes it from him.*

decided to sell your house down the road, then the buyer could assume your remaining loan balance. The buyer will just continue making the monthly loan payments right where you left them off when you sold the house. Generally all the buyer will have to do is pay a small "assumption" fee to the bank and fill out a new loan application. The buyer may not have to be approved and go through an entire loan process like

you did when you first borrowed the money. You **have to** be careful though with assumable loans. Sometimes the original borrower is still held accountable for the repayment on the loan after someone else assumes it from him. If this were the case and the person you sold your house to stopped making payments on the loan, then the bank could come after you for the remaining funds owed to them. If this happened, it could also have a negative impact on your credit rating. That's something that you certainly don't want to happen!

Blanket Mortgage is a mortgage that covers several properties.

Package Mortgage is a mortgage that covers the _Realty_ plus the _Personalty_. The Personalty is also called *Chattels*. A *Package Mortgage* includes more than the real estate. For example, a condominium that is sold with the appliances included in the mortgage could be called a package mortgage.

Conventional Loan is a loan from a bank that's not insured like an FHA or VA loan and it has the market interest rates. The *Veterans Administration* (VA), the *Federal Housing Administration* (FHA), the *Federal National Mortgage Association* (FNMA) also known as "Fannie Mae," the *Government National Mortgage Association* (GNMA) also known as "Ginnie Mae," and the *Federal Home Loan Mortgage Corporation* (FHLMC) also known as "Freddie Mac," are all government organizations that function on their own in the secondary mortgage market. The purpose of the secondary market is that they buy the mortgage loans from the banks. They then package a group of loans together and sell them off to investors in the bond market as mortgage backed securities. The benefit for the banks is that they get to replenish their funds after they sell off some loans in their portfolios. This is why banks have many of the current requirements for appraisals, termite inspections, etc. They need this documentation in order to meet the requirements to sell their loans on the secondary market.

Different Types Of Appraisal Accounts

1.   *Loan Origination Appraisals* - This type of appraisal account will be busier during good economic conditions and increasing sales of homes. During a good economy there will be higher employment percentages and more opportunity to make money. This leads to many people buying a nicer home or moving to a nicer area, which in turn leads to many new mortgage loan applications at the banks that will require appraisals.

2.   *Refinance Loan Appraisals* - This type of appraisal account will generally be busier during times of lower interest rates for mortgage loans. During lower interest rate times many homeowners will refinance their existing mortgage. They can take advantage of the lower interest rates to reduce their current monthly mortgage payments. This leads to many refinance mortgage loan applications at the banks that will require appraisals.

3.   *Foreclosure Appraisals* - This type of appraisal account will generally be busier during bad economic conditions and recessions. During a bad economy there will be higher unemployment which leads to many people falling behind with paying their bills and their mortgage loan payments. This in turn leads to bank foreclosure proceedings. New appraisals are needed after the properties are taken back by the lenders. It's a tragedy when someone loses their home due to foreclosure. However, as I've said earlier, you're not taking advantage of anyone or being unethical by appraising properties that are the result of a distressed sale or a foreclosure. All of these properties have to be appraised. Therefore, someone is going to be hired to do the job. Everyone will be much better off if the lender hires an **"A to Z Appraiser"** who does top quality work. Why make the situation worse by hiring another appraiser who is only concerned with the fee he earns and not the quality of his appraisal.

I do an awful lot of foreclosure appraisals for lenders. After the bank takes the property back, they have it reappraised to decide what price to list it at for a quick sale. They do this to sell the property quickly and get as much of their money back as possible. By doing foreclosure appraisals, I've seen some very interesting properties and situations. I'm referring to aspects other than the sad fact that someone has lost their home due to a distressed situation. You might want to consider getting an account to do some foreclosure appraisals because it's great experience and you may find it to be very interesting work.

I've seen everything from very low valued Condos and Co-Ops, multi-million dollar single family houses, a State Supreme Court Judge's house, and even funeral homes that have been foreclosed on that I had to appraise. Some houses are in great condition after a foreclosure. I have seen cases of people that have put a

> *Therefore, someone will be hired to do the job. Everyone will be much better off if the lender hires an "A to Z Appraiser" who does top quality work.*

lot of money into a house and then some bad luck hit them. They ended up losing their jobs or another unfortunate circumstance happened to them. Since they couldn't make the loan payments, the bank took the house back. I've also seen some houses that were *totally* destroyed after a foreclosure. I've seen cases of people who would destroy a house out of anger and revenge due to the bank foreclosing on them. I've also seen some dishonest builders and investors scam the banks out of millions of dollars. What they did was borrow the money and then just walk away from the house and kept the funds from the loan without even making one loan payment to the bank.

4.   *Tax Appraisals* - This type of appraisal account will generally be busier during times when the property taxes are raised. Many homeowners will dispute an increase in their property taxes or the current amount of their taxes. They may feel that their property has been "over assessed" and that their property taxes should be reduced. To dispute your property taxes, you need to have an appraisal done to estimate the market value of your property.

5.   *Commercial Appraisals* - This type of appraisal account will generally be busier in a good economy when businesses are doing well. A commercial real estate appraisal refers to the appraisal of a building and/or site that deals with a nonresidential property. This would generally be any building larger than a legal four family dwelling or a site that is commercially zoned by town hall. Commercial appraising is very involved and takes a lot more training, experience and classes than just doing residential appraisals. If you ever have the opportunity to work with a commercial appraiser you'll see what I mean. The fees charged for commercial appraisals are **much** higher than those charged for residential appraisals. However, along with the higher fees there

is a much higher liability that's assumed by the appraiser if a mistake is made with the report. As with anything else in life: *The greater the rewards, the higher the risk and sacrifice to obtain those rewards.*

Miscellaneous Notes

I remember Dr. Scribner responding to a question in our class about whether or not the appraiser should know the sales price of the subject property. Let's say the sales price is $91,000 and your appraisal is coming in at $90,000. Then you can make the value $91,000 because no one can measure value that accurately and why create problems with the deal for a 3-4% difference from the sales price. This is one reason why you should know the sales price as long as you're not biased by knowing it. Also, by knowing the sales price you can get some indication of the type of property and sales comparables you'll be evaluating ahead of time.

> *This is one reason you should know the sales price as long as you're not biased by knowing it.*
> *Also, by knowing the sales price you can get some indication of the type of property and sales comparables you'll be evaluating ahead of time.*

Contract Rent is the rent that's being paid according to the lease. Leases should have a *condemnation clause* in them. This will help protect the landlord in case the building gets condemned at a time when the tenant has below market rent. If this happened, the tenant could take the landlord to court to be compensated for the difference between what the market rent is for the area and what their contract rent is in the lease. If this happened a judge can award the tenant money since there's no condemnation clause in their lease. As the landlord, you certainly don't want that to happen!

Urban Space is space in a building in an urban area. For example, space in an office building in a built-up and populated city. *Floor Area Ratio*, (FAR) - how many feet of building can you put on a lot. *Loss Ratio* - the square feet of a building that is lost rental due to hallways, common areas, utility rooms, etc. Sometimes entire floors are called "mechanical floors" because they hold the operating systems for part of the building. These all reduce the total rentable square feet

in the building. The lower the Loss Ratio is, then the higher the efficiency of the building. The efficiency percentage is based upon the size of the building that you're dealing with. A 15% loss ratio could be considered low and a 25% loss ratio could be considered high.

The Reconciliation Process

Before starting to write up your appraisal report you should sit down with all of your notes, photographs and maps and review your data. This will give you some sense of direction before you jump into the report and end up leaving important items out. When you write an appraisal report use wording that is in a business like and professional manner. Remember the person reading your report will be someone trying to use the appraisal to help them in a business and investment decision.

You have to reconcile the entire appraisal report as you write it up. While you're filling out the back of the appraisal form, keep checking the front side to make sure that you're being consistent with what you write. You can always go back and change things while you're writing up the report, so take your time and be thorough. There will be times when you're writing up the report and you realize that you need to obtain some more information. You may need this information to make sure your conclusions are accurate and

You check for the accuracy and logic of your information to see that it makes sense and it's not way off base. You don't want any conflicting statements and/or measurements because then your entire appraisal report becomes questionable.

consistent. When this happens, stop writing the report until you go out and get the necessary data. You're much better off taking your time and delaying the report than just rushing it to meet a deadline. Remember "haste makes waste."

Since every phase of the appraisal report is being reconciled, you're constantly reviewing your data to come up with a supportive estimate of value. You check for the accuracy and logic of your information to see that it makes sense and it's not way off base. You don't want any conflicting statements and/or measurements because then your entire appraisal report becomes questionable. Just remember to <u>be consistent</u> in all of your reports and on the front **and**

back of the appraisal form reports!!! *(I think I've told you that enough times now, so I know you're never gonna forget it, right?)* There are items that are found in several areas on the form, such as, square footage, room count, garages, condition, location evaluations, etc. Be careful and make sure that you list them consistently or else your entire appraisal report will be in question. Also, be careful not to show two different viewpoints, such as, whether the market is increasing or decreasing in real estate values.

One of my instructors told our class that he was involved in a court case that had to deal with inconsistencies in an appraisal report for a commercial property. He said that the appraiser showed two conflicting viewpoints for the direction of the real estate market at the time of valuation for this property. Supposedly the lender had to foreclose on this property. After the foreclosure, the lender found out that the market value was worth much less than they were led to believe by the appraisal report. The lender filed a lawsuit against the appraiser. They sued based on the assumption that they wouldn't have lent the money in the first place if the appraisal report was accurate. The lender believed that the report failed to accurately estimate the market conditions and value "as of" the date of the appraisal. In some areas of the appraisal report there was supposedly data showing a declining market and in other areas there was data showing an increasing market. These types of inconsistencies put the credibility of your entire appraisal report in question.

Just use your **<u>common sense</u>** and think about your reconciliation analysis. Make sure that your estimates and comments in the report make sense. Don't let a calculator make your decisions for you!! You're the one with the mind that has the ability to think and reason, not the calculator or textbook. The calculator and textbook are only used to assist you in your appraisal report. You have to reconcile the **entire** appraisal report and not just one section, such as the grid area on the form for the sales comparison approach. All factors in your field notes and report must be considered to come up with a supportive estimate of value.

Nothing is cut into stone in performing good, quality and thorough real estate appraisals. The appraisal textbooks and techniques are guidelines and recommendations, not the final say. You're the one who has seen the subject property and the sales comparables firsthand with your own eyes. *(At least you better have or I'm comin' to get ya!)*. You're the one who has obtained the field notes and pertinent data. Therefore, you're the expert and the professional

All factors in your field notes and report must be considered to come up with a supportive estimate of value.

who has firsthand knowledge and experience with the property you're appraising. Use your own judgment on all appraisals to CYA. Now that doesn't mean that you shouldn't take advice from someone else who has more knowledge than you do. Especially, if there's a review appraiser who is looking over your reports and signing their name to them. Just remember that you put your John Hancock on the bottom line of every appraisal report. Therefore, it's your neck that's on the line if you screw up or cut corners. Cover Your Assets and do good, quality work on all of your reports.

The reconciliation process considers all three approaches to value but you don't have to use all three as long as you have a valid reason. Let's say you decided not to use the Cost Approach since the building is too old or for another reason. Well you still have considered the Cost Approach even though you didn't use it.

Signing-Off On The Appraisal Report

When you sign-off on an appraisal report you don't want to create a lot of problems for yourself later. Problems can arise later if the client finds out that your data is inaccurate or your market value estimate is way off base. So make sure you know what you're doing and that you have sufficient information about the subject property, the comparable sales and the local market. **Don't** include any data that's PFA, which stands for *Plucked From the Air*. Meaning, don't make up information just to fill out sections of the report. As I said before, if you need to obtain more data, then take the time to go and get it before finishing the report.

It's *very important* that you understand the fact that when you sign an appraisal report, you will be held accountable for everything in it. Also, when you sign-off on a report as the review appraiser, then you're just as liable for the accuracy of the data in that appraisal report as the appraiser himself. So don't just flip through a report and sign-off as the review appraiser. Make sure the data you're reviewing is accurate and that the appraiser that has viewed the property is competent and thorough.

Anyone can file a complaint against you for any of your appraisal reports if it's found to have serious inaccuracies and problems in it. It doesn't have to be your client who has to be the one to file a complaint

Don't include any data that's PFA, which stands for Plucked From the Air. Meaning don't make up information just to fill out sections of the report.

against you. If someone off the street was given a copy of your report by a client they can create problems for you if you do poor quality work. You don't want one of your reports coming back to haunt you down the road. The State Certification Committee in your state can bring you up in front of a review board. This will happen if you're guilty of doing poor appraisal reports that have serious inaccuracies and inconsistencies.

I had an experience with an *MAI* designated appraiser who was signing-off on appraisal reports as the reviewer and **he wasn't even reading the reports!!!** An MAI is a very high designation for an appraiser to get. I had gotten very busy at one point and I had to subcontract out some of my work. This was because my office couldn't handle all of the work we had and I didn't have the time to hire and train any new appraisers. The appraisal office that I had hired to do some of my appraisals ended up doing some of the worst appraisal reports I have ever seen. These appraisals were so bad that they weren't even worth the paper they were written on! There were so many inconsistencies and problems in these reports that it was amazing to me how anyone could sign-off on them. As a result, I had to throw away all of those reports. *(Of course I told them I wasn't paying their bill)*. I called their office and told them that I was considering filing a complaint against them with the Appraisal Institute and the State Certification Board. Coincidentally, they never sent me another bill for their work and I never heard from them again.

What apparently had happened was that this MAI and his appraisal office were only concerned with pumping out as many reports per day as possible. They couldn't care less about the quality of the appraisals. All they wanted to know was how much money they could make each day. So learn a lesson from this experience like I did. If you ever get very busy and have to subcontract out some appraisal work or hire new appraisers quickly, you better make sure that they do quality work. You'll be in just as much trouble as them if you send in bad reports to anyone!

If you do poor quality work like that you're going to get sued and you'll end up losing your license, your certification, and your designation. There's no doubt about it. You might get away with doing garbage work for a short time, but eventually you're going to pay for it. If you lose your State license and/or certification than no one will accept your appraisals and you'll be out of work! If this happens then no one is going to hire you with a black mark on your record. You also can't find work when you don't have the required State and Federal approvals to be a real estate appraiser.

I'll tell you another bedtime war story from my own experience in the appraisal business. This should definitely give you a good reason to verify all information yourself and not to rely on someone else's word about it. I was doing a foreclosure appraisal for a bank that had to take a property back from a borrower because they stopped making their mortgage payments. In this particular case I found out later that there was a very dishonest Realtor involved in the transaction. I had finished my on-site inspection of the property and I was leaving to obtain my sales comparables and other field data. This Realtor told me that she had some good comps for me to use back at her office. I said, *"Fine,*

I'll take a look at them." There's nothing wrong with having someone assist you on an appraisal report in obtaining your data. The more information you have, the better off you are. In fact you'll usually need someone at town hall, a real estate office or some other place to assist you on most of your reports. You just have to verify that the information they're giving you is accurate before you use it in your appraisal report.

Anyway, I went back to this Realtor's office and she gave me three sales comparables that she said were good comps to use. The only problem with these sales was that they were handwritten on a sheet of paper and weren't from a published data source that was widely accepted. This immediately raised a red flag in my mind about the validity of these sales comps and it should for you too if you ever encounter a situation like that. Coincidentally, the sales prices of these comps appeared abnormal for that area. So I asked her where she obtained this data and comps from and she said that they were all verified by her as recent sales.

I took the comps and went to another office in the area to try to confirm the validity of these sales. I couldn't find any published data source that had these sales listed. So I concluded that they were intentionally falsified by this dishonest Realtor to try to alter the final estimate of value for the subject property. The incentive for this Realtor was to *"move the deal along"* so she could get her commission on the sale. I went back to her office and questioned her more about these comps she had given me and suddenly she started fumbling for answers. She ended up taking the sheet of paper into the back room and then coming out later and telling me, *"Oh, maybe I was mistaken about these sales."* She then ripped up this paper with the false comps on it while I was standing there, obviously to destroy the incriminating evidence. This Realtor clearly intended to mislead me to line her own pockets with a sales commission on the deal. I'll tell you more about dishonest Realtors and other third parties later.

I was so angry about the dishonesty of that Realtor that I wrote a strong letter filing a complaint to the real estate authorities about her. You shouldn't hesitate to file a complaint against anyone who is dishonest in this, or any other business. If I had trusted that Realtor by not verifying her information, I could have been in big trouble down the road. Someone reading the appraisal report could have discovered later that those sales comparables were totally false!!

You have to keep all of your field notes in your file for every appraisal. You do the same amount of work for every appraisal no matter what type of report you're doing, such as, a written report, an oral report, one page update, etc. The five different types of appraisal reports are: Oral Report, Letter of Opinion, Form Report, Narrative Report, Demonstration Appraisal Report. A Letter of Opinion is an appraisal. An Opinion of Value is **not** an appraisal.

I'll give you some advice that one of my instructors gave our class about doing a *demonstration appraisal report*. A demonstration appraisal report is a narrative appraisal report that is required for candidates trying to get an appraiser designation from certain organizations. The purpose of it is to test the knowledge and competence of an appraiser on all aspects of appraising residential real estate. It's an extremely thorough and comprehensive report that must to be done if you wish to obtain a designation.

Our instructor told us that you should follow the check list located in the pamphlet published by the appraisal organization you will get the designation from. By using this checklist, you won't forget to include anything in your demonstration report. You must be consistent throughout your report and you can't have any disparities with your statements, facts, adjustments, etc. He also said that you should use a two-family house for your demonstration report.

> *When doing an appraisal, you have to mention any of the three S's in your report to CYA (Cover Your Assets). The three S's stand for: Structural, Safety and Sanitary problems or hazards in a building.*

Furthermore, you should find your vacant land and sales comparables **before** you choose the subject property that you'll use. Have someone who is a knowledgeable appraiser review your report before you send it into the appraisal organization for grading and evaluation.

When appraising a building based on the building plans and specifications you should get a copy of the plans to keep in your own files. This is because the plans are always changing so you need a copy to CYA, *(Cover Your Assets)*. You should disclose in the report that your estimate of value is based upon the plans that you have been shown. You should state that the estimate of market value does not take into account any changes that have taken place from the time you originally saw those plans.

When doing an appraisal, you *have to* mention any of the three S's in your report to CYA. The three S's stand for: $\underline{S}$tructural, $\underline{S}$afety and $\underline{S}$anitary problems or hazards in a building.

There is something else that you have to be careful of to CYA. You should never say that only one or two of the sales comparables were used as the strongest representation for the value estimate in an appraisal report. The reason for this is that attorneys will try to "knockout" the strong basis for your value estimate in your defense against a lawsuit. Do not strongly emphasize that your value estimate is based upon just one or two sales comps in your report. If you do, then if an attorney can knockout those comps, you'll be left with no defense in the case. This is another reason why you should <u>always</u> get more than the minimum number of sales comparables or data to fill out the appraisal form. The more sales comparables and market data you have, the stronger your appraisal report is. With a strong appraisal there will be much less of a chance anyone could question your report.

There's nothing wrong with making a true statement in your report if you provided some additional weight on a few of the sales comparables you included. You have every right to give some more emphasis on a few of the better sales comps in your report to estimate market value. You will always have some sales that are better comps than others in relation to the subject property. That's why the estimate of market value **is not** just an average of the adjusted sales prices for all of the comps you used. During your reconciliation process you have to decide which sales carry more weight and are a closer indication to the estimate of market value of the subject property. Then use an estimate of value for the subject property that's closer to the adjusted sales prices of *those* comps. Since they're a better representation of the subject property, you'll have a closer estimate of value.

Standards Of Professional Practice Parts A + B

Parts A and B of this course were another of the state appraisal courses that I took. I will use my own notes from my class notebook, along with my own comments and experience, as a guideline but I won't duplicate the Standards Course information. I will try to highlight the items that I made notes on while taking the class. These were the points raised by the class instructor's and my own experiences that I felt were important to write down and study. However, it must be noted, that I'm not going to cover all aspects of the Standards Course in this book. I am only going to highlight as much as possible from my own notes. You should definitely take the state appraisal courses taught by their own instructors to get the most benefit from their expertise and training. I will try to keep it in a flowing format by including additional comments.

The whole idea behind this course is to teach students the ethical requirements and the accepted minimum standards to be responsible and honest real estate appraisers. Unfortunately, some people have no concept of morals even after they take these courses.

> *Unfortunately, some people have no concept of morals even after they take these courses. Just don't be one of those people and you'll make plenty of money in this business and you'll sleep well at night.*

Just don't be one of those people and you'll make plenty of money in this business and you'll sleep well.

The appraisal report must be portrayed in a meaningful manner that is understood by the client. You **cannot** let the entire report nor any one section of the appraisal report be used to mislead the client nor anyone else. It is also unethical to knowingly use, or allow an employee or third party to use a misleading appraisal report, even if you don't sign the report.

You cannot report a predetermined market value nor any oral market value estimates before doing a full appraisal. You cannot give an estimate of market value unless you do _all_ of the aspects of an actual appraisal report. You're liable for any discrepancies if you quote someone a value and you end up being wrong. You're supposed to be an expert and professional in your field. So if someone asks you, *"What's my house worth?"* Just tell them that you cannot give them a market value estimate without doing all of the research and field work of a full appraisal report.

> *You cannot slant the estimate of market value, nor any other aspect of the appraisal report, to favor the client.*

You cannot slant the estimate of market value, nor any other aspect of the appraisal report, to favor the client. This is a very important aspect to remember. Don't try to "move any deals along" to benefit your clients. If the market value estimate is not a price the client wants to hear, then that's too bad. You can't alter the appraisal report just to keep someone happy.

Regardless of the type of appraisal your doing or the fee charged for the services it **must** be done according to the Federal and State Appraisal Standards. You can't cut corners just because you're not getting paid a high fee for additional work needed.

You cannot base your appraisal fee on the amount of the market value estimate or any other stipulated result. You cannot have any undisclosed fees for a report. Regardless of the fee you charge the work is always the same. You have to base your fees on the time and knowledge required to do the assignment, not on the value estimate. You can quote your fee on a range rather than a set price so you can have room for any additional work that is needed.

It's OK to give a client a range of the market value estimate _only_ if the client requests it and understands it. For example, you can appraise a house to be worth $195,000 to $200,000 if the client understands this estimate. The client also must agree that you will use a range for the market value estimate.

You cannot advertise to the public in a false, misleading or exaggerated manner. For example, you can't advertise that your an *MAI* appraiser unless you actually have been given that designation.

You must act in a disinterested and impartial manner for the appraisal assignment and report. If you have **any** interest at all in the subject property, appraisal assignment and/or report other than your regular fee, then you must disclose everything to the client and state it in the report.

You must disclose *everything* in your appraisal report that is an ethical or standards requirement.

You cannot discuss the value estimate or any other information of the appraisal report with anyone other than the client. This is another important point to keep in mind at all times. You *must* respect the confidential nature of the appraiser-client relationship. If you give out copies of an appraisal report to show a potential client the quality of your work, then you must *first* get the approval of the client the appraisal was for. An alternative is that you must "white out" the pertinent names and information, such as the property address, the client, the dates, and the estimate of value.

You must retain your written records of the appraisal, and any consulting work, for a minimum of five years after the appraisal assignment. This is needed in the event that you have to go back and reevaluate an old appraisal assignment.

It is the responsibility of the appraiser, before accepting any assignment, to identify the appraisal problem and have the experience and knowledge required to competently complete the assignment. If not, then you must disclose your lack of knowledge and/or experience to the client before accepting the assignment. You must take the steps necessary to complete the assignment competently. For example, if you were hired to appraise a commercial property and you have no prior experience in commercial appraising, then you will have to get help from an experienced commercial appraiser for this assignment. Furthermore, you're required to tell the client about your lack of experience before you take the job.

An appraiser's files are his primary data source. Other data is a secondary source. **You have to be consistent in your appraisal reports!!**

Reality Talk

I've included these last sections because I felt they're a very important part of giving you a complete picture of the real estate business in general. Some of these things you're going to have to experience for yourself to really see and understand what I mean. The school of hard knocks will always teach you the hard way, but you'll learn your lessons well!

After reading these sections you might say, *"This is just a bunch of negative and exaggerated examples of not trusting your fellow man."* Well I've got news for you sweetheart, it may be negative and it may make you wonder about trusting your fellow man; but no matter what you call it, I call every bit of it ***Reality, Reality, Reality!!!!*** Every single thing I mention in this book is from actual experiences that I have personally encountered or I have had friends in this business encounter them. I only wish that I had a nickel for each time I've seen it happen. If I did, I wouldn't need to work anymore! You can go through life with blind faith and leave yourself wide open by trusting everyone. But just remember the old saying, *"A fool and his money are soon parted."* I have a lot of experience in all aspects of residential real estate. From this experience I could tell you war stories that would make your head spin. I've learned from my years in business and life that **money** is definitely a *truth serum* that **always** brings out the <u>**true**</u> character and integrity of a person and will reveal what they are really like deep down inside. If you want to see what someone is really like deep down inside and if they're truly honest and have integrity, then look at the way they are when dealing with money. Don't focus on the front or image they portray in public because often that's not a good indicator. Instead look at their actions and how honest they are when dealing with money. That's the true person deep down inside! It's not how much money they have or don't have, because I know a lot more poor people who are far more honest and sincere than many of the wealthy people I've known. **Instead look at what the person does to get money and to keep money - that's the key to the truth serum!**

Third Parties To The Transaction

As I said in the beginning of the book, third parties to the transaction could be any number of people. The list includes but isn't limited to: the seller, the Realtor, the home inspector, the mortgage lender, the attorney, the seller's dog or cat *(well, maybe not),* and anyone else who has an interest in the deal.

I don't want any one person or any one group of people to think that they're being singled out when I use the term "third parties." I want to stress that this is a very broad term. I don't want anyone to think it's directed at them, or to take the term, "third party," personally. Realtors and third parties are very important people involved in the purchase and sale of real estate. They are a necessity and provide a vital service that helps the public to buy and sell property.

> *Every single thing I mention in this book is from actual experiences that I have personally encountered or I have had friends in this business encounter them.*
>
> *I've learned from my years in business and life that **money** is definitely a truth serum that **always** brings out the <u>true</u> character and integrity of a person and will reveal what they are really like deep down inside.*

The problem I have is that some Realtors and third parties can be very dishonest, incompetent, ignorant, or a combination of all three of these undesirable qualities. To make matters even worse, they go a step further and think that they're *experts* in every aspect of real estate. These are the third party people that I'm referring to. Just understand that Realtors and most third parties **are not experts** in real estate. Realtors only need about two days of basic real estate classes to get a license. So don't think they know all the important aspects of buying and selling a house.

I also want to make it clear for a second time, that throughout this book both males and females are being referred to whenever the pronouns *he* or *she* are used. Both males and females are also referred to when I give examples of war stories that I've encountered in the real estate business. The pronouns "he" or "she" are only used for the sake of brevity.

In case you didn't know, most of the time the Realtor works for the **seller**, not the buyer. Sometimes the Realtor will represent the buyer, but that's not as common in some areas, so check with your local real estate board on this. Some states now require the Realtors to sign an agreement with potential sellers and buyers clearly stating whom they're working for. One reason for this may be that some home buyers don't realize that the Realtor often represents the seller. This means that when they go into a real estate office to buy a house, the Realtor that shows them different properties has a fiduciary responsibility to the **seller** of the house. Even though the buyer came into the real estate office looking for houses, the Realtor works for the seller. In this case the Realtor is responsible for looking out for the seller's best interest, and not the buyer's. Some buyers don't know this and think that the Realtor is looking out for **their** best interest only!

I've seen plenty of ignorant, dishonest Realtors and third parties get angry because my clients wanted to take my advice and check everything out about the house they were planning to buy or sell. That's why I believe that the last thing a dishonest, ignorant and/or incompetent third party person wants is an "educated buyer." Because an educated buyer is a knowledgable person who checks everything out before making a big investment. This can take a few days to check town hall, get repairs estimates, etc. If a home buyer or seller wants to verify things and get a lot of repair estimates prior to closing, these Realtors and third parties criticize them and say, *"Oh, this buyer or seller is just a worrier."* These third parties can cost a home buyer or seller tens of thousands of dollars. They do this by pressuring your client into not checking everything out before the closing. Far too many people are buying and selling their homes with their eyes closed. Hopefully, my educational materials will open your eyes *nice and wide* when you decide to buy or sell your house!

Sometimes the seller of the house, the Realtor, or some other third party will tell you something, such as the air-conditioning system, works just fine. However you find that you can't operate the system by its normal controls. If the seller, Realtor, or other third party get very defensive about the situation and insist that the system works properly, just tell them to go ahead and turn it on so you can evaluate the air-conditioning. Don't get in an argument with them just say, *"Great, you turn it on and I'll be more than happy to evaluate the A/C for my client."* This way you dump it back in their lap and leave it up to them to turn on the system.

Now remember, I said this in the beginning of the book and I'll say it again. You're a guest in someone else's house! So don't be rude or get into an argument with anyone at the inspection site. You have to always be very diplomatic and professional in this or any other business to be successful. You also have to respect the seller's property. Don't go into someone's house and start taking the place apart by opening up walls and moving furniture all around. You have to treat their home and personal belongings as you want someone to treat your home and personal belongings during an inspection. Some seller's get very upset and worried during an appraisal and/or a home inspection because it can make or break a real estate deal. So remember to always be polite and courteous during an appraisal.

Now don't get me wrong when I tell you this by thinking you have to be a marshmallow during the appraisal. As an **"A to Z Appraiser"** you still have to do a very thorough inspection. This means that you have to evaluate all visible and accessible areas in the house and on the property. Don't be afraid to probe the

> In case you didn't know, most of the time the Realtor works for the seller, not the buyer.

visible wood beams on the inside and outside of the house. When you probe the wood beams and exterior trim work you're going to leave marks and some minor cosmetic damage. This can't be helped and it's a necessary part of properly evaluating the structural members for rot and wood destroying insect infestation. However, because probing will leave visible marks in wood, you don't want to go around damaging the interior finished floor moldings, doors and window sills. Just use your common sense when deciding what wood areas are finished coverings that shouldn't be probed and what wood areas have to be probed during your inspection.

I once did an inspection and I was probing the moldings at the base of the garage door trim work. This is a very common area to find rot and wood destroying insect infestation because the wood is in close contact with the soil. The wood was so rotted at the base of the door trim work that the probe went right through it. A hole that was a few inches in diameter was left in the wood. This is going to happen to you when you probe rotted and damaged wood. There's nothing wrong with you leaving this wood damaged because if the wood is very solid, then it won't fall apart when you probe it. However, if the wood needs to be replaced then it will fall apart and leave some damage. Don't worry about leaving the wood with some cosmetic damage because it has to be replaced anyway due to the rot and/or wood destroying insect damage. All your doing is showing your client and all third parties that it needs replacing.

Anyway, after I probed this garage door molding, I told the client and the third parties that this section of wood needed to be replaced because it was all rotted out. About three days later I got a phone call from the Realtor. She said that the seller's were going to have their attorney contact me because the seller's felt that *"I seriously hurt the market value of their property."* It was such a ridiculous comment that even the Realtor said the seller was crazy to make that claim. I was never contacted by the seller's attorney because the seller's must have realized that they had no basis for a complaint against me. They realized that the wood was rotted out and the probing damage was done during an inspection that they allowed me to do at their home.

Verify Everything With The Documentation

Often the seller or the Realtor will tell you or your client that something, such as the roof or heating system, was just recently replaced. Another example is that they will tell you that the asbestos was removed by a licensed EPA contractor. That's fine, then just tell the client to get copies of all of the receipts and documentation for the work performed. Recommend that the client call the contractors personally. This will enable them to talk with the contractors to find out important information. The client should ask the contractors if there was anything about the work they did at the subject property that would be helpful or important for the client to know. Sometimes the contractor will inform your client that the seller wanted to save some money on the job. This could be due to the fact that the house was being on the market. As a result, the seller may have told the contractor to cut corners and not do the proper repair work. This is often done just to cover up a problem so potential buyers won't see any inadequate repair work.

You also need to check with the local building department to make sure that this information is accurate and if any permits and final approvals were required. Almost *always* permits and approvals are required so don't take it for granted that everything was filed and taken care of. Often you'll have the seller, the Realtor, or another third party tell you or your client that all the building permits and approvals have been obtained for some work done at the site. Or else many times third party people will say that building permits and approvals were not needed for some work done at the site. That's fine, then just tell the client to obtain all receipts and documentation for the work done. Also, you and the client need to check with the local building department to make sure that this information is accurate and that all permits and *final* approvals were obtained if they were required for the work done.

Whenever you make **any** changes to a house or a site from the time of the original construction, you have to file the necessary permits and obtain all final approvals from the local municipality. *(Contrary to popular belief, this is an accurate statement and I'm the only guy I know of that tells his client's the facts about checking the records at town hall. Realtors don't want your client checking town hall records because then he may know too much and be an educated buyer.)* This pertains to *all repairs* done at the house and site, such as: replacing the heating or air-conditioning systems; upgrading the electrical system; replacing the roof shingles; finishing a basement or attic; putting an addition on a house; adding a deck or a swimming pool; installing or updating a bathroom or kitchen; and anything else other than minor maintenance like painting. The reason you have to obtain permits and approvals for this repair work is that the local building department inspectors have to check the work out. They have to make sure the work is done properly and safely.

Local building inspectors are needed to ensure that all construction and repair work at least meets the minimum building codes in that town. By meeting the building code standards, it will help protect the

Whenever you make ANY changes to a house or site from the time of the original construction, you have to file the necessary permits and obtain all final approvals from the local municipality.

occupants of the house from unsafe conditions. For example, let's say an electrician installs new branch wires and outlets in a remodeled bath or kitchen. How do you know the wires and outlets are properly installed? The answer is - you don't!! Once the walls are sealed up there's no way for the house occupants to see any loose or exposed wires. Unsafe electrical conditions could lead to a fire or someone getting electrocuted. This is why the local building inspector has to sign-off on repair work in stages. In most areas, the inspector will view the contractor's work before it's sealed up with a finished covering, such as sheetrock, flooring, etc. Then the building inspector will give the OK to seal up the work. A final inspection is conducted when the repair job is completed. It's similar to new house construction. The building inspector goes out to view the work in different stages during the construction process. Each inspection must receive an approval before further construction can continue. This process allows the inspector to sign-off on work that will be covered up when completed.

There is a second reason why the local muncipality wants you to file for permits and approvals for all repair work. When you put an addition on a house, add a deck, a pool, or upgrade the house, you're then increasing its market value. As a result, the tax assessor may want to raise your property taxes because now the house is worth more money.

The Sad Truth

I was doing an appraisal once, and a woman at town hall told me a few scary stories. They emphasize the importance of obtaining all permits and final approvals for repair work. She said that there had been two recent occasions with insurance agents that came by her office. These agents were checking the records on two houses in that town. One insurance company was involved in a lawsuit filed by a contractor against a homeowner. This contractor was doing some repair work in the attic area of a house. There had been work done a few years earlier by another contractor in this attic area. Well, the second contractor was working and he fell through the ceiling! This contractor sued the homeowner for millions of dollars. The basis of the lawsuit was that the prior repairs did not have a permit and final approval from the town building inspector for the work done.

The other insurance agent that came into this woman's office at town hall was also handling a lawsuit for millions of dollars. She told me that a child was swimming in someone's pool along with the homeowner's children. Unfortunately, something shot out of the pool water filter device and hit this boy in the eye. The boy is now blind in one eye. His family sued the homeowner because they didn't have a *final* plumbing inspection approval for the pool equipment which included the pool water filter.

An attorney gave one of my clients another very good reason why it's imperative to get all final permits and approvals. He said that someone could get hurt on your property due to repairs or upgrading that wasn't done properly or safely. If this happens and you don't have permits and approvals for the work, you could be sued. We've already seen this in the stories I just mentioned. However, to make matters even worse, your insurance company may try to refuse paying the claim if you lose in court. The insurance company may tell you that it's your negligence for not making sure that all valid permits and approvals had been obtained. You certainly don't want to get stuck in a position like that. Especially, when someone gets injured.

Check Town Hall ... Or Else

Don't just take it for granted that the permits and approvals have been obtained for any work performed. Many people will add to the original construction or make repairs without filing for permits. They might do the work themselves or else they hire a contractor who doesn't know what he's doing and he won't file any permits for the work. Recommend to the client that he verify this information and you should check it out as well. If it's true and all permits and approvals have been obtained, then great, everyone's happy. But if it's not true, then you don't want to get stuck holding the bag for the problems that will come up later.

Don't let any Realtors, sellers, or other third parties talk you or your client out of verifying this information. Almost always a seller or Realtor will say:

"Oh, yes they have all the permits for that work," or *"Oh, you don't need to file a permit for that in this area,"* or *"Yes, we do have a C of O,"* or *"The asbestos was removed by a licensed EPA contractor."* **Verify everything they say by looking at the written documentation with your own two eyes and tell the client to do the same!!!!** If the third parties information is wrong, then you and your client will end up paying the price for it. Just because someone has a Certificate of Occupancy it doesn't mean that the

> *Don't take it for granted that the permits have been obtained for any work performed. Many people will add to the original construction or make repairs without filing for permits.*

building department has approved all of the work done at the site. A *C of O* is issued when the house is built and it's generally only used to state the legal occupancy of the house. That's why it's called a *Certificate of Occupancy*. Even if a C of O is required

> *Don't let any Realtors or other third parties talk you or your client out of verifying this information at town hall.*

for any repairs done at the site, this **does not** mean that the contractor or the homeowner had the C of O updated to include the repairs that were done. If town hall isn't notified that the work is being done, then the C of O doesn't magically get updated on its own!

In some areas, a new C of O is not issued when repairs or upgrading is done at the subject property. These areas will just require that the homeowner obtain permits and approvals from the town building and zoning departments. So don't make the client think

that because there's a C of O, there are no violations or no missing permits and approvals.

You Have The Right To ...

You must go down to town hall **personally** to check *ALL* records pertaining to the subject property. This will enable you to verify all information in the real estate listing and any other data sources. You and the client can also confirm any other information that has been represented about the house. If you or the client send a third party to town hall to check the records, and they miss something, it's the <u>client's</u> neck and money that's on the line. So go and check the records yourself. Because if it's your mistake for not verifying certain information, then the client may want you to reimburse them for any expenses they incur.

Your client has a <u>right</u> to know everything about the subject property. Often a Realtor, or other third party to the transaction will say, *"Oh, you don't need to check the town hall records. The attorney, appraiser and the title company all take care of that for you."* DON'T BELIEVE THAT FOR A MINUTE!!!! If you or your client leave the town hall records check to someone else, then you'll both probably learn the hard way that important items are often missed. I went through this experience myself when my brother and I were selling one of our rental properties. The buyer was getting a FHA mortgage loan. With these loans, the lender requires a more extensive search into the property records than the search done for a conventional mortgage loan. This search turned up a list of building violations and missing permits that were from a prior owner of the property. Even though the violations were not caused by my brother and me, we still were held responsible for them. The reason for this is that the building department doesn't care who owns the house. All they care about, is that the property is safe and everything adheres to the local building codes.

After these problems surfaced, my attorney contacted the title company that we had paid for the title insurance policy and the title records search. Our title company said that there is a clause in just about all title policies dealing with this type of situation. The clause states that the title company **is not responsible** for any building, zoning or other violations. A title company is only concerned with the *ownership interest* in the subject property. Ownership interest is what is stated in the deed for the property. This has **_absolutely nothing_** to do with building permits, zoning, taxes, and many other aspects at town hall. As a result, we spent thousands of dollars and delayed the closing for months, in order to resolve these old violations created by a prior owner. This experience should put an end to any third parties trying to convince your clients that the attorney, appraiser, and title company check town hall thoroughly. That is, unless the appraiser is an **"A to Z Appraiser."**

I've done foreclosure appraisals for a bank, where they would have the house reappraised after they took back the title in the foreclosure process. During my appraisal, I turned up problems in the deed that weren't picked up when the bank originally lent the mortgage money. Now they're going to have to spend the time and money to correct a prior owner's mistakes. This situation could happen to you and your clients.

Is The Listing Accurate?

Let me give you another newsflash so I make this point very clear about checking all records at the town hall. Many people think the information in a real estate listing is always accurate. THAT'S NONSENSE!!!! If you read the bottom of all real estate listings and other data sources, you'll see a statement such as, *"Data Is Believed Accurate But Not Warranted."* Do you know what that means? Well I'll tell you anyway. It means that if the information in the real estate listing or data source is wrong, then you cannot hold the listing Realtor or data company accountable for the error. In most areas, Realtors are not required to check the records at town hall to verify the information that the seller tells them to fill out a real estate listing. I've seen many cases where a real estate listing would say: the subject property has a 200 amp electrical system, when it only had 100 amps; or the house was connected to the city sewer system, when it actually had a septic system; or the size of the lot was one acre, when it was less than one acre; or the square footage and age of the house was incorrect on the real estate listing, etc.

So, remember to tell your clients not to rely on the information found in real estate listings. If there is a *"know-it-all"* Realtor at the site they're probably going

> Let me give you another newsflash to make it clear about checking all records at the town hall. Many people think that the information in a real estate listing is always accurate. THAT'S NONSENSE!!!!

to tell your client that you're wrong. The Realtor will say that their real estate listing is 100% accurate. If any Realtors dispute the advice you give to your clients, then just tell that Realtor or other third party to put their money where their mouth is! Just about every time I get a Realtor who earns a commission on the sale disputing what I say, I prove them wrong. Once you respond confidently and firmly (but not rudely) to know-it-all Realtors, it usually shuts them up for the rest of the inspection or appraisal. I can't even count the number of times that I've had a know-it-all Realtor tell my clients and me, *"My real estate listing is 100% correct, I checked it myself."* Before the inspection or appraisal is over, I always seem to find something about the listing that's inaccurate. When this happens, these Realtors never seem to admit that they were wrong. Someone needs to inform ignorant Realtors that maybe they don't know as much about real estate as they think they do. We'll talk more about this later.

Realtors and other data source employees don't intentionally put inaccurate information into a listing sheet. They generally rely on the seller to provide the information or else the Realtor may think that they know what they're doing. The seller or the Realtor may unintentionally make a mistake. So it's not that anyone's trying to hide the truth from any buyers. It's just that someone can make a mistake with the data. That's why all records need to be checked at town hall. This will help prevent incorrect information from going unnoticed.

At town hall the records will show: the amount of taxes on the house, the square footage and age of the house, the acreage of the site, if there are any building violations, if there are any easements or encroachments, if there are problems with the title and deed of the property, and a lot more. All of this information is very valuable to you and the client. Most people don't even realize how much information is open for the public to view at their local town hall records department. If you're thorough in your trip to town hall and you end up finding something out that's important, then you'll look like a hero. Your client will thank you for finding the important information.

A Catch 22 Position

In just about any house you go into, you can find some upgrading or repairs that have been done which require permits and approvals. You'll also find that there are missing permits and approvals for some of this work in almost *every* house you go into! It's very common because there are very few homeowners who know that permits and final approvals are needed for all repair work done in a house. Many contractors don't bother with the permits, unless the homeowner insists on seeing them upon completion of the job. When you or your client find missing permits, just tell the client it's a very common problem. Don't make the client think this is the only house without all valid permits and approvals. Just tell them to find out what is required to obtain the final approvals from the town for the work done.

Sometimes your clients will ask you, *"What will happen if I do go to town hall to check about valid permits and approvals for the finished basement or*

> You'll also find that there are missing permits and approvals for some of this work in almost every house you go into! It's very common because there are very few homeowners who know that permits and final approvals are needed for all work done.

attic, the addition, deck, pool, extra apartment, etc. and they aren't on file in the building department." Well if you or your client tell the building inspector that you checked for the permits and approvals and you can't find them, you might raise a red flag in his mind. This could lead to the building inspector going to the subject property. The building inspector could file a building code violation against the property for the work done. A violation could be issued because there are no permits on file. Usually the only way to get building violations removed is to have the work pass the local building code standards. What will happen is the building inspector will tell the homeowner that if the work doesn't meet the local building code standards, then they must hire a licensed contractor to make the necessary repairs. Repairs will be needed to bring the work up to meet the minimum standards before a valid permit and approval can be obtained and the violation will be removed.

You can run into serious problems in certain situations when permits and approvals need to be obtained after the work has already been done. One

case is when the repair work was not permitted by the building or zoning codes. For example, the local codes may not allow the homeowner to finish a basement or attic to use as livable space, build a small addition or garage, etc. When this occurs, the only option is to remove all of the work done. The building inspector can't approve something that is against the law of the town. I've had clients that took my advice and checked town hall prior to closing. They found garges that were built too close to the neighbors' property line; pools that were not allowed on the site; additions and enclosed porches that had to be dismantled; finished basements and attics that were against the zoning and fire codes, etc. None of these problem conditions could be approved without getting zoning variances and changes made to the building and fire codes! In order to buy these houses, the sellers had to dismantle all the repair work done to the house and site. That can turn into a nightmare and take a lot of time, money and aggravation to accomplish.

A more common problem when permits need to be obtained after the work has already been done occurs when the work is not accessible to view. For example, if there has been some electrical wiring, plumbing or foundation repairs. Usually this type of work will be sealed over after the repairs are completed. The building inspector can't sign-off on something that he can't see! As a result, the only way to get the permits and final approvals will be to open up the walls, floors, ceilings, etc so the inspector can view the repairs. I've had this situation come up on many occassions when my clients were notified about missing permits. This also can turn into a nighmare.

So it can be a *Catch 22* for the client. If they don't raise a red flag at the building department, then the missing permits might not create a problem for the closing when the client purchases the property. However, if your client doesn't clear up this matter prior to buying the house, then it might come up when he goes to refinance or sell the house down the road. Then your client will be stuck wasting his own time and money fixing a problem that someone else had created! I wouldn't take the chance if I were buying the house. From your standpoint as the appraiser, you're **required** to mention the building code violations that you know about in your written report. It's true that only an inspector from the local town hall can do a building code inspection. However, you still need to inquire about any known violations. You also must take any violations into consideration when estimating market value because it will have an affect on the purchase price of the typical buyer. So whether the client clears up the problem isn't your concern. However, you must mention it in your report to CYA.

People Who Have No Right To Remain Silent

Sometimes you'll find that the seller, the Realtor, or another third party won't want to answer any preinspection questions. Or a dishonest Realtor will tell the seller not to be home for the appraisal appointment so they don't get involved in the appraisal process. They just say something like, *"I've been selling real estate for 10 years now and I've never seen it done this way before by asking the owner all these questions."* They are talking out of ignorance! The reason they've never seen it done this way is that they've never seen a good, thorough and knowledgable appraiser before!!!

Also, some people rationalize their actions to a point where it just blows my mind. They intentionally are dishonest and lie to you by <u>not</u> saying anything and by not answering any of your questions. I have done

> The Realtors may say, "I've been selling real estate for 10 years now and I've never seen it done this way before by asking the owner all these questions."
> They are talking out of ignorance!

many inspections and appraisals where I encountered Realtors, sellers, and other third parties who **intentionally** tried to hide something from my client and any other potential buyers. Once I was checking the lower level of a house that was located on the side of a hill. In one corner there were some plywood boards leaning up against the foundation wall. I moved the boards to see what was behind them and I found serious structural cracks in the foundation wall. I was really angry about the seller's attempt to hide this. The house was located on a hill and with a serious structural crack like that, it could have cost someone their life!!

Sellers and Realtors often don't tell home buyers about known problems with a house. They just keep quiet and hope the buyer's home inspector or appraiser don't detect the problem. I'll give you a few more examples that I've experienced. One was a client I had that was buying a house with an old, forced hot air

heating system. A thin layer of asbestos insulation was on the air ducts and in the lining of the furnace. This creates a serious health hazard because the asbestos fibers are blown throughout the house. The dishonest Realtor never mentioned a word to my clients about this asbestos problem. As soon as I saw the asbestos during the inspection, I told the client about this health hazard. Suddenly the Realtor jumps into the conversation and says, *"The owner already has found a contractor to remove the asbestos from the air ducts so the client doesn't need to worry about it."* When I asked the Realtor if the owner was going to have the asbestos in the livable rooms removed, she said, *"there was no need to do that."* It's so typical that the Realtor would say there's no need to do that. After all, the dishonest Realtor isn't going to be living in that house and breathing those fibers!

I did an inspection once and found severe rot and powder post beetle damage to the main girder beam of a house. My awl went right through the main girder while I was probing this beam in the crawl space. On the exterior of the house I found most of the siding had buckled and had to be replaced. This siding damage was from water problems due to the lack of a roof overhang on the house. My client had to spend a lot of time and money on the home inspection and in getting repair estimates. Afterwards, my client found out that the seller and the Realtor had known about these problems before the home inspection. Another buyer had backed out of a prior offer on this house because these problems were detected by their inspector.

I have done many inspections where I would find personal items intentionally placed by a third party to cover termite and water damage. Luckily I detected these problems so my clients didn't get hit with any surprises after they moved into the houses. However, since the third party never told me or my client about these problems and left it up to us to find them on our own, then what is that called? **Dishonesty, Dishonesty, Dishonesty!!!!** Plain and simple.

Let's say the appraiser and the client didn't happen to notice a problem condition that a third party to the transaction knew existed but never told them about. How can that third party justify their actions by not mentioning the problem condition to the appraiser and/ or the client? You can call it a business negotiating decision by the third party; you can call it a mistake that is the fault of the buyer's appraiser and/or home inspector; you can blame the buyer for not hiring a competent appraiser and/or home inspector; or you can call it luck. But no matter what you call it, and I don't care how you rationalize it, it **has to** be called one thing - *DISHONEST!* The third party person simply is not telling someone something they know that person should and would want to know about. Whatever happened to the golden rule in today's world? *"Do onto others as you would want others to do onto you."* People should just ask themselves: *If I were buying this house, would I want the seller to tell me about this problem?*

I'm not accusing anyone in particular of being dishonest or questioning their integrity. I'm simply using this example to make you realize there are dishonest and ignorant people out there that rationalize their unethical actions. Often the same person who refuses to answer your questions or doesn't tell you about a problem they know you should be informed about, is the same guy that brags how he goes to church every Sunday because he's such a good, ethical person in society.   BALONEY!!   They can't hide behind that cloak or that excuse.

There is something that you might consider when you're dealing with a dishonest person like that. You might want to inform them that if something comes up after your client buys the house that they knew about, then your client can sue the seller, the Realtor, and other third parties. That's because you cannot intentionally hide a problem from anyone, whether you're the buyer or the seller. Just about all houses are sold in *"As Is"* condition. This doesn't mean that the seller has a license to steal nor does it mean that the seller can commit fraud. A lot of people believe that an "As Is" sale means that the Realtors and sellers don't have to tell anyone about known problem conditions at the property. That's totally false! The old theory of "buyer beware" is no longer valid. When a house is sold in "As Is" condition, it means that the seller is **_required_** to disclose all known defects to the buyer and the buyer agrees to accept the house with its problems. The seller doesn't have to be a home inspector, however, they do have to inform you about the problems they know about and they cannot hide them from you.

Realtors and some other third parties have a *fiduciary responsibility* to lay all the cards out on the table for the client, whether it is the buyer or the seller. They are required to disclose to the buyer and the seller any problem conditions that they know about. Since they're professionals in the real estate business, they are held to a higher standard than the public. As a

result, they can be found liable for something they knew about, or that they should have known about, if they did not inform the buyer or seller about the problem condition.

Talk To The Neighbors

You can find out an awful lot about a house and the area it's located in by talking to the neighbors who live next to the subject property. I try to do this whenever I have the opportunity and I always encourage my clients to talk to the neighbors themselves. The people who live near the subject property usually have been there for at least a few years. They can tell you the good and bad points of the area. The best part about their responses to your questions is that they have no incentive to lie to you or your client! They're not involved financially in the sale of the subject property, and as a result, you'll get an unbiased second opinion for free!

Obviously, if the neighbor is a relative or close friend of the seller then their responses may be biased to help "move the deal along." But that's why you and

> *You can find out an awful lot about a house and the area it's located in just by talking to the neighbors who live next to the subject property.*

your client should talk to several neighbors in the area and not just one of them. Don't feel like you're being rude or imposing on the neighbors either. You'll be amazed at how people love to talk to someone who's truly interested in listening to what they have to say. It gives people a feeling of importance and makes them feel like they're doing someone else a big favor. Especially, if the person they're helping will be a future next door neighbor.

Some questions that you and your client's can ask the neighbors are:

1   Do you ever have any water problems in your house? *(This is a **great** question to ask. If the subject property gets water from a high groundwater table, then most of the houses in the area may have the same problem unless they're located on higher ground.)*

2   Does the local municipality raise property and/or

school taxes often?

3 Is it a quiet area or are there any noise problems?

4 How are the schools and public transportation?

5 *(If the house is located on a Private street)*, What are the rights and responsibilities of the homeowners to use and maintain the street? What are the fees for the street maintenance, paving, snow plowing etc.?

6 Is there anything about the area that you would find helpful to know if you were buying this house?

So you don't believe me that talking to the neighbors is helpful? Well I'll tell you another war story and then maybe you'll change your mind. I tell all my clients to speak to the neighbors before they buy a house. This will enable them to find out anything interesting about water problems, noise problems, etc. One client of mine was buying a house with a septic system on the site. He took my advice and asked a few of the neighbors about water problems and septic problems in the area. Well he was awfully surprised to find out that the area had a high groundwater table. This not only created water problems in their basements during heavy rains, but it also forced them all to have their septic systems replaced!! New septic tanks were needed due to the excessive water in the ground over the years. This client ended up having *a lot* more to calculate into his purchase price after finding out this information. He certainly was grateful to me for giving him that advice. So learn a lesson from this and recommend that **all** of your clients talk to the neighbors. They might end up finding out something very helpful and you'll end up looking like a hero for it.

Be Totally Objective - Part 1

Don't tell the client to buy or not to buy the house for any reason!!!!! This is one point that really bothers Realtors and I have to side with them on this one. Your job as an appraiser is to tell the client the estimated market value of the house only!! I'll repeat my statement again so you get it straight. Don't tell the client to buy or not to buy the house for any reason!

If the house is in poor condition just include the repair estimates and the effect on the market value in your appraisal report. The condition of the house does not make it a good deal or a bad deal. Price is the **ONLY** factor on whether it's a good deal or not! Here's why:

◊ I've seen people buy houses in great condition but they were over paying for the house. Therefore it's a bad deal because they were paying much more than the market value price of the house.

◊ At the same time, I've seen people buy houses that are a mess and need a lot of work. However, they were getting a great deal because they were buying the house well below market value. If you added up all the repairs and upgrading costs, and then added it to the purchase price, they could sell the house for much more than they paid for it.

The point is that you have no right telling the client whether or not to buy the house. You're hired to only

> *The condition of the house does not make it a good deal or a bad deal. Price is the ONLY factor on whether it's a good deal or not!*

estimate the market value - and that's what your training and expertise are focused on. As a result, **it's none of your business** if your client decides to buy a house that you don't like or that you wouldn't buy for any reason.

You may not like the house for several different reasons: it's too old for your tastes; or it's a Cape Cod style and you only like Colonial style homes; or you feel that there's a lot of work to be done to the house; or it's not in a good area of town that you'd want to live in. The point I'm making is that all of these are your own *subjective* judgments and opinions! You have to be totally *objective* when you're appraising a house. Even though you might not want to buy that house or condo, maybe your client has different tastes and likes than you do. Also, maybe the client can't afford to buy a house in great condition or in a good section of town.

I've inspected houses that when I'd write down the style of the house, either Ranch, Cape Cod, Colonial or Tudor, I'd be tempted to write down *"ugly"* because the house was so hideous looking. However, I'm not paid to tell the client whether I'd live in the house. So I keep my subjective comments and opinions to myself.

Be Totally Objective - Part 2

Don't ever tell any lender to give a loan or not to give a loan on a property!!!! This situation may come up if you do appraisal work for a bank. A mortgage lender may ask you if they should make a loan, or you may throw in your two cents on your own. I'll repeat it again so you don't forget it. Don't ever tell any lender to give a loan or not to give a loan on a property!

Every once in a while I hear an appraiser saying that they recommended that the lender approve or not approve someone's mortgage loan. That blows my mind when they do that! Your job as an appraiser is to only interpret the market data that you have obtained as it relates to the subject property. You don't include your own subjective opinions or biases.

As an appraiser, you know **nothing** about the potential borrower's income, personal debts, past credit history, possible court judgments and lawsuits against them, total monthly living expenses, job stability, etc. Only the borrower and the lender know that type of information. So I don't care how nice the house you're appraising is; or how bad the condition of the house is; or what type of area it's located in; or whatever else you find out about it during your field work. And I don't care if it's the nicest house in the world or the worst house in the world. If you tell the lender to make the loan just because the house is selling for a great price and it's in excellent condition, **then you better be willing to put your money where your mouth is!** Because what happens if that guy borrows the money and then destroys the house through lack of maintenance and then stops making his loan payments on the mortgage. The bank is going to get stuck holding the bag for the loan. The bank will end up losing money on the foreclosure sale, even though you told them what a great loan they'd be making!

It's the sane scenario if you stick your nose somewhere it shouldn't be by telling the lender not to make the loan. I don't care if it's the ugliest house you've ever seen or if it's in the worst section of town and you would *never* buy it. How do you know that the guy buying that house isn't some multimillionaire.

> *You can put all of the objective comments you want in the appraisal report. But just keep your subjective opinions and your nose out of the lender's and the borrower's business.*

What if he's going to renovate that house and donate it to a poor family or to a local charity. If the lender listened to you, then he wouldn't make the loan. *(Oh yes, I forgot you have a crystal ball at home. You can see that this loan will go sour for the lender after the money is lent out!)*

Don't take any of this personally. It's not meant to insult you. It's just meant to open your eyes to some of the realities of the real estate business. The point I'm trying to make is that you must estimate market value based upon the data you obtain and everything that effects the value of the subject property. You can put all of the objective comments you want in the appraisal report. But just keep your subjective opinions and your nose out of the lender's and the borrower's business. You're not hired to be a nosy "busy body." There are already FAR too many busy body, know-it-all Realtors and other third parties in the real estate business. You're hired to estimate market value ONLY! There are many times that I see people talk out of ignorance by thinking that they're a know-it-all. And I'm not being a hypocrite because I certainly don't think I have all the answers.

Negotiating Realities To Assist Your Client

I also agree with Realtors on the fact that it's none of your business if the client does or does not want to negotiate with the seller after your appraisal. You have NO right sticking your nose into anything other than the appraisal itself. If the client asks you to help him out further with some negotiations, then you can provide this service if you like. It's up to you. But let the client ask for your help, don't volunteer it.

Sometimes your client will ask you for your advice. They may want to know if any repairs or differences between the purchase price and the value estimate of your appraisal report should be negotiated with or paid for by the seller. Tell them that it all depends on the flexibility of the seller. Some people are negotiable and some aren't. However, if he asks the seller, there are only two answers he can get, and one of those is great!

It's similar to finding termite damage in a house. In many states the seller of the house is required by law to pay for the removal of any termites found on the property. However, the seller doesn't have to sell you the house if he doesn't want to. He can just say, fine I'll pay for the termite treatment but I'm going to raise the price by the same amount. The point is, just tell the client that whether or not something is negotiable will always depend on the flexibility of the seller.

However, there is a **very important** concept that you want to tell your client about negotiating repairs or other factors that come up during your appraisal. Most of the time, if the seller is flexible, the seller will agree to have the repairs done at his own expense. You want to inform your client that if the seller has the repairs fixed at his expense, then he's probably going to get several estimates. Which contractor do you think the seller is going to hire: the guy who does high quality work at a high price or the guy who does low quality work at a low price? I'd say the seller is more likely to hire the guy who's the cheapest to save himself a few bucks. After all, he's selling the house and he's not going to have to live with any poor quality repairs in the home. I think your client might agree with that conclusion as well. So you should inform your client about this possibility.

Also, if the seller hires the contractor and pays him with his own check, then that contractor is responsible to the seller and not to your client. Therefore, if the contractor does poor quality work and your client buys the house and finds problems with the repair work done, then your client has no legal recourse. That contractor was *hired and paid* by the *seller* of the house and not by your client. Therefore, that contractor is generally only liable to the seller for his work. What are your client's chances of getting the seller to come back from his new home to your area to file a complaint and demand compensation against that contractor for poor quality work? ZERO!!!! Now, I'm not an attorney so you have to check this and all other legal aspects I'm telling you about with your own legal counsel. But the point I'm making is pretty clear. Just inform the client of these ideas and let the client decide what action they want to take. You'll find that this type of information is very helpful to your clients and you'll look like a hero when you open their eyes to it.

When hiring repair contractors you need to notify your client about some basic concepts. In most areas,

The seller is more likely to hire the guy who's the cheapest to save himself a few bucks. After all, he's selling the house and he's not going to have to live with any poor quality repairs in the home.

contractors must be licensed and insured to do any repair work. The local town hall could verify this information. Insurance coverage should be for the general contractor plus any subcontractors they hire to assist them. For large construction jobs, the client should see if the contractor is bonded. *Bonding* means that the contractor can insure the quality of their work and that the job will be completed on time. A bonded contractor will have to place a bond before they start the job for it to be valid. For small construction jobs, bonding may be too much to ask from a contractor.

The client should check with the local Better Business Bureau and other organizations to determine if the contractor is reputable. The contractor should provide references of former clients they have done work for. This can help the client to find out about the contractors track record. However, if the contractor does provide your client with names, he's going to make sure he doesn't give them phone numbers of unhappy customers! This is where the client's own judgement will come into play in deciding if a contractor is reputable.

All aspects of agreements with contractors should be clearly stated in the written price estimate. The client should have a time limit and a price cap on the repair work. This will prevent the contractor from "dragging their feet" to complete the job. A price cap will prevent cost overruns and excess fees added after the work has begun. A statement should be put in the estimate that the contractor will provide the homeowner with all permits and final approvals from town hall. Any warranties for the repair work should be in writing. If the seller has hired contractors to make repairs, the client needs to speak with them about warranties. The client should find out how long the warranties are in effect and if they are transferable to the new owners.

There's another aspect that you need to inform your client about regarding negotiating with the seller. That is there will be times when some Realtors or other third parties will tell your client, *"Oh, there's no way the seller is going to reduce his price. He's already giving the house away and he has two backup offers waiting if you don't buy the house now."* HORSE MANURE!!!! I've heard that line used 100,000 times, not only while doing home inspections and appraisals, but also when buying my own rental properties. I've seen my own offers accepted by sellers that some know-it-all Realtor told me would never be accepted. I've also seen many clients get offers accepted when a Realtor or other third party told them the seller would never accept it.

So don't let yourself or your client be intimidated by anyone. It's your client's money and future, **he** has to be the one to decide how much he wants to pay for a house. Don't you or any third party make the decision for them. Any Realtors involved in the transaction have a *fiduciary responsibility* to the buyer or the seller. This means that they are **required** to present any and all purchase offers from all potential buyers to the seller that they know about. No matter how low or ridiculous the offer might seem, it still has to be presented to the seller. It doesn't matter if someone offers the seller less than 1/2 the asking price. They have to present the offer to give the seller the opportunity to accept it or reject it.

Don't Let Your Client Be Pressured

Tell the client not to be pressured or rushed into *any* decisions by the imaginary backup offers on the subject property. Some Realtors, sellers, or other third parties want your client to believe that imaginary backup offers really exist. Also, tell your client not to become too emotionally involved in any deal. They should look at the property as though it were a typical business decision. They should put their personal emotions aside because they're spending up to hundreds of thousands of dollars on this investment. You have to make the client realize that they're not buying a **_car_** they're buying a **_house_**!! There's a big difference between the two.

Harry Helmsley, who was clearly a brilliant real estate investor, was quoted as saying, *"The minute you fall in love with a building you're in trouble."* Meaning that if you get too emotionally attached to a property, you forget to look at it like a business decision. When this happens, you often end up paying too much for the property. You have to be objective all the time and be able to make the hard decisions and walk away from a deal at any time.

Since I do home inspections, appraisals, and have owned rental properties myself, I see this happen to

> They should put their personal emotions aside because they're spending up to hundreds of thousands of dollars on this investment. You have to make the client realize that they're not buying a car, they're buying a house!!!

potential home buyers all the time. Many people get too emotional about buying a house and they only look at the cosmetic appeal of the house or the location it's in. You have to take a step back and look at the purchase as though it was strictly a business decision. Too often people get convinced that if they don't make a high-priced offer on the house right away, then another buyer will come along and steal it right from under them. Sure, there's a potential that if the house really is a good deal then someone else will come along and buy it sooner than you will. But this happens a lot less often than most people believe, or are led to believe by some Realtors involved in the transaction.

Often a Realtor or seller will rush a potential home buyer into making an offer and/or signing contracts on a home sooner than they should. They tend to put the "fear of God" into the home buyer. They tell the buyer, *"You have to make a high offer and sign the contracts right away. If you don't, someone else will buy it because of a backup purchase offer on this house."* There are a million ways that a real estate deal can be killed. Many of those so called *"backup offers"* are either imaginary or will fall through. Some reasons real estate deals fall through are: the seller and buyer don't agree on a final price and terms; the buyer or seller gets *"cold feet,"*; problems come up during the home inspection and/or appraisal; the mortgage loan is denied; etc. I have personally seen an awful lot of real estate deals fall through due to any number of reasons.

I had an excellent real estate attorney, named Walter Kehm, that handled all of my legal work when I first started buying rental properties. He used to say that *"Real estate deals are like a trolley car, if you let one go there will be another one coming by in 20 minutes."* I have found this statement to be very true from my own experiences in the real estate business. Not only in my own investments, but in the home inspection and appraisal experience I have had as well.

Many times I've had clients who decided not to purchase a home because of the problems that were found during the home inspection and/or appraisal. The seller's of these houses would not renegotiate with the buyer, and as a result, the deal never went through. In every one of these cases, the client continued to look at other houses which were for sale. Within a few months, these clients eventually found a nicer home at a better price than the deal they walked away from. They had benefited by waiting to find the best deal that they could, rather than rushing to purchase the first decent house they could find. So learn a lesson from this and don't let yourself or any of your clients be rushed into buying a house. A home is the biggest investment most people will make, so it's prudent that they take their time and think it through completely.

Also, some sellers and third parties will just wait until they find a buyer that hires an appraiser and/or home inspector that isn't as good, honest and thorough as you are. When this happens then that buyer will be going into the deal with their eyes **closed**. You want your client to go into the deal with their eyes **open**. Just because someone else might come along and pay too much for the house, doesn't mean that your client should beat them to it and over pay for the property.

You have to assist your client in their investment decision. That's what you're being paid for. You want your client to know all of the good and bad points about the subject property. Sometimes the truth hurts and people don't want to hear bad things about a house that they've fallen in love with. But that's too bad because what you're telling them is *REALITY!!* So let them know that your job is to open their eyes to aspects about buying a house that many other buyers don't have a clue exist. If someone else goes in with their eyes closed and pays too much for the property, then all I can say is that they should have hired an **"A to Z Appraiser and/or Home Inspector,"** like your client did!

Now at the same time, if your client is still willing to pay the same price for the house even after you open their eyes, then fine. It's *none of your business* what the client does after you inform them about potential costs and problems with the subject property. You've done your professional and ethical responsibility by informing them ahead of time; and that's all you're required to do. It's their money and their future, so keep your nose out of it from that point on.

Lay All The Cards On The Table

An important concept that I want you to clearly understand, is that your job is to lay all the cards out on the table for your clients. Don't leave any skeletons hidden in the closet. Tell them about all the different aspects and realities of their investment, both good and bad, of what we've discussed plus any that you learn from your own experiences. If all the cards are laid out, then the client can make an intelligent and educated decision about their real estate purchase or mortgage loan. Don't make any decisions for the client. It's **their** money and **their** future, so let **them** decide. Your job is to just give the client the facts and your objective opinions, both good and bad. *(I've said that so many times by now I'm turning blue in the face. I just want to make sure you don't forget it.)*

If you're not sure about telling your client something, then just ask yourself: *"Is this something that can affect the market value of the subject property?"* and *"If I were the person buying this house or condo, would I want someone to inform me about this or not." "Would I feel this is something that I would want to know about?"*

If you, or any third parties, try to make the decisions for the client, then you're not really helping them out. It's similar to a person going to a doctor for a

> If all the cards are laid out, then the client can make an intelligent and educated decision about their real estate purchase. Don't make any decisions for the client. It's their money and their future, so let them decide.

routine physical. If the doctor finds a problem condition from the test results, he should tell the patient what he found and the possible treatments. The doctor should then let the patient choose what action or treatment to take. Now the doctor is the professional and an expert in this field of medicine. Therefore, he should provide the patient with some objective advice and alternatives. With the doctor's advice and alternatives, the patient can then make an intelligent and educated decision on their own.

However, what would happen if the doctor decided, on his own, to not tell the patient about the problem condition? Let's say the doctor just rationalized in his own mind that the patient didn't need to know about the problem condition. Maybe the doctor would think that if he told the patient, he would only worry the patient unnecessarily. Does that doctor have a right to make a decision like that with someone else's life? Or should that doctor lay all of the cards out on the table for the patient to decide? You tell me. I think the doctor should let the patient decide. When a doctor doesn't inform a patient properly about their health condition, it brings to mind the old saying, *"Doctors bury their mistakes."* Unfortunately, I've seen first hand experiences where some doctors buried their mistakes. The doctor shouldn't filter out anything the client should know. And neither should an appraiser, a home seller, a Realtor, an attorney, a home inspector, nor anyone else. Unfortunately, many times people do filter out information that someone has a **right** to know about.

Tony Fasanella was one of my instructors for the state appraisal course called *"The Standards of Professional Practice."* Tony constantly stated to our class that the key to honest, ethical and professional conduct was **disclosure, disclosure, disclosure** of all aspects in an appraisal report. This meant that you don't hide anything from the client or do anything that will give someone a false impression or lead them to a wrong conclusion. That includes what you say verbally and what you put in the written report.

I feel bad about creating headaches for the seller or Realtor when I detect problem conditions during an inspection or appraisal. I like to help people, not make their life more difficult *(unless they're dishonest)*. But it's not my fault when I find problems with a house during an inspection or appraisal. The way I look at it is I didn't create the problems - I only identified the problems which my client has a right to know about. So don't feel guilty about creating headaches for anyone if you're telling the truth. Your job is not to kill real estate deals, it's to identify all the negative and positive aspects of a house. Even though you don't create the negative aspects the sellers and Realtors still get angry at you . They look at you like you're an idiot merely because they're ignorant to what the facts are.

Safety Concerns

Remember that when you're doing an appraisal you **have to** mention any of the three S's in every appraisal report. You also have to mention anything that affects the value of the subject property. The three S's stand for: Structural, Safety and Sanitary problems or hazards in a building. Safety hazard items such as tripping hazards in the steps, walks and patios; loose and missing handrails; improper deck construction and guardrails; leaning retaining walls; loose electrical grounding cables, etc., may seem like minor items to repair. However, these are things that can cause someone to get seriously hurt if they're not repaired immediately and properly.

◊ An uneven section in a walkway might not seem like much but what happens if the person that trips, falls and hits their head?

◊ A leaning retaining wall will crush a child if it collapses on top of them.

◊ A missing or loose handrail could cause someone to fall down the steps.

If you think I'm overreacting then this story oughta jar ya. I heard this story from the ASHI National Seminar. A home inspector was sued because he neglected to check the deck on a house and it had very bad termite infestation. The woman who bought the house went out on the deck one day and it collapsed and left her paralyzed from the neck down. This is certainly a horrible tragedy for everyone involved in that incident. But the point I want to make very clear is do not take chances with safety items!! If you make a mistake and forget to include something in your appraisal report that negatively affects market value,

> *If you make a mistake and forget to include a negative aspect that affects market value, you could end up costing the client some money. However, if you miss a safety hazard, you could end up costing someone their LIFE!*

you could end up costing the client some money by buying a house or granting a loan for more than they should have. However, if you miss a safety hazard, you could end up costing someone their **LIFE!** Don't wait for accidents to happen. Just remember what your mother used to tell you - "An ounce of prevention is worth a pound of cure!"

Now I don't want you to think that you have to walk around the house with a microscope to detect every possible tripping hazard. Just do good, thorough appraisals and be honest. Don't let any dishonest Realtors to the transaction influence your decisions because you want them to refer some more of their clients to you. If you just move the deal along to satisfy a Realtor who may have recommended you for the appraisal, you're going to get sued eventually. There's no doubt about it. And if that's how your doing your appraisals, then you *DESERVE* to get sued.

Believe me, there are enough appraisers out there that either don't know what they're doing or are just plain dishonest. They're out to make as much money as possible without caring who gets hurt by it. Tony Fasanella and Dr. David Scribner were excellent instructors for the appraisal courses I had to take for the State Certification requirements. I remember Tony talking about dishonest appraisers. He said that people like that *"have no business being in this business."* I agree with him completely, and I hope you do too.

> *Don't let any Realtors influence your decisions because you want them to refer some more of their clients to you. If you just "move the deal along" to satisfy a Realtor, you're going to get sued eventually. There's no doubt about it.*

Don't Over Exaggerate Problems Or Repairs

Now at the same time, don't be like some appraisers and over exaggerate everything as being bad just to Cover Your Assets. This is another aspect that really bothers Realtors and I agree with them on this point as well. If you're a doomsday appraiser then you're not doing the client any good either, because you're over exaggerating things and your market value estimates will be way off base by being too conservative. Don't unnecessarily make the client think that the house is a dump and about to collapse on top of you when it really isn't so bad, or that the house isn't worth 10 cents.

All houses will have some problems because no house is perfect. So you want to be reasonable in your conclusions and evaluations to the client. If the house needs a new roof, don't make the guy think that no one would ever consider buying this house because they will have to sleep with an umbrella over their bed the whole time they live there! Just tell him to get an estimate for a new roof. Plain and simple.

You're going to see many houses that have older roofs that will need replacing. Don't make the client think that this is the only house around that needs a new roof. A roof might be an expensive item to repair. However, if he puts a new roof on the house, he'll increase the property's market value. He also won't have to worry about any roof leaks for 20 years. Replacing roofs, heating systems, appliances, etc. is all part of normal house maintenance. Some items are more expensive than others, and some items last longer than others. Whether your client buys this house, or the house next door, he's going to have to do the same basic maintenance to either one over time. The only difference may be how soon he has to do the repairs. Just tell him to get estimates on the items that need it, so he knows what his repair costs will be *before the closing*.

You're also going to see many houses that have negative aspects that affect their market value. Whether it is a locational problem, functional problem, physical depreciation, environmental problem, etc. Despite the problems, all houses will have **some** market value. If the house is located in a low income section of town, don't make the client think that no one would ever consider buying this house because of its location! Just make sufficient adjustments for the property location and any other negative aspects in your report. This way you can accurately estimate the market value. Don't make a big deal over something that merely needs an average adjustment in the report. Just be honest and reasonable in your evaluations, plain and simple. Don't make a seller, a Realtor, or other third parties life miserable, or cost them their profit, their fee or their commission for no-good reason.

There's risk in everything in life, even crossing the street. What you and your client need to do is eliminate

> All houses will have some problems because no house is perfect. So you want to be reasonable in your conclusions and evaluations to the client

as much risk as possible in their purchase or loan on the subject property. You can never eliminate _all_ of the risk, but you just want to narrow it down as much as possible. Having a good, thorough home inspection and appraisal done; checking the records at town hall; getting estimates for items that you determine need to be repaired; having certain things further evaluated; etc. all help to reduce the risk for you and your client. The more that is checked out then the more the risk is reduced. It's that basic. It's like buying an insurance policy for you and your client. So if you don't get lazy and cut corners, then at least if something goes wrong you won't look back and kick yourself for missing something that you should have checked out further.

You also have to make sure that you're knowledgeable enough so that you can give the client enough information to help him in his real estate purchase. You can't just tell the guy to get a whole host of contractors to come in and evaluate the different aspects of the house further because you're not sure about _anything_. I've seen this done by other home inspectors before and believe me, you're going to have an unhappy client if you do this to someone.

I once was doing a foreclosure appraisal for a bank and they sent me a copy of the home inspection report for this house. The bank had paid a very high price for the inspection. This bank didn't know that I did home inspections. They ended up hiring a home inspector that was recommended by a dishonest Realtor who wanted to move the deal along to get a commission. There were other factors that came up during my appraisal process which indicated further that this Realtor was dishonest. I told the banker that I couldn't believe it when I read this inspection report and found

out the price the bank paid for it. This inspector wrote a four or five page report that told the bank absolutely nothing about the house! This inspection report basically told the lender that since the inspector wasn't sure about _anything_, the bank needed to hire many different contractors to evaluate: the heating system, the well water system, the septic system, the electrical system, the structural beams, the swimming pool, the roof, etc. Do you believe that? I'm amazed that the bank even paid this incompetent crook that calls himself a home inspector! They should have told him to "whistle dixie" for his inspection fee and then fired the Realtor for recommending him.

There's nothing wrong with recommending to your client that they get estimates for repairs that are needed. Or if there are a few items that you think a licensed contractor should evaluate further. However, don't charge somebody a fee if you can't evaluate anything about the subject property!

Is It Possible To Build A ...?

There is something else that you need to be aware of. There will be times when your client will ask you if it's possible to make some changes or additions to the house or site. Virtually anything can be done from a construction standpoint. However, what your client needs to find out is:

1   What the costs will be for the work.

2   If the zoning and building department regulations will allow the work to be done.

For example, I often have clients ask me, _"Can we put an addition on the house?"_, or _"I'd like to build a dormer and finish the attic space to make another bedroom. Is that possible?"_, or _"Since there's a steep slope in the backyard, will we be able to build a large deck."_

When you get asked questions like that, just tell the client to check with the zoning and building departments. The client needs to find out if these departments will allow the work to be done. If the zoning and building department employees say _"yes,"_ then tell the client to get estimates from licensed contractors for the work they want done. There's nothing complex about it.

Don't over exaggerate your answer by responding with, *"Well if you want to put an addition on the house, then you might as well forget about buying this place. That will just be a lot of work and aggravation for nothing. Just go find yourself a larger house to buy."*

At the same time don't under estimate your answer by telling them, *"Of course you can put a dormer in the attic area Mr. Client. The zoning and building departments are really flexible around here. They always bend the rules to help out homeowners. My friend Joe is a carpenter and he can do all of the work needed for next to nothing."*

Report Writing

We've pretty much covered just about every aspect of the real estate appraisal business, and the appraisal process itself. Now we'll talk about writing up the appraisal report after leaving the job site. Don't hand the client a checklist style appraisal report at the site. You have to think about what you're going to write in your report, before you mail it out to your client. In my opinion, any appraiser that gives a brief checklist style report to their clients, gives a black eye to the whole profession. Appraisers who give their clients a brief, meaningless checklist report should be embarrassed!

An ***"A to Z Appraiser"*** provides a written appraisal report that's informative and useful to their

In my opinion, any appraiser that gives a very brief checklist style report to their clients, gives a black eye to the whole profession. Any appraisers who give a meaningless checklist report to their clients should be embarrassed!

clients. Your written report has to have narrative comments to assist the client and explain everything in an easy to understand fashion. That's why the checklist style reports are such a joke. Checklist style reports don't tell the client anything about the house! A narrative report will educate the client about the subject property in a manner that is easy for an average person to understand. Remember not to use construction jargon terms or have comments that only a professional in the industry will be able to understand. When writing your reports you have to think about what you want to say and think about the

person who will be reading it.

I'll use an analogy from high school that you probably can relate to. Do you remember when you were in school and you were given a homework assignment to do a written report? Well, you didn't give the teacher your report at the end of the class did you? You had to go home and think about what you were going to write, so that it would be a quality homework assignment. *(Or at least you should have).* If you shouldn't cut corners for a written report for school, then you shouldn't cut corners for a written report for an appraisal client.

A very important point to remember is this: ***What you put in the written report is what you will be held accountable for!!!!*** This simply means, that I don't care how many times you told the client over the phone that the railroad tracks in the guy's back yard have a negative impact on market value. If you don't put it in the written report, then you have **no defense** when you get an angry client calling you up 10 months later about not being able to sleep because the trains pass by his house every night at 3:00 in the morning and toot their horns! You won't even remember the house, let alone the locational problems of it 10 months later.

In appraisal reports, you're required to disclose everything that you know which has an effect on the market value of the subject property. Everything must be disclosed in a way that can't be misinterpreted or twisted around. You should always have a notepad at the job site and you should be taking field notes throughout the appraisal. Don't make the mistake of leaving anything to memory. You'll find out the hard way that when you get back to your office to write the report up, you'll have forgotten a lot. Moreover, you won't remember some of the details clearly. This is even more true when you start to get really busy and you sometimes have to do two appraisal inspections in one day. You'll have a hard time remembering if a problem condition was in the first or second house you inspected that day. That is, unless you have very detailed notes from the job site.

Organize your notes and your appraisal so that you don't forget to include anything in the written report. Make sure you take your time at the job site and in writing the report so you don't leave anything out. When you take field notes and write your report make sure to include anything the client mentioned that concerned them or that they had questions about.

When the client is concerned about a particular aspect of the house or condo, then it's an indication that this is an item they'll expect to see in the report. The client will also become angry if they buy the house and discover that you improperly evaluated the item.

For example, let's say the client asks a few questions about any possible easements in the front yard. Well you better make sure you evaluate the deed and all other pertinent documents at town hall to try to figure out if there's an easement. On top of that, make sure your conclusions are put in the written report. If you don't, the client may buy the house and discover you missed this item during your appraisal and didn't mention it in your report. When this happens, then at the very least, you'll have a dissatisfied client who won't recommend you.

I'm not trying to scare you. I'm just telling you the facts. Cover Your Assets in all of your written reports. You basically try to CYA on all appraisals due to the possibility of unreasonable clients. While taking the appraisal courses one of my instructors told me about a very good commercial appraiser who was threatened with a lawsuit by an unreasonable client. Apparently there were many loan foreclosures on properties taken back by this particular mortgage lender. The lender was threatening to sue many of the appraisers they had hired for the original market value estimates. This lender was claiming that these appraisers over estimated the market value at the time of the original appraisal reports. Many of these appraisers gave in to that type of threat. They just had their E & O insurance carrier payoff the lender to get rid of the matter rather than spend a lot of money on legal fees defending themselves. This particular appraiser knew he was right and simply told the lender that he was going to fight them in court. This appraiser also didn't want a "black mark" on his record for something that he didn't do wrong.

I take my hat off to that appraiser for having the guts and determination to stand up for what he knew was right. Coincidentally, the lender dropped the lawsuit because they had no case against the appraiser. Do you believe that! Some people have no concept of logic and they can be so unreasonable. An unreasonable client, such as the one in this case, will rationalize their actions by saying to themselves: *"Well, let's sue everybody in sight and see who breaks under the pressure and pays us a few bucks for nothing."*

If something isn't visible or accessible and/or can't be accurately evaluated, then tell the client that, and tell them to have it checked out further if any doubts exist. If you haven't been able to evaluate some aspect of the appraisal report to the point where you feel comfortable in telling them it's a thorough and complete report, then tell the client that. Ask the client for more time to check things out further.

Be very careful about giving cost estimates for repairs. You might end up paying the difference

> *Any areas of the house that are inaccessible due to furniture, personal belongings, finished areas, etc. should be stated in your report.*
> *This way the client will have a written record that you don't have a magic wand, X-ray vision, or a crystal ball.*

between what you quoted the client and what they ended up paying for the work. Tell the client to call a contractor and get estimates on their own. Otherwise, make sure you know what the costs will be and leave some margin for error. Be very careful about recommending any contractors. If you do, make sure they're very honest. If the client uses anyone that you recommend and the client ends up in court with that person, then your client might become angry with you. They could become angry with you for referring that contractor.

Don't let the war stories scare you, just be aware it can happen to anyone. It's just part of normal, everyday business problems to deal with in any business. You get paid more because a lot of knowledge is required to be a skilled appraiser. As a result, there's more liability. Look at the liability doctors have to assume in their profession. That's why they get paid so much.

Any areas of the house that are inaccessible or not visible due to furniture, personal belongings, finished areas, etc. should be stated in your report. This doesn't mean that you have to take out a ruler and write the exact location of every piece of furniture, carpeting, wall covering, picture, etc. Just use your common sense and mention anything that is hidden but would normally be accessible and visible on a typical appraisal assignment. For example, some of the inaccessible areas that should be mentioned would include: a finished basement or attic, a garage that's filled with storage items, a locked room, etc. Also, anything you couldn't evaluate properly during your field work should be stated in your report. This way the client will have a written record that you don't have a magic wand, X-ray vision, or a crystal ball, *(which some people might be surprised to find out).*

If you think it sounds strange to state in the written report that you can't see behind finished and inaccessible areas, then I'll tell you another bedtime war story so you understand why. I once did an inspection and there was a section of the ceiling on the top floor of the house that had some brown water stains. The water stain wasn't that large and it didn't appear to be recent. You'll find this condition often in attics where there will be old water stains from roof leaks that have since been repaired. I told the client at the inspection site and in the written report that there probably was some damage to the areas behind the sheetrock ceilings. I explained that I can't detect this damage because it's not visible. When the client applied for his mortgage loan, the bank appraiser went through the house and mentioned the water stains on the ceiling in the appraisal report as well.

About three weeks after the date I did the inspection, I got a phone call from this client. He said that he needed a letter from me stating that the roof was in good condition and that it wasn't leaking. He said that the bank read what the appraiser had put in his report about the water stains. As a result, they required this letter for a final approval to lend him the mortgage money to buy the house. I told the client that I can't give him a letter stating that the roof is definitely not leaking and that everything is in good condition.

He kept pushing the point of how he needed a letter because he felt that anything would help to satisfy his lender. I told him that I would not make any statements that could be misinterpreted. Furthermore, I said that the only thing I could write would be what I had stated in the written inspection report and that was: *"the water stains did not appear to be recent and appeared to have been from a prior roof leak but there could be damage behind the finished areas."* This statement turned out to be exactly what had happened. The seller of the house had a roof leak in that area before having the house last reroofed. After the new roof was installed, the water leak stopped. The only problem was that the seller was too cheap to pay to have the damage to the roof rafters repaired. There was no attic for me to view this damage due to the design of the house!

Well about a month later I got a phone call from this client. He told me that after he closed on the house, he had a contractor open that section of the ceiling. Beneath the ceiling covering they found extensive water damage to the roof rafters. The client was a little bit unhappy because he felt that I didn't tell him *"strongly"* enough that there could be damage behind the sheetrock ceiling. Do you believe that!!! What more do I have to do? I told him at the site and I put a statement in the written report! I guess he felt I should have beat him over the head with the idea to make him understand it more clearly. So learn a lesson from this and don't leave anything to the imagination. When you start to book a lot of appraisals you'll have a hard enough time remembering a house you appraised one month ago; let alone if you have to remember something about it one year later.

Your state appraisal commission may have booklets and information to assist you in writing an appraisal report that meets the federal and state appraisal standards. Call your state appraisal board and have them send you information. There might be a small fee but it's well worth the additional time and money spent.

The Report Is Totally Confidential

There is an important point to remember about the contents of the **entire** written report, as well as any other aspects you learn about during the appraisal process. That is the report and any other aspects of the appraisal are the property of the person who commissioned the appraisal and paid the fee, which is your client. Your client is the one who owns the contents of that report once he has received it and paid you for your services. Therefore, the contents of the report is confidential information for the client only!!! When I say that your client "owns" the contents of the report, it doesn't mean that they own the copyrights to the report text. It means that the information and data is the property of the client for their use in evaluating the subject property.

Many times a Realtor or seller to the transaction will ask you for a copy of the appraisal report or about some of the other aspects that you evaluated during your appraisal. **Don't give it to them without the client's consent!!!** It's none of their business to see what's in the written report unless the client wants them to see it. The client may want to negotiate with the seller on some items you noted during your appraisal and report. If the report gets into anyone else's hands, then it diminishes the client's negotiating position. It's similar to playing poker. You wouldn't show your hand to other players of the game, would you?

If you send a copy of the written report to a Realtor or seller, then you can weaken your client's position. Your client's position is weakened because the third party will know what's in the report. You

Many times a Realtor or seller will ask you for a copy of the appraisal report or about other aspects that you evaluated. Don't give it to them without the client's consent!!!

should also make your client aware of this when you book the job over the phone and at the job site. Tell your client about the poker game analogy so that you dump it back into their lap. This way the client makes the decision as to who gets any additional copies of the written report.

I recommend to my clients' that they don't give a copy of the written report to anyone but their own attorney. I've hardly ever seen a copy of the written appraisal report benefit my client when it was given to a Realtor, seller, or any other third parties. The reason for this is simple. Let's say the seller doesn't agree with me when I tell my client about a problem condition at the house. The seller is not going to change his mind just because he sees that I wrote the statement on paper. On top of that, I've often seen copies of the report hurt my clients' position when it was given to a third party. Let's say you told the client that the roof is very old but it's not leaking at this time. The Realtors and sellers will use this statement against the client. They'll say, *"As long as the roof isn't leaking, the seller isn't obligated to replace it."* This totally disregards the fact that the roof will leak and need replacing in the near future.

Tell your client there's a better approach to negotiate rather than giving the seller a copy of your report. A written estimate from a licensed contractor can be much more helpful and convincing. Your client gets two benefits from this. First, the client can show the seller and Realtor a second opinion in writing that confirms what you're telling them. Second, the client will have a repair estimate prior to closing. This way they'll know what the costs will be whether they do the work now or later.

There's another reason why you don't want to send a copy of the written report to any dishonest Realtors. The reason is that the written reports have a **very nasty** habit of floating around when they're not in your client's hands. You don't want your report ending up in someone else's hands, especially not another appraisal company. If you're an *"A to Z Appraiser"* then you have to worry about your competitors trying to steal your ideas and information that they find in your written reports.

I actually had a local Realtor _threaten_ me once about this topic. Along with my home inspection and appraisal reports I send out a letter to the client. This Realtor threatened me because this letter states some benefits and reasons why the client shouldn't give out copies of the written report to anyone else. Do you believe that!! This Realtor not only threatened me with legal action, but she even went a step further. She told all of the other people in her office to tell their client's not to use me on their home inspections. Talk about **dishonesty!** This Realtor was getting a commission on the sale and she represented the seller in the transaction. Realtors who represent the seller know that they have no legal right to see the written report nor any of the test results, such as radon and water tests. That's okay though. I get enough work from satisfied clients so I don't need any work from dishonest Realtors. As an *"A to Z Appraiser,"* you won't either.

Appraisal Referral Realities

You will find that the vast majority of Realtors and some other third parties won't recommend you for appraisals if you're too honest and too thorough. They won't recommend you because you may kill their deals by finding problems with the house or condo. If that happens, then they'll end up losing their commission, their fee, or their profit on the sale. People like that will only refer customers to you with strings attached. If you don't move the deal along by not telling the

> *You will find the vast majority of Realtors won't recommend you for appraisals if you're too honest and too thorough.*

client about any problems in the house, then they get angry and won't recommend you again. Don't bother with these types of people. It'll be very hard to avoid them in business, so just try to ignore them. You can get more than enough business from honest people. You don't want to *"sell your soul"* just to make money, so who cares if they don't recommend you.

Honest Realtors and third party people will recommend a good, thorough appraiser. They know that a good appraiser will satisfy the client that the estimated market value of the house or condo has been thoroughly evaluated. Unfortunately, you may find that the honest third party people who will recommend you if you're good, can be **extremely** outnumbered in some areas. And I'm not talking about your clients, because they'll *always* recommend you if you're good. You just want to do business with the honest third party people so you can sleep with a clear conscience at night.

The only way you're going to make big money on a steady basis in this business is to have satisfied clients who refer customers to you. If you have steady referrals from former clients, then you won't even have to advertise and your phone will ring off the hook for appraisal jobs. That's when you know you have a rock

> *There's a big difference between referrals from satisfied clients who you've done appraisals for, and referrals from Realtors who send customers to you just because you "move the deal along."*

solid business that's going to make you a lot of money for a long, long time. And you want to be in this for the long term. The people that make the most money in this business, are the ones who have the most satisfied clients. Even in a recession, they still make money, because houses are still sold when the economy is bad. The only difference is that houses sell for less money,

but they still need to be appraised.

There's a big difference between referrals from satisfied clients who you've done appraisals for, and referrals from Realtors and third parties who send customers to you just because you "move the deal along." If you just move the deal along and don't do a thorough and professional appraisal, then the client is going to know that after the appraisal's over. They might not say anything to you, but they just won't recommend you to their friends or business associates. I've seen it before in some other appraisal companies. They get all of their business from dishonest Realtors because they don't tell the client about anything wrong with the house or give an accurate estimate of the market value, and they just move the deal along. These appraisers end up being **owned** by dishonest Realtors and other third parties because the third parties have control over their income. I don't know about you, but I don't like anybody having leverage over me.

With these types of referrals from dishonest Realtors and third parties, you can't tell the client about anything being wrong with the house or you have to slant the market value estimate to favor the Realtor. If you do tell your client about repairs needed, and it creates *any* problems or kills the deal, then the third party gets angry and won't recommend you anymore. Regardless of the fact that you were being honest with the client, they still won't recommend you anymore. Dishonest Realtors and third parties don't want you to say anything that will throw a monkey wrench into their deal.

It doesn't matter how many other deals you moved along for the dishonest Realtor or other third party person. If you create problems with or kill, just one of their deals; then that's it, you're cut off. And if they cut you off after you've been catering to them for some time, then you're really in trouble. You're in trouble because you don't have any satisfied clients to refer you for any future appraisals. Then your phone stops ringing and your appraisal income goes down to nothing.

You don't believe me? I've heard quite a few war stories about appraisers who can't find any new business due to the poor quality of their work in the past. I've even seen it happen firsthand, my friend, with a local home inspection company in my area. When the older inspector left the business and the new inspector came in and started doing good, honest and thorough inspections, the phone stopped ringing. All of the dishonest Realtors and third parties stopped using the new inspector because he didn't cater to them and move the deal along like the older inspector had. The phone didn't ring from client referrals either. This is because none of the former clients would recommend anyone to this inspection company. They wouldn't recommend anyone because they knew the work was of such a poor quality from the older inspector. This created a terrible reflection on the company name, even after the older inspector left the business. To make matters even worse, the only phone calls that came in were from <u>unhappy</u> former clients of the old inspector. These people called to complain about the inspection services they had gotten.

There's another drawback to getting all of your referrals from dishonest third parties. What happens is, the client buys the house or makes the loan and then finds out after the fact, that there are some problems. The client decides that the appraiser should've noticed these problems during the appraisal and told the client about them. Or possibly the market value estimate was way off base. So what does the client do? He gets angry because he knows the appraiser wasn't thorough or professional, and he sicks his attorney on the appraiser. Appraisers like that end up being sued out of business.

So you see, the only way to make it in this, or any other business, is to do good, honest and professional work. If you *"sell your soul"* then your income and your reputation are going to pay dearly for it. And you won't even sleep well at night. I've found that some people have an **amazing** ability to rationalize their actions, no matter how bad they are. So let the dishonest Realtors and other third parties sell their

> *They get all of their business from dishonest Realtors because they don't tell the client about anything wrong with the house, and they just "move the deal along." These appraisers end up being owned by the dishonest Realtors.*

souls. Just don't ever compromise your own integrity. Too many people compromise their integrity for money. I think that money is like a truth serum. It brings out the true character of a person, deep down inside, whether they're good or bad. There's an awful lot of *"white collar crime"* that goes unnoticed because people rationalize their actions. They deliberately hide problems from the clients. Then they kid themselves thinking that there's nothing wrong with burying things underneath a blanket of deception.

I've had many Realtors and sellers complain because my home inspections take three or four hours. They also complain because of the amount of research and time I spend on my appraisals. They don't want you to be too thorough or to spend too much time in the house or on the report. My clients never complain because I spend three or four hours inspecting a house they're planning to buy. So why do Realtors and sellers complain about it? They seem to forget, that my responsibility is to my client and not to any third parties. However, if **they** were buying the house, well then, it would be a totally different story. I'll talk more about hypocrites later.

I'm certainly not being a hypocrite myself or talking out of ignorance. I let my track record and integrity speak for itself: Less than *one percent* of my clients have ever called me up to say that they were unhappy with my services. I've even **turned away** business by being honest with people. There are many

> *So you see, the only way to make it in this, or any other business, is to do good, honest and professional work. If you "sell your soul" then your income and your reputation are going to pay dearly for it.*

dishonest Realtors whose business I have turned away. I told these Realtors that I didn't want their referrals for clients. The reason for this is that I knew they would complain if I did a thorough inspection. Other examples are, I've done inspections on houses that were taken back in foreclosures or the houses were part of estate sales after someone had died. These houses had all of the utilities turned off at the time I arrived to do the inspection. You can't do a proper appraisal and/or home inspection on a house without any utilities turned on. The reason for this is that you won't be able to test any of the operating systems. I would be up-front and honest with my clients. I'd tell them that rather than go ahead with the inspection, they'd be better off waiting until the utilities were turned on. If they delay the inspection, I wouldn't have to charge them a fee for a limited home inspection. Sometimes these deals would fall through because another buyer would come along before the utilities were turned on, or some other reason. Therefore, as a result of being up-front and honest, I would lose money. However, I'd rather lose the money, then to do the inspection and not feel good about it. I hope that's the way you run your business as well.

If you go into this business, then you're going to come across many dishonest Realtors and other third parties who will try to get you to *"move their deals along."* I'm letting you know ahead of time that's it's going to happen, so don't say I didn't warn you about this. Often what dishonest Realtors will do is try to butter you up when you show first show up at the subject property. Sometimes they'll even call you up before you go out to the site and try to butter you up. What they say to you is, *"Oh, can I have one of your business cards. Our office is always looking for new appraisers to recommend to our clients."* They lie to you by saying this to make you think that they're going to refer their future clients to you for appraisal work. However, it's the same old game that they're playing. If you don't *"move their deal along,"* then your business cards will end up in their garbage can as soon as the Realtors get back to their office. *(I have an awful lot of business cards and brochures that have ended up in dishonest Realtor's garbage cans. My cards ended up in their garbage because I was too honest and thorough with my clients.)*

So remember, don't let any Realtors or other third parties butter you up on an appraisal. Be on your guard when they ask you for your business card so they can supposedly refer other clients to you. Translated into English, what they're really saying to you is, *"Don't tell the buyer that anything's wrong with the house and we'll give you some referral business. This way the both of us can cheat and deceive people and line our pockets with dirty money."* You'll also come across another offshoot for this type of Realtor and third party dishonesty if you go into this business. Dishonest Realtors will sometimes say to you, *"It's not **what** you say to the client, it's **how** you say it that matters."* Translated into English, what they really mean by saying this to you is, *"Don't tell the buyer that something, such as the heating system is old and can die at anytime. Just tell them that it's working properly now because that's all they need to know. Don't mention anything to them about getting estimates to replace it."*

Some Good Reasons For Federal Regulations

In my opinion, there is an *urgent* need for Federal legislation. The legislation should prevent anyone who will benefit by the sale of a property from recommending a home inspector or an appraiser. The reason I say this is that, **it is a total conflict of interest if they recommend an inspector or appraiser!!!** I can't believe that laws have not been passed which prevent this conflict of interest. If someone will gain a profit or a commission on the sale of a property, then don't you think that there's an obvious problem if they recommend a home inspector or an appraiser? The problem is due to the temptation of the third party to make sure the deal goes through, at any cost, so they can get paid. Furthermore, most of the time, third parties who get a commission on the sale work for the seller!! This means that their fiduciary and legal responsibility is to get the best deal possible for the **seller**, not the **buyer**. Therefore, how can these third

> *Legislation should prevent anyone who benefits by the sale of a property from recommending a home inspector or appraiser. I say this because, it's a total conflict of interest if they recommend an inspector or appraiser!!!*

party people say that they're looking out for the buyer's best interest, by recommending a thorough and unbiased home inspector or appraiser? Again, it's a total conflict of interest if they recommend a home inspector or an appraiser!

Believe me, I'm no rocket scientist and I can see as clear as day that there's a problem here that needs to be fixed. I also think that there is an *urgent* need for another type of Federal legislation. This legislation should require all third parties involved in a real estate transaction, who receive a commission on the sale, to make certain recommendations to the seller and the buyer. However, the recommendations *should not* be a conflict of interest.

◊ The recommendation they should be required to make to the seller is: *"The seller should hire an independent real estate appraiser that they select on their own, without any involvement or encouragement of the Realtors or any other third parties. An appraisal is recommended to give the seller an unbiased estimate of market value for the subject property. This appraisal should be done **before** the seller lists the property for sale."*

◊   The recommendation they should be required to make to the buyer is: *"The buyer should hire an <u>independent</u> real estate home inspector that they select on their own, without any involvement or encouragement of the Realtors or any other third parties. An inspection is recommended to give the buyer a thorough and professional home inspection of the subject property. This home inspection should be done **<u>before</u>** the buyer signs any contracts to purchase the subject property."*

If these ideas were enforced by Federal legislation, then it would greatly help everyone in the country with the biggest investment of their lives. This type of legislation would also improve the integrity of the real estate business *tremendously*. Now don't get me wrong here. If an attorney wants to recommend a home

> *Believe me, I'm no rocket scientist and I can see as clear as day that there's a problem here that needs to be fixed.*

inspector or an appraiser to a client they're representing, then that's fine. In a case like this, the attorney is only looking out for their client's interests. The attorney will get paid a fee, regardless of whether the deal goes through or not. Therefore, they don't have a conflict of interest to move the deal along by recommending an incompetent home inspector or appraiser. I hope you see the difference between these two situations.

In the front of the book I list the benefits of having an appraisal done by an independent, honest and thorough real estate appraiser. I think they're all valid reasons that are based on a foundation of solid facts. These facts reinforce my opinions about the need for Federal legislation. I've seen many examples of sellers who have been deceived by dishonest Realtors and other third parties. This deception could have been prevented, if the seller had been educated about the benefits of getting an unbiased appraiser to estimate the market value of their property. The way some dishonest third parties cheat sellers' is by deceiving them as to the true market value of their property.

I had a client that hired me to do an appraisal of their house before they listed it for sale. The woman who owned the house was a very nice, easygoing person. She told me that she and her husband purchased the house just three years earlier for about $500,000. There was a Realtor who was involved in the transaction. At the time they purchased the property, this Realtor told the couple: *"You're getting*

*a **rock bottom** price, and you're **stealing** this house for $100,000 below market value."* The woman who was my client told me, that she and her husband asked this same Realtor to list their house for sale, three years later. Well, this Realtor told them: *"The market has gone way down because of the recession. You're going to have to sell the house for $100,000 less than what you paid for it, three years earlier."*

Luckily, my client and her husband didn't believe that the real estate market had dropped that drastically in only three years. I did an extremely thorough appraisal, using six sales comparables that had sold within the past six months. These sales comps were all located within two blocks of the subject property. My appraisal market value estimate was just about the same price the client had paid for the house. There was a recession that caused prices to drop in the area. However, at the time my clients were going to sell the property, the market had rebounded so they wouldn't have to take a big loss. This is a perfect example of how the public can get cheated by dishonest and/or incompetent third party people who call themselves *"real estate professionals."*

This appraisal client made a statement to me about Realtors that I have found to be very true. She said that *"Realtors talk out of both sides of their mouth."* During all of my experience in this business I've found

> *I've seen ENDLESS examples of buyers who have been deceived by dishonest Realtors and other third parties to the transaction.*

that most Realtors will say anything to sell a house. It's similar to a prostitute - they screw people for money!!

I've seen **<u>ENDLESS</u>** examples of buyers who have been deceived by dishonest third parties. I'd be one of the richest people around if I had a nickel for each time I've seen this happen. All of this deception could have been prevented, if the buyer had been educated about the benefits of getting an unbiased home inspector to evaluate the condition of the subject property. The way dishonest Realtors and other third parties cheat buyers' is by deceiving them as to the true condition of the house they're purchasing.

For example, let's say a buyer wants to have an inspection done on a house they are thinking about purchasing. They will ask a Realtor or other third party that's involved in the deal to recommend a home inspector to them. A dishonest Realtor or other third party will give the buyer three names of home inspectors that won't say anything bad about the subject property. This way the deal won't be delayed or renegotiated due to problem conditions found during the inspection.

After the buyer closes on the house and moves-in, they find out the repairs that are needed and all of the problems with the house. The buyer then realizes that these are the things that the home inspector should have told them about. But by that time, it's too late. It's already a done deal.

The reason a dishonest Realtor or other third party gives the buyer a list of three names is another con game. All three of the inspectors on that list are incompetent crooks with no integrity or morals! The

> *The reason a dishonest Realtor or other third party gives the buyer a list of three names is another con game. All three of the inspectors on that list are incompetent crooks with no integrity or morals!*

dishonest Realtor or other third party has those inspectors in their back pocket. They're partners in crime. They're cheating the public by "moving deals along" and people don't realize they've been scammed until it's too late. The buyer can call the third party to complain about the incompetent home inspector they recommended. However, often the third party gets off the hook by saying, *"Well, Mr. Buyer, I'm very sorry you found problems with the house that didn't come out during the inspection. However, I gave you three names to call. You should have hired inspector #2 on the list instead of inspector #3."* If you don't believe all of this, then just ask other inspectors that are very thorough and knowledgeable. See what they tell you.

You Get What You Pay For

I don't mean to scare you by talking about dishonesty and lawsuits. But this is how the whole idea of Federal and State regulations and licensing came about for real estate appraisers. During the 1980's real estate prices were rising through the roof, *(pardon the pun)*. The banks and savings and loans kept lending mortgage money on over-priced real estate transactions. A reason for this may be that they figured they couldn't lose money. If the buyer didn't make the mortgage payments then the lender could foreclose. If that happened, then the property would be worth more than the bank had lent and they would make a profit anyway.

Well that's not how it turned out. Everybody ended up losing in a big way. When the recession hit the economy in 1989 an awful lot of banks lost billions of dollars due to real estate loans that had gone sour. The Savings and Loan bailout is currently estimated at 250 billion dollars. Banks could foreclose on the properties but they couldn't resell them to get their funds back. Everybody loses in that type of situation including the homeowner, bank, the economy, the local town, etc.

The whole reason the *Resolution Trust Corporation*, RTC, was created was to take over insolvent banks. After taking over these banks, the RTC would try to sell the bank assets to investors to recoup some of the losses. The *Federal Deposit Insurance Corporation*, FDIC, and the *Federal Savings and Loan Insurance Corporation*, FSLIC, had to pay the depositors in the insolvent banks. Customers that had bank accounts were paid the insurance amount for their deposited money. Any funds that the RTC could not recoup with the sale of assets from insolvent banks were left to the American taxpayer to pay.

To try to prevent this whole mess from ever happening again, the Federal Government set up the *Appraisal Foundation.* Its purpose is to design some minimum requirements for Federal and State licensing and certification for all real estate appraisers. The government had to regulate some occupational group involved in the real estate industry. Since the banks and savings and loans were already regulated, they looked to the real estate appraisers.

Many bankers felt that they would not have made many real estate loans that had gone sour if the appraisers had been more cautious. They felt that the appraisers erred because they kept arriving at inflated estimates of market value in their reports. On the other hand, many appraisers felt that some bankers and mortgage brokers had unfairly pressured them in the 1980's. The pressure on the appraisers was to arrive at high estimates of market value in their reports. The high estimates were necessary in some reports so that the lender or broker could grant the mortgage loan and earn a profit or a commission fee. Before the Federal requirements, just about anyone could call themselves a real estate appraiser. The only way to differentiate between appraisers and to measure their competence was to ask if they were designated by one of the large appraisal organizations that existed.

I hate to say it, but I don't think the current regulations are enough to eliminate the potential for future problems. Problems such as those encountered with bad real estate loans in the 1980's may happen again. I think a very important aspect that's being overlooked will all of the licensing requirements is the standard amount that mortgage lenders pay appraisers. Real estate appraisers are highly underpaid for the amount of work needed to do a thorough and high quality appraisal report. If you're a thorough appraiser, you can earn a six figure income in this business. However, I still think there are far too many lenders that are *only* concerned with how inexpensively they can have a licensed appraiser do their reports. **They're so penny wise and dollar foolish it's amazing!**

If you pay an appraiser more money than the lowest fee possible, then you can insist that he provide you with higher quality appraisal reports. If the appraiser's getting paid a reasonable fee for the work involved to do a thorough report, then he's going to spend much more time on the assignment. The appraiser will make a bigger effort to do the best work that he can.

I met an appraiser once who owned a business that did work for insurance companies. His appraisal firm did replacement value appraisals on homes. These are needed for insurance companies prior to writing some homeowner's policies. This appraiser was telling me about how insurance companies don't want to spend any money on these appraisals. He would get calls from insurance companies all over the country looking for someone to handle their appraisal work. When he told them his fee, their response was always, *"That's more money than we're paying now for these appraisals. You have to lower your prices."* After hearing this, the appraiser would ask the insurers why they called him if they already had an appraisal company handling their work. The insurers response would be, *"We're not happy with the quality of the work we're getting."* The appraiser would answer, *"That's why I charge more!"*

According to the Federal and State Appraisal Standards, an appraiser has to do the same amount of work for all of their reports, no matter what they're being paid. You can't cut corners because you're not getting paid enough on a particular assignment. If you take shortcuts, you're going to make mistakes and you'll end up regretting it. Unfortunately, many people forget this. That's why you have lazy and unqualified appraisers who are only concerned with mailing out as many reports as possible to clients. These appraisers don't have any concern about the quality of the work in their reports. The reason for this lack of concern is that these appraisers feel that they're not getting paid enough to spend sufficient time on each report. I think some lenders might want to refresh their memories about this old saying: *"You get what you pay for!"*

By doing so many foreclosure appraisals, I can tell you that I've seen the results of this problem firsthand on many occasions. I've seen what a nightmare it becomes for a mortgage lender to have to foreclose on a property. I've seen lenders lose a ton of money in foreclosures. One of the aspects that play a big part in those loans being granted in the first place is the appraisal report. Some of these lenders would never have granted the loan if they had hired a more thorough, competent appraiser to estimate the value of the property.

"Oh yes, but I forgot, those lenders are very intelligent businessmen. After all, they saved an extra $100 or $150 by hiring the cheapest appraiser in town. They didn't need to hire a competent, honest and knowledgeable appraiser and paying the extra amount by billing the loan applicant for the additional appraisal fee." All those lenders had to do was to charge the mortgage loan applicant $100 to $150 more for the appraisal reports. If they had, then they could have saved themselves tens of thousands of dollars in losses for many of the loans that had gone sour! And I'm not talking about the lender paying the higher fee to get a good, competent appraisal done. The appraisal fee for mortgage loan applications is passed on to the potential borrower when they hand in their loan application. I've seen this scenario happen so often. It makes me sick to my stomach to think that the American taxpayer is paying for this whole failure of the banking industry due to foreclosures.

Handling Client Complaints

No matter how good you are, you're going to get a few complaints from clients because you can't satisfy everyone all the time. It's the same problem in every other business. So you might as well get ready to deal with it now. The bright side is that the better you are, the fewer complaints you'll get. It's that simple. If you don't like headaches or aggravation, then just do good, thorough appraisals and you'll minimize the complaints as much as possible. As I've said earlier, I've only had less than one percent of my clients complain about my services. Of these complaints, I was only wrong one time. If you have a track record like that, then you'll be doing just fine. You will also be able to consider the quality of your work far superior to the competition.

When you get a complaint from a client after they have purchased the house you had appraised, it may be due to the fact that they didn't read the written appraisal report prior to the closing. Believe it or not, many people get so excited and emotional about

> *No matter how good you are, you're going to get a few complaints from clients because you can't satisfy everyone all the time. It's the same problem in every other business.*

buying a house that they tend to overlook very important factors. This is why you **have to** send your clients a thorough and professional written appraisal report. Don't be like a lot of other appraisers out there and send your clients a checklist report that doesn't tell them anything. If you send your clients a checklist report you'll end up regretting it if you get into this type of situation.

Some people will just assume that if they attended the on-site inspection, then they know enough about the house and they won't bother reading a long, narrative appraisal report. They also will just assume that they don't need to bother with getting estimates for any problem conditions prior to closing on the house. They'll just wait until after they move-in and worry about getting estimates later. This is a BIG mistake on the client's part because you know the old saying, *"When you **assume**, you make an **Ass** out of **U** and **Me**."*

I've had this exact situation happen with one of my

inspection client's. This client had purchased a house and didn't follow my professional recommendations. I had told this client, verbally and in the written inspection report, to have the siding checked out before closing by a licensed contractor. There were many damaged and missing shingles on the house. I also told this client that when I asked the seller the preinspection questions, the seller said that the house had been treated for carpenter ant damage a few years ago. I told the client to speak to the exterminator who did the carpenter ant treatment; get all documentation for the work; and find out the extent of the damage and the treatment. Furthermore, I told this client to hire their own exterminator to evaluate this information and treat the house again.

This client had decided they didn't need to worry about following any of my recommendations until *after* they moved into the house. Well wouldn't you know it, I got a phone call from them a few months after they moved into the house. They told me that the reason the shingles were falling off the house was because of the carpenter ant damage. I asked the client how they found out about the cause of this problem. He said that they had hired a contractor, after they bought the house, to evaluate the damaged shingles and the prior owner's carpenter ant treatment.

If this client had listened to me at the inspection site and read the written inspection report, they would have eliminated all these problems before they bought the house! However, the client either did not listen to me clearly at the inspection site and did not read the written report; or the client did listen to me and did

> *This is a perfect example of why you have to stress to your clients, and put a statement in the written reports, recommending that they get repair estimates and eliminate any questions, concerns or problems - BEFORE BUYING THE HOUSE!!!!*

read the report but they just decided, on their own, not to follow my professional recommendations. Therefore, in a case such as this, the client cannot blame anyone but themselves for being negligent and foolish.

This is a perfect example of why you have to stress to your clients, and put a statement in the written reports, recommending that they get repair estimates and eliminate any questions, concerns or problems - BEFORE BUYING THE HOUSE!!!! Just tell the client not to get too emotional or excited about their purchase and not to assume anything. If they check everything out before they buy the house, then it becomes the **seller's** responsibility to remedy any problems. However, if the client doesn't check everything out before they buy the house, then it becomes the **buyer's** responsibility to remedy any problems.

If you're a thorough real estate appraiser, then sometimes when you get a complaint from a client, it's because they have been deceived by a dishonest and/or ignorant contractor. All of your written reports should have a statement that warns your clients about this problem, before it's too late. What happens is this: The client closes on the house and then moves-in to their new home. While they're living there or during some remodeling work, they find items that need to be repaired that weren't identified in the appraisal report.

Most of the time, the reason these items weren't identified during the on-site inspection, is because they weren't visible or accessible during the inspection. This happens all the time with termites and water problems, unless it's a visible problem and you're a thorough **"A to Z Appraiser."** The client will open up a floor, wall or ceiling during remodeling work. When it's all open, they find damage from termites or water leaks. Obviously, the appraiser can't identify a problem if it's not visible. *(Well, at least you would think that it's obvious to people).* Unfortunately, there are some people who don't realize you can't see behind floors, walls and ceilings. These people always think they hired *Clark Kent*, alias *Superman*, to do their appraisal!

What happens next, is the client will then unknowingly call up a dishonest and/or ignorant contractor. They will ask the contractor to come to the house and give them an estimate for the repairs needed. The contractor goes to the house and looks at the damage. He sees dollar signs in his eyes and immediately turns to your client and says, *"You mean your appraiser didn't see this? Your appraiser should have seen this damage and told you about it. You should sue that appraiser to get reimbursed for the repairs I have to do."* Then to put the icing on the cake, this moron that calls himself a contractor, hands your client a ridiculous estimate for the repairs. The estimate is usually so high, that it's from the planet Mars!

What a dishonest contractor tries to do is distract your client's attention by pointing the finger at the appraiser for not seeing the damage. While your client is angry and furious with you, they don't even think about getting a second repair estimate to verify what this contractor is telling them. A dishonest contractor

> *What a dishonest contractor tries to do is distract your client's attention by pointing the finger at the appraiser for not seeing the damage.*

tries to look like the *Knight in Shining Armor* that rides in on his white horse to save your client from the evil real estate appraiser. Because of this, your client thinks the contractor knows what he's talking about and that the appraiser is wrong. Actually, it's the other way around!

The contractor knows **nothing** about what is involved with an on-site appraisal inspection. The contractor also wasn't even at the house at the time of your inspection. Moreover, the contractor has no idea if the damage was visible or accessible at the time of the inspection. The contractor has no idea if the damage **even existed** at the time of the inspection. Therefore, how can this ignorant contractor say that you should have seen the damage and notified your client about it?

All a contractor like that will succeed in doing is raise your client's blood pressure due to the client's anger. After that, they will then rip-off your client, unless someone else opens the client's eyes to the truth. When a dishonest or uneducated contractor scares a client, they do it to _steal_ their money. When an **"A to Z Appraiser"** scares a client, they do it to _save_ them money. What I mean by this is a contractor, such as the one I've described, will steal your client's money by deceiving them into paying a grossly overcharged repair bill. They get the client all emotionally pumped up with anger, and while the client's attention is distracted, they lower the boom on them with a gigantic repair bill.

On the other hand, an **"A to Z Appraiser"** will save your client money by opening their eyes to the true risks and realities of buying a house. You may get the client scared by telling them about the potential pitfalls and hazards of a huge investment like a home. It's to the client's advantage to know all of the problems and risks in purchasing or selling a home if they don't check all of the records at town hall; the potential for damage and termites behind walls, floors, and ceilings; the health concerns of radon and asbestos; the risks of not pumping and internally inspecting a septic system; etc.

You might be saying to yourself, *"OK, now this author has really gone over the deep end. He's talking about the emotional state of real estate appraisal clients."* Well, Mr. Smarty Pants, let me give you a few war stories that show you the reality of this situation. These are two of the clients that consist of the less than one percent that have ever called me to complain about my services. I think you'll see why I feel that I was right in both cases and the home inspection clients were misled by lying contractors.

A client of mine had moved into a house that I had inspected for her. She called to say that she had replaced the water heater and the oil burner for the boiler. She told me the price she paid for the repairs and I immediately knew that she had been cheated by a dishonest contractor. I asked her why the contractor said the repairs were needed and if she had gotten any other estimates, before hiring this guy. The contractor told her that the oil burner and the water heater were unrepairable and both had to be replaced. She then said that she didn't get any other estimates for the repairs and this contractor was the only person to evaluate the damage. I then told the client to check the written inspection report and let me know what it said about these two items. The water heater was only three years old and was operating fine at the time of the

> When a dishonest or uneducated contractor scares a client, they do it to steal their money. When an "A to Z Appraiser" scares a client, they do it to save them money.

inspection. The oil burner was also operating properly at the time of the inspection. Both items were covered under a warranty and service contract with the manufacturer and oil delivery company. My client ended up realizing that these items didn't need to be replaced at all. On top of that, this immoral contractor charged her more than twice what she should have paid, even if they did need to be replaced! Since this guy was such a crooked contractor, I am positive that these items may only have needed a minor repair in the first place. However, the client was told that it was my fault by the contractor. She didn't find out the truth until it was too late and the money was spent on the repairs.

(This next story is a real beauty). Another client of mine called me after they moved into their new home. They had a contractor come in to give them a price quote to remove the old carpets and install new carpeting. This contractor found some damage underneath the existing carpet in a corner and one other small area. The hardwood floor underneath had buckled in two places. The contractor had only lifted the one corner of the carpet and he told the client, *"Didn't your home inspector see this damage underneath the carpet? This entire hardwood floor and carpet are going to cost you $5,000 to replace. Your home inspector should have seen this."* Not surprisingly, my client was angry about not being told of this damage before closing on the house. Fortunately, the client called me up before he let this blockhead, that calls himself a floor contractor, replace the hardwood floor.

When I saw the damage in person, I could not believe anyone would have told my client that I was negligent. My client and I, both confirmed that the corner where the damage was found had been buried in boxes, toys and furniture at the time of the inspection. We also both confirmed, that the other damaged area was covered with a large couch at the time of the inspection. Impressions from the furniture were still visible in the carpets surrounding the damaged areas. Therefore, it became very clear to both of us that the seller *intentionally* made sure we didn't see the damage at the time of the inspection.

I was angry that the seller was such a crook and that he would stoop so low and hide damage on purpose. However, what really annoyed me, was the ignorance of the floor contractor! When I finally looked at the damaged area underneath the corner of the carpet, I realized that the contractor had no right to accuse me of being negligent. The damaged area could be easily repaired by replacing a few of the buckled boards. It didn't even matter if the wood matched exactly or not. The client had told the contractor they wanted to cover the floor with a new carpet anyway. Luckily the client had taken my advice and called a second contractor to give them an estimate. While I was there, the second floor contractor came by the house. His price quote was a $500 repair job, not a $5,000 repair!

You should have a statement in all of the written reports that you send out to warn your clients about this type of situation. Let them know that some contractors will try to blame the appraiser and/or the home inspector. These contractors will then grossly overcharge the client for repairs that may never have been needed in the first place. Tell your clients to call you before they have any repairs done which they believe you should have identified during the on-site inspection. If they call you before the repairs are done, both you and they will have a chance to clear up the situation before it's too late.

You also want to warn your clients if you find out that the seller or any third parties have intentionally lied about some aspect of the subject property. I've had this happen on a few occasions and it should immediately raise a red flag in your mind about the property and that person's integrity. If you catch someone lying about some aspect of the property, then there probably will be other hidden problems. There could be damaged areas or something that's not visible which can create a problem after your client moves-in. If this happens to you, then make sure that you and your client verify as much information as possible, before they sign contracts.

There's a very important point that you need to remember. If you get an angry phone call from a client who complains that you missed something during your inspection: **Don't jump down their throat and tell them they're crazy!** You have to stay calm and be very reasonable and diplomatic when you deal with an angry or hostile person. Don't make the mistake of telling the client that he's insane if he thinks you should have seen damage that was hidden at the time of the inspection. By yelling back at the client, all you will succeed in doing is getting him even more furious at you. Just calmly tell the client that you want to come by the house to see the problem in person. This is for your benefit, as well as, the client's benefit. By seeing the damage in person, it will enable you to help solve the problem before they make any unnecessary or overpriced repairs.

Your client can get angry and all pumped up because they're looking at a very large repair bill. Moreover, the contractor is blaming you for not seeing the problem. As a result, the client is told by the contractor that you should pay for the repair. An angry client is concentrating on what repairs you *didn't* tell them about, before they bought the property. You have to make them realize how much you *did* tell them about, before they bought the property. As an **"A to Z Appraiser"**: your on-site inspection lasted up to several hours; you used more than the minimum three sales comparables; you checked all records at town hall; you warned them about radon; you told them to get estimates and further evaluations for some items; you sent them a narrative and informative written report; etc. Would they have gotten that much information if they hired another appraiser in the area? How much risk did you help them eliminate? How

much money did you save them? How much more thorough and professional was your appraisal, as compared to the competition? Would any homeowner, including them, allow an appraiser to come into their house and rip up the carpets, move the furniture, and open up the walls, floors and ceilings?

As long as you're logical and reasonable, the client will understand that you didn't cheat them. Your client will be complaining because **they're ignorant**, not because **you're negligent**. There's a big difference between the two. The client is ignorant because they don't know the Standards in the industry for performing an appraisal. When they're annoyed, they might not stop, take a step back, and think about the situation in a logical fashion. The client might not realize that an appraiser can't pull up carpets, or move furniture, or open up walls, floors and ceilings. You have to look at the situation from their perspective. The client is looking at a big repair bill and they think it's your fault. Once you explain the limits of an on-site inspection and ask the client questions, *(like the ones mentioned above)*, your client will understand that you haven't been negligent. After that your client will

A client of this limited mentality cannot comprehend that an appraiser doesn't travel on a magic carpet with a wand, emerald slippers, and Aladdin's lamp.

gradually calm down and recognize that you're the best appraiser in the area that they could have hired. Therefore, if you didn't see the damage, or if it wasn't visible, then no other appraiser would have identified the problem either.

Now, let's say that after you calmly explain all of this logic and reason, your client is still angry with you for missing something that you clearly had no way of identifying. If this is the situation, then I hate to have to clue you in. But you're dealing with a basket case! You have to tell this type of client that they need to call *"Super Man"* for their next real estate appraisal. This is the type of person that I've been warning you about. A client of this limited mentality cannot comprehend that an appraiser doesn't travel on a *magic carpet* with a *wand*, *emerald slippers*, and *Aladdin's lamp*. So bite your tongue, say your prayers, and try not to lose your patience with a person like that.

Know-It-All People

There will be times when you'll get a hostile seller, Realtor, or other third party to a transaction who will become very defensive by saying the market value of the house is higher than what your appraisal comes in at for a prepurchase appraisal; and lower than your market value estimate for a prelisting appraisal. You'll find that these types of people are all experts in everything, yet they have no facts or knowledge to back up their statements. Just don't be intimidated by anyone. Not even the client. If you're knowledgeable enough, you'll have plenty of confidence. So don't let anyone "ruffle your feathers" doing an appraisal.

Once you learn this material well enough and you get 10 or so appraisals under your belt you'll start to get a lot more confidence. That's why you shouldn't let any know-it-all Realtors or other third party people try to contradict you on any of your appraisals. When I say know-it-all people, I'm talking about people involved in the transaction, other than your client.

You don't want to be rude with your attitude. There will be times that you'll think you're right but you might find out later that you're wrong. You don't want to end up putting your foot in your mouth later. So just be confident, knowledgeable and honest. Don't imitate them by being a know-it-all yourself because two wrongs don't make a right. If that person is honest and sensible, they will realize that you are much more

> *You'll find that these types of people are all experts in everything, yet they have no facts or knowledge to back up their statements.*

knowledgeable than they are. For example, lets say you're looking for good, comparable sales for the subject property that have sold within the last six months. Many times some Realtors and other third parties to the transaction will give you some comps to assist you in your report. After reviewing these comparables, you may feel that they aren't good enough to use in order to properly estimate market value for the subject property. You will want to look for some better comps yourself or at least you have to try to find better sales to use in your report. You can't just take someone else's word that the comparables they give you are the only sales to use. After all, it's your neck that's on the line when you sign-off on that appraisal report!! This isn't uncommon and it happens all the time. Since the person giving you the sales comparables is not a State Certified Appraiser, then

they don't know what you have to look for to properly evaluate the comparables you use in an appraisal report.

If this were the case, and you had a know-it-all person involved in the deal, they might say to you, *"Well I've been in the real estate business for 10 years now. I know this area like the back of my hand and these are the ONLY good comps you can use for that house."* Just tell that person that if they want to guarantee to your client that these are the best comparable sales to use and if the market value estimate is inaccurate due to the sales comparables that they're giving you, then go ahead and put it in writing for my client. But don't expect me, the appraiser, to get

> *It's amazing to me when I come across Realtors who have taken a few basic classes related to aspects of real estate and - Abracadabra - they're instant experts in every aspect of real estate!!!!*

stuck holding the bag in eight months after this guy buys the house or grants the loan and then finds out the estimate of market value was way off base!

That type of comeback will usually put an end to any know-it-all's comments. Basically you're telling that person that if they know so much more about appraising than you do, then they should be willing to put their money where their mouth is. A know-it-all's reaction will be totally different when it's **their** neck and money that's on the line, as opposed to yours or your clients.

It's amazing to me when I come across ignorant Realtors and other third party people who have taken a few basic classes related to some of the different aspects of real estate and - *Abracadabra* - they're instant experts in every aspect of real estate!! *(Or at least they think they are.)* They become **legends in their own minds**. They think that after they take a few real estate related classes and tests, *(that just about anyone with a pulse can pass)*, they instantly have more knowledge than: every home inspector, every real estate appraiser, every real estate investor, every real estate attorney, every home buyer and every seller. I don't know how they do it. They must be giving out some magical pills or secret potion at these classes!

You may also come across sellers that get hostile. Sellers can get hostile when you try to tell your client about some problem conditions and items that need to be repaired at the subject property. Don't let them ruffle your feathers. My original real estate attorney used to say that there are two things that you can't tell a man: One is: That his property is overpriced; The other is: *(Well, I've decided that it wouldn't be appropriate for me to repeat the other item in this book. So I won't tell you. I'll just leave you in suspense.)*

Certified, Licensed Or Just A Dreamer ?

As an appraiser you'll come across Realtors and third party people who will say to you, *"Oh, I'm a certified real estate appraiser too. I don't work for an appraisal office, but I've done many appraisals for my clients."* They usually make a comment like that when they think they have better comps or information than you do to estimate market value of the subject property. I've found a problem with these people saying this to me. The problem is that I've never seen one of them that have an actual Certification or License number issued to them by the State they work in. That can only lead to one conclusion. <u>They're not state certified or licensed real estate appraisers!!!!</u> **<u>Period</u>.**

Some people have an amazing ability to kid themselves and rationalize things. If you're a State Certified or Licensed real estate appraiser, then you

> *Some people have an amazing ability to kid themselves and rationalize things.*

would have a State license number and documentation to prove it. This would verify that you have taken all the required classes; you have all the required fee-paid real estate appraisal experience; and you have passed all the required State appraisal examinations. There's no *if, ands* or *buts* about it! So the next time some third party tells you that they know what they're talking about and you don't because they're an "appraiser," ask them the following questions:

1.　Did you take the equivalent of the state appraisal **Course 1** and did you successfully pass the course examination?

2.　Did you take the equivalent of the state appraisal **Course 2** and did you successfully pass the course examination?

3.　Did you take the equivalent of the state appraisal **Course Standards of Professional Practice Part A and Part B** and did you successfully pass both course examinations?

4.　Have you done at least **250 Fee-Paid Real Estate Appraisals** that have all of the requirements necessary to be considered as actual appraisal reports?

5.　Did you pay the required application fees and did you take the State Certification real estate appraisal examination and did you successfully pass the exam?

6.　Do you have a State Certification or License number issued to you?

After they get finished answering *"No"* to all of the above questions, ask them a few more. This way they might realize that they don't know more than you do about appraising. Ask them questions like:

7.　What's the proper appraisal definition of market value?

8.　How do you estimate the Physical Depreciation using the Age/Life Method?

9.　What's the difference between Physical, Functional and External Depreciation?

10.　When is the Cost Approach effective and should it be used to estimate the market value of single family houses?

11.　What are the standard three different approaches to estimate market value?

12.　What price per square foot do you use to accurately reflect this market when you're adjusting for the different gross living area sizes between the subject property and the comparable properties?

Now don't be rude about it, or be a wise guy yourself, just politely make them realize that **you're the knowledgeable and professional real estate appraiser**. It's fine if any Realtors or other third party people offer you some advice and try to assist you on your appraisal. There's nothing wrong with that, and often it'll help you out a lot. Just don't let anyone push you around or get an attitude with you. You don't want anyone to have an attitude like they've got all the answers and you're out to lunch or on cloud 9.

Most States have a minimum experience requirement of 250 Fee-Paid appraisals. These appraisals must have all the requirements necessary to be considered actual appraisal reports for State and Federal Certification experience. What this means is that you have to do at least 250 **actual appraisal reports.** These consist of appraisals that a client has hired you to do for them. Furthermore, the client has to have paid you specifically for doing the appraisal report. To elaborate further, it's when you're commissioned by a client to do an appraisal report only and not in combination with another real estate related service. The purpose of their payment to you is just for the appraisal and you're not being paid for some other real estate related service that you provide the client. Also, the appraisal *must have all the requirements* of a full appraisal report. Meaning that you must at least have all of the information, addendums, adjustments, math calculations, the three approaches to value, etc. that are found on the standard appraisal forms.

Many Realtors improperly think they do appraisals. They think that an appraisal consists of taking a few recent sales in their area and then writing a brief description of what they believe someone's house is worth based on these comps. CHICKEN FEED!!!! That is not an appraisal report and you might want to clue them in on this. Also, tax assessors for the city have to reassess houses occasionally for tax increases. What the assessor will do is simply make across the board increases based upon rising prices and tax rates. They don't even have to go out and look at the property in many cases! They just punch in some new tax rates into a computer and it updates all the property tax files. These **are not** appraisals either.

As I said in the beginning of the book, the reason for the Federal and State certification and licensing process is that they basically want you to take some classes and work under someone else's guidance. It is recommended that you do this until you get some experience under your belt. This has many benefits to it and it will really help you out in your beginning stages. You won't spend a lot of time *"spinning your wheels"* trying to learn the business.

Tell Your Client To Ignore The Hypocrites

I'm bothered by dishonest and/or ignorant Realtors and other third party people who inaccurately tell your client that everything is just fine and dandy about the house they're interested in buying. They may tell your client that nothing needs to be repaired when in reality there are repairs needed. They may also tell your client the market value is what they estimate and not the price you have arrived at. I'm bothered by this because they're such **hypocrites!** *(Of course these third party people know better than you as to what's good for your client. You're just very well trained and experienced in doing appraisals, but somehow they know more than you do.)* Do you think they would make the same comments and statements if they were buying the house or making the loan and not your client? NOT A CHANCE!!! That's what makes them such hypocrites. I'll give you some imaginary examples that will make you laugh but you'll have to agree that they do get the point across.

What if they were your client at the inspection and you said to them, *"According to the owner, the*

> Do you think they would make the same comments and statements if they were buying the house and not your client? NOT A CHANCE!!!

septic system hasn't been pumped clean in two years. The septic system is underground and can't be seen. The typical buyer in this area would hire a septic contractor to pump the system and do an internal inspection just to make sure it's OK. Therefore, my recommendation is that you have it checked out further to be sure everything's all right."

Could you picture that third party person, *(if they were your client)*, turning to you and saying, *"Oh, well I don't need to get the septic pumped and internally inspected. This loan application will be approved anyway because there's no way the borrower will default on the loan. After all the septic only has to be pumped every 2-3 years so there's still another year before any maintenance is needed on the system."*

What if you said to them, *"I tried to turn on the air-conditioning system by using the normal thermostat control on the wall. It won't turn on so you should have the system checked out by a licensed A/C contractor to determine what repairs are needed."*

Could you picture that third party person responding to that by saying, *"You're wrong Mr.*

Appraiser, I don't need to get a contractor to check out the A/C system. The seller and the third party both told me that it works fine. They just can't seem to turn it on now. It must be a loose wire inside the thermostat. My husband can fix that himself after we move in."

How about if you told them, *"You have a lead water main line in the house. You have to get an estimate to have a new water main line installed. Lead is a very serious health concern for adults and **especially** for children."*

Of course they'd answer this by saying, *"You're totally over exaggerating. My friend lives right down the block and he has four children. They have been living with a lead water main in their house for 14 years and not one person in his family has been sick a day in their life."*

Let's say you found asbestos and you informed them, *"There is some asbestos on the visible heating pipes in the lower level. The Environmental Protection Agency recommends that you have it professionally removed by an EPA licensed contractor for safety. It will not only be a health benefit but it will also help when you go to sell the house down the road to have the asbestos professionally removed."*

Of course they would answer this by saying, *"Oh no, I only have to wrap some duct tape around the asbestos. I don't need to hire EPA licensed contractors. That whole asbestos thing is just an over reaction by some alarmist people in the asbestos removal business who are trying to make money by scaring people."*

What if you found termite damaged wood and you said to them, *"There is some termite damage in the base of the garage door. I didn't see the termites crawling inside the wood but then again, it's very, very rare to actually see them in the damaged areas. It's highly recommended that you have the house treated by a licensed Pest Control Operator because the termites could be in nonvisible areas of the house."*

Upon hearing this, their response would be, *"As long as there are no active termites crawling around in the visible areas of the house or in the damaged wood, then I have no need to be concerned with getting the house treated by a PCO. My friend Ralph told me the only time a treatment is necessary is when you actually see the termites. Ralph knows what he's talking about; he teaches math at the university."*

Now these examples may seem a little bit carried away and they do have some humor in them. There is a

point that I'm trying to make with these examples. That is there's no way any third party who contradicts you on an appraisal would have the same reaction and comments if **they** were the ones buying the house or granting the loan money, as opposed to your client. I had a teacher in one of my religion classes in high school who used a great example that fits this type of situation perfectly. He was talking about how some people hide behind the Bible with their actions and use it only when it's convenient and when it benefits them. He said, *"They wheel the Bible out when it's good for them and then they wheel it back in when it's not good for them."* People who do that are kidding themselves and are hypocrites by their actions.

It's no different with a third party that contradicts the facts during an appraisal. They're simply being hypocrites when they contradict you. They're hypocrites because the vast majority of times they're contradicting you is because it benefits their pocket book and not your client's. All you're trying to do is tell your client the facts and realities about buying a house or securing a mortgage loan with the property. It doesn't matter if he's buying this house or the house down the block. You just want him to go into the deal with his eyes open.

Don't over exaggerate things but at the same time don't let some ignorant seller, Realtor, or another third party try to sugar coat anything either. And if you ever have a real problem with a seller, a Realtor, or another third party contradicting what you say to your client just ask them, *"What if the tables were turned and you were buying this house and my client told you not to worry about the asbestos,* (or whatever else you're discussing). *Would you take his word for it and not listen to the appraiser that you hired who is the expert in his field?"* Don't be surprised if they swallow their tongue or fumble for words to answer a question like that.

Straight Talk

Not all people who dispute or contradict what you tell the client will be dishonest. They may just be ignorant about the topic their discussing. This will happen all the time throughout your life. Some people think they've got all the answers to <u>everything</u>! But what's funny about it, is that these kinds of people never have anything to prove that they know what they're talking about. There's an old saying that describes the difference between a Wise Man and a Fool: *"A Wise Man **Knows** He Doesn't Know Everything, But A Fool **Thinks** He Does."* So be a Wise Man in everything you do. Don't be a Wise Guy or a Fool in life.

When I bought my first real estate book and tape series while I was in college, I heard all of the negative comments, criticism and laughter from everyone! These negative comments and criticism came from family, friends and anyone else I mentioned the books

> There's an old saying that describes the difference between a Wise Man and a Fool: "A Wise Man Knows He Doesn't Know Everything, But A Fool Thinks He Does."

and tapes to. I practically had to *hypnotize* my brother to buy that first house with me, because the critics were starting to worry him too. You'll probably hear some of the same negative comments and criticism from buying **this** material as well! Everyone gave me 10,000 reasons why I would fail with the real estate tapes and *"lose it all."* They all said it was a *"get rich quick scheme"* that was just a pipe dream. Not one person ever stopped to even think of just **one** reason why it would work!! I had enough guts, confidence and foresight to go ahead and listen to those tapes and read those books anyway, despite all the criticism around me. Thank God I did, because I proved to myself that I was right all along. Things did work out well, as I had anticipated.

That experience, and many others as well, have taught me a very good lesson that I'll never forget. I've learned that you have to follow your own gut feelings and instincts with all of your decisions in life. Anytime you do something that's out of the norm of some people's standards, they criticize you for it. I think it's because some people have no foresight or ambition. You just have to ignore people like that, let their narrow minded and negative thinking limit **them** and not you. You have to dare to be your own person and to be different if you feel strongly about something.

Now don't get the wrong impression by this. I don't want you to think that you shouldn't listen to anyone in life and think that you've got all the answers yourself. I'll listen to advice from anyone, but whether I follow that advice is my decision to make. I won't just take someone else's advice with blind faith, because free advice is often only worth what you paid for it. What I'll do is take advice from anyone and then use my own gut feeling and judgment from my experiences to make a final decision. This way, if I find out later that the decision I made was a mistake, then I can't **blame** anyone else but myself for it. However, if I find out later the decision I made was correct, then I don't **owe** anyone else but myself for it.

I'll give you some actual examples from history that I read about. These examples are from a *Dale Carnegie* book with a chapter titled: *"Remember That No One Ever Kicks A Dead Dog."* That phrase refers to the fact that when you're kicked or criticized it's often done because it gives the kicker a feeling of importance. It often means that you're accomplishing something that's worthy of attention. Many people get a savage satisfaction out of denouncing those who are better educated or more successful.

A former president of Yale University, Timothy Dwight, apparently took huge delight in denouncing a man who was running for President of the United States. This president of Yale warned that if this man were elected President of the United States, *"We may see our wives and daughters the victims of legal prostitution, soberly dishonored, speciously polluted; the outcasts of delicacy and virtue, the loathing of God and man."* Sounds almost like a denunciation of Adolph Hitler, doesn't it? But it wasn't. It was a denunciation of Thomas Jefferson, the author of the Declaration of Independence and the patron saint of democracy. Pretty incredible that someone, who was well educated, could have made a statement like that about Thomas Jefferson.

What American do you suppose was denounced as a *"hypocrite,"* *"an impostor,"* and as *"little better than a murderer?"* A newspaper cartoon depicted him on a guillotine, the big knife ready to cut off his head. Crowds jeered and hissed at him as he rode through the streets. Who was he? George Washington. Do you believe that! I think it's absolutely amazing how some people say things out of sheer ignorance without knowing the truth or the facts. We're all guilty of doing it at one time or another. Just remember those two stories from history so you don't do it too often.

So, the next time someone criticizes you or disputes something you're saying, don't get angry and argue back. Just look at where it's coming from and ask yourself:

◇ Is this person more successful than I am?

◇ Does this person have any background or experience in the topic they're disputing?

◇ Does this person really know what they're talking about, or do they just <u>think</u> they know what they're talking about?

If the person has nothing to prove that they know what they're talking about, then just ignore them because they're talking out of ignorance. You don't want to get aggravated over someone or something trivial.

Motivational Talk

I hope you're beginning to see the inner workings of the different aspects of Real Estate from a point of view that the vast majority of the public doesn't have a clue exists. These are the realities of the real estate business in general. I could tell you the truth or I could paint a perfect picture that you'd rather hear about instead, but then I'd be lying to you. I don't mean to be negative. I just want to open your eyes to some important information. You might want to inform your clients about some of this information when they call you for price quotes. You'll find that they appreciate it and will thank you because they didn't know or realize some of the realities of the real estate business in general.

If you find some of these things hard to believe, then don't take my word for it. Talk to other home inspectors and appraisers in your area that are honest and do good, quality work. See if they confirm or dispute what I'm telling you. It's no different from any other business. Every business has aspects about it that the public is unaware of. This makes the uninformed public susceptible to being taken advantage of, due to their lack of awareness.

Now, I'm not a doomsdayer by any means. I

<u>strongly</u> believe that anyone, from any background can achieve anything they want in life. But I do have an awful lot of battle wounds and scars from trusting people too much. My battle wounds aren't all from my

> *Every business has aspects about it that the public is unaware of. This makes the uninformed public susceptible to being taken advantage of, due to their lack of awareness.*

experiences in the appraisal and home inspection business, but are also from past experiences in my personal and business life. After learning my lessons, I got up every day and licked my wounds and kept moving forward. By the time I got into the appraisal and home inspection business I wizened up a lot.

It's OK to lose a few battles. You just want to make every effort you can to win the war. And don't take any prisoners along the way. Like the saying goes, you have to *Go For It* with everything you do! Don't sit around and **let** things happen, you have to go out and **make** things happen in your life. I started with nothing and made it on my own and I'm certainly no rocket scientist. Therefore, I firmly believe that anyone, no matter who you are or where you come from, can become successful. You can provide a real benefit to society in just about anything that you set your mind to doing. The only key is that you have to be willing to work very hard. You also have to make all of the sacrifices necessary to attain the level and

> *I read a quotation from Teddy Roosevelt that said "It's hard to fail, but it's worse never to have tried."*

success that you're looking for. If you live an honest life and leave this world a little better off then when you got here, then you can consider yourself a success.

I remember when my brother and I bought our first rental property. There was a perfect example of how anyone could become successful, despite their current situation or where they came from. The woman who sold us the house had two sons. One son had worked hard to move out of the low income area he was born in. This son then went on to medical school and became a successful dentist. He later married another dentist and was living a nice lifestyle with his wife and children. The other son, who grew up in the same house, was a total failure in life. This second son was living in his mother's house and was receiving money from welfare and other public assistance programs. He was too lazy to work and his mother actually had to **evict** him from her house to sell it! This son refused to move when his mother told him she was selling the house. Because of this, we had to wait an extra four months to buy the house until the seller could evict her own son. So here were two people, from the exact same home, where one became successful and happy and the other was a failure and miserable in life. It's all up to you. Your own ambition will make the difference. I had a friend that used to say, *"You live by the consequences of your own actions."*

I read a quotation from Teddy Roosevelt that said *"It's hard to fail, but it's worse never to have tried."* Albert Einstein, the most profound thinker of our day, confessed that he was wrong 99% of the time. I read that Thomas Edison tried over a thousand different ways before he got a light bulb to work. Can you imagine the difference it would've made in history if they just gave up on their efforts.

You're going to make mistakes in your personal and business life no matter how careful and honest you try to be. It's just a part of life that everyone experiences so don't let it get you down. Try to look at it in a different way by saying *"You don't make mistakes, you just learn lessons."* What you want to try to do is have more successes than failures. Mistakes and failures aren't bad, they just give you more experience to make better decisions in the future. Don't be like a cat that sits on a hot stove. It'll never sit on a *hot* stove again, but it'll never sit on a *cold* stove either.

I met someone once that told me that *"Nothing is Bad, Everything Has A Purpose."* That's a very true statement. Look back at the majority of the mistakes you've made, and all the bad things that have happened to you over the years. At the time they happened, they seemed much worse then they do now. Often those mistakes or bad experiences led to something better or more profitable for you in the long run. They say that things that happen to us aren't bad. It's the way that we react to them, that makes them seem bad.

As I said in the beginning of the book, this isn't a *"get rich quick scheme."* It takes a lot of time, sacrifice and hard work to make a lot of money in any

> *You may wonder whether the hard work and sacrifices will be worth it. If you do, just remember this old saying, "You don't pay a price for success, you pay a price for failure"*

business. If it was easy to become rich, then everybody would be doing it! When you do become successful, you'll look back at all the hard work and sacrifices that you made and it will seem like a small price to have paid. It's like taking an exam in school. While you're

studying for the exam it seems like such hard work. But when the test is over and you do well, then you look back on the studying you had to do and it doesn't seem so bad after all. You may wonder whether the hard work and sacrifices will be worth it. If you do, then just remember these sayings, *"You don't pay a price for success, you pay a price for failure"* and *"Every dog has his day."*

Take care of the important things in your personal and business life and the little things will take care of themselves. Don't spend all of your time worrying about minor problems. People spend 90% of their time harping on a problem and only 10% of their time trying to find a <u>solution</u> to the problem. Don't step over dollars to pick up pennies either. People spend 90% of their time worrying about saving pennies and cutting costs and only 10% of their time concentrating on *increasing their income* with new opportunities.

Conclusion

Now I hope you feel we've covered every aspect of the real estate appraisal business from A to Z. I hope now you realize what I meant when I said in the beginning of the book that I wasn't going to paint some fairy tale, rosy picture. Also, that I was going to tell it like it is without holding anything back. You might have found some of this information to be very surprising to learn. I certainly did when I started out in this business. I hope I've given you enough information so that you don't make the same mistakes that I did.

I can't think of anything we've missed. However, as I've said earlier, you have to keep feeding your mind with the new technologies and aspects of this business that are coming into the market. Don't get lazy now. Remember to keep feeding your mind with new information and training. The more knowledge you have, the more money you'll make. If you're knowledgeable <u>and</u> honest, then you'll really make some big money.

I want to take the time now to commend you on getting this far through the book. I've heard statistics that have shown that **less than 10%** of the people who purchase self-improvement books and tapes, ever even read the books and/or listen to the tapes one complete time. To me that's an amazing statistic. People spend their hard earned money on something, and then they get lazy or distracted and they don't follow through with it. They purchase books and tapes and read 1/2 of the book or listen to 1/2 of the tapes, and then they put them on a shelf to collect dust.

I take my hat off to you. You have the ambition, willpower and the foresight to make an attempt at improving your own life, as well as the life of others. By getting this far in this book, you've shown that you're part of the minority within the majority. And that's a unique group of people who really want to have a positive impact on their own lives and the lives of the people around them. Abraham Lincoln said that *"A man who follows a crowd will never be followed by a crowd."* So be a leader in everything you do.

As I said in the beginning of this book: Please send me an email and let me know what you think of this book and any recommendations you might have for improvements or new products. I accept positive and negative comments since both help me to improve the next version of my products. I am always looking to improve my products and services and I greatly appreciate customer feedback and suggestions. I appreciate the trust and confidence that you placed in me by purchasing this book. Due to your referrals our business keeps growing, and so will yours. Good luck, and I wish you the best in all your endeavors. I hope someday I'll get a chance to meet you at a real estate appraisal seminar.

> *I want to take the time now to commend you on getting this far through the manual. I've heard statistics that have shown that less than 10% of the people who purchase self-improvement books and tapes, ever even read the books and/or listen to the tapes one complete time.*

The prior edition of this book was dedicated to *Midnight* who died on Wednesday, October 28, 1998. I'll always remember you.

Top: Is this what they meant when they said:
"A man's home is his castle"

Bottom: That's me, the author, doing a home inspection
and appraisal for a client - in 3 feet of snow!

Narrative Report Generator *and* On-Site Checklist

Includes: CD-Rom with the *best* Narrative Report Generator and On-Site Checklist on the market! These documents will enable you to *easily* do 30 page narrative, professional home inspection reports to send to your clients. The On-Site Checklist will assist you at the inspection site to be sure that you properly evaluate the subject property. Designed to walk you through the entire inspection process with very detailed instructions on how to properly evaluate the condition and status of **all** aspects of a home in a fool-proof, step-by-step system. The most thorough and professional Report Generator in the business!

Home Buyer's Survival Kit

Includes: One video tape plus one audio cassette tape which are over 2 hours long. The video and audio tapes will assist you with the biggest investment of your life - your own home! Learn how to determine the true market value and condition of any home. Whether you are buying selling or renovating a home, identifying the hidden problem conditions can save you thousands of dollars! As an added bonus, you get the *Video Companion Guide* plus a sample real estate appraisal report to help you evaluate a house.

Complete *Real Estate Appraising From A to Z Kit*

Includes the in-depth book + four audio CD's + two video tapes: Textbook Manual that tells you the truth and covers *every* aspect of the Real Estate Appraisal Business from A to Z. *"The **real facts** the other appraisal books don't tell you!"* Starter Kit with a large assortment of appraisal supplies. This will get you up and running with your new appraisal business. The appraisal supplies you receive include: Single family URAR forms, a variety of appraisal photo forms, sketch addendum forms, certification and limiting condition forms, and a variety of property stencils.

Complete *Home Inspection Business From A to Z Kit*

Includes the in-depth book + four audio CD's + two video tapes + inspection report and checklist: Textbook Manual that tells you the truth and covers *every* aspect of the Home Inspection Business from A to Z. *"The **real facts** the other home inspection books don't tell you!"* Report Writing Document (condensed version) that enables you to *easily* do narrative, professional inspection reports to send to your clients. On-Site Checklist booklet (condensed version) to assist you at the inspection site to be sure that you properly evaluate the subject property.

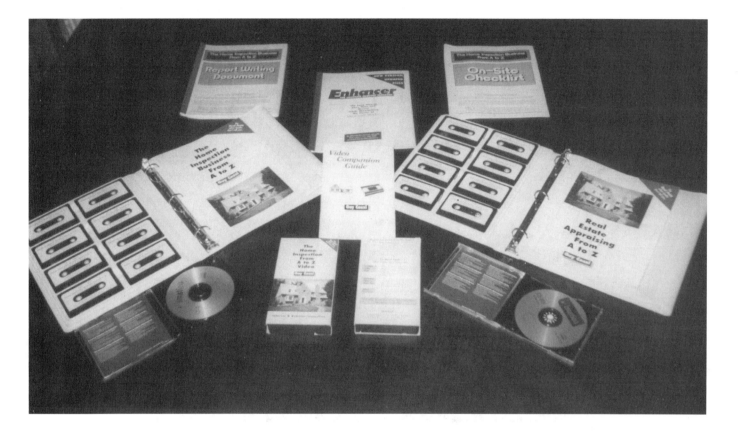

Just some of our books, video and audio tapes, CD's, and much more!
Email nemmar@hotmail.com for prices.
Visit us at www.nemmar.com

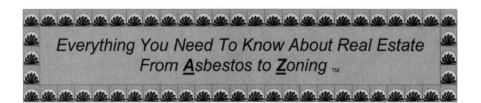

Everything You Need To Know About Real Estate
From __A__sbestos to __Z__oning ™

The Home Inspection Business From A to Z ™

Real Estate Appraising From A to Z ™

Real Estate Investing From A to Z ™

NeMMaR Real Estate Training
Email: nemmar@hotmail.com
www.nemmar.com